INSIDE TALIGENT TECHNOLOGY

SEAN COTTER

with

MIKE POTEL
Vice President, Technology Development
Taligent, Inc.

Addison-Wesley Publishing Company

Reading, Massachusetts   Menlo Park, California   New York
Don Mills, Ontario   Wokingham, England   Amsterdam   Bonn   Sydney
Singapore   Tokyo   Madrid   San Juan   Paris   Seoul   Milan   Mexico City   Taipei

Sponsoring Editor: Martha Steffen
Cover and text design: Taligent Technical Communications Group, Gary Ashcavai
Set in 10 point New Baskerville

Library of Congress Cataloging-in-Publication Data

Cotter, Sean.
  Inside Taligent technology / Sean Cotter with Mike Potel.
     p.   cm.
  Includes bibliographical references and index.
  ISBN 0-201-40970-4
  1. Object-oriented programming (Computer science) 2. Systems
software. 3. CommonPoint.   I. Potel, Michael J., 1948-
II. Title.
QA76.64.C67 1995
005.1'1–dc20   94-45876
                                                     CIP

 1 2 3 4 5 6 7 8 9 -CRS-99 98 97 96 95

First printing, June 1995

Addison-Wesley books are available for bulk purchases by corporations, institutions, and other organizations.
For more information please contact the Corporate, Government, and Special Sales Department at (800) 238-9682.

Contents

Chapter 2
The Taligent programming model

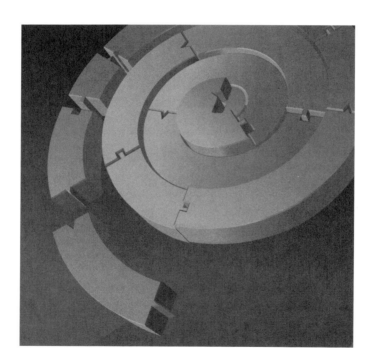

FOREWORD

Taligent represents the culmination of years of work by many talented people with whom I have had the good fortune to be associated. I was the Director of Software Engineering for Apple Computer in early 1988 when my staff and I set about developing a new software strategy for Apple. The story of the blue and pink index cards, mentioned in Chapter 1, marked the beginning of two ambitious undertakings: the Macintosh System 7.0 project to develop a major revision of that platform; and a longer-term project to develop an all-new application programming model based on object-oriented technology.

About two dozen intrepid souls formed the original skunkworks team charged with developing what became known in industry lore as "Pink." This effort centered on a combination of new ideas that we thought could change the nature of software development. These included object-oriented toolkits; compound documents; pervasive networking and collaboration; innovative user interfaces; advanced graphics, multimedia, text, and imaging; multilingual text capabilities; tools optimized for iterative development; and a design center based on a modern operating system (OS) foundation. Pervading everything was the principle that the entire programming model, as well as the implementation of the system itself, would be fully object oriented and designed around the concept of *frameworks:* customizable and extensible object designs for all aspects of the system and the applications built with it.

Over time, the project was nurtured and grew at Apple and eventually attracted the attention of IBM, which had strong object-oriented technology interests and history of its own. In early 1992, the two companies created Taligent, Inc., a new company devoted to bringing Pink to market. IBM brought several key elements to the venture: a strong commitment to the enterprise customer, a wealth of OS and object technologies, and multiple hardware and software platforms with which to leverage Taligent's capabilities.

Not long after Taligent was formed, Hewlett-Packard became interested in the undertaking for many of the same reasons. In early 1994, Hewlett-Packard became the third investor in Taligent and provided a further infusion of technology and expertise, particularly in the areas of distributed computing, object-oriented environments, and enterprise solutions.

Taligent started with 170 employees and has since grown to a 400-person company. A major milestone was achieved in the summer of 1994 when we shipped our initial developer release of the CommonPoint™ application system. In so doing, we expanded our partnership to include those first brave developers who would help us refine our fledgling system into a real product. As I write this in early 1995, we are well on our way to fulfilling our original commitment to deliver the first product release of the CommonPoint system by the mid-1990s and to begin what we hope will be a generational change for our industry.

Acknowledgments

Although my name appears on the cover, the engineering work this book describes was done by a large number of very bright and creative people who should all share credit for the result. My role in creating the book has been to direct and shape this telling of the Taligent® technology story, and I want to acknowledge personally some of the key people who made this book happen.

First and foremost, I want to state my appreciation of and admiration for Sean Cotter, the true author of this book. Sean deserves great credit for taking my rambling ideas and organizing them into the coherent story told here. He has put up with me for over a year of taped conversations, countless drafts, and endless pink scribbles. He has also spent many hours with scores of other people at Taligent and plowed through quantities of documentation, memos, specifications, presentations, videotapes, and demos to assemble this story. Beyond his tireless work and good cheer, he has truly internalized and given expression to our Taligent vision. On behalf of all of Taligent, I thank him for the superb book he has produced.

In his Preface, Sean has listed the names of the many people who have helped us with *Inside Taligent Technology,* to whom I also extend my sincere thanks for all their efforts. I owe special thanks to Cathy Novak, whose original inspiration and sponsorship set this book in motion; to her Technical Communications team, whose developer documentation provided much of our source material; to Gary Ashcavai for his wonderful artwork and willingness to do endless revisions; to Jim Showalter for giving us the benefit of his teaching materials and experience; to Doug Brent and his Product Development team for providing considerable content and reviewing numerous drafts; to Stratton Sclavos and his Marketing team for their contributions to the industry story, product strategy, and positioning; to Martha Steffen and our friends at Addison-Wesley for their patience; to my boss Joe Guglielmi and his staff for their support and guidance; and especially to my wife, Cathy Frantz, for her encouragement, wisdom, and understanding throughout.

Finally, this book is dedicated to all the Pink team members, past and present, and all our friends, partners, families, and supporters who have encouraged us to produce the system described in these pages. We hope it lives up to your expectations.

Mike Potel

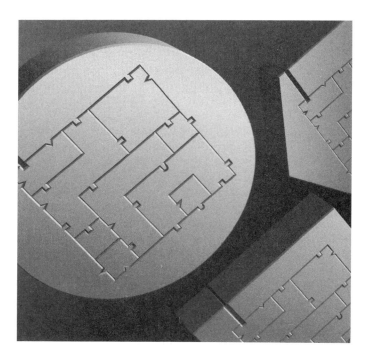

PREFACE

This book presents Taligent's own story, as I've come to understand it, about Taligent technology: what it is, why it's important, and where the people who created it intend to take it.

Although this book is required reading for some of Taligent's programming classes, it isn't a programming manual. Instead, it presents a snapshot of Taligent's business, marketing, and technical plans—a snapshot taken before the beta versions of Taligent's first products were completed. However, the technical information in the book isn't limited to the first Taligent product release. It describes both technology that is part of the first release and, wherever possible, the rough outlines of technology under development for later releases.

Audience and structure   *Inside Taligent Technology* contains useful information for anyone who wants to begin learning about Taligent technology, including knowledgeable users, managers who make decisions about information systems, and computer professionals. It has two parts. Part I, "Introduction to Taligent technology," is for both programmers and nontechnical readers:

- Chapter 1, "A new generation of applications," discusses recent trends in the computer industry and Taligent's vision of the role it can play.
- Chapter 2, "The Taligent programming model," summarizes Taligent's approach to object-oriented programming (OOP) and introduces frameworks, the structures that underlie all Taligent programming.
- Chapter 3, "A human interface for organizations," introduces some of the benefits for users that Taligent technology makes possible.
- Chapter 4, "Taligent market development," describes the business and marketing strategy Taligent has adopted to achieve rapid high-volume deployment of its software products.
- Chapter 5, "Development tools and approaches," introduces Taligent's development tools and describes how to get started as a Taligent developer.

You don't need to be an expert to understand these chapters. Anyone with an interest in computers should be able to grasp the basic concepts that underlie Taligent technology.

Part II, "CommonPoint system architecture," presents an overview of the CommonPoint application system, Taligent's flagship software product. These chapters are intended primarily as a reference for readers who have some familiarity with the principles of object-oriented programming and want to know more about CommonPoint capabilities in specific areas:

- Chapter 6, "Introduction to the CommonPoint application system," introduces the CommonPoint system architecture and the notation conventions used in Part II.

- Chapter 7, "Desktop frameworks," introduces the CommonPoint frameworks that are at the heart of the Taligent programming model. It explains how Taligent applies the OOP and framework concepts introduced in Chapter 2 to basic programming tasks such as representing data.

- Chapter 8, "Embeddable Data Types," introduces some of the CommonPoint frameworks that provide ready-made data types for specific application domains such as text and graphics.

- Chapter 9, "Graphics," describes CommonPoint capabilities in the areas of 2-D and 3-D graphics, graphics device drivers, fonts, and color.

- Chapter 10, "Text," introduces the CommonPoint mechanisms for storing, styling, displaying, and inputting multilingual text.

- Chapter 11, "Time media," describes the CommonPoint frameworks that support various kinds of time media, including audio, MIDI, video, and telephony.

- Chapter 12, "Other Application Services," introduces the ways in which CommonPoint applications can interoperate with non-Taligent applications. It also describes CommonPoint capabilities in the areas of printing, scanning, and localization.

- Chapter 13, "Enterprise Services," describes the high-level distributed computing services available to CommonPoint applications, including data access, concurrency control and recovery, system management, messaging, and remote object calls (ROC).

- Chapter 14, "Foundation Services," describes basic programming services used by all CommonPoint applications and frameworks, including the notification mechanism, identifiers, storage, testing, and numerics.

- Chapter 15, "OS Services," introduces low-level CommonPoint services such as communications, the file system, time services, runtime services, and microkernel services.

Part II doesn't describe how to program the CommonPoint system. You can find that kind of detailed information in the CommonPoint developer guides and related publications.

Acknowledgments

Mike Potel, my coauthor and guide to the depths of object-oriented technology, has spent many hours regaling me with stories, industry lore, and spontaneous disquisitions on complex technical questions. Most important, he helped reorganize the entire book several times, pored over every draft, and made countless substantive contributions. I could not have completed *Inside Taligent Technology* without his enthusiasm, encouragement, and participation at every stage.

I owe special thanks to Jim Showalter, most notably for his contribution to Chapters 2 and 7, and to Gary Ashcavai, for his work on the book's illustrations and design. Many other people at Taligent helped me locate information, explained technical concepts, reviewed pieces of the book as it developed, or contributed their own words, pictures, and ideas. For their generous contributions I thank Deborah Adair, Tom Affinito, Lorenzo Aguilar, Dave Anderson, Anthony Armenta, Jeremy Ashley, Bryan Atsatt, Steve Boyle, Doug Brent, Tom Chavez, Jerome Coonen, Tom Cronan, Debbie Coutant, Mark Davis, Rosario De La Torre, Rob Dickinson, Mike Dilts, Jeff Elliott, David Goldsmith, Jack Grimes, Joe Guglielmi, Roger Harvey, Stephen Holland, Bayles Holt, Victoria Igle, Dan Keller, Peter Kellogg-Smith, Morgen Kimbrell, Julie Knaggs, Deborah Knoles, Steve Lemon, Judy Lin, Donna MacInnis, Steve Milne, Sandeep Nawathe, Alix North, Scott Patterson, Monica Pawlan, Kate Payne, John Peterson, Christopher Pettus, Jim Quarato, Jack Robson, Kennan Rossi, Sara Sazegari, Stratton Sclavos, Kirk Scott, David Sharp, Andy Shebanow, Roger Spreen, Keith Stephens, Tom Taylor, Hemant Thakkar, Holly Thomason, Esther Tong, Tony Tseung, Rob Turner, Anne Tweet, Joyce Uggla, Mark Vickers, Greg Voss, Roger Webster, John Werner, and Jeff Zias.

I would also like to thank William Adams at Adamation, Sharon Everson at Apple, and Randall Flint at Sundial Systems for reviewing work in progress; Loralee Windsor for copyediting the final drafts; Martha Steffen and Keith Wolman at Addison-Wesley for giving me the chance to embark on this adventure; and Cathy Novak and Odile Sullivan-Tarazi at Taligent for helping me navigate.

Above all, I thank my wife, Nancy Warner, and my son, Colin Warner, for their affection, humor, and patience throughout the 14 long months it took to write this book.

Sean Cotter

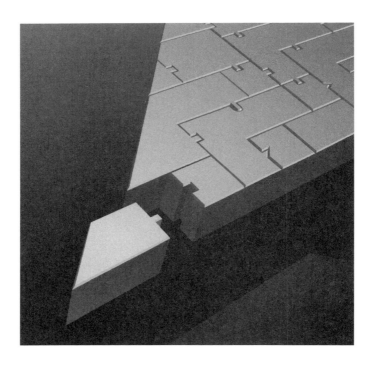

PART I

INTRODUCTION TO TALIGENT TECHNOLOGY

4

Chapter 1

A new generation of applications

Taligent was founded in 1992 by Apple Computer and IBM to help both companies address what is sometimes called the "software crisis": the fact that, from many customers' point of view, software applications take too long to create and maintain and are too difficult to learn and use.

This has been a familiar refrain since the earliest days of computing, and such criticism is part of the evolution of any new technology. But the software crisis has come to a head in the 1990s. New customer needs in the areas of workgroup collaboration, workflow automation, information management, multimedia, and data access and visualization are driving market growth for 32-bit, multitasking computers and related hardware and software, to the tune of half a trillion dollars so far in this decade. Unfortunately, most application software for these new computers hasn't caught up with their capabilities. Customers are clamoring for new kinds of solutions. They're not looking for a better spreadsheet, word processor, or other "personal productivity" software; they're looking for integrated enterprise solutions that can handle the accelerating information needs of a global economy.

The applications that customers want are very difficult to create with traditional software development technology. Sophisticated applications take years to develop and millions of lines of code, and when they finally get finished they are difficult to maintain and modify for new business requirements. At the same time, the economics of commercial software development are exacerbating the problem. Only the largest application companies are making money.

In fiscal 1994, for example, Microsoft's revenue from the applications portion of its business increased by more than $650 million to about $2.9 billion, while the total revenue for the software applications industry—including Microsoft—increased by only about $550 million to about $8.3 billion (Dataquest estimates quoted by O'Connor, 1994). In other words, the rest of the industry experienced a collective decrease in revenue of about $100 million. Small companies are being gobbled up by larger ones or going out of business, and even some of the larger ones are facing severe losses. Both the risks and the price of entry for software developers who want to bring innovative technology to market are getting higher every day. This is a problem for the entire computer industry.

A BRIEF HISTORY OF TALIGENT

When Taligent was founded in early 1992, Apple and IBM had already committed substantial resources to the exploration of object-oriented programming (OOP) as the basis for a new generation of applications. At Apple, this commitment went at least as far back as the early 1980s and the Lisa® Toolkit. Other object-oriented projects included the Object Pascal programming language, the MacApp® application framework, and (in spirit, if not in detail) the HyperCard® "software construction kit."

After furious internal debates in the late 1980s, a new project, code-named "Pink," emerged. It was called Pink because, at a meeting in 1988, key Apple engineers and managers settled on a direction for the company by jotting down ideas on index cards and pinning the cards to the wall in two groups: blue cards, representing technologies that could be supported as extensions to the current system software for Macintosh® computers, and pink cards, representing technologies for a future dream system. The technologies listed on the blue cards eventually formed the core of System 7, Apple's current system software. The pink cards listed precursors of Taligent's object-oriented system software.

IBM's involvement with objects also extended back to the early 1980s and a series of pioneering projects that were incorporated into software for System/38™ and eventually the AS/400®, one of IBM's most important hardware platforms. Projects in the late 1980s included work with the object-oriented programming language Smalltalk, joint research with the company Metaphor/Patriot Partners, and cross-platform standards like the System Object Model (SOM) and Distributed System Object Model (DSOM).

Apple and IBM joined forces to form Taligent because they shared an interest in catalyzing the development of a new generation of applications, based on object-oriented technology, that would work the same way across an entire organization, regardless of the underlying hardware platforms. In early 1994 Hewlett-Packard decided that it could also benefit from this approach and became Taligent's third major investor and partner.

Hewlett-Packard had also undertaken pioneering work in object-oriented technology throughout the 1980s. This included the development of the NewWave® operating environment and user interface; cofounding the Object Management Group, an important standards organization for the industry; early adoption of C++ for use with the SoftBench™ development environment; and, by the 1990s, the release of HP® Distributed Smalltalk. As it also does for Apple and IBM, the Taligent® approach fits naturally with Hewlett-Packard's goals in terms of both technology and marketing.

Programming for the enterprise desktop

All of Taligent's investors recognize the limitations of the current generation of applications for handling the increasing information needs of businesses and other organizations. They also recognize that graphical user interfaces modeled on a single user working at a single virtual "desktop" on a single computer don't always work very well for groups of users who need to interact with each other electronically. Although the personal desktop metaphor has achieved great success in terms of the personal productivity of individual users, it tends to break down in networked environments with hundreds of users simultaneously using different kinds of computers that run different kinds of system software.

The personal desktop must evolve into an enterprise desktop. Customers need powerful distributed applications that require both hardware and software support. Modern operating systems can support 32-bit (and higher) hardware and high-speed networks, but application development is not keeping up with hardware and network capabilities.

Today's software development techniques evolved from high-level procedural languages and structured programming techniques that first achieved widespread acceptance about 25 years ago. At the time, procedural techniques involved a new learning curve for programmers who were used to older styles of programming. Nevertheless, the new approach succeeded because the practical advantages it provided far outweighed the retraining costs involved.

Like procedural programming in its time, object-oriented programming is creating a new generation of programming techniques, radically changing the way programmers work, the kinds of software they produce, and the way they maintain and upgrade software products. Taligent and its investors are committed to object-oriented technology as the best long-term technical solution for the software problems plaguing all segments of the computer industry today.

**Protecting the
customer's investment**

When the Pink project first got under way at Apple in 1988, few existing operating systems could meet the new system's basic requirements, which included preemptive multitasking, lightweight threads, fast interprocess communication (IPC), large numbers of protected address spaces, dynamic shared libraries, and the like. The team therefore began to develop both a new programming model for application development and a new microkernel-based operating environment that could drive power-hungry applications by taking full advantage of 32-bit (and higher) multitasking computers.

Since that time the low-level capabilities of a number of existing operating systems have caught up with the basic processing requirements of the new kinds of applications that customers want. Taligent's investors have continued to develop their own operating systems, sometimes using Taligent technology and sometimes supplying technology to Taligent for further development. Most important, customers interested in Taligent technology have made it clear that in addition to their need for new application capabilities, they need to preserve their investment in existing data and associated applications and operating systems. Any new kinds of applications must not only run on a variety of existing operating systems but also be capable of interoperating with existing procedural applications.

Although Taligent is still focused on its original goal of making applications easier to create and use, the company's strategy has evolved in response to the expressed needs of its customers. Instead of developing a traditional operating system from the microkernel up, Taligent has created a new category of system software, called an *application system,* that provides a comprehensive set of services for building flexible, portable application solutions. Some aspects of the microkernel-based operating system that are still under development may be incorporated into the operating systems provided by Taligent's investors and into other Taligent products.

The rest of this chapter surveys some trends in the computer industry, explains how the concept of an application system has evolved, and describes how Taligent is laying the foundation for a new generation of applications.

AN INDUSTRYWIDE DILEMMA

Commercial software developers, corporate software developers, users of the software created by both kinds of developers, and original equipment manufacturers (OEMs) such as Taligent's investors are all becoming aware of some disturbing trends in the computer industry. This section summarizes these trends from the point of view of each group.

✔ NOTE   As used in this book, the term *commercial software developers* means developers who write and sell commercial software. Synonyms include "shrink-wrapped software developers" and "independent software vendors" (ISVs). The term *corporate software developers* includes both developers who write software for in-house functions (such as inventory control) and developers who write software that is part of or closely tied to the goods and services sold by a corporation (such as the switching software used by telephone companies). In addition to corporations, a variety of other organizations include software developers with similar characteristics and concerns.

Commercial software developers

Commercial software developers face a mature and unforgiving software market in the mid-1990s. Innovative new products are becoming more and more difficult to develop and market successfully. The software needs of many users aren't being met. In many ways, the state of commercial software development reflects the state of the industry as a whole.

Ten signs of trouble

Anyone involved in creating, marketing, or using commercial software packages can recognize the signs of trouble described here.

Fewer new applications

Check out your favorite computer trade magazine. What are the software mail-order houses selling these days? Version 6.0 of a popular word processor. Version 4.0 of one presentation program, version 5.0 of another. New versions of two or three big spreadsheet applications, of page-layout applications, of low- and high-end graphics programs, of utilities and communications packages and financial applications. But how many listings can you find for brand new, version 1.0 applications? You'll have to look hard; there aren't many.

How many new application categories have emerged in the past few years? For example, how many new kinds of applications solve group and enterprise problems? Is everyone so busy revising their current applications or porting them to new platforms that they don't have time to develop new ones? Have all the important applications already been written? Or have thousands of markets not had their needs addressed or even recognized?

Bigger applications and bigger manuals

Six or seven years ago you could fit your whole operating system, an application, and a few documents on a 400K disk. After a while you needed an 800K disk. Today a 1.44-MB disk usually isn't enough for the application by itself, and you're lucky if a major business application package comes on fewer than five disks of compressed files. Many occupy 20 MB or more of disk space after they're installed.

Why such big applications? Because each new version is loaded with more and more new features. Most users don't use or even know about the added features despite forests of dialog boxes and menus and submenus that hit the bottom of the screen. All those new features have to be documented, so of course manuals keep getting bigger too. You don't hear companies boasting about their featherweight manuals anymore. Software manuals can run to several volumes of hundreds of pages each—and users need to spend lots of time reading those pages to use the applications effectively.

Despite all the new features, users aren't getting the kinds of capabilities they need in areas such as workflow management, real-time collaboration, decision support, and business-specific distributed computing applications.

Long time to market

As the complexity of system software and applications increases, so does the time it takes to bring a new product or a new release of an existing product to market. Two or three years between releases is common. In the interim, users may switch to a competing application. More importantly, the time it takes to get a 1.0 application to market can easily exceed the funding window of a startup company with a good idea and specialized understanding of a particular market. This is especially true of applications for business computing environments.

Rising upgrade prices

Another consequence of the length of time between releases is that upgrade prices are approaching what applications themselves used to cost. Companies that used to send out upgrades free may now charge a hundred dollars or more for each one, depending on how recently you bought your first version. This isn't to say that upgrades aren't worth the money; they always include new features, some of which you may even use. Prices have risen because the effort of producing an upgrade to a successful commercial application is beginning to approach and even exceed the effort required to get the original release out the door.

Expanding engineering teams

Ten years ago, a couple of typical programmers with a good idea could create an application and have a chance of establishing a successful commercial-grade product. Now it's more common to see 10-, 20-, or even 100-person teams working on applications. Good applications still emerge from time to time that are written by one or two gurus—but there have never been and never will be enough gurus to write all the software that needs to be written.

Substantial testing requirements

The number of testers on some software teams is beginning to equal or exceed the number of engineers, and many projects can't afford all the testers they really need. In the old days, you could create an application, test it in a few configurations, and you'd be through. But now there are so many possible configurations of hardware, system software, networks, and installation options, that testing—even for a single platform—has become a nightmare. With multiple platforms, the problem is compounded. Frame tests dozens of different versions of FrameMaker for its markets. Lotus tests Lotus 1-2-3 for hundreds of printer configurations. All this work takes many highly skilled people, a lot of time, and a lot of money.

Applications adding OS features

Another reason applications are getting so big is that software developers are often forced to add what amount to operating system capabilities. No matter how quickly system software vendors like Apple, IBM, or Microsoft develop system software extensions and refinements, they can never meet all the specific system software needs of the big commercial developers—not to mention the more specialized needs of corporate developers or small companies developing for vertical markets.

Some developers claim that over half of their application code is really system software needed to get their applications to work. They have to extend the existing operating system, or work around bugs, or shield themselves from parts of the system that work against what they're trying to do. Rather than hiring people with expertise in a particular domain, such as publishing or accounting, developers have to hire computer systems experts to write user interface elements, printer drivers, line layout systems, fixed-point graphics models, help systems, and so on. Application teams routinely include more specialists in various areas of software engineering than in the tasks that an application is supposed to perform.

Economics stifling innovation

The economics of software development are beginning to dictate the kinds of applications that will and won't be developed. The cost of developing, testing, documenting, duplicating, and legally protecting a major commercial-grade horizontal or vertical application can exceed $50 million, and that's just for development; marketing and support can require similar expenditures.

Not many companies can raise that kind of capital. An application that involves an innovative concept for a new, unproven market isn't likely to attract such sums. Instead, the economics of software development increasingly favor large, feature-laden applications for large, established markets. In general, a successful mainstream application requires something on the order of 100,000 units per year in sales to amortize the development costs, which implies a market of, say, a million units per year if the application claims a 10 percent share of a given segment. This means that certain kinds of applications are likely to get written, and other kinds don't stand a chance. Most software companies can't afford to target markets of 10,000 or 1,000 or 100 units per year.

Yet there are many more potential customers in focused, vertical markets than in traditional horizontal markets. Despite the personal computer revolution of the past decade or so, over half of the business workers in the United States still don't even have computers on their desks. This isn't necessarily because they can't benefit from computing. It's more likely due to the absence of software adapted to their specific business needs.

Users ignoring upgrades

People who do use computers are continuing to buy machines, but they aren't upgrading their applications at the same rate. For example, in recent years hardware unit volume has increased substantially as prices have decreased. But the increase in software unit volume hasn't kept pace. Plenty of customers are buying second machines and faster replacement machines to run their existing applications, but fewer seem to see the value in upgrading their applications. When they do upgrade, it's often because they need to maintain compatibility with their colleagues, not because they intend to use the new features.

Fewer profitable software companies

The logical consequence of these trends is fewer and fewer profitable software companies. Over the past several years, software market share has become increasingly consolidated within a few large companies. A very small percentage of software titles command the vast majority of total software sales. Big companies are buying up little companies at an increasing rate, because only the biggest companies can afford the scale of organization and expenditure it takes to develop and sustain successful applications for today's computer systems.

In the limit . . .

It's not hard to imagine where the commercial software industry is headed if these trends continue to their logical extreme. Eventually, only one software company will be making money—the company selling version 10.0 of its single all-purpose application, WordSheet. WordSheet 10.0 is developed by the top 100 software gurus in the world, who all work for the company. Tested by 250 test engineers, four years between releases, and costing $500 per upgrade, WordSheet 10.0 doesn't fit on floppies anymore. You have to buy it on a CD.

The inevitable consequence: Users stick with 9.0.

Corporate software developers

These trends are bad enough for commercial software developers, but they spell disaster for corporate software developers and developers in other institutions, such as laboratories and universities, that create their own software. In-house development teams most commonly consist of just two or three people per project, although they can range up to thousands of programmers in rare cases. Whatever their size, these teams usually develop custom programs for use only within their own companies or as part of their company's products, which may not sell in the high volumes common in the retail software market. Fast turnaround is critical. They can't take two or three years to get an application developed. Product cycles as short as three to six months are desired.

Corporate developers are frequently developing software for the largest-volume application environment, Microsoft Windows. But Microsoft itself specializes in writing large, sophisticated applications. It writes them for Windows and for the Mac® OS, and it is the leading application vendor in both markets. Not surprisingly, Microsoft continues to add new application features to Windows, such as Object Linking and Embedding (OLE), that can be most efficiently exploited by virtuoso multiapplication development teams like its own.

Microsoft isn't alone in this respect. Companies that create traditional system software strive constantly to add new features that increase the things their systems can do—features that small development teams often have difficulty exploiting successfully. This situation favors large commercial software companies and penalizes corporate developers with small teams, short product cycles, and limited product deployment.

As David Taylor and others have pointed out, the volume of information that corporations and other rapidly evolving information-based organizations must handle is exceeding their capacity to process it (Taylor, 1990). Most corporate developers are facing a growing backlog at the same time that they're facing budget cuts and increasingly frustrated users. As much as 80 or 90 percent of most information services (IS) budgets goes to maintaining existing software, so it's very difficult to get ahead. Corporate developers are also under pressure to downsize to less expensive machines. Off-the-shelf libraries and software packages provide generic solutions for some processing tasks, but they are often just as difficult to adapt to new circumstances as custom packages developed within a company; and because they are generic, they provide little or no competitive differentiation.

Frequently late, over budget, and in many cases obsolete before they ever get used, corporate software projects are notorious for creating bottlenecks. When software is an essential part of a product, the slow pace of development directly impedes a company's ability to differentiate itself and compete in new markets. An article by W. Wayt Gibbs in the September 1994 issue of *Scientific American* lists some of the more spectacular software disasters in recent history, including the California Department of Motor Vehicles attempt to merge the state's driver and vehicle registration systems, which cost over $43 million and was abandoned without ever being used; the failed $165 million attempt by American Airlines to link its flight-reservation software with the reservation systems of Marriott, Hilton, and Budget; and the Denver airport's computerized baggage system, which contributed to the delay in the airport's opening at a cost of hundreds of millions of dollars. These are extreme examples, but similar disasters on a smaller scale are now part of everyday life in corporate America. The software crisis affects everyone, including millions of people who never touch a computer.

Users

Users, especially those trying to work together in businesses and other enterprises, are becoming more sophisticated and demanding, and they're not happy. Often they must make do with applications that don't quite fit their needs. Standard accounting packages are fine if you run a standard business, but accounting for many businesses requires additional categories and relationships that just can't be anticipated by large software companies targeting mass markets. The same thing holds true in every software category. Software companies keep adding complicated features to their big applications, but customizing for specialized purposes is still very difficult.

Even if they don't use all the extra features, customers pay for all those extra bytes. The vast majority of commercial software shipments go to existing users who are less and less pleased with what they get. Well-established applications get larger and more difficult to use, and applications that expand the use of computers into new areas such as collaboration are rare. As a result, the software market for both individual users and business customers is becoming a replacement market with little growth.

Applications still don't work together as well as they should. Even copying and pasting can't always be relied on. If you're working with text, you will probably get the ASCII characters, but not always the fonts, styles, and sizes, and hardly ever the tabs, margins, and line spacing. If you're working with graphics, you'll probably get the lines and rectangles, but not always the colors or more complex curves, and rarely the alignment, grouping, or snap-to-grid information. Considering the difficulties at this trivial level of cooperation, it's not surprising that distributed applications used with diverse databases and hardware platforms over large networks have severe limitations from the point of view of both users and system administrators.

For example, programs written for traditional operating systems can implement limited collaboration capabilities, but they must use a complex conversion process that involves sending millions of bits over a single connection with one other computer. Two users in different locations can view and annotate a document using special tools, but only one can make real-time changes to the document itself, and there is little or no support for collaboration among more than two users.

New technologies like OLE promise to improve interapplication communication, but their additional capabilities cost the developer more time writing code. OLE is difficult to program and therefore works best when a given company controls the applications that are trying to communicate. As a result, OLE is best suited for large software companies that sell several major horizontal high-volume applications, especially highly integrated application suites. It tends to hurt small companies doing more specialized applications for smaller markets, because they must support this expensive technology to remain competitive, without reaping the benefits across several successful applications.

This situation directly affects the options available to users: if you want your applications to work smoothly together, you have to buy a standard package that addresses some, but not all, of your needs. If you take a chance on more specialized applications, they may not work together as reliably.

Like their counterparts in corporate software development, users in large organizations are especially vulnerable to the limitations of the current generation of applications. Multiuser collaboration across corporate networks faces all kinds of obstacles, including incompatible platforms, multiple email systems, multiple network protocols, and security problems. Corporate users working together over a network must deal with a tangle of rules and procedures and long lists of names—all things that computers are supposed to be good at but aren't.

OEMs

Original equipment manufacturers that are known for hardware innovation, such as Apple, IBM, and Hewlett-Packard, are also affected by the slow pace and increasing complexity of software development. Hardware development technology made great strides in the 1980s. Hardware engineers now routinely create silicon chips that work as specified the first time, and development cycles for new hardware products are much shorter than they used to be. But system software engineers can't keep up with the pace of hardware innovations. In many cases, new hardware features go unused because the system software doesn't support them.

Macintosh examples

Some examples from the history of the Macintosh computer, itself an innovative hardware platform, illustrate this problem. The Macintosh II, which Apple introduced in 1987, was the first Macintosh computer that included a memory management unit (MMU). An MMU allows a computer to use virtual memory, which involves treating hard disk memory as if it were additional RAM. But it was several years before Macintosh system software used this capability. Millions of MMU chips went unused until System 7 was introduced in 1991. Even then, support for virtual memory was only partial, because System 7 didn't provide protected address spaces, shared memory, memory-mapped files, locking of pages, or other features that take full advantage of the MMU.

The floating point unit (FPU) also became a standard hardware feature starting with the Macintosh II. FPUs are good for intensive calculations like those involved in drawing complex graphics. But the standard Macintosh graphics system continued to be based on screen coordinates and integer arithmetic; only a few specialized applications could take advantage of the FPU's capabilities. Because so few people were benefitting from the FPU, Apple's hardware engineers eventually began making it optional in some CPUs.

Soon after introducing the Macintosh II, Apple introduced the SuperDrive® disk drive across its entire product line. This drive could read floppy disks formatted for either MS-DOS or Macintosh system software. But it wasn't until 1993 that the icon for an MS-DOS floppy would actually appear on the Macintosh desktop when you inserted the disk.

These kinds of hardware support problems aren't the fault of Apple's system software engineers, who have learned to perform miracles with the legacies they must live with. The problems arise because the original Macintosh system software didn't anticipate the need for supporting new hardware capabilities. For example, it didn't support color, multiple monitors of varying size, hard disks, bus slots, or advanced networks. Despite these limitations, Apple engineers came up with inventive solutions that support all of these features today. But this support comes at a cost in terms of both the engineering effort and the complexity of the solutions required.

PC examples

IBM and other OEMs in the Intel-based PC market face the same kinds of problems. Millions of PCs capable of supporting 32-bit addressing were designed, sold, bought, used, and thrown away without ever running a single 32-bit application, because system software never took advantage of it.

The Macintosh MMU and FPU examples have parallels in the Windows market. All 386 and faster processors have a built-in MMU. However, with the exception of Windows NT users (and Windows 95 users, when it becomes available), most Windows users still have no virtual memory capability. Similarly, millions of existing Intel-based systems have at least a slot for an FPU, but the Windows graphics environment is still based on screen coordinates and integer arithmetic and can't take advantage of FPU capabilities.

Many patented hardware technologies have faced a similar fate. One example is the Micro Channel® architecture (MCA) bus that IBM invented. It provided autoconfiguration, slot independence, high performance, and other capabilities that represented a significant improvement compared to the standard architecture. But IBM couldn't persuade enough developers to build add-on cards that supported the bus. It wasn't part of the standard PC clone hardware manufactured by dozens of companies around the world, so it didn't sell in as large volumes, and it's very difficult to write drivers for MS-DOS, so many card developers didn't bother.

Many factors affect the success of any commercial product, and system software can't take all the blame for the fact that sophisticated hardware doesn't get used. But the tendency is disturbing. People who invent something new and better shouldn't be penalized for their efforts. Companies that lavish expertise and innovative technology on hardware today face a commodity market for personal computers, especially in the IBM-compatible world, in which it's very difficult to build anything besides another clone that adheres to the standard. If only companies that have thin margins and very low R&D budgets can make money, everyone in the industry ends up losing. Innovation gets punished rather than rewarded, and market growth slows. The benefits to the user of cutthroat pricing are offset by slowing innovation and the fact that many clone system suppliers stay in business for only a few years.

The emergence of application systems

The sad stories in the previous section can all be traced to the same problem. The problem isn't the hardware, which keeps getting cheaper and faster and more reliable. It's not the users, who are more computer literate than they've ever been. It's not application developers, who generally have many more ideas than they can successfully develop. User interfaces can share some of the blame; computers are becoming more difficult to use as they become adapted to more complex tasks, especially in multiuser environments. But a single problem lies behind nearly all the difficulties faced by the computer industry: the dominant paradigm for developing, marketing, and deploying application software is stifling innovation.

Increased frustration and slower productivity are common as a technology matures. It was equally true of the technology that preceded today's procedural development methods. Twenty-five or thirty years ago, most computer programs basically consisted of a long list of instructions and data. The processor would start at the beginning of the list, follow all the instructions, and output a result. This worked well for solving problems such as preparing a payroll or performing a series of complex calculations, but not for other tasks that people wanted computers to perform. As the hardware became more sophisticated and more powerful, this kind of programming also became increasingly difficult for programmers, who often wrote programs in relatively low-level languages or even assembly language.

These frustrations led to some dramatic changes in programming techniques. Within a few years, high-level procedural languages and structured programming techniques, previously the domain of academics and a few teams of researchers, achieved general acceptance in the marketplace. Rather than writing a list of arcane instructions for the machine to read from top to bottom, programmers could work in higher-level languages that made it easier to work with logical abstractions such as loops and data structures.

Application program interfaces (APIs)

Personal computer operating systems, such as CP/M, ProDOS®, and MS-DOS, began to emerge in the late 1970s and early 1980s. At first these operating systems consisted of abstractions that represented hardware devices, such as the terminal, printer, or disk drive. For example, instead of writing a lot of code to move a specific kind of disk drive head from place to place on a disk, programmers could write simpler code that used an operating system abstraction to write a file to the disk. They could concentrate more on the needs of the applications they were writing, using the operating system to manipulate the hardware as necessary.

This led to the three-tier arrangement shown on the left side of Figure 1, with clear-cut barriers between the hardware, the operating system, and an application. To communicate across the barrier between the application and the operating system, programmers learned to use *application program interfaces (APIs)*, the commands and definitions supported by the operating system. This arrangement provided high-level abstractions of the hardware for programmers to use instead of dealing with it directly. The operating system took care of the hardware, so the application didn't have to.

FIGURE 1
THE EMERGENCE OF
APPLICATION SYSTEMS

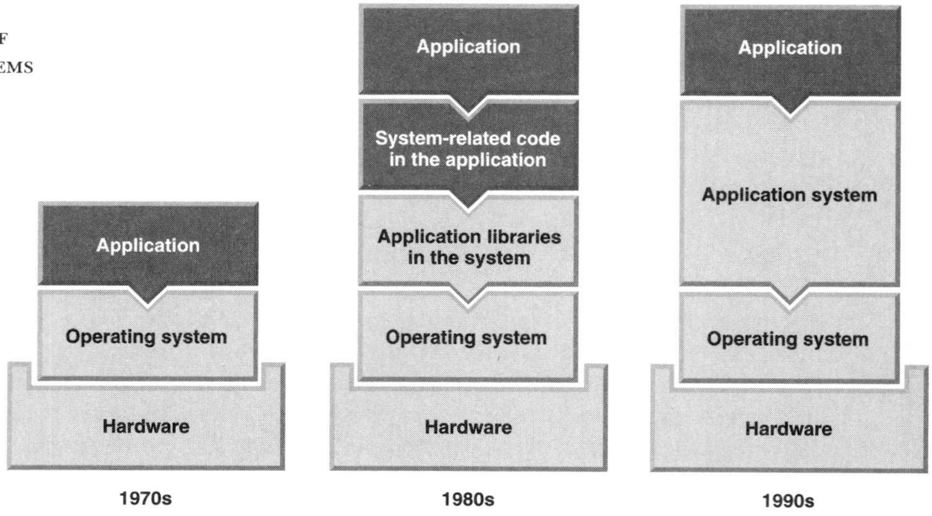

1970s	1980s	1990s
Application	Application	Application
Operating system	System-related code in the application	Application system
Hardware	Application libraries in the system	Operating system
	Operating system	Hardware
	Hardware	

Application libraries in the system

As time passed, operating system designers began to add more and more abstractions to handle file management, printing, graphics, and other programming tasks. Programmers in turn began to create more complex applications that took advantage of these capabilities and added new ones. In the 1980s, as shown in the middle of Figure 1, system software such as Mac OS, Windows, and OS/2® expanded to include application libraries that developers could use to add new capabilities to their applications, including menus, windows, dialog boxes, networking, telecommunications, interapplication communication, and so on.

For example, a Mac OS programmer needs to call just one function to display a standard dialog box that allows users to scroll through lists of files, directories, and disk drives; responds appropriately when the user clicks or double-clicks various fields and buttons within the dialog box; and returns control to the application only after the user has made an appropriate selection. Although some tasks may require calling lower-level operating system functions directly, in general the applications written for this kind of system software include more calls to application libraries than to the underlying operating system libraries.

System-related code in the application

As the application libraries and the underlying operating systems continued to mature and acquire more capabilities, the number of APIs and programming reference manuals and the complexity of the programming task began to increase exponentially. But if an application needed more specialized capabilities than some part of the system happened to provide (for example a printer driver or a high-end graphics engine), the programmer usually didn't have the ability to modify the underlying library. Instead, the programmer either had to live with it as is or had to create a new one from scratch, essentially replacing part of the operating system.

For example, Aldus Persuasion writes all its printer drivers from scratch. Adobe Illustrator, which runs on both the Mac OS and Windows, ignores QuickDraw™ (the Mac OS graphics engine) and GDI (the Windows graphics engine) and uses its own PostScript graphics system instead. Developers spend a lot of time trying to make their programs work with (or around) the underlying operating system, and therefore less of their time working on the tasks their application performs for the customer. Whether it calls application libraries or the underlying operating system, half or more of a modern application's code is essentially a form of system software.

Application systems

All this has resulted in the large operating systems and large applications that dominate the market today. In effect, application developers are pushing down into the domain of system software, spending more and more energy filling in the pieces they need to build advanced applications. At the same time, system software designers continue to expand their application libraries to meet new user demands, pushing up into the application domain. As the system expands, it becomes more difficult for proliferating teams of software engineers to make all the pieces work together seamlessly, so costs and time to market keep increasing, especially for multiplatform development efforts. Complex new system solutions don't address the portability needs of distributed applications.

It's as if system software engineers have built a wonderful house of cards as high as it can possibly be built. Now only a few gurus have hands steady enough to reach into the interior and change something without knocking the whole structure down. And if you can't get a guru when you want to insert a new card, you have to hire armies of people to hold all the cards steady.

The tension between the needs of developers and the increasing complexity of operating systems is leading in the 1990s toward a new category of system software that Taligent calls an *application system,* as suggested by the right side of Figure 1. Instead of requiring programmers to incorporate system-related code into their programs, an application system provides a comprehensive set of integrated application and distributed services capabilities, freeing the programmer to concentrate on code related to a single application's problem domain.

Environments such as HyperCard for the Mac OS, IBM's CICS™, Lotus Notes, and Smalltalk each resemble certain aspects of an application system, because they allow application developers to create applications without necessarily using the underlying operating system directly. Although the lines between these application environments and their underlying operating systems aren't always clear-cut, they provide many default behaviors that save application developers time and effort and ultimately benefit users as well.

Unlike any of these precursors, however, a comprehensive application system must facilitate the rapid construction of full-featured distributed applications for deployment across heterogeneous peer-to-peer and client-server environments. In addition, the application system should provide for a high degree of interoperability among applications—both those built with the application system and existing applications running locally or remotely on the host operating system.

Traditional operating systems like those introduced in Figure 1 abstracted the underlying hardware for application developers, and in some cases, such as the UNIX® system, allowed the applications to be portable across different hardware platforms. Taligent's application system abstracts the underlying operating system for application developers and thereby allows applications created with those abstractions to be portable across different operating systems.

THE TALIGENT PRODUCT SUITE

Taligent has created a new kind of system software: the CommonPoint™ application system. Portable across multiple host operating systems and capable of interoperating with applications running on those systems, the CommonPoint system provides robust support for distributed computing and a user environment designed for people working together over a network.

CommonPoint application developers develop software by using either host development tools or tools in the CommonPoint Developer Series. The CommonPoint Developer Series includes the *cp*Professional™ development environment for prototyping and development and the *cp*Constructor™ user interface builder for creating user interface elements.[1] All CommonPoint Developer Series tools are capable of running on any CommonPoint host.

Figure 2 shows some of the host operating systems that can support the CommonPoint system and the CommonPoint Developer Series. Taligent has also been developing a set of OS technologies, called Taligent Object Services (TalOS™), optimized for hosting the CommonPoint system and portable across multiple hardware platforms. Taligent plans to make these technologies available to its investors and other licensees.

FIGURE 2
HOW TALIGENT
FITS IN

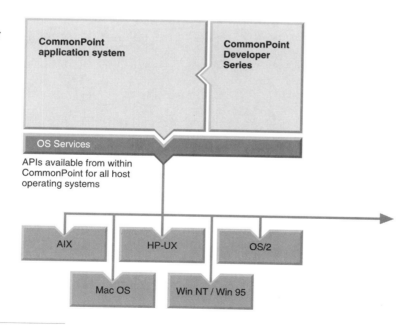

1. During development and in early product literature, the CommonPoint application system, *cp*Professional development environment, and *cp*Constructor user interface builder were known as the Taligent Application Environment (TalÆ™), Taligent Development Environment (TalDE™), and Taligent User Interface Builder, respectively.

CommonPoint application system

The CommonPoint application system supports a comprehensive set of features, including compound documents, 2-D and 3-D graphics, and real-time document sharing and collaboration. It also provides a complete programming model that is designed to work the same way on all host operating systems. Taligent's investors plan to ship the CommonPoint application system with AIX®, OS/2, HP-UX®, and Mac OS systems, and Taligent plans to sell it as a separate software package that runs on other 32-bit systems such as Windows NT and Windows 95. Taligent is vigorously pursuing ports to all popular 32-bit operating systems and is building a network of OEM and distribution partners to deliver its products.

Whenever the CommonPoint system (or a CommonPoint application) needs something from the host, such as file system or networking services, it uses the standard calling APIs provided by OS Services. These APIs are represented in Figure 2 by the gray layer below the CommonPoint and CommonPoint Developer Series boxes. The CommonPoint implementation for each host translates those API calls into the appropriate calls to the host system's APIs.

No matter what host it is running on, the CommonPoint system requires only the lowest portion of host system software—file system calls, driver calls, kernel calls, and so on. It doesn't rely on any of the host system's higher-level features, such as graphics packages. Programmers writing applications for the CommonPoint system don't need to call the host APIs directly (though they can), and applications developed using the Taligent programming model can be designed to be source-code compatible across all host operating systems. Taligent's goal is to allow developers who follow the rules to port their software simply by recompiling their code, although as a practical matter some testing on different platforms will still be necessary.

In addition, as suggested by Figure 3, applications written for the host operating systems can run at the same time as CommonPoint applications and can interoperate with them, thus preserving customers' software investments. Both the host operating system and the CommonPoint application system use the same low-level host protocols (labeled "Host OS core services" in Figure 3) to communicate with the underlying 32-bit (and higher) hardware.

FIGURE 3
COMMONPOINT
APPLICATIONS
RUN ALONGSIDE
HOST APPLICA-
TIONS AND
INTEROPERATE
WITH THEM

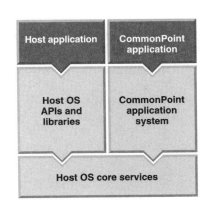

Taligent provides its investors and other key partners with a reference release, currently running on AIX, for each new version of the CommonPoint application system and the CommonPoint Developer Series. When Taligent or any other company ports a Taligent reference release to a new host operating system, the newly ported version provides the interface code required to map the standard CommonPoint and *cp*Professional APIs to the low-level host protocols. Before Taligent or any third party can make such a port available commercially, the ported version must pass a suite of tests to certify that it supports the APIs and other standards established by Taligent's reference release.

Taligent will administer these tests at first, with the goal of eventually making them available to an independent organization such as the Object Management Group or the X/Open standards organization. This testing process ensures that all CommonPoint implementations work the same way and provides branding for certified implementations, which can then use the CommonPoint logo.

CommonPoint Developer Series

The CommonPoint Developer Series includes the *cp*Professional development environment and the *cp*Constructor user interface builder, which are briefly summarized here. For more detailed information, see Chapter 5, "Development tools and approaches."

*cp*Professional

The *cp*Professional development environment is a tightly integrated suite of customizable development tools that are optimized for rapid prototyping and development of CommonPoint applications. Programmers can use these tools to browse through the parts of the CommonPoint system that interest them and assemble programs by customizing preexisting pieces of code. All *cp*Professional tools are built around an object-oriented project database that supports many of their key capabilities, including incremental compiling and linking at the granularity of individual functions.

The *cp*Professional development environment provides these benefits for developers of CommonPoint software:

- **Easy to use and customize.** All tools are tightly integrated and share a consistent user interface. They include a browsing environment that developers can customize to suit their work preferences. This environment also provides built-in links among all related information.
- **Accelerates the learning process.** *cp*Professional viewers provide multiple program views to aid developers in the visualization and comprehension of object-oriented systems. For example, subsystem views are organized according to the standard CommonPoint taxonomy, which is particularly useful for developers programming with the CommonPoint APIs for the first time.

- **Automates complex programming tasks.** *cp*Professional tools automate many complex activities that accompany conventional development environments. For example, the automated build system frees developers from having to specify module dependencies and build rules, a time-consuming and error-prone activity when performed manually.

- **Reduces turnaround times.** The *cp*Professional incremental build system greatly reduces the turnaround time required for changes by making build times truly proportional to the magnitude of changes. A simple change to a C++ function, for example, requires recompilation and linking of that function only, not the entire class or file containing the function.

- **Facilitates team programming.** The *cp*Professional source control system doesn't require team members to check modules in and out. Instead, it keeps track of dependencies related to any change at the granularity of individual functions. Conflicts are less likely because of this fine granularity; if any do occur, merge tools help the programmer merge new code with the project.

The *cp*Professional development environment also lays the foundation for third-party development efforts. For more information, see the section beginning on page 136.

cpConstructor

The *cp*Constructor user interface builder streamlines the creation and layout of visual interface elements such as buttons, text fields, windows, dialog boxes, and menus. The appearance and other characteristics of these objects can be changed at any time without affecting the implementation of their behavior.

Working with the *cp*Constructor user interface builder is much like working with a drawing program. A user interface designer can copy and paste visual elements, modify them, arrange them on the screen, and perform preliminary testing. The *cp*Constructor user interface builder also greatly simplifies localization of CommonPoint applications.

For more information, see the section beginning on page 146.

**Taligent Object
Services**

The Taligent Object Services (TalOS) technologies are being built around a new Mach-3.0-based microkernel, used by IBM as part of the Workplace technologies, that's designed to exploit the latest 32-bit microprocessors and to support object-oriented system architectures. As explained at the beginning of this chapter, Taligent's strategy with regard to this low-level system technology has evolved since the early days of the Pink project at Apple. Instead of creating a single system from the microkernel up, Taligent has created the first comprehensive application system and has focused its first product offerings on versions of the CommonPoint application system and CommonPoint Developer Series tools that run on existing host operating systems.

Nonetheless, TalOS technologies can eventually provide an extensible and portable operating system for customers seeking the best performance and smallest footprint in a focused CommonPoint solution. TalOS technologies also bring the benefits of the Taligent programming model to operating system and hardware developers, such as developers of drivers for hardware devices.

TalOS technologies use object-oriented techniques to implement basic host services for the CommonPoint system such as device driver support and low-level network protocols. Runtime and microkernel services, also designed for optimal support of objects, supplement the microkernel in managing system resources.

Hardware dependencies are primarily confined to the microkernel, runtime services, and a few object service I/O frameworks. This confinement allows TalOS technologies to extend the benefits of frameworks to a broad range of desktop and transportable hardware platforms, including those based on the Intel, PowerPC™, and PA-RISC microprocessors used by Taligent's investors.

Taligent plans to make TalOS technologies available to its investors and other licensees. For example, IBM has announced that it plans to use TalOS technologies in its new versions of OS/2 and AIX® for PowerPC computers.

For more information about TalOS technologies, see Chapter 15, "OS Services."

HOW TALIGENT IS DIFFERENT

Taligent products facilitate new ways of working for both application and system programmers. Most importantly, everyone plays by the same set of rules. Code written by a developer for the CommonPoint application system stands on the same technical footing as any code written by Taligent or by Apple, IBM, or Hewlett-Packard for their versions of the system. Taligent's use of object-oriented technology throughout all of its products, especially its use of frameworks, makes this possible.

Frameworks

All Taligent products are built from OOP abstractions known as frameworks. A *framework* is an extensible library of cooperating classes that make up a reusable design solution for a given problem domain. Taligent uses frameworks not only for application domains such as user interface, text, and documents, but also for traditional system domains such as graphics, multimedia, fonts, and printing; low-level services such as drivers and network protocols; and development tools. Virtually everything that is implemented as a library in a traditional operating system is implemented as a framework in the CommonPoint system.

Nearly everything in the real world can be described in terms of conceptual frameworks—that is, within a frame of reference. Shopping in a grocery store, driving a car, playing baseball, buying a house, starting a business, or flying the space shuttle all involve working within clearly defined rules and relationships while permitting great flexibility. You can buy a lot of groceries or just a few; shop at a big supermarket, a corner store, or a fruit stand at the side of the highway; pay with cash, check, credit card, or coupons. Despite such variations, everyone knows what shopping for groceries means, how it works, and how to interact with the other people involved.

Similarly, an experienced driver renting an unfamiliar car takes only a few minutes to adjust the seat and mirrors and adapt to the new locations of controls and dials, the feel of the steering, and the location of the car's edges in relation to other vehicles and the edge of the road. By following some simple rules and paying attention, the driver can interact safely with other drivers of different kinds of vehicles going in different directions at different speeds and navigate many different roads and freeways to reach one particular destination among many possibilities.

Baseball teams know how to play baseball, home buyers know how to look for and purchase a house, executives know how to set up businesses, and astronauts know how to perform complex technical feats in space, all because they work within a recognized frame of reference for each domain. Yet all of these processes work a bit differently each time, allowing flexibility within clearly defined limits. In this sense, everything in life is a framework, and we all work with frameworks every day without even thinking about it.

Everything, that is, except software, and everyone except software developers. It's as if programmers have to grow the food, build the store, stock the shelves, and invent a monetary system each time they want to buy groceries. Computer software may be the last major industrial product that's still built from scratch each time.

Although the preceding comparisons may seem exaggerated, most programmers would agree that developing software requires much more work than it should. Taligent is attempting to change the programming paradigm by using object-oriented frameworks for everything—not only for developing applications but also for developing the CommonPoint system itself.

Taligent frameworks provide generic code at all levels of the system that programmers can reuse and customize easily. Instead of using thousands of interrelated APIs to write monolithic applications for a monolithic operating system, developers can use individual framework APIs to create smaller, more specialized programs that are fully integrated with the rest of the system and with other programs. And instead of writing only applications that sit on top of the operating system, developers can customize the application system itself to create new kinds of tools, utilities, drivers, file formats, networking protocols, data types, graphics primitives, drawing algorithms, and the like, any of which can be products in their own right.

Taligent's approach to frameworks is described in more detail in Chapter 2, "The Taligent programming model."

Shifting the burden of complexity

Larry Tesler, one of Apple's best-known OOP gurus, once pointed out that you can never actually make things easier in software. You can only shift the burden of complexity from one place to another. For example, the development of very-large-scale integration (VLSI) technology shifted much of the complexity that was formerly the domain of computer system engineers to the domain of integrated circuit designers. This in turn freed computer system engineers to create more complex kinds of hardware. Eventually, the building-block approach that VLSI made possible led to the pervasive use of integrated circuits in ways that were previously inconceivable, for example in appliances, cars, toys and many other products.

In a similar fashion, Taligent wants to shift much of the complexity of software development from application developers to application system engineers. Figure 4 shows another way of looking at some of the relationships shown in Figure 1 on page 18, this time in terms of the way in which the total complexity of each system is distributed among the user, the application developer, and system software.

Twenty years ago, a typical operating system for a personal computer was relatively simple, as shown by the leftmost column in Figure 4. An operating system like MS-DOS or CP/M could run in 64K of RAM and from a floppy disk. Because they had to fit in the same 64K of RAM, applications were also simple. But users had to work hard to use the applications. They had to memorize commands, keep track of obscure file names, and learn all kinds of esoteric details and tricks to accomplish relatively simple tasks. Moving data from one application to another was always difficult and often impossible. Users had to bear much of the burden of complexity involved in running applications.

After the Macintosh computer and operating systems with graphical user interfaces arrived on the scene, these relationships changed, as shown in the second column in Figure 4. System software companies realized that if they could make computers easier for users to use, many new users might buy their products. To this end, they added user interface capabilities to their underlying system software in the form of application libraries or "toolboxes."

FIGURE 4
SHIFTING THE
BURDEN OF
COMPLEXITY

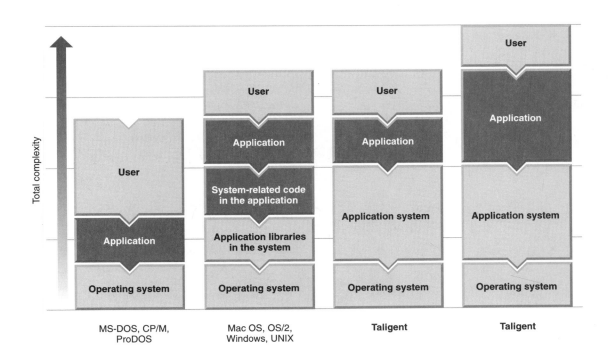

Now applications could take advantage of windows, dialog boxes, input devices like the mouse, and other innovations that greatly simplified things from the user's point of view. But the complexity didn't just disappear; instead, it was shifted to the application developers, who had to work a lot harder to create applications, and to system software engineers, who had to provide the new capabilities. The work was worth it though, because more users could use computers with less effort, and applications could meet a wider variety of user needs, leading to a net increase in the total complexity of the problems that the applications could be used to solve.

Taligent maintains that half or more of what application developers are doing today is system software work that no longer has to be their responsibility. The computer industry can't expect this situation to continue if it intends to meet customer demands for innovative, distributed applications that run in networked environments. Taligent would like to shift the complexity of computing once again, away from the application developer and into the application system. The third column in Figure 4 illustrates one consequence of this approach. Users still don't have to bother with the technical details of the system, and the applications they use provide the same kinds of capabilities as before, but small engineering teams can deliver a product in perhaps 6 to 12 months that might take a bigger team two years or more to develop for the previous generation of operating systems. This by itself can dramatically change the economics of software development.

Another consequence, illustrated by the rightmost column in Figure 4, is that some application developers will make a more extensive effort. But rather than squandering their resources fighting with the underlying operating system or reinventing the wheel, they can build on Taligent technology to provide innovative application capabilities and a richer user experience. Just as the Mac OS and Windows and other user-friendly operating systems have led to thousands of new applications that couldn't have existed in the world of MS-DOS and CP/M, Taligent technology will help create a new generation of applications that address more complex needs—in particular, the needs of users working together in an organization—than traditional applications can.

Application frameworks vs. a full application system

Object-oriented technology has been evolving for a long time and has many precursors in the current generation of system software. The left side of Figure 5 shows the basic model used in today's procedural systems: an underlying operating system, libraries and APIs built on top of that system, and applications written using those libraries and APIs.

The middle part of Figure 5 shows how object technology has been introduced for writing applications that work with the current generation of operating systems. An *application framework* provides a preassembled generic application that a developer can modify to create a real application. For example, the application framework includes basic menus and windows and code for basic operations, and the programmer adds the new code required for a specific application. Because the developer starts with robust code that's been tested and debugged, the new code is more likely to work reliably both with the system and with other applications built from the same base.

This is a big improvement over the model shown on the left of Figure 5. Examples of application frameworks include Apple's MacApp, Microsoft Foundation Classes (MFC), and NextStep. These frameworks in turn provide class libraries, or collections of ready-made objects, that make the frameworks easier to work with. (Objects and class libraries are discussed in more detail in Chapter 2.) The class libraries are built on top of the same procedural operating systems as before.

FIGURE 5
APPLICATION FRAMEWORKS VS.
FULL APPLICATION SYSTEMS

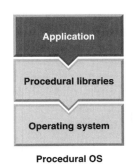

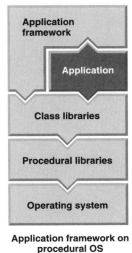

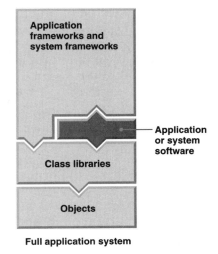

Procedural OS

UNIX, OS/2, Mac OS,
Windows NT

Application framework on
procedural OS

MacApp, MFC, NextStep

Full application system

Taligent

At first glance application frameworks seem to have the best of both worlds: they make use of OOP, so they're easier to use and maintain, but they can coexist with the older procedural operating systems and applications that are based on them.

However, application frameworks running on a procedural operating system have some drawbacks:

- The application framework controls the underlying operating system not by manipulating objects in the system, but by mapping object behavior to the underlying procedural libraries. This creates a certain amount of overhead and loss of fidelity.

- Because the framework generally doesn't provide everything required to write a real application, programmers must still make calls to the underlying procedural libraries (the box below "Class libraries" in the middle part of Figure 5). For example, MacApp developers must still make QuickDraw™ and other Mac OS calls, NextStep developers must still make Display PostScript and UNIX calls, and so on. In effect, the programmer must master two programming environments, one object-oriented and one procedural, including two sets of manuals, two kinds of debuggers, two sets of courses to take, and so on.

- Because the creators of the framework must figure out how to map the behavior of the framework to the underlying procedural system and then test the resulting mechanism, there is often a time lag between upgrades to the operating system and corresponding upgrades to the application framework. MacApp developers, for example, had to wait six months after the first release of System 7 before they received a version of MacApp that gave them the system's new capabilities "for free."

The right side of Figure 5 illustrates Taligent's approach. Taligent has built its entire programming model around objects. A foundation layer of basic system objects supports a rich set of class libraries, which in turn support frameworks designed to build not only traditional applications but also extensions and additions to any part of the application system. Taligent not only asks its developers to use OOP, but also uses exactly the same techniques throughout its own application system.

As mentioned earlier, Taligent has designed the CommonPoint application system to run on existing operating systems such as OS/2 and HP-UX. This means that applications written for the CommonPoint system can run on the same computer with applications written for that computer's native operating system, as shown in Figure 3 on page 23. However, unlike applications written with most traditional frameworks, CommonPoint applications don't need to use the host operating system APIs. The CommonPoint application system provides a complete programming model, and applications developed with it are fully portable across multiple host operating systems. Because the CommonPoint application system maps to host systems at a very low level, rather than repackaging host capabilities, it avoids mapping overhead and time-lag problems associated with traditional application frameworks.

HOW TALIGENT CAN HELP

One way or another, the software crisis described at the beginning of this chapter must be solved. The ever-increasing flow of information on which our society depends is overwhelming our ability to process it. Computing has become so fundamental to the way we live and work that software limitations affect everyone, whether directly because of system failures or indirectly because the high cost of software development inflates the cost of goods and services.

Taligent technology can help all four of the industry groups mentioned at the beginning of this chapter. It can:

- Help commercial developers extend existing markets and stimulate new ones.
- Help corporate developers develop applications more quickly.
- Help users working together in networked environments perform complex business tasks that the current generation of applications can't handle economically.
- Help OEMs sell innovative hardware solutions that are difficult or impossible to deploy profitably today.

However, technology is not enough, by itself, to create the new kinds of applications customers are demanding. With its investors, Taligent has adopted a business and marketing strategy for launching the CommonPoint system on multiple hosts and achieving high-volume deployment rapidly. This strategy, which is outlined in Chapter 4, depends on the development leverage and improved user experience that the CommonPoint system provides.

Development leverage

Commercial developers, corporate developers, and OEMs need to develop software more quickly and with greater responsiveness to specialized needs, especially the needs of enterprise customers. Unfortunately, writing procedural software is still largely a labor-intensive, hand-crafted activity. Programmers must write a lot of code and integrate it themselves so it can run successfully on the underlying operating system. Application frameworks can alleviate this problem, but, depending on how complete the framework programming model is, programmers must still replace or work around parts of the underlying operating system, and operating system development still proceeds under the old rules.

Taligent believes it can best help software innovation not by creating yet another monolithic operating system, but by facilitating changes in the way both application programmers and system programmers work. These changes won't happen overnight. Procedural programming required developers to learn new languages and new ways of working, and so does Taligent's application of OOP to system software. But just as procedural programming changed the nature of application development, Taligent believes that the intelligent use of objects can dramatically improve the speed with which all developers create software.

FIGURE 6
INCREASING DEVELOPMENT LEVERAGE

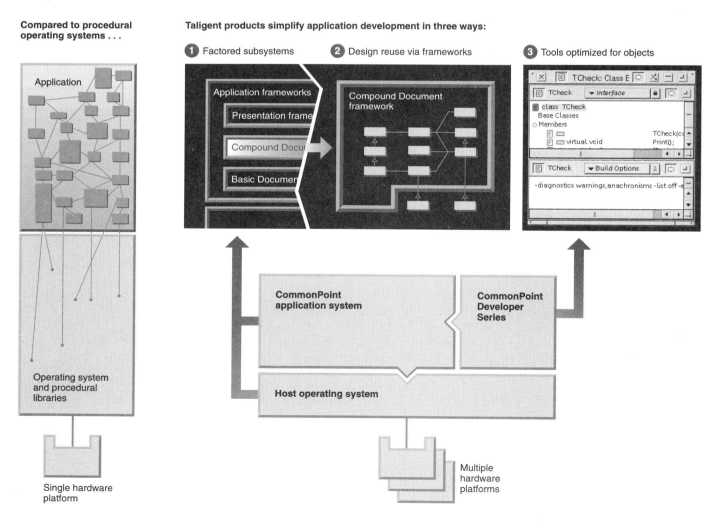

Compared to procedural operating systems . . .

Application

Operating system and procedural libraries

Single hardware platform

Taligent products simplify application development in three ways:

1 Factored subsystems

2 Design reuse via frameworks

3 Tools optimized for objects

Application frameworks

Presentation frame

Compound Docu

Basic Documen

Compound Document framework

CommonPoint application system

CommonPoint Developer Series

Host operating system

Multiple hardware platforms

Figure 6 illustrates the three major ways that Taligent products increase development leverage compared to traditional development environments:

1. **Factored subsystems ("Divide and conquer").** With the help of its investors, Taligent has carefully examined existing application and system environments, factored them into appropriate subsystems, and organized the subsystems into an integrated object-oriented architecture. Instead of facing a monolithic system with complex intrasystem relationships that must be mastered programmatically, application developers can deal with more manageable independent parts that are designed to work together. If a developer's domain requires dealing with only two or three subsystems, development can focus on modifying and extending those parts rather than making sure everything works correctly with the rest of the system.

2. **Design reuse via frameworks ("Don't reinvent the wheel").** For each subsystem, Taligent provides an implementation based on a framework, so that the developer doesn't have to start from scratch. Instead, development starts with prefabricated, preassembled units that are designed to be customized. Rather than having to do all the work themselves, programmers only have to write the extra pieces unique to their requirements. They don't have to reinvent basic elements such as menus, windows, text and graphics tools, or distributed computing capabilities on their own. Because Taligent's frameworks are designed for use on multiple hardware and operating system platforms, the resulting software is guaranteed to be portable without major development efforts for each platform.

3. **Tools optimized for object development ("You're only as good as your tools").** Finally, to ensure that developers can take full advantage of these benefits, Taligent also provides development tools that are optimized for its object-oriented approach. Most development environments today are organized around text editors—that is, applications designed for writing and editing code. They work this way because most operating systems define the programmer's role as writing new lines of code. In Taligent's view, the programmer's primary role should not be to write new code but to reuse existing code in new ways. So the *cp*Professional development environment is designed to let the programmer browse through working pieces of code, making small modifications along the way and seeing their effect without having to recompile the entire program. Like the CommonPoint system, the *cp*Professional development environment itself is built from frameworks that can be used and extended by tool developers.

For a more detailed discussion of the potential benefits of Taligent technology for commercial software developers, corporate software developers, and OEMs, see "Benefits of CommonPoint development," beginning on page 125.

More choices for users

The benefits that Taligent's approach to software development provides for developers of all kinds can also help them address users' needs more effectively. All CommonPoint applications can take advantage of integrated capabilities in most major application domains, including multilingual text, graphics, time media, and distributed computing. Users can mix a variety of rich data types in any document rather than creating separate documents for each type with a specialized application. Instead of struggling with software protocols and incompatible applications, they can concentrate on getting their work done.

The most important benefits for users are in the following areas:

- **More effective solutions.** All users stand to benefit from the increased consistency and reliability that the CommonPoint application system makes possible across a variety of host operating systems.
- **New classes of solutions.** The CommonPoint application system facilitates new kinds of applications in areas such as collaboration, workflow management, and information access.
- **Incremental enhancement.** CommonPoint applications can be easily modified to meet new business needs as they arise. The ability to make incremental changes also avoids the tendency of related custom applications to get out of sync with each other when developed serially using conventional programming.

OOP has proved to be uniquely adaptable, among programming technologies, for modeling all kinds of human activities in all kinds of organizations. The Taligent human interface employs these capabilities to extend today's user interface metaphors in ways that make it easier for people to work together.

An example of software limitations

Telephones and computers sit side by side on millions of real business desktops in every industry, but these two essential pieces of equipment can communicate with each other at only the most rudimentary level, if at all. The computer may be able to dial the telephone with the aid of a modem and communicate with other computers, but it has no other information about what the telephone is being used for.

The telephone company's proprietary software provides various useful communication services, including conference calls, call forwarding, paging services, voice mail, and so on, but the computer on the desktop has no information about what those are or how they're being used, and the telephone has no information about how its actions are related to those performed on the computer. Moreover, the computer itself is still perceived as a personal productivity device, whereas the telephone is perceived as a communications device that makes it possible for groups of people to share their work, exchange ideas, and run an organization.

A new kind of solution

What kinds of interactions might be possible if telephones and computers could share some basic information about the people who use them to communicate? Suppose you are an illustrator and I need to talk to you about a drawing you have prepared for a book I'm writing. Instead of printing out the drawing and arranging a face-to-face meeting with you, I can open the drawing on my computer, then dial your number by dragging an icon that represents you over an icon that represents my telephone.

When you answer the phone, our computers also connect with each other automatically, and the drawing document on my screen appears in a window on your screen. Any changes you make to the document are instantly visible to me as you make them, and anything I do to the document is instantly visible to you; we are sharing the actual document in real time, not just a bitmapped image. When I move the pointer, your pointer moves, and vice versa. We can both talk on the telephone while treating our computer screens as if they were one shared piece of paper, pointing, making notes, and making corrections just as we would in a face-to-face meeting.

When we're finished and hang up the phone, we each retain a copy of the original drawing document, a copy of the new version that we worked on together, and even (if we both agreed to it explicitly) a digital recording of part of our conversation. No need to travel 50 yards (or 50 miles) for a face-to-face meeting. No need to discuss visual problems without a visual reference. No printing, photocopying, uploading, or downloading.

This example gives just a taste of the kind of solution that Taligent technology can deliver effectively in a multiuser environment. Chapter 3, "A human interface for organizations," introduces the Taligent human interface in more detail.

GUIDING PRINCIPLES

Taligent has developed its products in accordance with these five guiding principles:

- **Fully object oriented.** Taligent system software products implement a completely new application programming model based on object-oriented technology. This means not only that developers can create new solutions more quickly, but also that the CommonPoint application system and other Taligent products can be extended by adding new technology without making development tools temporarily obsolete or requiring two or three years between releases. The system is constructed for growth. It's not intended to solve everyone's problems right away. Instead, Taligent is starting out with a highly flexible architecture, listening carefully to its customers as they begin using it, and planning for growth as new technologies emerge.

- **Open and extensible at all levels.** The CommonPoint application system is open and extensible at all levels. It is designed to promote third-party innovation in system software domains as well as traditional application domains, and it provides frameworks explicitly designed for this kind of development.

  This approach should provide many new kinds of opportunities for developers. Some may be happy to give up fighting with traditional system software, use only the CommonPoint frameworks they need without extensive customization, and continue developing software solutions for the domains in which they have expertise. Others may decide to customize certain application system frameworks to provide additional capabilities for their applications. And still others may discover that they can develop system software products by creating new frameworks or extending existing frameworks to implement more specialized solutions of their own.

- **Portable, adaptable, and scalable.** Any Taligent framework can be customized or entirely reimplemented by any developer. If someone has special insights into databases, for example, the Data Access framework is just as accessible as any others. This allows vendors of different SQL connectivity modules to support their proprietary interfaces via the data access frameworks, but it also means that individual programmers who want to provide new kinds of database services to users can do so in a variety of ways that are independent of any specific SQL implementation.

  The CommonPoint application system is fully portable across multiple host operating systems and across multiple hardware platforms. A developer who writes a CommonPoint application can target multiple operating systems without having to rewrite the application each time.

■ **Integrated development tools.** The *cp*Professional development environment is built around an object-oriented project database designed to help programmers explore, reuse, and extend existing code, rather than creating code from scratch. Taligent's development tools are fully object oriented and framework based, like the CommonPoint system, so that tool developers can extend and replace these frameworks just as they can extend or replace system frameworks. In addition to providing a state-of-the-art object-oriented programming environment of its own and encouraging third-party tool development, Taligent supports host system tools for the operating systems on which the CommonPoint application system runs.

■ **Rich capabilities.** The CommonPoint system includes a wide range of software capabilities that developers can easily incorporate in their applications, including object embedding and linking, drag and drop, multilevel undo, and many other basic human interface features; collaboration; scriptability; interoperability with OpenDoc™ and OLE; 2-D and 3-D graphics; international Unicode text throughout the system; time media support; sophisticated data access querying abilities; and broad support for distributed computing.

These capabilities are key requirements for the next generation of applications that will emerge as software moves beyond the personal computer desktop into the realm of business processes in modern enterprises. For details about capabilities in specific domains, see Part II, "CommonPoint system architecture."

The next chapter introduces the programming model that Taligent uses to support these principles.

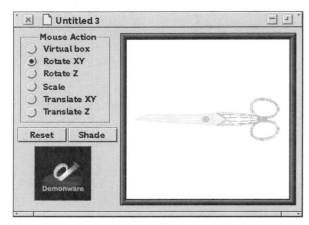

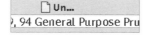

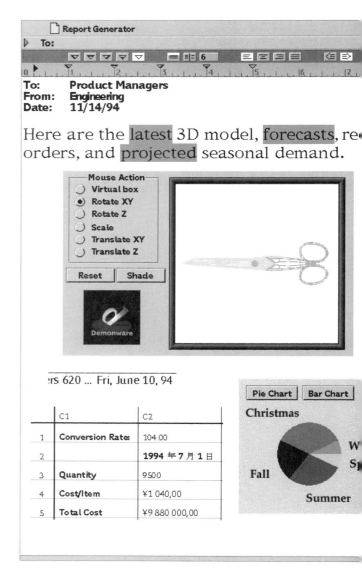

Writing a data-centered CommonPoint application involves using frameworks to assemble a set of related components and tools.

CHAPTER 2

THE TALIGENT
PROGRAMMING MODEL

Object-oriented programming (OOP) has evolved from disparate theories and techniques. Different approaches interpret key concepts and define terminology in different ways. Even standard OOP languages such as Smalltalk, C++, and Object Pascal differ significantly in their implementation of the basic object model.

This chapter defines Taligent's standard OOP terminology and introduces Taligent's approach to objects and frameworks. It is the most technical chapter in Part I. You don't need to understand all the details described here to understand Chapters 3, 4, or 5. However, if you aren't familiar with object-oriented technology, this chapter gives you the basic information you need to understand the Taligent programming model. If you are already familiar with object-oriented technology, it provides a quick review of basic OOP concepts from Taligent's point of view.

If you are a software engineer, you should also consult some of the other books about OOP listed in the Bibliography and the CommonPoint developer guides before attempting to write CommonPoint programs.

BASIC OOP CONCEPTS

This section introduces basic OOP concepts as Taligent defines them.

Objects

Objects are software entities made of data (nouns) and definitions of actions that can be performed on the data (verbs). Together, the data and actions associated with objects allow them to simulate the characteristics and behavior of almost any real-world entity, including concrete items, such as computers, people, and physical places, and abstract concepts, such as geometric shapes and data structures.

Data abstraction

Much like the cells that make up living organisms, to which they are often compared, objects hide their internal details from other objects. Just as cells communicate with each other via chemical messages that the cell membrane recognizes and allows to pass through to the inside of the cell, objects communicate with each other by means of messages (evoked by calling member functions associated with each object). If one object needs to trigger some particular action on the data within another object, it simply sends that object the appropriate message. The message's sender doesn't need to know anything about the recipient or its data other than the names of the member functions to which it responds.

This capacity for *data abstraction*—the organization of data into small, independent objects that can communicate with each other—helps software developers break complex programming problems into many smaller, simpler problems. Data abstraction is one of the primary benefits of OOP. By learning how to use the member functions that control an object, a programmer can concentrate on what the object does rather than on how it does it.

Encapsulation

The enforcement of the data abstraction provided by objects is called *encapsulation*. Just as a cell membrane protects the cell's interior from all external chemical signals except those the membrane recognizes, encapsulation prevents activities in the rest of the program from accidentally damaging an object but allows other objects to interact with that object by calling its member functions.

Figure 7 shows how encapsulation works. The left side of the figure shows the appearance of a hypothetical window object of type TWindow, and the right side shows the implementation of that object. The implementation shows some of the *members* that the TWindow object provides. These include four *data members* that hold the coordinates for the left side, right side, top, and bottom of the window and several *member functions* that operate on the window. The member functions define the actions that a TWindow object can respond to. The Open function opens the window, the Close function closes it when the user clicks the box in the upper-left corner, and the Resize function adjusts the size of the window when, for example, the user drags its lower-right corner.

✅ NOTE   Although the TWindow objects in Figure 7 and later figures reflect the Taligent convention of beginning with "T" for "Type," they present a highly simplified view of window programming and are not real CommonPoint objects. In reality, the details of window implementation depend on the development system, the role of the window, and so on.

The Resize member function in Figure 7 has arguments that specify the window's coordinates. The only way to change the actual coordinates from outside the object is to call the Resize member function; the program can't do anything to the data members directly. The data in any object can be changed only by that object's member functions.

Encapsulation protects an object's data from accidental or inappropriate changes, which in this case could mean that the values of the coordinates might not match the way the window actually looks, and text or other data inside the window might run over its edges. Because there is only one way to change a window's coordinates—by using the Resize member function—the drawing of the window and its location on screen are guaranteed to match. Consistency is ensured.

TWindow includes several other member functions. The Zoom function is triggered when a user clicks the box in the window's upper-right corner to enlarge the window so it fills up the whole screen or clicks the box again to shrink it to its original size. The Zoom function in turn calls the Resize function, specifying coordinates that are inset slightly from the sides of the screen and keeping track of the original coordinates so it can restore them when the user clicks the Zoom box again.

FIGURE 7
ENCAPSULATION
ENFORCES DATA
ABSTRACTION

Appearance

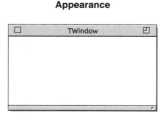

Implementation

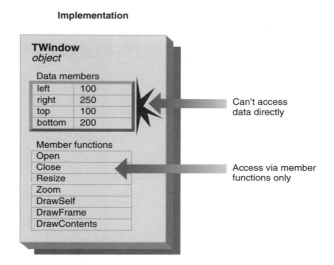

Three member functions take care of actually drawing the window shown in Figure 7. The DrawSelf member function can be called to redraw the entire window and its contents. The DrawSelf function in turn calls DrawFrame and DrawContents. DrawFrame draws the window's frame and controls, and DrawContents draws its contents, adjusting automatically for the window's current size.

Classes

An object is defined by a *class,* which is a description of the data and actions shared by all objects that belong to that class. Each object created from a class is called an *instance* of that class. Programmers use classes like cookie cutters to create, or *instantiate,* objects with particular data members and member functions.

Figure 8 shows how this might work with the TWindow object described in the preceding section. To create an object from a class like TWindow from within a program, a programmer instantiates it—that is, uses the definitions provided by the class to create a single working window object that has all those characteristics.

Instantiation saves the work of recreating the data members and member functions each time the program needs to create a window. Instead, one line of code instantiates or "stamps out" the object in a form that's ready to use. Each actual window on the screen corresponds to a separate instance of an object instantiated from class TWindow.

Every instantiation creates a new set of data members but shares a single copy of the code that implements the member functions. Every TWindow object has the same data members as all other TWindow objects, but the values of its data members are different, corresponding to its unique size and position on the screen.

FIGURE 8
PROGRAMMERS
USE CLASSES
LIKE COOKIE
CUTTERS TO
CREATE OBJECTS

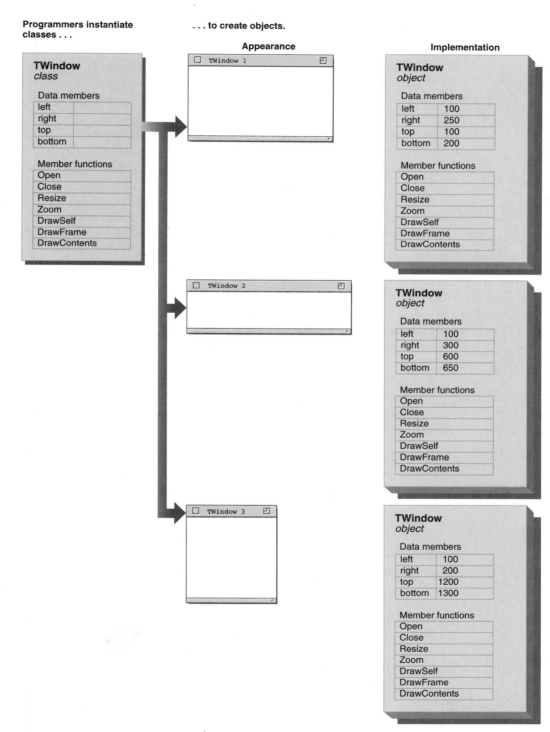

Programmers instantiate classes . . .

. . . to create objects.

Appearance

Implementation

TWindow
class

Data members

left	
right	
top	
bottom	

Member functions

| Open |
| Close |
| Resize |
| Zoom |
| DrawSelf |
| DrawFrame |
| DrawContents |

TWindow 1

TWindow
object

Data members

left	100
right	250
top	100
bottom	200

Member functions

| Open |
| Close |
| Resize |
| Zoom |
| DrawSelf |
| DrawFrame |
| DrawContents |

TWindow 2

TWindow
object

Data members

left	100
right	300
top	600
bottom	650

Member functions

| Open |
| Close |
| Resize |
| Zoom |
| DrawSelf |
| DrawFrame |
| DrawContents |

TWindow 3

TWindow
object

Data members

left	100
right	200
top	1200
bottom	1300

Member functions

| Open |
| Close |
| Resize |
| Zoom |
| DrawSelf |
| DrawFrame |
| DrawContents |

Subclassing and inheritance

Some software vendors who say they use "objects" really mean that they provide libraries of object classes that can be used by simple instantiation as described in the previous section. But one of the primary benefits of objects involves the ability to extend and modify them: that is, to derive new kinds of objects from the standard objects available in the system, thereby creating new capabilities without having to start from scratch.

Because characteristics shared by different classes are factored into shared base classes, one of the benefits of classes is code reuse through *inheritance*. Each class that derives from the base class inherits the parent's structure and behavior. Derived classes represent increasingly specialized entities founded on more abstract or general base classes.

The ability to derive new classes from existing classes makes it possible to extend the capabilities of any part of Taligent's system software. If a CommonPoint class does exactly what an application requires for a particular purpose, the programmer can use it as is. If it does some but not all of what's needed, the programmer can derive a new class from the existing one and add new data structures and actions to extend its capabilities.

For example, suppose you want to create a scrolling window. You can derive a new class called TScrollingWindow from the TWindow class, a process called *subclassing*. Figure 9 shows how this works.

The new TScrollingWindow class inherits all the characteristics of TWindow. This means you start with (reuse) all the same data members and member functions and just add the new ones you need or replace the ones whose behavior you want to change. Inheritance relationships like this allow many different classes to share common characteristics. Two new data members, scrollX and scrollY, represent the horizontal and vertical scroll positions, which indicate what part of the content should be drawn inside the window. A new member function called DrawScrollbars draws the scroll bars, including the position of each scroll bar's "thumb" (the small box that moves up and down or left and right inside a scroll bar), which depends on the values of scrollX and scrollY. Finally, you need to replace the original TWindow DrawSelf member function with a new DrawSelf function that draws a scrolling window.

The new DrawSelf function calls DrawFrame as before to draw the basic window, then calls the new DrawScrollbars member function to add the scroll bars, then calls the original DrawContents, but with slightly different arguments. The new arguments reflect both the reduced content area due to making room for the scroll bars and the shift in the contents indicated by the current values of scrollX and scrollY.

In the programming language C++, the class from which a new class is derived by subclassing is called a *base class*, and the new class derived from a base class is called a *derived class*.

FIGURE 9
SUBCLASSING
A NEW CLASS
FROM AN
EXISTING
CLASS

This symbol
means
"subclassed from."

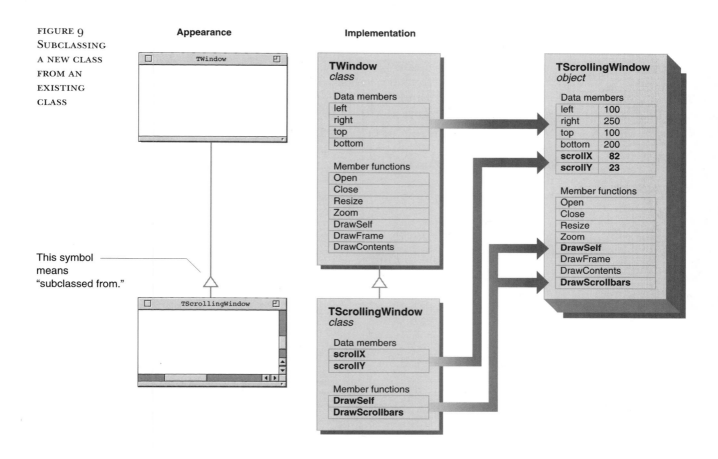

Overriding

Because TScrollingWindow inherits all the characteristics of the TWindow class, a program that uses TScrollingWindow ends up using the TWindow definitions of inherited functions such as Resize. When a program calls the DrawSelf function for a TScrollingWindow object, however, it doesn't use the original TWindow's DrawSelf function; instead, it *overrides* the original function: that is, it skips over the original and uses the new function definition provided by TScrollingWindow. Figure 10 illustrates this process.

In C++, a function that can be overridden as shown in Figure 10 is called a *virtual function,* because it can (but need not) be replaced. If a base class provides no default implementation for a function, it is called a *pure virtual function,* because it's really just a "stub" or placeholder that can't be used as is and must therefore be overridden with an implementation provided by the programmer.

FIGURE 10
OVERRIDING

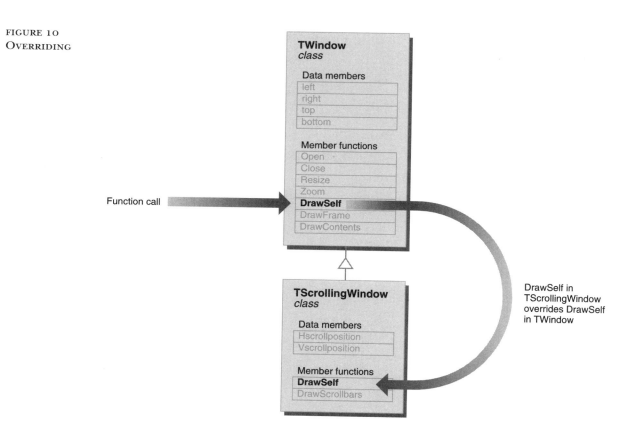

Polymorphism

Different kinds of windows that have different drawing requirements can each implement their own DrawSelf functions as shown in Figure 10. Thus, to draw any window object derived from the TWindow class, no matter what special drawing requirements it may have, you simply call its DrawSelf function. This ability to hide different implementations behind the same name, called *polymorphism,* greatly simplifies communication among objects. You can use the same name with many different kinds of objects to trigger the same effect without having to deal with the underlying mechanisms, which may be quite different. Polymorphism allows programmers to create their own custom versions of objects that plug back into the system and work in place of the originals.

Multiple inheritance

Suppose you want to derive a new class from the TScrollingWindow class. Objects of this new class, called TScrollingDrawingWindow, track mouse movements within the window whenever the mouse button is down. Suppose also that you have another class available, called MMouseTracker, that provides these mouse-tracking capabilities within a given area on screen but doesn't provide any of the capabilities provided by TScrollingWindow.

Figure 11 shows how OOP addresses this kind of situation, which requires a form of inheritance called *multiple inheritance.*

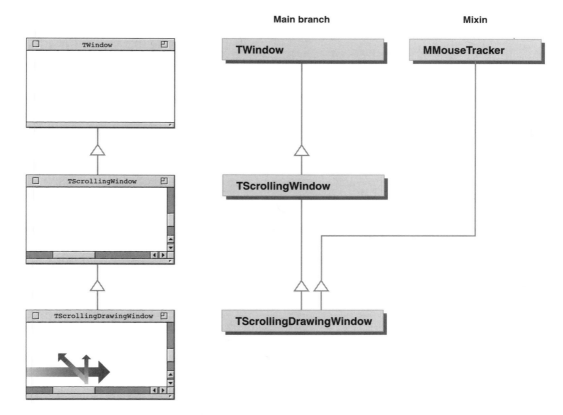

FIGURE 11
MULTIPLE
INHERITANCE
AND MIXINS

TScrollingDrawingWindow inherits characteristics of TScrollingWindow, which in turn inherits characteristics of TWindow. These three classes represent the main branch of the inheritance hierarchy for TScrollingDrawingWindow. But TScrollingDrawingWindow also "mixes in" the characteristics of the class MMouseTracker with the characteristics it inherits from TScrollingWindow, thus providing its own hybrid capabilities. Classes such as MMouseTracker that are designed for this purpose are called *mixin classes*.

TScrollingDrawingWindow uses the capabilities inherited from MMouseTracker to keep track of the location of the mouse and overrides the DrawContents member function inherited from TScrollingWindow (which was in turn inherited from TWindow) to draw lines when the mouse button is down. TScrollingDrawingWindow inherits all the other scrolling and drawing capabilities of TScrollingWindow without changing them.

✅ NOTE   Although Figure 11 follows the Taligent convention of beginning the names of mixin classes with "M," the example is highly simplified and doesn't reflect the way mouse tracking is actually handled in the CommonPoint system.

Class hierarchies and containment hierarchies

Many products that support OOP provide *class libraries* that you can use and reuse by instantiation and subclassing as described in the previous sections. Inheritance and polymorphism are important benefits of these libraries, which allow you to create and use families of related objects that share the same interface even though their contents and behavior differ. A *class hierarchy* describes the patterns of inheritance within a family of related objects. These patterns are also called "is a" relationships; for example, the TScrollingWindow discussed earlier "is a" TWindow. Each class defines the objects that belong to that class in terms of inherited characteristics that are either used as is or replaced (overridden), plus new characteristics.

After you've instantiated an object, its inherited behavior is determined by its place in the class hierarchy, but it may also be part of a *containment hierarchy:* that is, it can contain and be contained by other objects. Containment relationships are also called "has a" relationships. For example, a window that contains a text object "has a" text object. The text object might in turn contain graphics or multimedia objects, and the window that contains it is in turn contained within a particular application.

Grady Booch (1994) describes this combination of class and containment hierarchies as "the canonical form of a complex system." It turns out that an amazing variety of artificial and natural structures, from cells to spacecraft, can be modeled by using similar complementary hierarchies. Virtually anything in the real world can be described both as "part of" something else and as one instance of a category of related things.

For example, an individual cardiac cell is part of a heart, which is part of a circulatory system, which is part of a body made up of many complex interdependent systems. At the same time, a cardiac cell is one of three basic kinds of muscle cells—cardiac, smooth, and striated—and it has some properties in common with those kinds of cells and some properties that are different. Similarly, a valve is part of a car engine, which is part of a car, and the valve itself is made up of still smaller parts. A valve can also be described as a particular kind of valve that resembles other valves in some ways and differs from them in other ways.

This natural correspondence between the hierarchical yet flexible relationships among classes and the relationships we perceive in the real world give OOP its unique ability to model or simulate complex systems.

Benefits of class libraries

The benefits of class libraries can be summarized as follows:

- Objects and their corresponding classes break down complex programming problems into many smaller, simpler problems.
- Encapsulation enforces data abstraction: the organization of data into small, independent objects that can communicate with each other. Encapsulation protects the data in an object from accidental damage, but allows other objects to interact with that data by calling the object's member functions.
- Subclassing and inheritance make it possible to extend and modify objects: that is, to derive new kinds of objects from the standard classes available in the system, thereby creating new capabilities without having to start from scratch.
- Polymorphism and multiple inheritance make it possible for different programmers to mix and match characteristics of many different classes and create specialized objects that can still work with related objects in predictable ways.
- Class hierarchies and containment hierarchies provide a flexible mechanism for modeling real-world objects and the relationships among them.

THE EVOLUTION OF FRAMEWORKS

Libraries of reusable classes are useful in many situations, but they also have limitations:

- **Complexity.** In a complex system, the class hierarchies for related classes can become extremely confusing, with many dozens or even hundreds of classes. Unless the programmer has access to detailed documentation or some other way of organizing the class library, it can be difficult to figure out what was intended by the class library developers—for example, which functions call other functions and when. It can also be difficult to figure out how to derive new classes within the class hierarchy. The programmer has to understand a lot about relationships among classes to make changes and additions.

- **Flow of control.** A program written with the aid of class libraries is still responsible for the *flow of control*—that is, it must control the interactions among all the objects created from a particular library. The programmer has to decide which functions to call at what times for which kinds of objects, because the library is basically passive and doesn't do anything unless the programmer figures out how to make it happen. This can become a significant problem in a program that involves multiple derived objects with many slightly different kinds of data and behavior.

- **Duplication of effort.** Although class libraries allow programmers to use and reuse many small pieces of code, each programmer puts those pieces together in a different way. Two different programmers can use the same set of class libraries to write two programs that do exactly the same thing but whose internal structure (that is, design) may be quite different, depending on hundreds of small decisions each programmer makes along the way. This becomes a maintenance problem, especially for developers working on a series of related programs. Inevitably, similar pieces of code end up doing similar things in slightly different ways and don't work as well together as they should.

Class libraries provide lots of flexibility, but the more complex the program, the more programmers are forced to reinvent basic solutions to basic problems over and over again.

Frameworks, which were introduced in Chapter 1, represent the next level of abstraction beyond class libraries. They were first developed to free application programmers from the chores involved in displaying menus, windows, dialog boxes, and other standard user interface elements for personal computers. Frameworks also represent a change in the way programmers think about the interaction between the code they write and code written by others. Figure 12 shows how this interaction has evolved over the years.

FIGURE 12
EVOLUTION OF
APPLICATION
PROGRAM
STRUCTURES

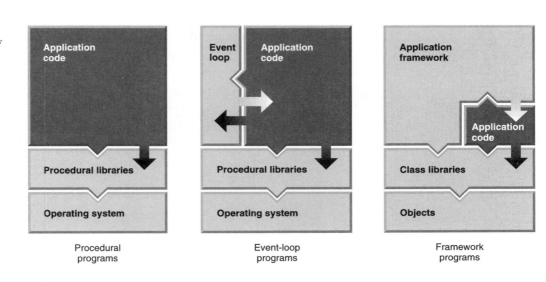

Procedural programs

In the early days of procedural programming, as shown on the left side of Figure 12, the programmer called libraries provided by the operating system to perform certain tasks, but basically the program executed down the page from start to finish, and the programmer was solely responsible for the flow of control. This was appropriate for printing out paychecks, calculating a mathematical table, or solving other problems with a program that executed in just one way.

The flow of control under this arrangement is illustrated by Figure 13. The system has no information about a program's code. The programmer is responsible for providing the overall behavior and flow of control for an application, with the system providing only fine-grained capabilities.

FIGURE 13
PROCEDURAL
PROGRAM
STRUCTURE
FOR A
TRADITIONAL
OPERATING
SYSTEM

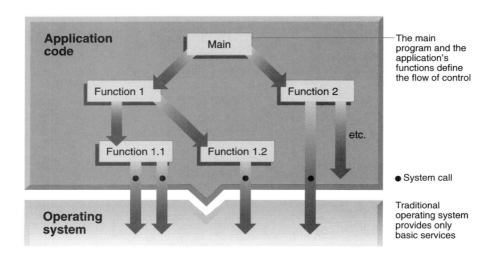

Event-loop programs

The development of graphical user interfaces began to turn the arrangement shown in Figure 13 inside out. These interfaces allow the user, rather than program logic, to drive the program and decide when certain actions should be performed. Today, most personal computer software accomplishes this by means of an event loop, illustrated by the middle part of Figure 12.

An *event loop* monitors the mouse, keyboard, and other sources of external events and calls the appropriate parts of the programmer's code according to actions that the user performs. The programmer no longer determines the order in which events occur. Instead, a program is divided into separate pieces that get called at unpredictable times and in an unpredictable order.

By relinquishing control in this way to users, the developer creates a program that is much easier to use. Nevertheless, individual pieces of the program written by the developer still call libraries provided by the operating system to accomplish certain tasks, and the programmer must still determine the flow of control within each piece after it's called by the event loop. Application code still "sits on top of" the system, and the programmer must know what system services are available and when to call them.

Framework programs

Even event loop programs require programmers to write a lot of code that shouldn't need to be written separately for every application. The concept of an application framework carries the event loop concept further, as suggested by the right side of Figure 12. Instead of dealing with all the nuts and bolts of constructing basic menus and windows and dialog boxes and making them all work together, programmers using application frameworks like those provided by the CommonPoint system start with working application code and basic user interface elements in place, and then build from there by replacing some of the generic capabilities of the framework with the specific capabilities of the intended application.

As Figure 12 suggests, application frameworks reduce the total amount of code that a programmer has to write from scratch. However, because the framework is really a generic application that displays windows, supports copy and paste, and so on, the programmer can also relinquish control to a greater degree than event loop programs permit. The framework code takes care of almost all event handling and flow of control, and the programmer's code gets called only when the framework needs it—to create or manipulate a proprietary data structure, for example.

A programmer writing a framework program not only relinquishes control to the user (as is also true for event loop programs), but also relinquishes the detailed flow of control within the program to other programmers—namely, those who wrote the framework. This approach allows the labors of different programmers to be combined to create more complex systems that work together in interesting ways, as opposed to isolated individuals creating custom code over and over again for similar problems.

A classic application framework

MacApp, from Apple Computer, was one of the first commercially successful application frameworks. It provides working code for a generic Mac OS application, which is not easy to write from scratch. The generic application is built from objects, so MacApp programming involves using object-oriented techniques even though the objects are implemented on top of a procedural operating system. The generic application includes a working menu system that takes care of pulling down menus, highlighting, dimming items that aren't active, implementing command-key equivalents, and so on. It also includes standard File and Edit menus.

The File menu includes working New, Open, Close, Save, and Save As commands and the dialog boxes for locating files and disks that go with them. The File menu also includes the Print and Page Setup commands, with the corresponding code for printing multiple copies on various sizes of paper, portrait or landscape orientation, and so on. The last default command in the File menu is the Quit command, for exiting the program.

The Edit menu includes Cut, Copy, Paste, and Undo, all supported by "boilerplate" code—that is, the code that sets up and runs the commands, with stubs for the code to be provided by a specific application.

A programmer doesn't have to write any of these menu commands from scratch. They're working and ready to use, although in some cases they can't really do much without additional application-specific code. To make an application do anything useful, it's necessary to override at least some of the application framework's member functions.

For example, if you're writing a drawing application using MacApp, you need to add only the additional parts that give the application its drawing capabilities; you can use everything else as is. You would add a Tools menu for the graphic objects your program can draw and pieces of code that determine what each tool in that menu does when the user chooses the tool and moves or clicks the mouse within a window. You would also override MacApp's boilerplate code for the data your program reads and writes when the user opens, closes, and saves files, replacing it with code that can read and write the actual data for the graphics objects your program knows about. By just subclassing and overriding these few parts of the MacApp framework, you can create a complete, well-behaved drawing application with much less effort than it would take to create it without the framework.

FRAMEWORK CONCEPTS

MacApp is a typical solution to the kind of problem frameworks were first invented to address: writing an application with a graphical user interface designed for a single user. Taligent has extended this approach to all levels of system software.

To appreciate the significance for programmers of Taligent's pervasive use of frameworks, you should understand the basic concepts of framework technology described in this section.

Properties of frameworks

A *framework* is a collection of cooperating classes that make up a reusable design solution for a given problem domain. It typically includes objects that provide default behavior, like MacApp's menus and windows, and programmers use it by inheriting some of that default behavior and overriding other behavior so that the framework calls application code at the appropriate times.

There are three main differences between frameworks and class libraries:

- **Behavior versus protocol.** Class libraries are essentially collections of behaviors that you can call when you want those individual behaviors in your program. A framework, on the other hand, provides not only behavior but also the protocol or set of rules that govern the ways in which behaviors can be combined, including rules for what a programmer is supposed to provide versus what the framework provides.

- **Don't call us, we'll call you.** With a class library, the code the programmer writes instantiates objects and calls their member functions. It's possible to instantiate and call objects in the same way with a framework—that is, to treat the framework as a class library—but to take full advantage of a framework's reusable design, a programmer writes code that overrides and is called by the framework. The framework manages the flow of control among its objects. Writing a program involves dividing up responsibilities among the various pieces of software that get called by the framework rather than specifying how the different pieces should work together. This relationship is expressed by the principle: "Don't call us, we'll call you."

- **Implementation versus design.** With class libraries programmers reuse only implementations, whereas with frameworks they reuse design. A framework embodies the way a family of related programs or pieces of software work. It represents a generic design solution that can be adapted to a variety of specific problems in a given domain. For example, a single framework can embody the way a user interface works, even though two different user interfaces created with the same framework might solve quite different interface problems.

A framework often embodies specific domain expertise. Application code customizes the framework in a way that solves a particular application problem within the general domain of the problem the framework was designed to solve. In the case of an application framework like MacApp, the expertise is in the domain of writing programs for the Mac OS that display menus and windows and perform other basic tasks consistently and reliably. In the case of a framework developed by a bank, the domain expertise embodied in the framework might be how customer accounts or certain kinds of financial transactions work. In this case, a programmer might customize the framework to create specific kinds of accounts or financial instruments.

How frameworks work

Figure 14 shows a highly simplified view of the way an application and an application framework work together. The application framework includes the main event loop and passes events around as necessary. For example, its HandleUpdate function talks to every TWindow object and causes it to update by calling its DrawSelf function. The application gets all of this behavior simply by instantiating TApplication and subclassing whatever additional classes, such as TWindow, it needs to provide its unique capabilities. Like a master puppeteer, the application framework pulls the "strings" provided by the application's subclasses whenever it needs the behavior they provide.

FIGURE 14
LIKE A MASTER
PUPPETEER,
AN APPLICATION
FRAMEWORK
PULLS THE
"STRINGS"
PROVIDED
BY THE
APPLICATION'S
SUBCLASSES

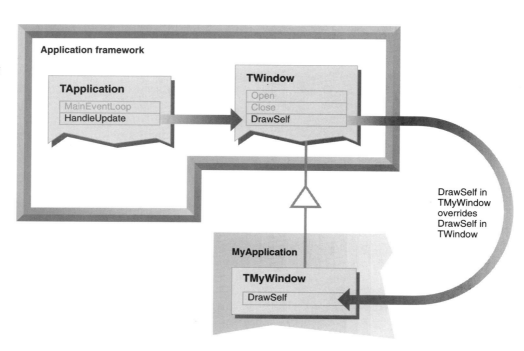

When you examine the behavior of an application framework with the aid of a debugger, you see a series of calls to internal framework member functions, with only the occasional call to your code when the framework calls one of your object's functions.

The bottom part of Figure 15 illustrates this situation. In a conventional operating system like the one illustrated in Figure 13, the debugger would show the opposite arrangement: a series of calls within your code and an occasional call to a system function, as shown in the top part of Figure 15.

FIGURE 15
VIEWED FROM
A DEBUGGER,
CALLS TO
APPLICATION
FRAMEWORK
FUNCTIONS
OUTNUMBER
CALLS TO
YOUR CODE

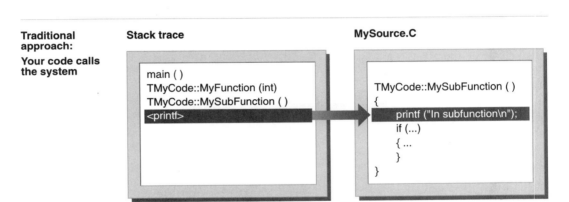

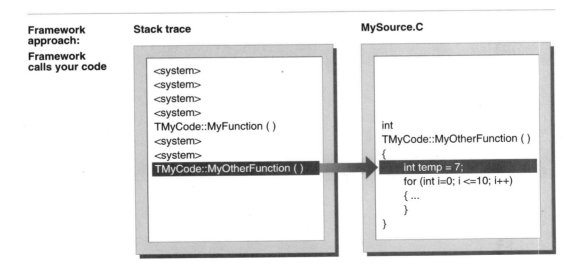

Calling API vs. subclassing API

Frameworks can be thought of as having two APIs: a *calling API,* which resembles a class library, and a *subclassing API,* which is used for overriding framework member functions. The calling/subclassing distinction describes the mechanism by which functions are invoked: call or be called. Figure 16 provides a simplified picture of the way programmers use these APIs.

FIGURE 16
CALLING
API vs.
SUBCLASSING
API

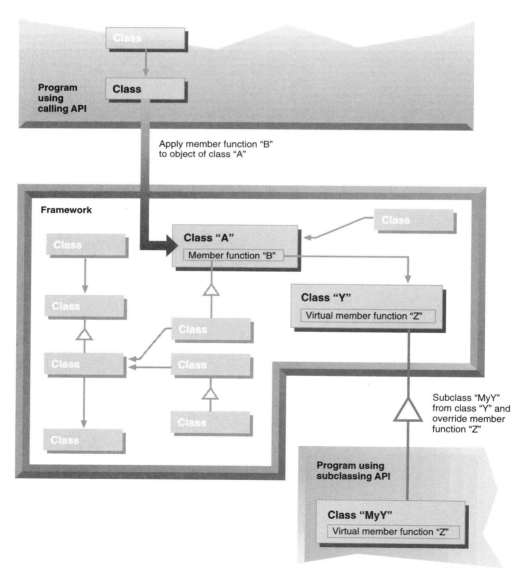

The L shape in the center of Figure 16 represents the framework, which consists of multiple classes that cooperate intimately to address a particular problem domain. The box above the framework represents a program using the calling API. This program could be another framework or any program that requires the services of the framework in the center of the figure.

For example, the Data Access framework in the CommonPoint system allows applications to access multiple Structured Query Language (SQL) software modules by using a single calling API that resembles a class library. Programmers can instantiate standard connection, command, and statement objects with little modification and use them to construct their own queries and database documents. Programs constructed with the calling API work the same way with all SQL connectivity software modules supported by the Data Access framework.

The box underneath the framework in Figure 16 represents a program using the subclassing API. The subclassing API looks very different from the calling API. A programmer uses the subclassing API by subclassing existing classes and overriding particular member functions. The resulting code is called by the framework when it calls those member functions polymorphically.

In the Data Access example, the subclassing API consists of virtual member functions for a generic implementation of the SQL interface. The appropriate innards of the generic interface are exposed, via the subclassing API, so that they can be customized for different SQL connectivity software modules. Because the calling API is the same for different software connectivity modules (such as ODBC or SQL*NET®) that are subclassed from the Data Access subclassing API, programs that use the calling API work the same way no matter which subclassed SQL software is actually providing the services. This is the essence of polymorphism.

In practice, the distinction between the calling API and the subclassing API is not always as straightforward as Figure 16 suggests. A member function called as part of the calling API may itself be overridden by a function provided by the same program's extension of the subclassing API; or it may end up calling other functions that the program has subclassed via the subclassing API; or it may use member functions from calling APIs for other frameworks that in turn rely on virtual functions that the program has extended via those frameworks' subclassing APIs.

Various approaches can be used at the same time by a single program, as discussed in "An application is an ensemble of framework-based code," beginning on page 64. However, CommonPoint programmers don't need to deal with the full complexity of multiple frameworks. The *cp*Professional development environment, which is introduced in Chapter 5, facilitates browsing through the classes provided by various frameworks to pick out and assemble the parts you want to work with.

**The class library–
framework continuum**

While clear differences exist between class libraries and frameworks, some libraries exhibit framework-like behavior, and some frameworks can be used like class libraries. You can view this as a continuum, with traditional class libraries at one end and sophisticated frameworks at the other, as suggested by Figure 17. All frameworks, including Taligent's frameworks, fall somewhere along this continuum.

For example, the higher-level application frameworks in the CommonPoint system are designed for customization (usually but not exclusively by subclassing) and therefore fall toward the framework side of the continuum shown in Figure 17. In contrast, lower-level parts of the system, such as Data Structures and Collections, tend to be used by most programmers as libraries and therefore fall toward the library side of the continuum (though system programmers and other specialists may customize them). Mid-level frameworks such as those provided by the Graphics system tend to be subclassed and customized by developers for subsequent use as libraries elsewhere in the same program.

FIGURE 17
CLASS LIBRARY—
FRAMEWORK
CONTINUUM

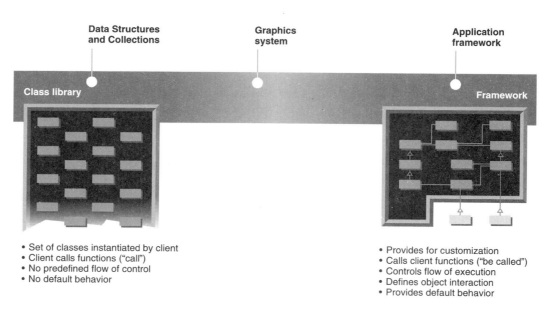

Data Structures
and Collections

Graphics
system

Application
framework

Class library

Framework

- Set of classes instantiated by client
- Client calls functions ("call")
- No predefined flow of control
- No default behavior

- Provides for customization
- Calls client functions ("be called")
- Controls flow of execution
- Defines object interaction
- Provides default behavior

Framework programming

Another way to look at the class library–framework continuum is to think of a framework as having two additional APIs that are orthogonal to the calling and subclassing APIs: the client and customization APIs. Whereas the calling and subclassing APIs describe the mechanism by which functions are invoked, the client and customization APIs describe the way developers use a framework's functions.

A framework's *client API* is employed by a programmer who wants to use the framework as it is intended to be used. Using a client API can in turn involve using both the calling and subclassing APIs, but without changing the fundamental internal operations of the framework.

The *customization API* is employed by a programmer who wants to modify, enhance, or extend a framework's behavior. Using a framework's customization API usually involves using the subclassing API, but in more complex ways that end up changing some portion of the framework into something completely different. However, the customization API can also involve the calling API if customizing the framework requires the programmer to provide new calling API functions. This kind of arrangement is analogous to "delegation" or "callbacks" in procedural programming.

In practice, the distinction between client and customization APIs gets blurry. A CommonPoint programmer can use a framework in a range of ways:

- **Use as is.** Use the framework as is, like a specialized class library. For example, the CommonPoint system's Text Editing framework provides ready-made text boxes, text tools, and full-featured text-editing components that a programmer can use as is. The Text Editing framework's calling API can be used by instantiation to create standard text objects, and the calling API in turn manipulates those parts of the Text Editing framework and other text frameworks that provide those services.

- **Complete.** Add code to the framework to implement specific capabilities. For example, the Presentation framework draws windows but not their contents. To display anything in a window, the programmer uses the framework's subclassing API to override the framework's virtual member functions that draw into the window. Similarly, to support specialized connectivity software for a particular database via the Data Access framework, the database provider subclasses from the generic classes provided by the framework's subclassing API.

- **Customize.** Replace parts of the framework implementation. For example, the Graphics Editing framework provides standard graphics tools that allow users to create multiple objects, select them, drag them around the screen, and so on. To customize the behavior of some of these tools, a programmer can replace some of the code in the framework. It's possible to replace a little or a lot, or even the entire implementation. It's even possible to implement some or all of the code in hardware, such as the graphics rendering algorithms. In all cases the same calling API is preserved.

An application is an ensemble of framework-based code

A single application can use many different frameworks, and it can do so with a mixture of approaches, as suggested by Figure 18. Pieces of the application's code "hang from" or are "nestled among" the frameworks provided by the system. The application consists of an *ensemble* of these pieces. The application code calls calling APIs of various frameworks, some of which the application has customized, and some of which it uses as is.

For example, one part of the code might use some part of a framework's calling API whose implementation has been modified by another part of the code that uses the framework's subclassing API. The end result is an ensemble of pieces that get called only when the system needs them, and only for use within that application's address space. In the CommonPoint system, several applications running at the same time can use the same frameworks in very different ways without interfering with each other.

FIGURE 18
AN
APPLICATION
IS AN
ENSEMBLE OF
FRAMEWORK-
BASED CODE

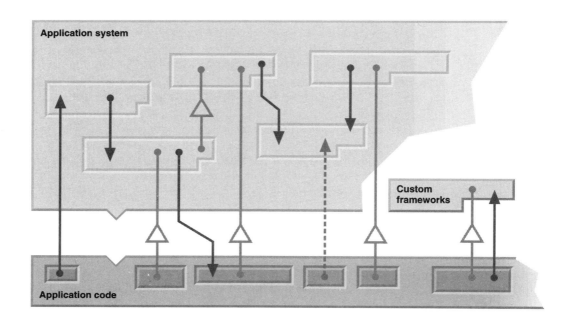

Benefits of frameworks   The benefits of frameworks can be summarized as follows:

- **Less code to write.** Much of the program's design and structure, as well as its code, already exists in the framework.
- **More reliable and robust code.** Code inherited from a framework has already been tested and integrated with the rest of the framework.
- **More consistent and modular code.** Code reuse provides consistency and common capabilities between programs, no matter who writes them. Frameworks also make it easier to break programs into small pieces.
- **More focus on areas of expertise, less focus on areas of system compatibility.** Developers can concentrate on the specific handling and presentation requirements of the data in a particular problem domain. They don't have to be experts at writing user interfaces, networking, or printing to use the frameworks that provide those services.
- **Generic solutions that can be reused for other, related problems.** Programmers who are used to dealing with frameworks tend to think in terms of generic solutions rather than special solutions. They can even design their own programs as frameworks to be reused by themselves or others.
- **Improved maintenance and orderly program evolution.** When you fix a bug in a framework, you fix the same bug in all the software derived from it. Similarly, when you add new features or capabilities to a framework, they just show up and work in all applications on the same system that are derived from that framework.
- **Improved integration of related programs.** Because all programs based on a particular framework inherit not only common code but also common design, programmers who are working on similar programs have a better chance of understanding and working with each other's code, and the programs they develop are more likely to work together consistently and reliably.

The last point is worth emphasizing. Frameworks can permit a high level of integration among multiple customizations. Much as individual objects hide their internal complexity and present a simplified interface for use by other objects, frameworks allow programmers to take advantage of preassembled complex relationships among objects without necessarily having to understand all the details of those relationships. Frameworks are designed to be subclassed and used by many programs at the same time in a way that allows programs to share common behavior without interfering with each other's specialized implementations.

This contrasts with class libraries, which are generally designed for use by one program at a time. Because they share the same underlying code, framework-derived programs work together reliably even though their designers don't know each other and may customize the framework in very different ways.

USING THE TALIGENT PROGRAMMING MODEL

Taligent frameworks provide generic solutions in a wide range of problem domains. In effect, programmers can pick and choose from a comprehensive set of integrated application capabilities without having to design, write, or debug any of the code that provides those capabilities. Because Taligent frameworks are designed as a "matched set" that work cooperatively, programs written with a particular framework work consistently with each other and with all of Taligent's other frameworks. Instead of having to worry about how the various pieces of an application work with the underlying operating system, programmers start with robust code that already works seamlessly with the rest of the system and then modify it as necessary.

The ease with which an individual programmer can learn to use Taligent's frameworks depends on that person's previous object-oriented design experience, knowledge of framework programming, and knowledge of C++ and OOP. After mastering a few frameworks, most programmers find new ones much easier to learn. The long-term benefits of frameworks far exceed the initial difficulties involved in learning this new way of programming.

Part II, "CommonPoint system architecture," provides an overview of the frameworks in the CommonPoint system. The rest of this section describes some of the benefits that Taligent frameworks provide in addition to the general benefits of framework programming described in the previous section.

Pervasive, integrated frameworks

Nearly everything that is implemented as a library in a traditional operating system is implemented as a framework in the CommonPoint application system. In most cases CommonPoint frameworks call other CommonPoint frameworks to obtain services. Unlike an application framework such as Microsoft Foundation Classes (MFC), which sits on top of the procedural Windows programming architecture, CommonPoint frameworks pervade the entire system from kernel services to the details of the user interface.

Each CommonPoint framework not only implements specific services but also provides a high degree of integration with the rest of the CommonPoint system. This means, for example, that anything displayed on the screen can be printed accurately, any data can be linked with any other data, and global text tools work on all text. This kind of integration among frameworks underlies many of the capabilities of the Taligent human interface, especially its ability to handle complex interactions among multiple users running multiple operating systems on multiple hardware platforms.

Compartmentalized effects of subclassing

In the Taligent programming model, subclassing affects a framework's behavior only for the program that's doing the subclassing. Unlike Windows or the Mac OS, for example, which allow any program or INIT file to patch the system and alter the behavior of all applications running on a given computer, the Taligent programming model permits system modifications only within an application's own address space, as suggested by Figure 19.

Taligent system software maps a copy of a framework into the virtual memory address spaces of all applications that are using it. There is only one physical copy of the original framework, and it is shared simultaneously by all these applications. An application can modify its mapped copy of the framework for use within its address space without interfering with other applications' modifications of the same framework for use within their address spaces.

FIGURE 19
SUBCLASSING AFFECTS A
FRAMEWORK'S BEHAVIOR ONLY
WITHIN THE SUBCLASSING
APPLICATION'S ADDRESS SPACE

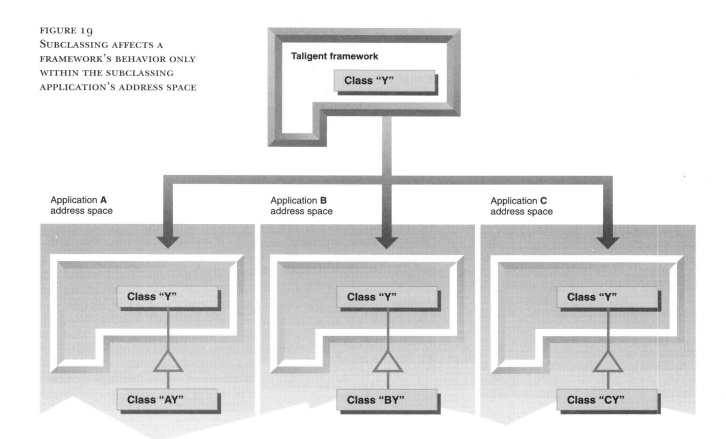

This conservative approach makes for a more robust system than would otherwise be possible. Applications can be written and tested assuming one reliable version of the system libraries rather than having to take all possible combinations of patched system libraries into account. Similarly, if an application crashes, it is isolated from the rest of the system and generally can't affect other applications.

In the Taligent programming model, programs do not typically need to "patch the system" on a global basis, except for some areas, such as installing fonts, that involve the system as a whole. Nevertheless, it is possible for knowledgeable programmers to replace libraries on a global basis with specialized runtime implementations.

Desktop frameworks

Programmers can use the Taligent programming model without having to learn all of the Taligent frameworks. They can begin with the high-level Desktop frameworks, which are introduced in Chapter 7, and learn others only as necessary for a particular problem domain.

The Desktop frameworks typically provide half or more of the code a developer would have to write to create an application for a procedural system. Instead of starting from scratch and following an elaborate set of rules to make sure their applications work reliably with other applications, CommonPoint developers start with code from the Desktop frameworks that already works reliably with all the other frameworks in the system and build out from that. As a result, applications written with the Desktop frameworks have much more code and design in common than, for example, Windows applications written by different companies, and therefore can cooperate reliably no matter who writes them.

Embeddable components

In the Taligent programming model, an *embeddable component* is an ensemble of framework code that constitutes a self-contained functional unit roughly equivalent to an application plus data. The Compound Document framework, which is one of the Desktop frameworks, supports the creation and integration within a single document of embeddable components with different capabilities: for example, a text component, a graphics component, and a spreadsheet component. The embeddable component is the key programming abstraction used in data-centered CommonPoint applications.

✅ NOTE   The term *component* is also used in the computer industry to describe any software entity, including objects such as buttons and menu items, that can be connected with other programmatic entities with the aid of visual programming tools. Taligent's approach to this broader category of component software is described in Chapter 5.

From a user's point of view, a component created with the Compound Document framework is similar in many respects to an OpenDoc "part" or OLE "server." It contains native data and possibly one or more other embeddable components. Users can create embeddable components explicitly by using stationery pads or tools and implicitly during paste or drag-and-drop operations. They can also embed any embeddable component within any other embeddable component.

A *document* is any freestanding embeddable component that isn't embedded within any other component; therefore, any embeddable component has the potential to be a document. Any degree of complexity is possible within a single document. A user can create a custom document that contains multiple components and multiple data types, such as text, graphics, video, and sound, without having to open separate applications to create and edit each type. A document that contains more than one embedded component is a *compound document.*

Figure 20 shows how a typical compound document might be organized. For an example of a real compound document, see page 40.

FIGURE 20
A NEWSLETTER
IN THE FORM
OF A
COMPOUND
DOCUMENT

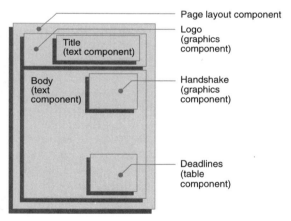

Enclosure and embedding   There are two ways a component can maintain its separate identity and still be contained by another component:

Enclosable icon

Enclosure occurs when one component contains another, which still exists as a completely separate object. A component represented as an *enclosable icon* is enclosed by another object. Typically, an object encloses other objects to organize them, as in a file folder.

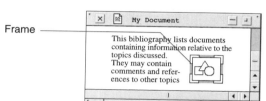

Frame

Embedding occurs when one component is incorporated into another, but its unique behavior, such as editing and presentation, remains available via menus or global tools. A component represented as a *frame* is embedded within another component.

In some cases one component can completely absorb another:

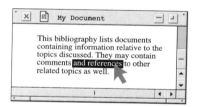

Absorption takes place when one object is completely incorporated into another, so that it's no longer identifiable as a separate object. For example, absorption occurs when a text string object is dropped into a paragraph.

A component might change its representation when it's moved or copied from one location to another. The component's container determines what form the component should take. For example, dragging a frame from a document into a folder changes the frame to an icon.

The four questions

To create an embeddable component, a programmer writes an ensemble based on the Compound Document framework. Most of the new code required answers four basic questions:

1. **Model.** What is the structure of the data? For example, the data might be a text string, an array of numbers, graphics data, or a sound file.

2. **Selections.** What discrete pieces of the data can the user select? In a table, a user might want to select cells; in a bar chart, a user might want to select each bar; in text, a user might want to select a range of characters.

3. **Commands.** What operations can the user perform on the data? For example, after selecting a cell in a table, the user might want to edit its contents or change its format by choosing commands from a menu.

4. **Presentation.** How is the data to be presented? For example, if it's an array of numbers, it could be presented as a bar chart, pie chart, or table.

Chapter 7 explains the terms *model, selections, commands,* and *presentation* in detail. Just as other dynamic systems based on very simple rules can achieve complex behaviors, the four questions and the object designs that answer them facilitate the modeling of complex business functions and other real-world processes.

Advantages of embeddable components

Embeddable components based on the Compound Document framework inherit a comprehensive set of features with little or no additional programming:

- Cut, Copy, and Paste commands work reliably for a myriad of standard data types.
- The user can embed any component in any other component.
- Any component can be linked with any other component.
- The user can drag and drop any component over virtually any other object.
- Frames are "live": that is, activity in visible frames continues in real time even when the frames aren't selected.
- The user can edit any component in place with any tools designed to work with the data structures that the component supports.
- All components support multilevel undo and redo up to whatever limit the developer chooses to set.
- All changes to a component are saved automatically to disk without any need for a Save command.
- All components can be used collaboratively—for example, by sharing data or commands, thereby allowing two or more users to work on the same document at the same time.
- All components automatically support any scripting languages ported to or created for the CommonPoint system in the future.
- Plans for future versions of the CommonPoint system include supporting the embedding and manipulation of OpenDoc parts and OLE servers, thus ensuring interoperability with operating systems that support those standards.

See "Interoperability Services" on page 284 for more information about Taligent's support for OpenDoc, OLE, and other industry standards.

Taligent's embeddable components also give developers several significant advantages over other development approaches:

- **Standardization.** The Compound Document framework provides working code with a consistent set of built-in capabilities for all embeddable components.

- **Increased reuse.** Because the resulting components have so much common code, they work together reliably no matter who writes them and inherit rich capabilities that take full advantage of other CommonPoint frameworks.

- **Narrower focus on areas of expertise.** As more components become available, many of the components required for a particular program may already be available. For example, a developer of scheduling programs may not need to provide basic text tools and text components that users may already own, or that the developer can acquire from alternative sources for incorporation in the scheduling application. Instead, the development effort can be restricted to the scheduler's core capabilities. Developers can concentrate on their own areas of expertise and leave other areas to other experts.

- **Ease of upgrading.** Users need not replace an entire program solution when a specific component or tool is upgraded. Instead, they need only replace the old component or tool.

- **Reduced time to market.** To create a component with the Compound Document framework, a developer just needs to provide a code ensemble that answers the four questions described in the previous section. To create equivalent components for other operating systems, a developer must write more code and must also take full responsibility for all the programmatic wiring required to hook that code into the rest of the system.

- **Component software.** Embeddable components are a form of component software—that is, components that component assemblers can script and wire together with visual tools without the need for extensive programming. For more information about component software and component assemblers, see "Development tools and the component software market," which begins on page 134.

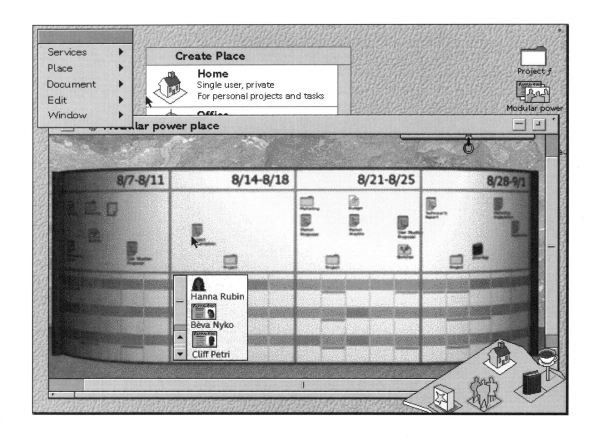

A new Place environment created by a user. For a description, see page 82.

CHAPTER 3

A HUMAN INTERFACE
FOR ORGANIZATIONS

The typical CommonPoint user works with a networked 32-bit multitasking computer in a business or other organization. Before beginning to use the CommonPoint system, this person may have used some simple distributed computing applications, such as email, decision support tools, and scheduling tools, that run on the host operating system. From this user's point of view, CommonPoint applications superficially resemble those host applications. They include familiar elements, such as windows, menus, dialog boxes, controls, tools, and icons, that anyone familiar with traditional graphical user interfaces can easily recognize and use.

In addition, CommonPoint applications provide immediate benefits in comparison with other applications running on the host, especially in areas such as real-time collaboration with other users over the network, workflow automation, project management, and other forms of distributed computing. Even users working with different operating systems can work together electronically via the CommonPoint system without worrying about incompatible data formats, networking protocols, or user interface implementations.

This chapter introduces some of the concepts that underlie the Taligent *human interface policies*—that is, the rules and conventions that govern the way a user communicates with and controls a computer running the CommonPoint system and other Taligent products. The first release of the CommonPoint system implements some but not all of these concepts. Taligent and its investors plan to continue developing the Taligent human interface in future releases to achieve and move beyond the vision described here.

A HUMAN INTERFACE SCENARIO

The scenario described in this section illustrates some of the benefits the CommonPoint system can provide for users in a business environment. It is one of many such scenarios created during CommonPoint development to explore potential directions for the Taligent human interface. It is not intended to illustrate specific details of the Taligent human interface implementation. Instead, this scenario illustrates Taligent's vision of the way a company might use and extend a mature version of the CommonPoint system in the future.

The scenario is based on a fictional company, the Cutting Edge Corporation, that manufactures lawnmowers and other powered garden equipment. It sells its products through multiple channels, including catalogs, hardware stores, and nurseries. For the last several years, Cutting Edge has researched the operations of line workers and the diverse computing platforms in use across the company. The need for cross-platform collaboration capabilities led Cutting Edge to early evaluation and test deployment of the first version of the CommonPoint application system.

Since then, Cutting Edge has created its own customer service system by customizing commercial CommonPoint applications with the aid of system integrators and in-house programmers. Some of these applications use CommonPoint frameworks that provide comprehensive support for *People, Places, and Things®*, the central metaphor of the Taligent human interface.

The People, Places, and Things metaphor is discussed in more detail later in this chapter. The basic concept is quite simple. All tasks performed in business environments involve working with other people (colleagues, customers, and suppliers) in various kinds of places (offices, meeting rooms, or auditoriums) with specialized things or tools (fax machines, telephones, pens, documents). The People, Places, and Things metaphor allows the Cutting Edge Corporation to model its employees' computing environments according to the contexts in which they need to interact with each other, the physical places in which those interactions take place, and the tools and resources they need to perform cooperative tasks.

The rest of this section describes a few moments in the computing experiences of three Cutting Edge employees: Martin Wong, a customer service representative; Rodney Sinclair, a customer support specialist; and Hanna Rubin, a product manager. It describes how they perform a range of tasks as individuals and as part of an overall business process workflow. It also describes how a manager can use a generic Places™ representation to construct a new virtual work environment and customize it for specific tasks involving a more ad hoc, give-and-take style of collaboration.

A department's common area

When Martin Wong first logs on at the beginning of a shift, he sees the Customer Service Department's common area shown in Figure 21. This electronic Place representation functions like common areas in real office environments. It has a bulletin board notice and a map that contains icons for navigating to several other Place representations. It also includes Martin's personal schedule for the day, which shows some of the same map icons for the other Place representations in which he will be working and a window showing the other people who are currently using the common area.

The bulletin board notice announces that some new software enhancements have come on-line, including highlighting tools, annotation stationery, and smarter call routing (described in later sections).

FIGURE 21
CUSTOMER
SERVICE
DEPARTMENT'S
COMMON AREA

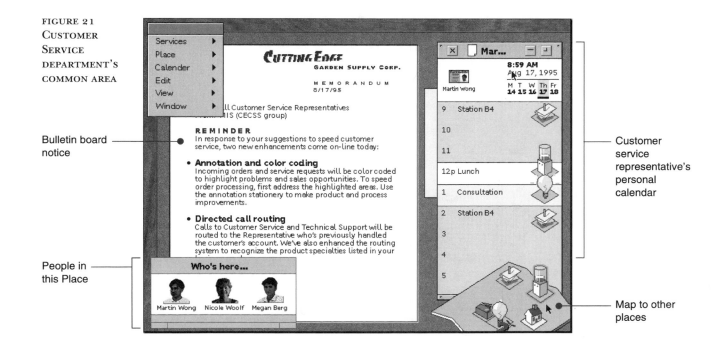

Bulletin board notice

People in this Place

Customer service representative's personal calendar

Map to other places

After reading the notice and checking his schedule, Martin clicks an icon on the map to travel to his desktop in the Customer Service Place representation, which is shown in Figure 22. His Customer Service desktop includes telephone, fax, and in-box appliances, a product catalog, and a map (folded shut in Figure 22) that allows him to go to other Place environments he may need to visit in the course of his work. Martin's Customer Service desktop also includes a pop-up routing menu that allows him to route calls or objects to different departments, such as order fulfillment, shipping, and technical support, as well as workflow routing icons at the upper right. The desktop models only those aspects of the Cutting Edge business process that are relevant for a customer service representative.

The customer order form shown in Figure 22 is the first one Martin has removed from the top of the pile in his in-box. The system has highlighted a problem with the order (an example of the new highlighting feature mentioned in the bulletin board notice), and Martin has opened the customer history file, which is automatically retrieved from the customer database and attached to the bottom of the form, to investigate the problem further. The Catalog and Notes icons in the lower-left corner of the screen allow him to look up relevant information, make notes on the catalog itself to communicate corrections or comments to other people in the company, and stamp orders with his authorization.

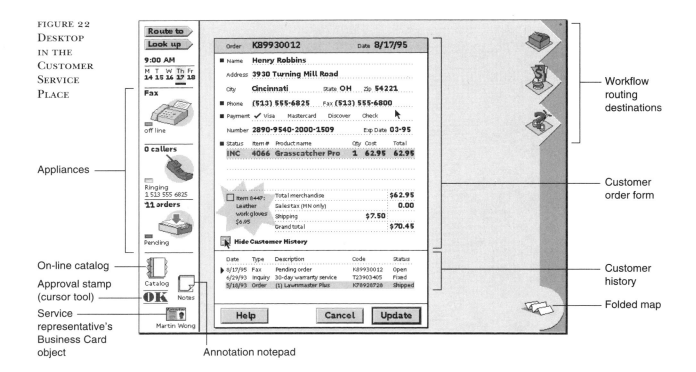

FIGURE 22
DESKTOP
IN THE
CUSTOMER
SERVICE
PLACE

Appliances

On-line catalog

Approval stamp
(cursor tool)

Service
representative's
Business Card
object

Annotation notepad

Workflow
routing
destinations

Customer
order form

Customer
history

Folded map

Martin discovers that the grasscatcher the customer wants to order isn't compatible with the lawnmower model the customer recently purchased, so he clicks the telephone appliance to call the customer and sort out the problem, updating the order form in the process.

After he finishes dealing with his first order, Martin notices he has a call on hold and answers it. The customer describes a problem with a noisy lawnmower. Martin checks his top-ten trouble list, but the noise problem the customer describes doesn't appear on the list. At this point Martin opens the routing menu as shown in Figure 23 to examine which technical support specialists are currently working in the Technical Support department, shown as a submenu of People™ representations. Instead of opening a separate application to route the call, Martin just chooses one of the available specialists from the menu and goes on to his next task.

FIGURE 23
PREPARING
TO TRANSFER
A CALL TO
TECHNICAL
SUPPORT

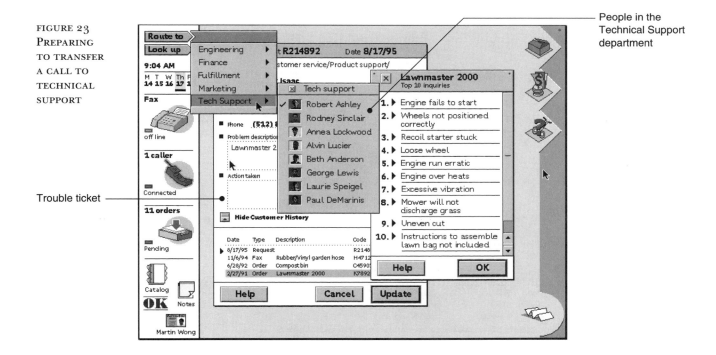

People in the Technical Support department

Trouble ticket

Martin's actions caused the call to be routed to Rodney Sinclair. Figure 24 shows Rodney's desktop shortly after he picks up the call. Notice that the phone call and problem form ("trouble ticket") show up on Rodney's screen exactly as they were when transferred by Martin. Rodney initiates a search of his troubleshooting database with the aid of the query document near the bottom of the screen, which returns a list of sounds. Because of the integrated multimedia and telephony capabilities of the CommonPoint system, Rodney can play the sounds for the benefit of the customer on the line. Each time he clicks a sound, the manual turns automatically to the page that describes the solution to the problem. When the customer recognizes the problem, Rodney uses other tools available on his desktop, including fax stationery, a mapmaking appliance, and a fax appliance, to assemble the relevant repair and service center information and fax it and the page from the service manual to the customer's fax number.

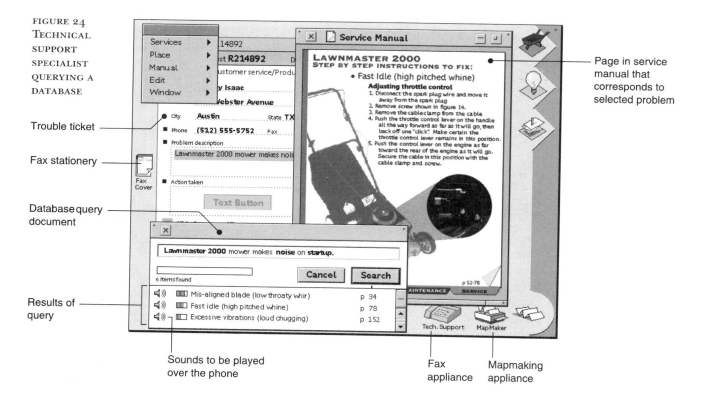

FIGURE 24
TECHNICAL
SUPPORT
SPECIALIST
QUERYING A
DATABASE

Trouble ticket

Fax stationery

Database query
document

Results of
query

Sounds to be played
over the phone

Page in service
manual that
corresponds to
selected problem

Fax
appliance

Mapmaking
appliance

The scenario up to this point demonstrates several key capabilities of the CommonPoint application system:

- **Custom desktops.** A systems integrator has assembled a variety of commercial packages to create the customer service system, including a workflow application, forms package, telephony system, fax appliance, and other tools and components. Cutting Edge customized the system with its own data, with specialized Business Card™ objects for company employees, by creating links to a catalog framework the company had bought and customized separately, by creating database documents to access inventory and customer history, and by purchasing additional commercial products such as the common area Place package.

- **Workflow automation.** Martin handed off the trouble ticket for the customer's call to Rodney, who had a whole new set of tools suited to his step in the process. Underlying mechanisms that support workflow control include store-and-forward messaging.

- **Integrated multimedia.** Rodney's diagnostic tools included integrated multimedia capabilities: the sounds of the noisy lawnmowers and the telephony system that routes calls between employees.

- **Integrated components.** Routine tasks involved manipulating a variety of data types that were intimately combined and connected, including electronic sticky notes, images, text, database queries, and financial data.

Figure 25 shows another part of the same scenario. A third Cutting Edge employee, the product manager Hanna Rubin, has been examining some of the data collected by the Customer Service department and other information about the lawn care business. She has concluded that there may be an opportunity to create a new generation product that has fewer mechanical parts and is quieter. To kick off the project, she has decided to set up a project coordination Place environment, because developing the new product will involve coordinating the work of several people inside and outside the company.

Hanna starts by creating a project coordination Place window from a gallery of Place templates purchased as a shrinkwrapped commercial product. The Place template she chooses provides built-in collaboration capabilities as well as a project management time line. Figure 25 shows the new environment as Hanna works on customizing it. She drags Business Card objects into the Place window for the members of the engineering team who will be involved and will need access. The Place software automatically sends the team members invitations and notes their availability over the next two months based on information obtained from the company meeting scheduling software. She also visits the company store Place representation (not shown), which allows her to select a software product and use her authorization credential to purchase it for use in her project. She drags an icon for the product, which is a video projection appliance for presentations, into her new Place window along with icons for various relevant documents.

FIGURE 25
A NEW PLACE
CREATED
FROM A PLACE
TEMPLATE

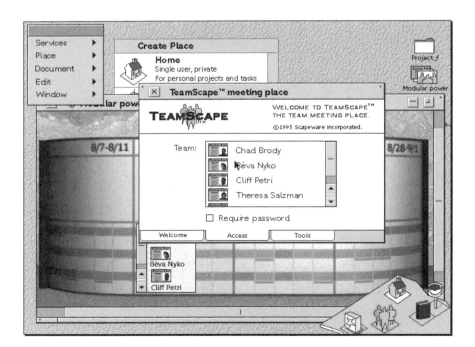

The project coordination Place software distributes the icons along the time line according to their creation date, then Hanna fills in the time line with dates for future revisions of the documents and meetings with team members where they will be discussed. The completed project coordination Place environment is shown on page 74. Many of the meetings will be virtual meetings conducted in this Place environment, with the team members participating electronically from their separate physical offices.

Over the next several weeks, the team members use the project coordination Place environment to plan the project, report on progress, discuss schedule and resources, work together on documents, and make collective decisions. Figure 26 shows Hanna's view of the project coordination Place environment at a key decision point, when the participants have to vote on the design proposal they have developed. Hanna is preparing for the vote, using a ballot maker module that came with the Place software and conducting the meeting with the aid of the projector appliance she bought separately. The other members of the team see the ballot she generates and use it to register their opinions.

FIGURE 26
THE TEAM
LEADER
PREPARES FOR
A VOTE IN
THE PROJECT
COORDINATION
PLACE

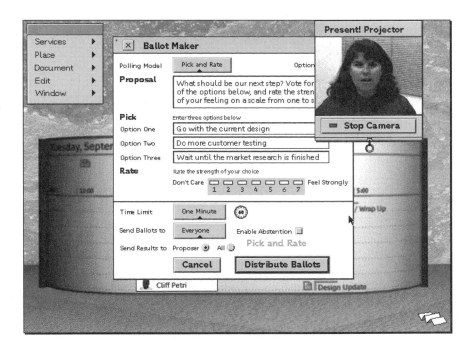

Hanna's use of the project coordination Place environment illustrates several additional aspects of the Taligent approach to the enterprise desktop:

- **Customized Place environments.** In just a few minutes, Hanna was able to create a collaborative environment and customize it for use on a particular project.
- **Software licensing.** Hanna purchased some of the components she used to create the project coordination Place representation at an electronic company store. The Licensing Services frameworks, which are introduced on page 314, support this kind of commercial transaction, triggering licensing and payment arrangements automatically when a user with the appropriate authorization makes a purchase.
- **Real-time collaboration.** Unlike the Place environments used by Martin Wong and Rodney Sinclair, which were designed to play specific roles in a workflow, the project coordination Place environment permitted various kinds of real-time interactions, including use by individual team members to obtain information, ad-hoc discussion, scheduling, presentations to the group by one person, and voting.

The rest of this chapter explains some of the human interface concepts that underlie the capabilities illustrated in this scenario.

EXTENDING THE DESKTOP METAPHOR

Until now, the key benefits of graphical user interfaces have been consistency and ease of use. Users have learned to rely on icons, menus, and other graphic representations that behave in predictable ways from one program to another within the same software environment. However, today's personal computer operating systems were originally designed to support the needs of a single user working alone in an office at a single computer. Most graphical user interfaces present the computer as an extension of the user's desk, with folders, documents, a trash can, and other objects such as clocks and in and out baskets that correspond to real objects on real desks. This simple metaphor has been highly successful with individual users, but it doesn't meet all the needs of multiple users in many different kinds of work environments working together on a common set of tasks.

Application-centered approach

Most graphical user interfaces for personal computers are application centered. To accomplish almost any task, the user must launch a sequence of separate applications to create and process the desired content. Each application comes with its own set of menus and dialog boxes, its own set of tools, and its own set of data types. Because each kind of data is tightly bound to the application that created it, users often have difficulty integrating data from different applications into a single document. And because developers are limited to the application model provided by system software, they have basically only one way to deliver value to their customers.

As segments of the software market mature, application developers get caught in escalating feature wars. Applications get larger and more complex, and each application's tools, menu commands, and other interface elements tend to become more specialized and difficult to learn. Instead of focusing on their work, users must learn many data formats and techniques to run applications and make them work together.

Document-centered approach

System software extensions like OLE can alleviate some of the drawbacks of an application-centered interface by allowing developers to divide applications into smaller components (called "servers" in OLE) that have their own separate areas in a single document. To work on such documents, the user activates one component, such as a chart in a word-processing document, and the available menus and tools change as appropriate for that component. As application developers use these technologies to factor their applications into smaller pieces, users can mix and match components for text, graphics, spreadsheets, and so on rather than having to use a separate full-featured application for each kind of data.

This approach makes some tasks easier, but until all applications are successfully factored, each component will still tend to have separate menus, tools, and data types, even though many of them are used for similar purposes, such as choosing fonts or drawing lines. As currently implemented on traditional operating systems, the document-centered approach still tends to reflect the underlying application structure.

Limitations of the desktop metaphor

Both the application-centered and document-centered approaches have proved useful in different ways. However, both are designed primarily for an individual working alone in an environment that is a metaphorical extension of the desk surface. The desktop metaphor helps an individual user keep track of files, folders, applications, windows, and so on, but it provides limited support for a user who wants to pull together a group of documents and tools related to a task, share them with others, or save and restore them as a whole. Extensions to support sharing information are difficult to implement and use.

For example, the current generation of graphical user interfaces doesn't represent other people consistently. Many user tasks involve working with others—sharing ideas, adapting information, or communicating the results. But when they need to communicate with each other via their computers, users are often confronted with scrolling lists of names and complex communication protocols. Certain applications, such as email packages, provide references to people, but they tend to do so inconsistently. For example, the list of names in a user's internal mail application tends to differ from the lists in the same user's scheduling and external mail applications, which in turn differ from the lists of users on servers.

New communications technologies such as PowerTalk™ for the Mac OS and Lotus Notes for Windows provide better collaboration capabilities, but they are limited by the differences among underlying operating systems. The ability to communicate and collaborate is not pervasive. At best, it's spotty even within a single operating system, let alone between systems and hardware platforms. The collaboration that is possible has been achieved only through heroic efforts on the part of developers to incorporate new technologies into their applications and on the part of users to learn and take advantage of them.

The Taligent human interface takes account of the fact that work in any organization involves not just one person, but many people; not just one place (an office with a desk in it) but many different kinds of places (other offices, meeting rooms, libraries, departments, and so on); and not just folders and documents, but many different kinds of tools and devices, including pens, pencils, markers, self-stick notes (analogous to Post-it notes), telephones, fax machines, printers, copiers, audiovisual equipment, manufacturing equipment, and so on.

TASK-CENTERED COMPUTING

The Taligent human interface incorporates and extends the document-centered approach described in the previous section. Users who are familiar with Mac OS, OS/2, or Windows environments will quickly feel at home. However, as they work with their colleagues electronically, they will experience a new sense of community—an active connection with other people in their organization and with the electronic places in which various people work, just as if they had all moved into a new office building or neighborhood. They will also discover that many tasks are easier to perform than they are in traditional user environments, especially tasks that involve collaboration among several users.

Instead of dividing the world into applications and their documents, Taligent has organized its human interface metaphors around human tasks. The *Task-Centered Computing*™ model for human interface design uses the completion of tasks as an organizing principle. Instead of learning to manipulate applications, users can bring their knowledge of the real world to their computing environment and can rely to a greater extent on the rules and expectations they take for granted in their everyday lives.

For example, if you're sitting at a desk in an office and you want to make a mark on a piece of paper, you can simply pick up any pen or pencil lying on the desk and make the mark. You don't have to choose a pen that goes with that particular kind of paper, or have access to the factory that made the piece of paper, or learn any special rules about what kinds of marks you can make on it. You just pick up the pencil and write. Until you begin working with a computer, you can pick things up, use them, and move around from one place to another and interact with other people in intuitive ways. But when you sit down at a traditional personal computer, you must learn various complicated rules about each application that are all slightly different and have nothing to do with the way you would otherwise work.

Users should be able to concentrate on the task at hand rather than the mechanics of using the computer. People should be able to use a computer just as easily and directly as they use other tools and objects in their working environments. In the CommonPoint system, a single pencil tool can make marks on a word-processing document, a database record, a spreadsheet, an email message, a digitized photograph, or any other electronic "paper"—unlike traditional applications, which each provide a slightly different pencil tool that works only on the "paper" produced by that application. In addition, several CommonPoint users can share the same piece of paper and watch each other make marks on it, just as if they were working together in the same room.

Extending familiar concepts

Taligent builds on users' knowledge of traditional human interface gestures and concepts and at the same time uses the CommonPoint application system's built-in features to reduce complexity and eliminate barriers. The goal is to extend existing metaphors in ways that make it easier to map knowledge of the world to representations on the screen.

The CommonPoint system doesn't require application icons familiar to Mac OS or Windows users. Instead, the user can start with icons for customizable stationery pads, which are templates for various kinds of objects the user works with. To create a new object, such as a memo, the user double-clicks the appropriate stationery pad, and the new object appears.

Such objects created by a user are distinct entities that combine characteristics of documents and applications in traditional human interface metaphors and also provide other capabilities. For example, users can put almost any object inside any other object, link objects with other objects across the network, or share objects with other users. The user doesn't have to deal with the myriad of similar but not quite identical tools, menus, and dialog boxes that traditional application- and document-centered computing still require. When a CommonPoint user selects an object such as a table inside another object, only the menus that are relevant to manipulating that object appear—not the entire interface for an industrial-strength spreadsheet program. In many cases no additional menus will be necessary, because the user can use standard tools and gestures to edit the object. Similarly, because global tools are completely independent of the objects they act on, users can use a few global tools and a few specialized tools rather than switching among complex tool palettes that duplicate each other's features but work in subtly different ways.

**Removing barriers
to communication**

In a real office environment, you can mark a draft document with your favorite highlighter, stick Post-it notes on pages of the draft, clip it together with comments from some other people and some photographs, and carry the whole set of documents down the hall to your colleague's office. If no one's there, you can leave the clipped documents on the person's chair so they can't be overlooked.

The CommonPoint system gives users the same kind of flexibility. A user can assemble complex documents without being overwhelmed by menus, dialog boxes, and tools that duplicate similar functions for each component. Similarly, the CommonPoint system allows a user to "visit" another user's office electronically and leave objects where they're sure to be noticed. That user can view all of those objects immediately, without first going through unpacking procedures such as saving files enclosed with a mail message on the hard disk.

Consider how you must go about these tasks with a conventional personal computer system. You write the draft document in a word-processing application. You can embed notes in the text, but you must manually set them off from the rest of the text with angle brackets or boldface type or some other convention. You can't easily highlight parts of the text, stick notes to it that can be peeled off later and stuck somewhere else, or print a copy with or without the annotations. To attach other people's comments and some photographs, you have to leave the word-processing application, open an email application, and follow that application's procedures for attaching additional files to a message that you can send over the network. The additions are relegated to separate files rather than appearing in the original document at the spots were they are relevant. When the message arrives, your colleague must detach the files and store them somewhere on the desktop before viewing them, which depends in turn on running the appropriate applications.

Task-centered computing not only makes it easier for users to work together in a collaborative environment but also makes it easier to engage in more complex interactions electronically than are possible with more conventional human interface metaphors. Most users don't care whether a particular program or system uses OOP, but they do care about getting their work done in ever more interdependent business settings. Taligent human interface policies are designed to facilitate complex interactions without forcing users to learn complex new rules.

PEOPLE, PLACES, AND THINGS

Many basic OOP concepts were developed in the 1960s by two Norwegian computer scientists, O.-J. Dahl and Kristen Nygaard. They invented the first object-based programming language, Simula, to model and simulate complex real-world entities such as manufacturing systems. OOP has proved to be uniquely adaptable, among programming technologies, for modeling all kinds of entities and interactions in all kinds of organizations. It had a strong influence on the early graphical user interfaces developed at Xerox PARC and by Apple for the Lisa and Macintosh computers. From the point of view of a user, OOP permits the use of familiar metaphors that facilitate complex human interactions via computers while minimizing the artificial procedures that seem to come with typical networked computing environments.

Taligent is using the modeling capabilities of OOP to develop human interface metaphors that meet the needs of the enterprise solutions market. Extending the desktop metaphor to the enterprise involves modeling the human relationships, contexts, and entities that exist in organizations. To this end, Taligent has developed the human interface metaphor called People, Places, and Things.

The People, Places, and Things metaphor implements Taligent's vision of task-centered computing for oraganizations. Based on the traditional schoolbook definition of a noun, this metaphor represents objects and relationships in ways that correspond to real objects and relationships. Instead of learning elaborate rules for making the computer do things, users interact with a diverse range of familiar objects using a consistent language of gestures and representations. The OOP technology that underlies the People, Places, and Things metaphor makes it easy to model complex processes and thereby extend the traditional human interface metaphors to meet the unique requirements of organizations and communities.

"A human interface scenario," beginning on page 76, shows how the People, Places, and Things metaphor might be used to model a specific business environment. The complete set of frameworks that support the People, Places, and Things metaphor will be available in future versions of the CommonPoint system.

The remainder of this section introduces basic concepts related to People representations, Places environments, and Things™ objects.

People

People elements will provide a consistent representation of people throughout the CommonPoint system. A People element represents a unique living, breathing person. A person's attributes, such as name, telephone number, address, email address, and so on can be summarized in Things elements such as Business Card objects that provide references to particular people. Collections of such references can be organized into network phone books, group icons, mailing lists, departments, organization charts, and so on.

Such references to people typically encapsulate the information required for working with those people. For example, when two people meet electronically, they might exchange electronic Business Card objects, just as they would exchange business cards in a real meeting, that contain the information they need to communicate effectively via a range of media, including name and title, phone number, fax number, email address, postal address, and so on.

Figure 27 shows some icons related to People elements: a Business Card object, a group object, and an object indicating that the person represented is "present" electronically in a particular Place environment. The first two icons represent Things objects that provide references to people. The third icon represents a true People element, because it indicates the presence of a living, breathing person in a particular elecronic location.

FIGURE 27
ICONS RELATED
TO PEOPLE
OBJECTS

 Beva Nyko   Modular power group   Megan Berg

Because People data types will be standard throughout the system, People elements and references to them will be universally recognized by other objects without any additional work on the part of the programmer. For example, a user might embed a Business Card object in a document, drop it into a form to fill in information about a person automatically, or drop it on a telephone to dial the person's phone number. In the scenario at the beginning of this chapter, Martin Wong's Business Card icon (shown at the lower left of Figure 22 on page 78) can be used in any of these ways.

People elements can be extended in many ways. In real life, one person can delegate his or her authority to another. People elements can support similar arrangements. For example, one person might be able to give another person an electronic credential that allows that person to take over some of the first person's roles in an organization, such as accessing certain reports or servers or approving expenditures up to a specified amount. As the next section explains, People objects are also associated with Place representations.

Places

Place representations are collaborative environments, based on real-world models such as meeting rooms, stores, and offices, that allow users to organize shared information and tasks in meaningful contexts. A Place representation is distinguished by the presence of one or more users and a unique organization of the interface objects that appear within it. Users can create a standard Place environment and modify the behavior of its interface objects and data to reflect the requirements of a particular task or set of tasks.

The illustration on page 74 shows a Place environment for a project calendar that has been created and modified by a user. "A human interface scenario," beginning on page 76, shows other Place environments that facilitate workflow among people playing different roles in an organization.

Like places in the real world, different Place environments can have different rules, usually based on the implicit rules of the real-world places on which they are modeled. We've all learned complex behaviors for the different kinds of places we live and work in every day. Taligent's task-centered computing model builds on behaviors that people already know, thus keeping the need to learn new behaviors to a minimum. For example, if you're in your own office, you know that you can do anything you want with the objects it contains. You can pick up pieces of paper and write on them, throw objects away, or take objects with you when you leave. If you go to your colleague's office, you may be able to leave something there, but you know you can't take anything away with you or throw it away without first asking permission. If you go to a store, you can take things away with you, but first you have to pay for them. Other places, such as movie theaters, require payment before you can enter.

Place representations are designed for flexible and scalable modeling of disparate real-world places and the rules and behaviors they embody. For example, some Place environments are for small group meetings, where participants can speak whenever they want to. Others, much like auditoriums, are designed for one person to talk while everyone else sits quietly and listens, except perhaps for a question-and-answer period during which people raise their hands to be recognized. Some Place environments require nothing more than a whiteboard and some markers that everyone can use, and others require complex tools that provide projection capabilities, live video and sound, database access, and so on. Basic capabilities of the Compound Document framework, such as real-time editing of shared documents, facilitate collaboration across all CommonPoint documents built with that framework.

Individual users who aren't interacting with a group can also benefit from the Places metaphor. As in real life, a user may want to clear everything off the computer desktop and concentrate on a single task, such as preparing a review. In future versions of the CommonPoint system, a user will be able to create a personal Place environment for doing reviews, with all the relevant information, tools, and objects such as personnel files ready to hand. If the phone rings, or if someone comes into the room, the user can return instantly to his or her home Place environment or switch to a different one to get information about some other task.

A Place environment can be represented by an icon that the user double-clicks to go there. Each user can have a collection of personal Place environments available, including a home (desktop) Place representation and various customized work areas, and can also go to other Place environments provided by the user's company or colleagues or purchased like other software. A user can give other users access to a particular Place representation by giving them a "postcard" that will take them there.

People in Places

When an individual user needs something, he or she can visit a Place environment where that object might be located and look for it, just as in real life. For example, if you need a specification from the engineering department, you can go to that department's Place environment, identify the people who are currently there, get some help from one of them by telephone, locate the specification, and bring it back to your home Place environment. This is possible because a Place representation always shows the people who are currently in that place, including information like phone numbers and responsibilities. Place representations can be designed to encourage the serendipitous personal interaction that all organizations depend on without requiring the physical presence of the people involved.

Representations of people in Place environments can also be customized for specific purposes. For example, the Routing menu shown in Figure 23 on page 79 allows the user to route a trouble ticket to a specific technical support specialist currently working in the Tech Support Place environment.

Places at all scales

Place software can be designed for any number of users, from one or two up to, potentially, hundreds. Place environments for single users, organized by project or other convenient categories, have already been discussed. Place environments for use by a handful of participants are appropriate for tasks such as one-on-one meetings, group design, project management, or budgeting that a company normally performs with small groups. Place classrooms can be designed to hold 10 to 30 students, and Place auditoriums can hold hundreds of people. Each Place representation at any of these scales provides appropriate tools and rules, like similar real-world places, for the tasks it is designed to facilitate.

Larger-scale Place environments can model bulletin boards, mail rooms, help desks, sales tracking systems, and other forms of collaboration that involve hundreds or thousands of people. At a national or global scale, Place software can potentially be used to model information services, retail stores, mass media broadcast facilities, voting, or Internet resources. The recent growth of the World Wide Web reflects the ad hoc self-organization of the Internet into entities that resemble Taligent Place representations in many respects.

Just as People elements can be referenced by Business Card objects and other Things objects, Place environments can be referenced by postcards, by icons on a map, by items in the standard Place menu, and in a variety of other ways. Users can customize their own Place objects and their own navigation tools, such as maps or menu entries. Place representations also provide a suitable context for dealing with complex issues of security and access control, which can be handled like similar real-world issues (for example, with credentials, ID cards, invitations, reservations, or tickets) and can therefore be made easier to understand and use. Place representations can also maintain information about usage, such as hourly charges, visitors, items sold or added, and so on, to facilitate electronic commerce. Taligent expects specialized and configurable Place representations to become a new category of software for solving practical problems at all scales of human organization.

An architecture for building shared spaces

Designing and building software, especially object-oriented software, has sometimes been compared to the growth of cities. The work of Christopher Alexander (1987), a Berkeley architect who has written extensively about urban design, and Kevin Lynch (1960), an urban planner at MIT, strikes familiar chords for many software designers. The specific applications of their ideas to computer science are beyond the scope of this book, but the general similarities between urban design and software design are easy to grasp.

Software and cities both tend to grow in a piecemeal way to express the changing needs of the people for whom they are built. Their growth is unpredictable, because large groups of people tend to change their collective behavior in unpredictable ways. Sometimes a city or a piece of software grows as an organic whole into something beautiful and useful at all scales, from doorknobs to transportation arteries, from the user interface to the microkernel; and sometimes it disintegrates into unrelated ugly pieces that are difficult to maintain and frustrating to use. Most cities, like most software systems, end up somewhere in between.

The Internet is the most famous and most successful example of this kind of "urban growth" in cyberspace. It consists of separate computers and networks of computers that are cobbled together, for the most part, with the aid of arcane UNIX protocols into a giant planetwide network. Protocols like the World Wide Web and programs like Mosaic allow users to navigate literally from one computer to another anywhere on the Internet simply by clicking on words in a document, and to download and view formatted text and information from other computers all over the world. Agent programs like Gopher can search the net for information on specific topics. Other programs and protocols allow users to join specialized discussion groups, search databases, shop, participate in political campaigns, play games, and take part in literally thousands of other activities whose variety and complexity increase every day.

Working with relatively crude, mostly text-based tools, Internet users have created a network of virtual communities that help people work and communicate on a global scale. The CommonPoint system, and especially its support for Place representations, applies the simulation capabilities of OOP to problem domains much like those that the World Wide Web and related software such as Mosaic and Netscape address. Place classes will provide a rich set of programming structures for building shared electronic spaces.

Things

The *Things* objects that are part of the People, Places, and Things metaphor fit easily into traditional user interfaces and also provide new capabilities unique to the CommonPoint application system:

- **Familiar desktop elements** include documents, folders, disk drives, trash can, menus, and windows. These resemble similar objects on traditional systems.
- **Extensions of desktop elements** include stationery pads, programmable containers, and embeddable components created with the Compound Document framework. These resemble similar objects on traditional systems, but also provide additional capabilities. (Embeddable components are introduced in Chapter 2, beginning on page 68.)
- **Appliances** include printers, scanners, telephones, answering machines, dictation machines, fax machines, in and out boxes, data compactors, cameras, recorders, and projectors. Appliances can be implemented entirely in software or as controllers for corresponding hardware.
- **Cursor tools** include selection, pencil, eraser, text, and rotation tools; approval stamps; and so on. Cursor tools can be application-specific or global.
- **Business objects** include forms, reports, invoices, routing slips, ballots, machines, instruments, books, magazines, movies, audiotapes, business cards, credit cards, money, catalogs, calendars, and so on. This is the most important category of Things objects—those used to model unique entities, both physical and conceptual, that are part of real-world human activities, as opposed to typical computer "things" such as applications and documents.

This section introduces some of the Things objects supported by the CommonPoint system.

Stationery pads

Stationery pads are templates used to create new documents and other interface objects. An object created from a stationery pad has the same properties as the original: layout, fonts, and the like. Users can create new objects from stationery in several ways. If the user double-clicks a stationery pad icon, a new document icon for that type of stationery appears in the same container as the stationery pad and opens in a window, as shown in Figure 28. Alternatively, if the user drags a stationery pad icon into a window where the preferred representation is a frame, a new frame for that type of stationery is created in the window.

To make a new stationery pad, the user creates an object from another piece of stationery or with an appropriate tool or menu command, modifies the object as desired, and chooses Make Stationery from the Document menu. The new stationery appears in the same container as the original object.

FIGURE 28
CREATING A
DOCUMENT
FROM A
STATIONERY
PAD

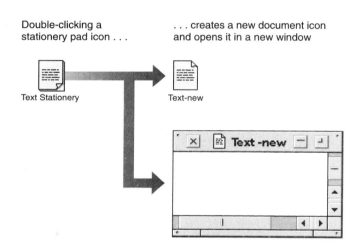

Double-clicking a
stationery pad icon . . .

. . . creates a new document icon
and opens it in a new window

Text Stationery

Text-new

Containers

A *container* in the CommonPoint system is any object that can enclose other objects, including other containers. Examples include folders, frames, documents, places, maps, and the trash. As in the Mac OS desktop, folders can contain other folders without any limitations. However, in the CommonPoint system, any document can be a container in the same sense that a folder is a container. This means you can store icons for documents, folders, stationery pads, and so on inside any document that is implemented as a containable, and they will behave just as if they were stored inside a folder. You can drag and drop icons, select them, and open them no matter where they're located.

This may seem like a subtle change from conventional human interface metaphors, but it has significant implications. For example, an email application running in the CommonPoint system won't need to provide a complicated mechanism for enclosing, saving, and opening files that are attached to messages. Instead, the sender can just drop file icons into the message document, and the recipient can just double-click to open them. Users won't have to deal with files that originally came with some message and end up cluttering the desktop. Rather than being forced to deal with dialog boxes, file management chores, and additional applications every time a message arrives with attachments, the user can just leave the attachments in the original message and use them there. A message can be the permanent home for other documents it contains, and a presentation can contain supporting documents like spreadsheets or charts without ever needing to store them separately on the desktop.

A *containable* is any object that has been explicitly implemented so that it can be placed in any container. Users can choose to filter the containables in a given container, such as a folder, so that only certain kinds are fully visible; the filtered containables are gathered together in a single icon until the user turns filtering off.

Containers can also be programmed to act much like agents or "smart folders," performing actions on contained objects or retrieving objects from a variety of sources over a network based on the objects' attributes or content. For example, a container can be programmed to retrieve aliases or originals of all word-processing documents on a volume, all the files larger than 100K, all files more than one year old, all files that have been changed since they were last backed up, and so on.

Cursor tools

A *cursor* is a graphic symbol that can be moved around the screen by a pointing device such as a mouse. As in traditional graphical user interfaces, cursors provide visual feedback on the current mode, the current cursor tool, the current context, or the object beneath the cursor. For example, the cursor may change to a pencil after the user chooses a pencil tool, but only when it's over a frame in which the pencil can write.

A *cursor tool* is a graphic symbol in a floating nonmodal window (that is, a window that can be deactivated) called a *palette*. Cursor tools represent modes in which the user can create and modify a particular kind of data. Common tools include the selection tool, the pencil, and the eraser. To use a tool, the user first clicks the tool's icon to select it. Then the user applies the tool to the content area of a frame by moving the cursor over the frame and using it to manipulate the frame's data. Typically, the cursor changes shape whenever it's over a frame a tool can act on to indicate which tool the user is "holding." Figure 29 shows a palette and a cursor tool in action.

FIGURE 29
A PALETTE
OF CURSOR
TOOLS AND A
TOOL IN USE

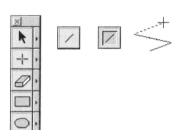

Cursor tools can also create new embedded components within an existing component. For example, Figure 30 shows a text cursor tool that can be used to create a new word-processing component within another component.

FIGURE 30
USING A
CURSOR
TOOL TO
CREATE AN
EMBEDDED
COMPONENT

You can use a text component tool . . .   . . . to create a new text component and type into it.

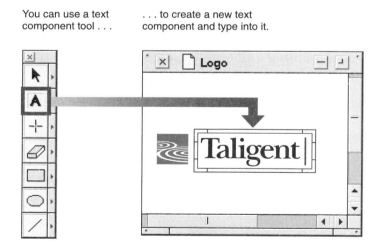

Taligent's support for cursor tools makes it possible to design *global tools* that, unlike tools supported by traditional user interfaces, are completely decoupled from specific kinds of embeddable components and the stationery from which they are created. There are three kinds of global tools:

- Tools that are applicable across a wide variety of data types. Examples include highlighter or colorpicker tools.
- Tools that are applicable to a common data type, like an I-beam tool for text.
- Tools with narrow applicability that are available only when components that support them are active.

Global tools are globally available, but they aren't necessarily globally applicable; some frames won't recognize a given tool. If the frame recognizes the data type that the tool acts on, the user can either edit the contents of the frame or use the tool to create new objects in the frame. If the frame doesn't recognize the data type that the tool acts on, the user may still be able to use the tool to create new frames within the first frame.

These kinds of global capabilities are built into the CommonPoint application system. For example, most text-editing components inherit their characteristics from the Text Editing framework. This means that all applications with text-editing capabilities support the standard characteristics of editable text in a uniform fashion. A global tool designed to operate on editable text can be designed to work on all editable text in the system, even if the text is in a component designed by a developer who is completely unknown to the text tool developer. The component inherits the ability to be manipulated by global tools along with all the other characteristics of the Text Editing framework. Global tools can rely on the inherited internal structure of a text-editing component even if the tool developer and the component developer haven't explicitly coordinated their product designs.

Aliases

An alias is a reference to another CommonPoint object and behaves much like an alias in the Mac OS. The CommonPoint system supports aliases on all host operating systems whose file systems also support them. Aliases allow users to represent an object outside of its original location without having to make a copy of it. Aliases are popular with users because they make it easier to keep track of objects and perform actions on them. When a user opens an alias, for example, the original object opens. Deleting or copying an alias affects only the alias, not the original object.

The CommonPoint system supports an object called a *proxy*™ that resembles an alias in some ways but is accessible from a document window's title bar. See "Windows" on page 103 for more information about proxies.

Appliances

An *appliance* is an object that typically performs some self-contained, automated operation on data in other objects. For example, a printer appliance prints a document, and an OCR appliance extracts text from an image. Appliances can be used for many purposes, including the automatic creation and transformation of data and other routine operations. Figure 31 shows some appliance icons.

FIGURE 31
APPLIANCE
ICONS

Laser Printer   Trash   Trash   Map Maker   Fax

Taligent appliances represent a range of functions. Some represent physical devices, such as telephones, fax machines, printers, and scanners, but others are completely self-contained, such as data compactors or alarm clocks. Users frequently use appliances by dragging something onto the appliance icon, such as a document, frame, snippet of data, or even other appliances. What happens after the user drops the object depends on the appliance. Its output may simply be the processed input, or it can be a new creation.

For example, if you drop a document onto a printer appliance, the appliance prints the document to the printer it represents, leaving the original document unchanged. A fax appliance behaves in a similar fashion, although the output is different. But if you drop a document on a data compactor, the output is the compacted original. An alarm clock appliance may not accept documents at all; instead, it might serve as a drop site for sound objects used to change the alarm sound or scheduler objects that set the alarm. These actions don't trigger the alarm; instead, they change its behavior. A scanner appliance doesn't accept input at all from the user; it simply outputs scanned documents.

Appliances can be designed to anticipate a user's needs and goals. For example, a mailbox appliance might forward mail to the appropriate destination (which it looks up in its own internal database) without forcing the user to specify the full name and address of the recipient. It might "learn" new addresses as it encounters them.

Appliances provide an easy and flexible way to perform repetitive tasks—something like a macro wrapped in a user interface object, which the user can turn on, let run, and turn off. The implementation of appliances depends heavily on the Drag and Drop frameworks, which are briefly introduced on page 178. Appliances can accept multiple object types, and draggable objects can be dropped on a variety of appliances.

MENUS, WINDOWS, AND CONTROLS

The CommonPoint User Interface frameworks provide familiar menus, windows, and controls, such as sliders and buttons, that resemble similar objects in other graphical user interfaces. This section provides a brief overview of some of these objects as they are implemented in the first version of the CommonPoint system.

✅ NOTE   Windows, icons, menus, and other user interface elements illustrated in this chapter are based on pre-beta versions of the User Interface frameworks. The appearance of some of these elements may change.

The system supports a variety of implementations; for example, menus can be implemented within a window rather than as floating palettes. The first version of the CommonPoint system implements menus as palettes, but future versions are expected to introduce fixed menus within windows. In some cases users might be able to choose between palette menus and menus within windows on a systemwide basis. From a developer's point of view, such differences among user interface implementations are transparent and don't affect application code.

Menus

Menus in the first version of the CommonPoint system are displayed in floating menu palettes like that shown in Figure 32.

FIGURE 32
THE MAIN
MENU PALETTE

At the highest level, the main menu palette contains a list of the available menus:

- **The Services menu** provides access to globally available services such as printing. In future versions of the CommonPoint system, these can include fax, email, online help, and services common to multiple Place environments.
- **The Document menu** lists commands that apply to the active container. The name of this menu changes to reflect the container type. For example, if a folder is selected, the menu name is Folder.
- **The Edit menu** lists commands for changing the contents of the current selection, such as Cut, Copy, and Paste.
- **The Window menu** lists commands that apply to windows, such as Tile and Cascade, and a list of current windows.

This menu arrangement is designed to provide as much information to the user as possible about the current context. The content of menus and submenus changes to reflect the current context.

Developers can provide additional context-sensitive menus for items that don't fit in the standard menus. These menus appear after the Window menu, as shown in Figure 33.

FIGURE 33
ADDING
CUSTOM
MENUS

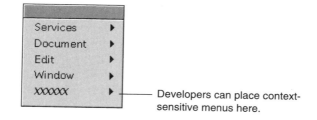

Developers can place context-sensitive menus here.

The main menu palette is always visible. The user can move any menu palette around by dragging its top, and can select an item in the menu by dragging. If a menu item includes a right-pointing arrow, a submenu appears when the user drags through that item, as shown in Figure 34.

FIGURE 34
USING MENUS

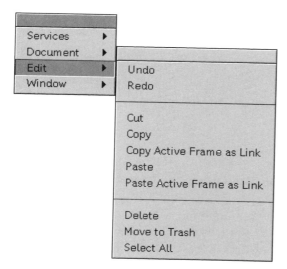

A "sticky menu" mode allows the user to choose a menu item just by clicking it. If the menu item has an associated submenu, the submenu appears, and the user can click again to choose one of its items. For repeated use, the user can also tear off any submenu to make it a separate menu palette.

The Copy Active Frame As Link and Paste Active Frame As Link commands are used to establish links between different selections. The Taligent human interface policies for linking are modeled on the OpenDoc human interface policies for linking. For more information about the Taligent linking mechanism, see "Connecting and navigating among components," which begins on page 194.

Windows

The CommonPoint system provides several kinds of windows for presenting and manipulating data. Figure 35 shows a typical document window, which is the primary window for presenting data to the user. A document window can include other containers, including embedded components.

FIGURE 35
MAIN
PARTS OF A
WINDOW

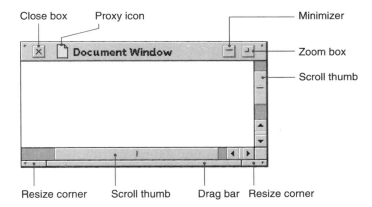

A window's title bar contains a title, a proxy icon, a close box, a minimizer, and a zoom box. The proxy icon acts as a *proxy* for drag-and-drop operations. For example, if a user wants to fax a window and its contents, the user can drag the proxy icon to a fax appliance without having to find the document's icon in the container, such as a desktop folder, where it resides. The *minimizer* lets the user reduce the window to its title bar. Other title bar controls behave much as they do in other graphical user interfaces.

Other kinds of CommonPoint windows, which include varying combinations of the basic parts shown in Figure 35, include the following:

- **A panel** presents controls for manipulating data, such as setting data attributes or work preferences.
- **A dialog box** solicits information from the user to complete a task.
- **A palette** presents tools for manipulating data or a set of data attributes (such as a color palette).

Controls

Controls are user interface elements that let users initiate actions or make choices. They include buttons, check boxes, pop-up menus and scrolling lists, sliders, and text entry fields. The standard Taligent controls work much the same way they do in other user interfaces. The *cp*Constructor user interface builder simplifies the assembly and modification of controls. For more information about the *cp*Constructor user interface builder, see page 146.

Figure 36 shows some standard Taligent controls. Controls work by sending commands or actions to other objects. An action is a text string used to communicate a user action, such as selecting a radio button, to a handler provided by an application. For more information about the way the CommonPoint system handles controls, see page 207.

FIGURE 36
SOME
COMMONPOINT
CONTROLS

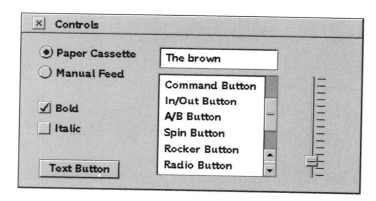

CSPACE—A COLLABORATIVE SPACE

Some aspects of the People, Places, and Things metaphor are implemented in the first release of the CommonPoint system, and each subsequent release will enhance the implementation further. The first release also includes powerful collaboration capabilities that are unique to Taligent.

Applications built with the Compound Document framework are automatically capable of being shared by multiple users across a network. To provide this capability, the Compound Document framework is closely tied to the Shared Document framework, which is in turn built on the Caucus framework (described briefly on page 380). The Caucus framework provides a multicast transport mechanism that broadcasts commands executed on one computer to all other computers registered in the same collaboration session. This mechanism allows users to share a single document at the same time and see the results of a change any of them makes as soon as it occurs.

As explained in Chapter 7, commands are high-level semantic entities that are relatively small and economical and therefore don't require high network bandwidth. As a result, Commonpoint collaboration is practical even on networks with relatively modest performance profiles, unlike "screen sharing" and other traditional collaboration mechanisms that require large numbers of pixels to be transmitted between machines.

FIGURE 37
CSPACE

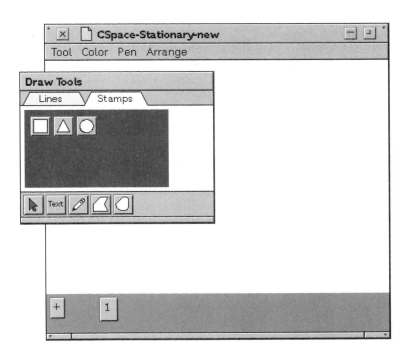

CSpace is one of several simple applications included with the first release of the CommonPoint system. It provides a container for managing collaboration among small groups of people, and it demonstrates some of the CommonPoint system's potential for collaboration solutions.

Figure 37 shows a typical CSpace document. A user can create such a document by tearing off a piece of CSpace stationery. To work on the document with other people, a user typically arranges a session time, makes sure each user who wants to participate in the session has access to the document, and conducts a telephone conference call during the session. Any user who opens the same CSpace document is automatically connected to the corresponding CSpace session as a participant; no other action is required. Current participants are listed in a Participants window that each user can choose to view or hide.

Any object placed in a CSpace document automatically appears in the shared area for all participants. The CSpace tool palette (available from a menu) provides a basic set of tools for creating text and graphics and annotating objects that have been dragged into a CSpace document.

During a CSpace session, whoever starts work on an object first can edit that object. While one user is editing an object, other users can edit other objects. The other users' versions of the CSpace document automatically update to reflect changes to an object as they are made. For example, if one user changes a formula in a spreadsheet component, all users see the resulting changes in the spreadsheet as they occur, even if that component isn't currently active in their view of the document.

Embeddable components created with the Compound Document framework can be dragged into a CSpace window and shared in this way. Although programmers don't need to take any extra steps to take advantage of this capability, they do need to think about the implications of collaboration if they expect multiple users to be able to share a particular component. For example, a movie player generally has Play and Stop commands. If the player is to be used by a single user only, the Play and Stop commands simply start and stop the movie. But if the player is intended for use in a collaborative environment such as CSpace, the Play and Stop commands should indicate a specific frame to ensure that the versions viewed by each user remain synchronized. Stop and Play commands that don't indicate a specific frame might leave the movie in a different state on different computers, depending on network traffic and other constraints on the underlying multicast mechanism.

INTEGRATION WITH HOST USER ENVIRONMENTS

The People, Places, and Things metaphor and related concepts and implementations are not intended to replace existing host user interface elements. Instead, the CommonPoint application system extends host user interface capabilities to support real-time access to distributed users, data, and resources.

CommonPoint applications and objects interoperate at various levels with host-based applications, including the exchange of data via cut-copy-paste operations and drag-and-drop capabilities supported by the host. The CommonPoint system will also support data translation, data interchange, and mutually embeddable components between host applications and CommonPoint applications. For more details about CommonPoint interoperability with host systems, see "Interoperability Services," beginning on page 284.

CommonPoint documents and their windows bear a familial resemblance to the those of the host environment but have a distinct look that helps the user identify them as CommonPoint objects. The relationship between the CommonPoint system and the host system superficially resembles the relationship between HyperCard and the Mac OS. HyperCard documents, called "stacks," have a distinctive look on the Mac OS desktop and provide integrated, customizable capabilities unique to HyperCard, but in other respects they behave like traditional Mac OS applications.

Desktop integration

Appliances, stationery pads, programmable containers, global tools, business objects, and other CommonPoint objects will be integrated with host desktop objects or added to the existing desktop. To achieve maximum desktop integration, the user experience of the CommonPoint system may vary slightly from one host to another.

For example, if a host system provides a trash can for deleting files, the CommonPoint implementation for that system can supplement the standard trash can's capabilities, so that it can delete both CommonPoint desktop objects and host desktop objects. If the host doesn't provide a trash can, the CommonPoint system will support whatever deletion mechanism the host supports and can also provide a trash can capable of deleting both CommonPoint and host objects.

Similarly, if the host supports printer appliances, the CommonPoint system transparently adds the capabilities of its printer appliances to the host appliances so that they can print either host documents or CommonPoint objects. If the host doesn't support printer appliances, the CommonPoint system can support them as a new kind of item on the desktop that can print both host documents and CommonPoint objects.

Portability and intraplatform consistency

Superficial differences between the CommonPoint user experience on one host and the user experience on another don't affect the portability of a CommonPoint application, which can be designed for compilation from identical code for multiple hosts. Glue code provided by Taligent takes care of differences among host user interfaces transparently, with no additional coding by the developer.

This approach emphasizes a consistent intraplatform user experience. Users can easily move back and forth between host applications and CommonPoint applications, taking advantage of new CommonPoint capabilities without having to learn new ways of performing routine tasks such as manipulating windows or printing documents. Intraplatform consistency is more important than interplatform consistency (that is, consistency among CommonPoint user interface details on different hosts), because most users work within the same environment on the same hardware platform for extended periods of time and are accustomed to the host user interface implementation.

Integration of Places

Place software encompasses a new category of applications that will grow in variety and importance over time. At first, users are likely to perceive Place environments as customizable organizing tools that work exceptionally well for certain kinds of tasks. As Taligent extends CommonPoint capabilities and more Places products and other CommonPoint applications become available, users will begin to experience the full range of possibilities that the People, Places, and Things metaphor can support, and they will spend more time working in Place environments.

Place environments can contain both CommonPoint objects and host objects; for example, Taligent plans to allow a user to drag an OLE object into a Place window. The user can then choose either to open the OLE object as an OLE part or to convert the OLE object to a CommonPoint component and open the converted component. Similarly, CommonPoint objects can be dragged anywhere on the host desktop.

To manipulate and organize CommonPoint objects, whether they appear on the host desktop or within a Place environment, users can run the host utilities they already know how to use. For example, searching for files involves using the host file-searching mechanism. At the same time, they can use CommonPoint objects in ways that host objects can't be used; for example, documents based on the Compound Document framework can be dropped into any collaborative Place environment and shared dynamically with other users over a network.

As the CommonPoint sy0stem matures, the Workspace frameworks (introduced briefly on page 178) will provide additional support for Place software. In the long term, the Workspace frameworks are designed to support cross-platform enterprise desktop capabilities for each host that can be extended and customized along the lines suggested by the human interface scenario described at the beginning of this chapter.

Enterprise Computing Community

Business Computing Users and Target Industries

Telecom Energy Financial Services Manufacturing Transportation Healthcare Higher Education

Solution Partners:
Business operations
Collaboration
Document management
Workflow
Information services
Vertical solutions

Tools:
Professional C++
Client-Server
Visual Assembly

Application System:
CommonPoint

AIX HP-UX OS/2

Mac OS Win NT / Win 95

CHAPTER 4

TALIGENT
MARKET DEVELOPMENT

Taligent faces the same fundamental marketing task that any company faces: identifying a customer set and solving one or more problems for those customers.

Chapter 1 introduces Taligent's vision of this task. The typical CommonPoint user works with a networked 32-bit multitasking computer in a business or other organization. Such users and the developers and OEMs who serve them face two problems:

- Sophisticated software solutions take too long to create and maintain, especially distributed applications that support multiple networked users and real-time information needs (often called "client-server" applications).
- These kinds of software solutions are too difficult to learn and use, especially for groups of people working together over a network.

Chapter 2 introduces the programming model that Taligent is using to help solve the first problem, and Chapter 3 describes how the People, Places, and Things human interface metaphor that Taligent technology makes possible can help solve the second problem.

Technology is not enough, by itself, to ensure the success of a commercial venture. A new way of developing applications doesn't spring into the world full grown from the brow of an engineer. Like other forms of software, the CommonPoint system has been born in a messy encounter between pure research and commercial necessity. At first it may resemble a new building with wires and pipes sticking out of the walls and rooms without floors and sockets without lights. Taligent's success depends on the success of the first developers who roll up their sleeves and create software that both demonstrates the CommonPoint system's potential and makes it useful from the first time a user tries it out. These early developers will also have a direct and powerful influence on the evolution of the system.

This chapter introduces Taligent's initial marketing plans, including information about target markets, plans for CommonPoint deployment, commercial CommonPoint software, and some of the benefits for developers and OEMs who adopt Taligent technology.

MARKET OVERVIEW

Taligent distinguishes two primary markets in the computer industry:

- **The personal productivity market:** 16- and 32-bit operating systems and related hardware and software designed for a single user working alone.
- **The enterprise solutions market:** 32-bit (and higher) multitasking operating systems and related hardware and software designed for multiple users working together over a network.

The personal productivity market targets individual users working with traditional applications such as word processors and spreadsheets to generate reports, analyses, and other documents for their own use and to present to others. Although for many years this market enjoyed growth of 30 to 40 percent per year, growth has now slowed to single digits in terms of the number of new applications being sold. Approximately 80 percent of the revenue from personal productivity application software is going to the top three application vendors. It is a mature, upgrade market in which the established vendors make most of the money.

In contrast, the enterprise solutions market targets groups of people working together to generate collaborative documents, make decisions, manage workflow, access data from a variety of sources, and cooperate in other ways in real time. Application software for this market helps users run their organizations, including areas such as information management, decision support, business-specific transactions, project management, manufacturing control, and human resources administration.

The enterprise solutions market is poised for dramatic growth through the rest of the 1990s. This growth represents the confluence of several trends, including the ever-increasing amount of information that corporations must process to compete effectively in the global marketplace, hardware advances such as RISC architectures, and new technologies that can take advantage of hardware advances to support sophisticated distributed applications in networked environments.

Spending trends confirm the significance of this growth. According to the InfoWorld '94 Operating System Survey, 87 percent of corporate customers queried were adopting client-server technologies, 84 percent planned to install 32-bit operating systems, and 50 percent were evaluating RISC. International Data Corporation (IDC) has estimated that client-server tools will form a $5 billion market by 1998. Other studies commissioned by Taligent project that annual shipments of networked computers with fast processors that can run the CommonPoint system will double between 1995 and 1998 from 22 million to 40 million units, for a compound annual growth rate (CAGR) of 23 percent and an installed base soaring well beyond 100 million units.

As the installed base increases, customer demand for software that can take full advantage of this new infrastructure is taking off even more dramatically. Depending on the specific category of solutions, industry analysts predict that the enterprise solutions software market will achieve 50 to 150 percent growth per year over the next three years. The CommonPoint application system is designed to address this market.

A new class of enterprise solutions

Taligent's research indicates that these will be high-growth software categories in the enterprise solutions market through the end of the 1990s:

- **Business operations.** Supports common line-of-business processes such as project management, business administration, servicing products, looking up customer records, and other transactions.

- **Collaboration.** Allows two or more users to share data interactively across a network and participate in electronic meetings, facilitating, for example, collective changes to a single document in real time.

- **Document management.** Supports the creation and distributed management of complex multiauthor documents composed of a variety of data types, including multilingual text, 3-D graphics, and time media.

- **Workflow.** Supports automation of various complex processes in an organization, such as those involving the flow of material and information, and incremental modification of those processes over time to adapt to changing business needs.

- **Information services.** Helps users retrieve data from diverse data sources, organize it, and present it in a coherent form to facilitate decision-making.

- **Vertical solutions.** Supports solutions for specific industries, such as insurance, construction, or hospital administration, that can be rapidly customized by or for individual companies.

"A human interface scenario," which begins on page 76, includes examples of software solutions in most of these categories.

These new kinds of enterprise solutions have the following requirements:

- **Multiple operating systems.** Users who need these solutions work with different kinds of networked hardware platforms and a variety of operating systems.
- **Industry standards.** Different kinds of machines must be able to communicate with each other over a network even though they use different networking protocols and other standards.
- **Rich data types.** Multilingual text, 3-D graphics, multimedia, and other rich data types that can be easily intermingled in a single document are required for many enterprise solutions.
- **Distributed computing.** Directory services, messaging, communications, data access, system management, collaboration, and other forms of support for users working together over a network underlie all enterprise solutions.

Why "CommonPoint"?

The name "CommonPoint" reflects the characteristics of the CommonPoint application system that support the emerging enterprise solutions:

- **A common foundation** for rapid development and ongoing customization of enterprise solutions. Rich built-in capabilities and increased productivity for developers mean not only less development time for applications but also more time for innovation in a developer's target domain.
- **A common platform** for distributed computing across different operating systems on a network. No matter what operating systems they happen to be running, users can share information and collaborate, access data in existing mainframes and minicomputers, deploy applications written for the CommonPoint system easily across multiple host operating systems, and move data easily between host applications and CommonPoint applications.
- **A common environment** that allows people in an organization to complete tasks together electronically. CommonPoint frameworks permit development of sophisticated multiuser environments based on task-centered computing and the People, Places, and Things metaphor.

Target industries

Taligent has evaluated the capabilities of its technology and has identified six key industries with urgent software needs that closely match CommonPoint capabilities. Other criteria used to select these industries include their substantial ongoing investment in information technology, knowledge of and experience with object technology, and extensive allocation of in-house resources for developing and maintaining software.

The following key industries are driving the demand for object-based enterprise solutions:

- **Telecommunications.** Telephone companies and phone companies also have OOP experience and rely heavily on software innovation to drive new products. Typical software solutions include billing systems, customer service applications, network management, and new information services.

- **Energy.** Utilities and fuel companies are committed to OOP and have an ongoing need for application development in the areas of exploration, seismic analysis, visualization, and process control.

- **Financial services.** Leading money centers, investment banks, brokerage houses, and insurance companies have the most extensive OOP experience in the Fortune 1000 companies, which they have leveraged in areas such as financial instruments, investment analysis, claims adjustments, and insurance policy development.

- **Manufacturing.** Auto manufacturers and other large-scale manufacturing companies are aggressively pursuing OOP for computer-integrated manufacturing (CIM), computer-based training (CBT), manufacturing simulation, and process control.

- **Transportation.** Airlines and air freight delivery services have extensive experience with objects, including prototyping and production of software for logistical and scheduling systems.

- **Healthcare.** Pharmaceutical companies, medical instrument companies, and large healthcare providers have taken an active interest in object-oriented technology for use in areas such as research, clinical trials, diagnosis, and patient management.

- **Higher education.** Although not, strictly speaking, an industry, higher education represents a microcosm of computing needs in the larger society, including students on a budget, administrators, curriculum planners, professional schools, and state-of-the-art research facilities in a variety of disciplines. Taligent's goal is to promote education in object technology and its application to all aspects of computing in universities and other institutions.

These industries represent a significant percentage of the U.S. gross national product (GNP), and in the mid-1990s they are collectively spending hundreds of millions of dollars per year on information technology. In addition to seeking industry-specific solutions, these industries are seeking new kinds of horizontal solutions that enhance group productivity and business processes.

Taligent has identified these target industries for its initial market development efforts. However, Taligent technology is suitable for many kinds of computing environments. Taligent is also targeting additional industries and nonbusiness sectors such as government and home computing for long-term market development.

Taligent marketing advantages

As the new enterprise solutions market develops, the computer industry is at a crossroads. The information infrastructure to support the global economy of the 21st century is being installed now, but the applications that can take maximum advantage of that infrastructure have not yet begun to reach their potential. The computer industry must deliver new kinds of applications that meet customer demands to justify ongoing customer investment in information technology.

Everyone in the computer industry is aware of this challenge, and Taligent is not alone in targeting the new enterprise solutions market. However, Taligent has three unique marketing advantages: timing, leverage from its investors, and a compelling product.

Timing

The CommonPoint application system is being released well ahead of major object-based products from Microsoft and other companies. Taligent is not only entering the market early, but entering at a time when other technologies that are crucial to its success are becoming pervasive. Most customers in this market are installing 32-bit operating systems. Volume operating systems such as Windows and Mac OS are crossing over to full 32-bit multitasking environments. New users are being seated at 486, Pentium, and RISC machines that can support these new operating systems. And the software development community is rapidly adopting object-oriented technology.

Leverage

Taligent's investors provide unmatched marketing leverage in the six key industries that Taligent is targeting. They have committed their worldwide distribution systems to Taligent products, and they all stand to gain from making the CommonPoint system a strong presence in the marketplace. The investors are also committed to building complementary tools, applications, and services around the CommonPoint system and bundling it appropriately for their own customer sets.

Compelling product

CommonPoint applications will be measured against traditional applications running at the same time on the host operating system. Taligent doesn't expect host-based applications to go away. Rather, users will rapidly discover that CommonPoint applications are far easier and more effective to use for tasks such as collaboration, creating compound documents with multiple rich data types, workflow control, and so on.

In a similar manner, developers will discover that they can create certain kinds of multiplatform CommonPoint applications much more easily than they can create similar applications for host operating systems—without having to give up their commitment to products that run directly on those host systems.

Taligent has a compelling product suite that can hold its own in the enterprise solutions market by improving productivity for both users and developers.

DEPLOYMENT OF TALIGENT PRODUCTS

As this book goes to press, Taligent's investment partners are in the process of porting the CommonPoint application system to their operating systems, and Taligent is in the process of porting it to 32-bit systems such as Windows NT.

In general, the CommonPoint product staging for any host follows the pattern shown in Figure 38. Stage 1 in Figure 38 shows the host operating system running directly on a modern 32-bit microprocessor using its own low-level protocols (labeled "Host OS core services" in Figure 38).

Stage 2 shows the CommonPoint application system running side by side with the entire host operating system, so that users can simultaneously run applications written for the host system and applications written for the CommonPoint system. Users can also copy and paste and share data in other ways between host and CommonPoint applications. The CommonPoint system in Stage 2 maps its OS Services APIs to the low-level host protocols to communicate with hardware. While the host may not provide a true microkernel, it meets CommonPoint system requirements such as protected virtual memory and fast interprocess communication.

Stage 3 shows the CommonPoint application system and the host operating system running side by side on top of microkernel services and related object services (labeled "Object-enhanced host OS core services"), which replace the low-level host protocols used by both systems in Stage 2. This reflects the tendency of operating system vendors to modernize their proprietary operating systems and provide optimized support for objects.

FIGURE 38
PRODUCT STAGING FOR THE COMMONPOINT APPLICATION SYSTEM

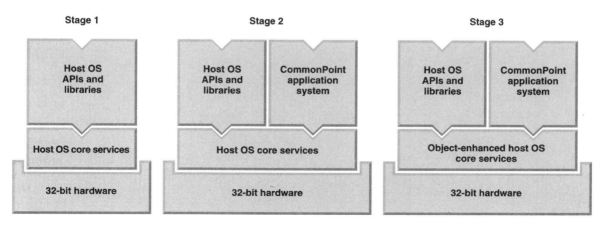

These stages, or variations on them, represent the basic CommonPoint deployment strategy as host systems migrate from a traditional kernel to a more compact and efficient microkernel design center. For example, IBM plans to incorporate its new microkernel into new versions of OS/2 and AIX, Apple is developing its own microkernel as the basis for future releases of the Mac OS, and Hewlett-Packard is adding kernel-level threads to HP-UX. Regardless of the host or the stage of deployment, CommonPoint applications always use the same APIs and work the same way.

As the CommonPoint system is deployed on a new host operating system, developers who wish to develop CommonPoint applications on that host can choose to use either host tools with which they are already familiar or a version of the CommonPoint Developer Series that's optimized for the host.

Deployment by investors

This section provides a general outline of investor plans for CommonPoint at the beginning of 1995. For up-to-date information about specific products and schedules, check your favorite computer press publications or contact the companies directly.

Apple

Apple is renowned for its innovative products, especially in the area of human interface design. It has unique market leverage with small and medium businesses and in application domains where the Mac OS has a strong presence, such as graphics and publishing. CommonPoint is one of several new technologies that Apple is adopting to gain market share in the enterprise solutions market.

When Apple migrates to a microkernel-based operating system, it plans to deploy the CommonPoint application system and to incorporate Taligent technology in versions of the Mac OS that run on its PowerPC-based systems.

Developers who want to create CommonPoint software for the Mac OS can use either native Mac OS development tools or the CommonPoint Developer Series. Apple plans to provide its own support program for CommonPoint developers. For more information, contact Apple directly or see page 154 for information on contacting Taligent.

Hewlett-Packard

Hewlett-Packard has extensive experience with object technology, including pioneering work with frameworks using the Fusion method (Coleman et al. 1994), so Taligent frameworks find a natural home with HP technologies. Hewlett-Packard is a major leader in the development of open object standards such as CORBA. It has a strong presence in the enterprise solutions market, especially the market for UNIX-based systems.

Hewlett-Packard is deploying the CommonPoint application system on its UNIX operating system, HP-UX, running on the PA-RISC-based HP 9000 platform.

Developers who want to create CommonPoint software on HP-UX-based systems can use either Hewlett-Packard's SoftBench development tools from within HP-UX or the CommonPoint Developer Series. Hewlett-Packard provides its own support program for CommonPoint developers. For more information, contact Hewlett-Packard directly or see page 154 for information on contacting Taligent.

IBM

IBM regards Taligent technology as a pivotal means of delivering fast and flexible solutions to its business customers, leveraging its broad product line, strong presence in the enterprise solutions market, and superb global distribution and customer support.

IBM is deploying the CommonPoint application system on both OS/2 and on its UNIX-based operating system, AIX. In addition, IBM plans to support access to OS/400® (system software for the AS/400 platform) data and services from within CommonPoint applications.

IBM's plans for Taligent technology are also linked to its plans for microkernel-based versions of OS/2 and AIX on PowerPC-based platforms. IBM and Taligent are exploring the use of TalOS technologies for device drivers, networking protocols, and so on. Similarly, Taligent is investigating proprietary technologies developed by IBM, such as the IBM microkernel and multiplatform file system protocols, for use in its products.

Developers who want to create CommonPoint software on AIX or OS/2 systems can use IBM's AIX CSet++ from within AIX, OS/2 CSet++ from within OS/2, or the CommonPoint Developer Series running on either system.

IBM provides its own support program for developers who want to create and market CommonPoint products that run on its implementations of the CommonPoint system, including products that need to interact with OS/400. For more information, contact IBM directly or see page 154 for information on contacting Taligent.

Deployment by Taligent

In addition to the deployment efforts of its investors, Taligent is deploying the CommonPoint application system on other 32-bit operating systems, such as Windows NT and Windows 95 (when it's available), that are capable of supporting it. As Figure 39 suggests, this arrangement is similar to the investor deployment strategies in the sense that the CommonPoint application system runs side by side with the native environment (such as Windows), using low-level host protocols to communicate with hardware.

Developers who want to develop CommonPoint software for Windows NT, Windows 95, or other host systems can use host development tools such as Microsoft Visual C++ with the Metaware C++ compiler from within the host environment, or they can use the CommonPoint Developer Series running on the host system.

Taligent plans to provide its own support program for developers who want to create and market CommonPoint products that run on Windows NT, Windows 95, and other platforms that Taligent will support in the future. Taligent also plans to license its Windows NT– and Windows 95–based CommonPoint system to OEMs, distributors, and other licensees. For more information, contact Taligent as described on page 154.

FIGURE 39
DEPLOYMENT OF THE
COMMONPOINT
APPLICATION SYSTEM
ON WINDOWS NT
AND WINDOWS 95

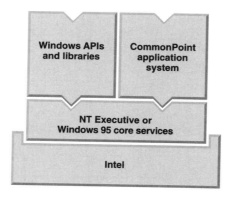

COMMERCIAL COMMONPOINT SOFTWARE

The CommonPoint application system makes it possible to design entirely new kinds of software products that take advantage of new kinds of markets. It opens up so many possibilities that commercial developers sometimes don't know where to begin. In reality, they can start developing for Taligent in much the same way they are already developing for other operating environments.

Although all CommonPoint developers must invest some time in learning object-oriented design and Taligent's programming model, commercial developers don't necessarily have to make significant changes in marketing and distributing their products. As time goes by and they become more familiar with Taligent technology, they can begin taking advantage of the additional architectural, packaging, distribution, and business opportunities that it brings to their areas of expertise.

This section introduces some of the design and marketing issues faced by commercial developers who decide to take advantage of Taligent technology. Some of the marketing options available to CommonPoint developers depend on the leverage provided by Taligent development tools. For information about Taligent's development tools strategy, see page 132.

An opportunity for long-term growth

The CommonPoint application system represents the first significant opportunity since the introduction of the Macintosh computer for small, flexible companies to promote innovative software aggressively and achieve significant growth on the scale of a Lotus or an Adobe. The price of entry for a developer is much lower for the CommonPoint system than it is for any other system software today.

Because the CommonPoint system marks the beginning of a new generation of applications, CommonPoint software development is a long-term proposition. But the potential rewards are enormous, not only for commercial developers but also for system integrators, corporate developers, training services, OEMs, and other players who get involved early and adapt their business plans to take advantage of Taligent's long-term product deployment strategy.

In addition to making its technology available as widely as possible, Taligent is acting as a catalyst in creating a complete market opportunity for all CommonPoint developers. These efforts range from facilitating development hardware discounts to help with distribution, advertising, and bundling packages. Taligent is also evangelizing venture capitalists and other investors who are interested in learning more about its technology.

**Product design
and marketing**

Figure 40 illustrates several different ways commercial developers can take advantage of their proprietary technology and expertise to develop products for the CommonPoint system.

The solid box on the left side of Figure 40 represents a developer's existing product on a non-CommonPoint platform. This product sells to markets and customers with which the developer is already familiar.

One option the CommonPoint system provides for commercial developers is to reengineer their original applications to run on the CommonPoint application system by dividing them up into smaller pieces, as suggested by the middle part of Figure 40. This involves learning how to use CommonPoint frameworks to create stationery, tools, and components that provide the same capabilities as the original. Once they have learned the system, developers can leverage their knowledge to reduce development costs and speed up product cycles, especially for applications that require strong support for distributed computing.

In addition to whatever capabilities the original application may provide, every application developed with the Compound Document framework also supports embedding, collaboration, automatic saving, multiple undo and redo, global tools, and all the other default features of embeddable components. Most important, the built-in distributed computing capabilities of the

FIGURE 40
COMMONPOINT
PRODUCT
DESIGN AND
MARKETING

Non-CommonPoint product

Existing markets
Existing customers

Reengineered product

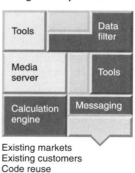

Existing markets
Existing customers
Code reuse
New product suites
Technology acquisition

New product options

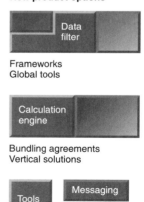

Frameworks
Global tools

Bundling agreements
Vertical solutions

Appliances, tools, places

CommonPoint system add significant value to any reengineered application. In other respects, however, the CommonPoint product shown in the middle part of Figure 40 would be familiar to users of the original non-CommonPoint application, and it would be sold to similar customers in similar ways.

In some cases, instead of using in-house expertise to customize CommonPoint frameworks, developers can purchase or license third-party frameworks that provide more specialized capabilities. Because CommonPoint frameworks are designed to be open and extensible, both commercial and corporate developers can "buy," "make," or selectively "buy and make" according to their needs without having to deal with independent, incompatible implementations of core technologies. The inherently modular form of CommonPoint applications allows developers to create product suites of highly integrated software from several different sources.

The right side of Figure 40 shows some possible results of such an approach. Developers can choose to leverage their expertise in particular problem domains to develop custom frameworks. Custom frameworks not only simplify further product development for vertical markets, but also potentially have value as products in their own right for other developers working in related domains. In addition, commercial developers can apply their expertise to a wide variety of products, including applications for vertical markets, custom frameworks for other developers, global tools, Place software, appliances, and marketing and bundling agreements with other companies.

Customizing the system

Many application developers have developed expertise in a particular area of system software, such as printing or telephony. Traditional operating systems require such developers to write all such system-related code themselves. The fact that the CommonPoint application system provides reliable default behavior for these areas doesn't mean companies with specialized system expertise are left out. Because the CommonPoint system is designed to be customized at all levels, developers can use their insight more efficiently to customize or replace system capabilities provided by CommonPoint frameworks and thereby give their applications a competitive advantage.

CommonPoint developers can rely on more robust compatibility among applications, parts of system software that particular applications modify for their own use, and specialized hardware than is possible with traditional operating systems. Instead of replacing whole areas of system software, developers can extend or override just those elements they need to change, leaving everything else in the framework intact and thereby ensuring that the framework will continue to work smoothly with the rest of the system and with other applications.

Developing system products

Having developed applications that customize the system in unique ways, some developers will discover that their customizations can become products in their own right, such as tools and components for users and tools, frameworks, and components for other developers.

Adobe Type Manager (ATM) is an example of a successful product of this type. It is a system software extension for high-quality font rendering that previously appeared within Adobe products such as Illustrator and PostScript printing software. The Mac OS and Windows happen to have "hooks" that allow a product like ATM to customize the underlying operating system and bring the benefit of high-quality fonts to all applications running on the system. The CommonPoint application system provides tens of thousands of such hooks for all kinds of system and application behavior.

All CommonPoint frameworks have the potential for this kind of system product development. Examples of such products include global tools for working with fonts, color, or graphics; appliances that control hardware such as printers or fax machines; and appliances that provide services such as data encryption and data compression.

BENEFITS OF COMMONPOINT DEVELOPMENT

CommonPoint application development has three major advantages for all developers:

- **Productivity and innovation.** Applications developed with the Compound Document framework automatically support many useful features, such as embedding and collaboration. Some developers may choose simply to take advantage of improved productivity to write CommonPoint applications for familiar markets and categories. Others may choose to leverage CommonPoint productivity and innovation to create new products they couldn't create before.

- **Built-in support for distributed computing capabilities.** The System Services frameworks in the CommonPoint system support a wide variety of distributed computing capabilities, including directory services, messaging, data access, system management, collaboration, and the cross-platform communication support that underlies all these features.

- **Superior user experience.** In addition to pervasive system support, innovative distributed applications require a user interface designed for multiple users working together. The People, Places, and Things metaphor provides the basis for a superior user experience in distributed environments.

Even the intrepid developers who began CommonPoint development before the first beta release of the system have experienced these benefits, despite the inherent problems of working with a system that's still under development. With very little coding, they have been able to write robust collaborative applications, networked multimedia applications, and cross-platform data access applications that incorporate both CommonPoint features and information retrieved from traditional databases. For the most recent examples of developer success stories, contact Taligent as described on page 154.

Chapter 1 discusses problems faced by commercial developers, corporate developers, and OEMs. The rest of this section summarizes some of the ways in which Taligent technology can help each of these constituencies.

New markets for commercial developers

Taligent's approach to software development can help commercial developers create distributed applications that can't be developed economically with traditional development techniques. The growing enterprise solutions market is in turn likely to stimulate new business strategies and alliances that increase the options available to all developers.

Parallels with VLSI technology

The object-oriented technology used to create software and the VLSI technology used to create hardware have many parallels. Both represent a dramatic improvement over the labor-intensive technologies that preceded them. Both involve an initial learning curve but also deliver major benefits in terms of the power and quality of the solutions they make possible. Both permit the use of integrated modules that can be reused over and over again for very different purposes. Just as VLSI technology and VLSI CAD tools facilitated a dramatic increase in the commercial use of microprocessors in household appliances, cars, factories, hospitals, and so on, Taligent believes its object-oriented application system and powerful development tools will help facilitate an explosion of new software categories and market opportunities.

One measure of Taligent's success will be the number of innovative applications that succeed in the marketplace. Rather than merely asking developers to port their existing applications, Taligent encourages them to investigate ideas that can't be implemented (or can't be implemented economically) on today's systems and to use Taligent's technology to develop those ideas into viable products.

Smaller, less expensive applications

Taligent's frameworks can provide most of the code that traditional applications must include to work efficiently with the underlying operating system. Applications developed for the CommonPoint application system can therefore be smaller and more focused on specific customer domains than the current generation of commercial applications. Manuals in turn can become smaller, because applications won't need to have so many features to compete effectively. Fewer bytes for programmers to develop means lower development costs, which means better profits for both new applications and upgrades.

Faster time to market, easier to customize system

Fewer bytes to develop also means smaller engineering teams, less code to test, and faster time to market, especially for distributed applications. Because all aspects of the operating environment are customizable and reusable, developers don't need to live with the system as is, and they don't need to replace whole pieces of it outright. Instead, they can adapt the parts they need to change relatively easily. Some may even want to create new system software products as well as (or instead of) application-level products.

Economics stimulates innovation

If companies can develop applications more quickly and economically, developers can afford to target vertical markets where no applications exist yet, rather than established horizontal markets that are already crowded with big, complex applications. This in turn means users are more likely to end up with programs written by people who understand their particular domains rather than by system software specialists.

Similarly, CommonPoint multilingual text and localization capabilities provide significant leverage in penetrating worldwide markets that systems with less comprehensive text capabilities may get to slowly or not at all.

Both small and large software companies can benefit from the more focused, less labor-intensive approach that the Taligent programming model makes possible. Instead of being limited to horizontal markets dominated by suites of industrial-strength applications, software development can expand into areas such as tools, frameworks, and system extensions that allow them to bring specialized expertise to bear on specialized problems.

Fourth-party alliances

Various kinds of "fourth-party" solutions are likely to emerge as third-party developers cultivate their own supporting partnerships. One company might decide to form an alliance with a number of smaller companies, which would create customized solutions for the main company to sell to customers. Another company might prefer to encourage smaller companies to build their own integrated packages around the main company's frameworks and sell them directly to customers whose needs they know intimately. Still another might prefer to deal directly with corporate developers, making tools and frameworks available for in-house solutions.

Companies like Quark and AutoDesk have already pioneered this approach by encouraging other companies to develop extensions for their products that meet the needs of specific market niches and thus help sell the main products in areas that they haven't had the resources or expertise to pursue themselves. Taligent believes that its use of frameworks throughout its products will make it much easier for other companies to adopt this kind of model. Any commercial software developer can publish APIs for its frameworks that allow fourth parties to integrate specialized capabilities into larger generic products. This kind of arrangement extends the reach of a developer's products to vertical markets, especially those involving specialized solutions.

Faster development for corporate developers

Developers working for corporations and other organizations have to produce specialized, reliable applications quickly that can coexist peacefully in multiplatform environments. Many are already familiar with OOP and are using application frameworks such as Apple's MacApp, Microsoft Foundation Classes (MFC), and Borland's Object Windows Library (OWL). Like small commercial developers working on vertical applications, corporate developers must minimize risk while working quickly to meet constantly changing customer needs. Object technology has already proved that it can help meet these goals.

Robust applications that are compatible with existing systems

For corporate developers who haven't yet begun to investigate OOP, the CommonPoint application system is a good place to start. Any new frameworks or applications they develop will run on multiple operating systems and on a variety of hardware platforms.

For corporate developers who are already knowledgeable about objects, Taligent can increase the development leverage that knowledge gives them. For example, although application frameworks such as MacApp have speeded up application development, programming that requires modification of the underlying system can still be a daunting task. Graphics, printing, and networking are typical examples of operating system domains that still eat up programming hours even if a programmer uses a high-level application framework. The CommonPoint application system allows programmers to take advantage of the long-term economies that frameworks provide at all levels of the system.

Taligent is not attempting to replace existing application environments. Instead, the CommonPoint system coexists with the current generation of application environments and operating systems. This is one of its major attractions for all kinds of organizations. Corporate developers must make difficult decisions about incorporating new technologies into their development cycles. Taligent gives them a new set of options. The tangible benefits of the CommonPoint system will vary depending on the corporation's needs, the current state of its software projects, and its long-term strategy for adopting object-oriented technology.

More options for software development

As mentioned previously, Taligent hopes to encourage new forms of collaboration between large commercial developers, smaller "fourth-party" commercial developers, and corporate developers. In addition to the benefits that corporate developers can gain by using Taligent's system for in-house projects, new opportunities are likely to emerge as these business alliances form and mature.

Until now many corporations have been limited to two choices when making decisions about software: either purchase standard libraries and commercial applications that are usually difficult to customize, or build libraries and applications from scratch. Taligent's approach to software development allows for other possibilities. For example, a corporate developer might be able to purchase a standard accounting package and customize it using customization APIs published by the company that sells the package. Thus, instead of writing a specialized application from scratch, the developer can reuse most of an existing application's code and rewrite only the parts that the corporation needs to handle differently. Or a corporation might find that an outside consultant or a small commercial developer that knows the corporation's needs can provide economical and reliable solutions that previously had to be developed in-house or not at all.

Support for hardware innovation

The benefits that Taligent provides for OEMs are critical for Taligent's investors. Apple, IBM, and Hewlett-Packard have demonstrated for years that they can add value to hardware. They want to create innovative computers whose features will be well supported by system software. Until now, operating systems have hindered rather than facilitated this goal. Taligent has developed its system with the complaints of hardware engineers in mind. Support for future hardware innovation has been a high priority throughout development.

Automatic compatibility with new CommonPoint releases

After an OEM introduces an innovative product and customizes Taligent's system to support that product, it doesn't need to rewrite that custom code each time Taligent releases a new version of the system. And if third parties must support the product to make it a success in the marketplace—by developing hardware boards, for example—they can develop prototypes and experiment with the product's capabilities without making a major investment in rewriting drivers or other parts of system software.

Innovative hardware can compete on its own merits

Consider Hewlett-Packard's advanced printing and imaging technologies. Instead of WYSIWYG (what you see is what you get), Hewlett-Packard's printer engineers would rather have WYWIWYG (what you *want* is what you get), because their printers produce much better graphics than any computer monitor can display. But because standard graphics engines like QuickDraw for the Mac Os or GDI for Windows are oriented toward what the user sees on the screen rather than the capabilities of high-end printers, printer engineers must often "dumb down" their machines or printer drivers to avoid conflicts with system software.

This kind of conflict doesn't exist in the CommonPoint application system. Whether they are developing printers, 3-D graphics hardware, graphics acceleration cards, or components of a high-end medical instrument, the hardware developer has the same technical standing as any other developer (including Taligent's engineers). Even the lowest levels of the system can be customized without compromising compatibility, and innovative hardware can compete on its own merits.

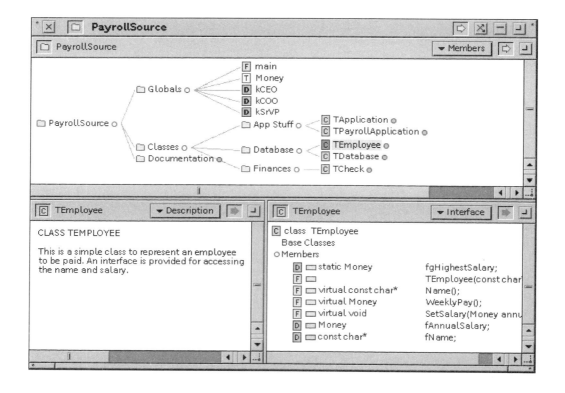

*The **cp**Professional development environment is a highly integrated system that supports rapid prototyping and development, graphic visualization of framework and program relationships, and customizable browsers. For details, see page 136.*

CHAPTER 5

DEVELOPMENT TOOLS AND APPROACHES

Computer hardware development has changed dramatically in the last 25 years. Computers used to be built from tubes, transistors, and wire-wrap boards using tools such as oscilloscopes, soldering irons, and custom logic. VLSI technology led to dramatic improvements in computer manufacturing techniques. Now computers are built from microprocessors, which are created from standard cell libraries and gate arrays by using CAD systems, in-circuit emulators, and other modern tools designed to assemble complex structures from preassembled parts.

In contrast to hardware developers, software developers are still using the equivalent of tubes and transistors to create software whose complexity equals or even exceeds the complexity of the modern hardware on which it runs. It is as if hardware engineers were still sitting at a bench doing custom logic. Each new application consists largely of custom code built from scratch. Application frameworks like MacApp help reduce the load, but developers write nearly everything anew for each application. Meanwhile the hardware engineers, who have long since moved on to the next generation of hardware construction technology, are cranking out new designs at a prodigious rate.

Taligent is building the foundation for a new generation of development tools that are optimized for object-oriented application systems—the equivalent for OOP of CAD tools for VLSI. The CommonPoint Developer Series is a significant step in that direction, but it is only the beginning. Like all Taligent software, CommonPoint Developer Series tools are built from customizable frameworks, and third-party development based on those frameworks is essential to the rapid evolution of new development tools.

This chapter introduces Taligent's development tools strategy and the first tools available in the CommonPoint Developer Series: the *cp*Professional development environment and the *cp*Constructor user interface builder. It also describes how to get started as a Taligent developer.

DEVELOPMENT TOOLS STRATEGY

Although the CommonPoint Developer Series will simplify CommonPoint development for most developers, not all CommonPoint developers will want to use Taligent tools exclusively. Those who have already written software for CommonPoint host operating systems can benefit from the ability to use the host development tools with which they're familiar. Taligent or its investors typically use standard host development tools to port the CommonPoint application system to each host operating system.

CommonPoint Developer Series tools, retargeted as necessary to the underlying host protocols for linking, compiling, and debugging, are designed to run on the CommonPoint system for each host. In the long term, Taligent, Taligent's investors, and third parties will write additional tools built, like the CommonPoint Developer Series, with CommonPoint frameworks. In a similar fashion, it will be possible build additional tools on top of CommonPoint Developer Series products, such as the *cp*Professional development environment, that provide extensible frameworks.

The dark gray boxes in Figure 41 illustrate the three broad categories of tools that commercial developers (also called independent software vendors, or ISVs) and Taligent's investors plan to provide in addition to the CommonPoint Developer Series tools.

FIGURE 41
TOOL DEPLOYMENT

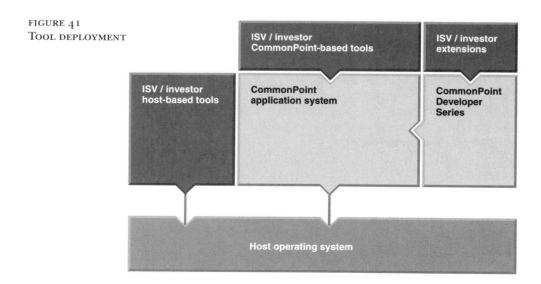

Cross-platform development

To develop a CommonPoint application for several host platforms, a developer can first use CommonPoint Developer Series tools, host tools, or both to develop it for whichever CommonPoint host is most familiar, then export the sources and do the final building and testing on each of the target CommonPoint hosts. For example, a company using Windows NT can develop an application with the *cp*Professional development environment and CommonPoint application system running on Windows NT, then export the source code to OS/2 and perform the final building and testing with either the *cp*Professional development environment running on CommonPoint for OS/2 or the IBM OS/2 CSet++ development environment.

For more information about the host tools available for CommonPoint development on each CommonPoint host, see "Deployment of Taligent products," which begins on page 117.

Additional languages and development environments

The *cp*Professional development environment supports C++ and C and can be extended to support additional languages. In addition to supporting such *cp*Professional extensions, Taligent is working with companies that have created other successful language and runtime environments to provide equivalent products for the CommonPoint application system. These include object-oriented language environments that can exploit the underlying CommonPoint system as well as procedural environments for supporting existing libraries and other non-CommonPoint code.

Development tools and the component software market

Software developers who use C++ and other "third-generation" programming languages require a range of development tools for analysis and design, building graphic user interfaces, configuration management and version control (CMVC), core programming needs (editors, build systems, compilers, and so on), and testing. They use such tools not only to create traditional applications but also to create *component software*—that is, commercial or custom components that less experienced programmers can wire together with visual programming tools, thus reducing or eliminating the need for handcrafted code.

The market for component software is growing rapidly, even though it is currently limited by incompatible architectures and related problems. Figure 42 illustrates Taligent's approach to this market.

FIGURE 42
TOOLS FOR
COMPONENT
ASSEMBLERS
AND COMPO-
NENT BUILDERS

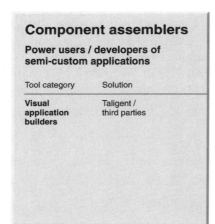

Component assemblers

Power users / developers of semi-custom applications

Tool category	Solution
Visual application builders	Taligent / third parties

Component builders

Programmers working with C++ and other third-generation languages

Tool category	Solution
Analysis and design	Taligent / third parties
User interface builders	*cp*Constructor / third parties
Advanced CMVC	Taligent / third parties
Core programming	*cp*Professional / third parties
Testing	Taligent / third parties

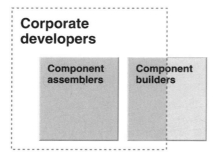

Corporate developers

| Component assemblers | Component builders |

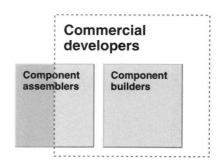

Commercial developers

| Component assemblers | Component builders |

Figure 42 divides developers who work with component software into two groups. *Component builders* are the programmers who create applications and component software. In contrast, *component assemblers* are typically corporate developers who work with visual application builders such as Visual Basic or PowerBuilder. They need to assemble applications quickly for specialized purposes, such as running scientific instruments or accessing a company database. Most component builders are commercial developers and most component assemblers are corporate developers, but there are substantial numbers of both in each environment.

Before they can begin to take advantage of CommonPoint components, component assemblers need a variety of components to choose from. Therefore, the first target customers for CommonPoint Developer Series tools are component builders. The top part of Figure 42 also shows how Taligent and third parties are meeting component builders' needs for a broad range of development tools.

The *cp*Professional development environment and the *cp*Constructor user interface builder are optimized for core CommonPoint programming and interface construction. Taligent plans to make them available for every CommonPoint host. The *cp*Professional incremental build system, team programming support, configurable browsers, and source-level debugger reduce turnaround times for prototyping and coding and for later maintenance and upgrading of existing programs. The *cp*Constructor user interface builder allows developers to decouple a program's user interface from its code, which helps to support rapid localization as well as experimental modification of a program's visual interface while the program is running.

The *cp*Professional development environment also provides basic CMVC capabilities. The *cp*Professional frameworks provide a foundation for more advanced CMVC and for analysis and design tools. To facilitate development of such tools, Taligent is working with third parties that have established track records in these areas. The Test framework (introduced on page 359) provides basic support for testing, and Taligent is also encouraging third parties to provide support in this area.

As more tools become available and component builders begin producing CommonPoint components, Taligent and its strategic partners will focus on creating visual programming tools for the growing component assembler market.

cpPROFESSIONAL

The *cp*Professional development environment is a highly integrated system for CommonPoint development. It supports rapid prototyping and development, graphic visualization of framework and program relationships, customizable browsers and viewers, and hypertext links among all related information.

*cp*Professional tool designers have been influenced by many development environments and approaches, including:

- Successful OOP development environments, such as Smalltalk, that provide integrated browsers that make it easy to figure out what objects are, what their member functions are, what calls them and what they call, what classes they are subclassed from, what additional classes are subclassed from them, and so on.
- Extensible development environments like UNIX and SoftBench. These systems have encouraged a proliferation of specialized tools from many different sources that can work together in a common environment.
- Tools that, like the Symantec and Borland development environments, support automated builds.
- Graphical user interface builders such as AppMaker and NeXT's Interface Builder that allow for interactive construction of user interface elements such as menus, windows, and dialog boxes.

cpProfessional problem domain

Four aspects of the CommonPoint application system present specific challenges for *cp*Professional designers:

- **Long build times.** Comprehensive systems like the CommonPoint application system can require very long builds with conventional tools because of the large number of interface header files. Incremental compiling and linking is essential for CommonPoint development. CommonPoint applications are likely to be developed in stages, with new features being added incrementally by subclassing and overriding CommonPoint frameworks.
- **Extensive APIs.** The beta version of the CommonPoint application system includes about 100 frameworks and object services that declare about 1,900 public classes and about 27,000 member functions. These in turn embody many complex relationships within and among frameworks, involving inheritance, reuse, subclassing, cooperative behavior, and many other dependencies. Developers require sophisticated tools that hide most of this complexity while permitting them to explore and experiment with specific pieces of code that are relevant to their programming domains.

- **Object-oriented framework programming.** Programming with Taligent frameworks involves new approaches to fundamental concepts such as the flow of control within a program. Development tools should make it easy to learn what a framework does and how to use it.
- **C++.** Initially, CommonPoint programming requires the use of C++, a complex language with many sophisticated features. One goal of the *cp*Professional development environment is to transform C++ programming from today's traditional batch development style to the interactive, incremental style that is typical of Smalltalk and appropriate for all object-oriented programming.

The next section describes how the *cp*Professional development environment addresses these challenges.

*cp*Professional tools and capabilities

*cp*Professional tools are built around an object-oriented project database that supports many key capabilities. Instead of storing code at the level of flat files or classes, the *cp*Professional project database stores code at the granularity of member functions and data members and keeps track of dependencies at the same level. This means, for example, that a change to a member function implementation requires recompilation of only the implementation, not the whole class definition. Similarly, a change to a class definition requires recompilation of only that definition, not the whole file. You can add a new function to a class and compile it without recompiling the whole definition. This fine granularity results in much less code being recompiled as a result of any given change.

With traditional development systems, any change to a single line in a file requires recompilation of the entire file and other files that depend on that file in any way. Because the *cp*Professional build system keeps track not only of which other pieces are dependent on a given piece, but also of how they are dependent, it can recognize which pieces need to be recompiled when a change is made and which don't.

For example, the build system recognizes that adding a comment to a line doesn't require recompilation of all related information. With traditional systems, programmers frequently avoid documenting their source code because new comments cause the same kind of lengthy recompilations as changes to the code itself. The *cp*Professional build system's automated dependency analysis can also keeps track of much more subtle dependencies. For example, changing the size of an object doesn't cause recompilation of code that depends only on references to that object.

Automated incremental build system

The *cp*Professional incremental build system automates the build process, eliminating the need for maintaining make files, a time-consuming and error-prone activity when performed manually. The system determines the correct order in which to build source components and the minimum number that must be rebuilt for a given change.

Because the build system can track dependencies with the aid of the project database, it also controls incremental compilation. Instead of feeding a whole file or class at a time to the compiler, it gives the compiler only the portions of code that have changed or are affected by changes, resulting in build times that are proportional to the magnitude of the changes.

Optimizing C++ compiler and linker

The compiler and linker produce highly optimized CommonPoint code. The compiler is ANSI/ISO compliant and supports current C++ language features, including templates, exceptions, and Run-Time Type Identification (RTTI). It also supports ANSI C.

Dynamic browsers and viewers

The *cp*Professional development environment supports multiple user-configurable program displays and pervasive navigational links among related data. These program displays help developers visualize and understand the CommonPoint frameworks.

As previously mentioned, the *cp*Professional development environment stores developers' program elements in an object-oriented project database. These include all class interfaces, source and object code for functions, documentation, and even project history and build information. Each kind of program element has a set of associated properties. For example, the properties of a function include its name, interface, source code implementation, description (documentation), a set of other functions it calls (references), a set of other functions that call it (clients), and so on. The properties of a class include its name, interface, description, references, clients, a list of base classes from which it is derived, a list of classes derived from it, and so on.

*cp*Professional programmers can look at a property of a program element by opening a *viewer* that displays that property: for example, a source code listing or a class hierarchy diagram. In addition, multiple viewers can be arranged inside a given window and wired together in an arrangement called a browser.

A *browser* allows two or more viewers to be arranged as panes inside the browser window, set up to show different properties, and linked so that selecting a program element in one viewer causes the display of a particular property of the selected element in another viewer. For example, a source code browser can display a list of function names in one viewer so that clicking on any name in that viewer displays its source code implementation in a second viewer. Similarly, a class hierarchy browser can display a list of class names in one viewer and show any selected class name's base classes and derived classes in two other viewers. Viewers are updated dynamically when the elements whose properties they display are modified.

Classic Smalltalk development environments allow programmers to view class names, their data members and member functions, and their source code implementation in a standard four-viewer browser. Other object-oriented development environments provide similar capabilities and may provide alternative browsers for other purposes. During the design of the *cp*Professional development environment, user input suggested that no single or fixed set of browsers satisfied all the needs of all programmers. Programmers want one kind of browser for designing a class hierarchy, another for writing programs, others for studying or modifying an existing class hierarchy or program, and still others for debugging or for learning the underlying system.

The Taligent solution to this problem is to let browsers be dynamic. Programmers can create their own custom browsers by splitting windows into multiple panes in arbitrary arrangements and sizes. Different properties can viewed in different panes and changed on the fly or wired together and saved as custom browsers. This allows programmers to create and customize their favorite browsers for different programming situations. The figures that follow illustrate how this works.

Figure 43 shows a browser window containing the top-level hierarchical overview for a project called PayrollSource.

FIGURE 43
HIERARCHICAL
OVERVIEW OF
A PROJECT

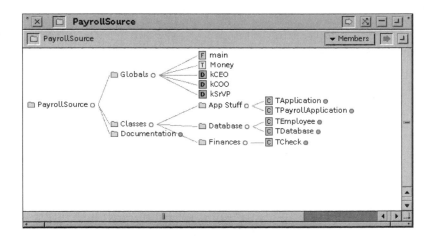

A programmer can use the hierarchical overview to connect containers and program elements with each other and include them in a project, or can double-click any element shown in the overview (or in any *cp*Professional viewer) to open a window that displays its contents (if it's a container) or its properties (if it's a single program element).

Figure 44 shows the same window split into two panes. The top pane shows the same hierarchical overview shown in Figure 43. A splitter control allows the user to create the new pane at the bottom of the figure.

To display information about the TEmployee class in the new pane, the user simply selects TEmployee in the top pane and drags its image to the input port at the top left of the bottom pane. The user can then view any property of TEmployee by selecting its name from the pop-up menu near the top right of the bottom pane. These operations cause the top viewer to be wired to the bottom viewer independently of its specific contents, so that selecting any element in the hierarchical overview will cause the viewer to display the selected property for that element. If a pane contains something other than a class, such as a function or a program, the menu changes to show the choices for that item.

FIGURE 44
SPLITTING
A WINDOW

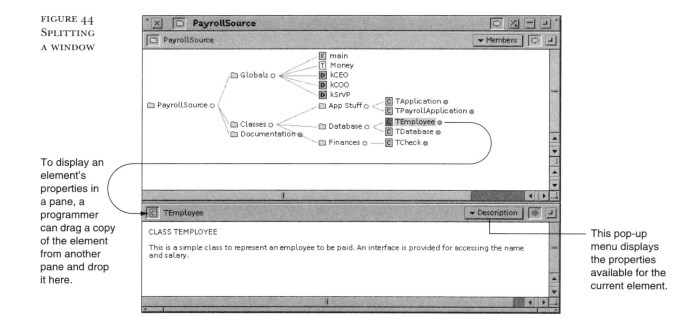

To display an element's properties in a pane, a programmer can drag a copy of the element from another pane and drop it here.

This pop-up menu displays the properties available for the current element.

If the user wants to display some additional information about TEmployee in the same browser window, the user can create a third pane as shown in Figure 45 and set it up in the same way to show a different property. Any number of custom browsers can be created in this way for specific programming needs and then saved for future use.

Future versions of the *cp*Professional development environment are being designed to allow third parties to create and sell specialized viewers and browsers, such as program visualizers, analysis and design tools, or other source code control systems.

FIGURE 45
USING
MULTIPLE
PANES

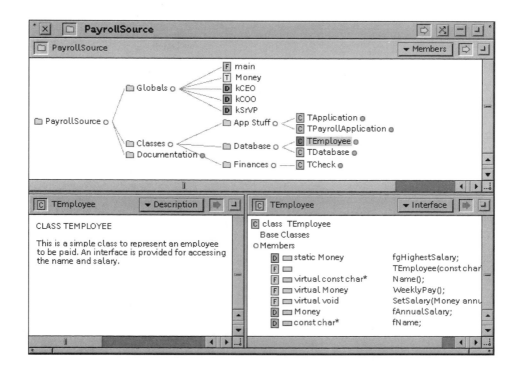

**Integrated source
level debugger**

The source level debugger allows *cp*Professional users to analyze C++ programs at the source level. It is also integrated with other *cp*Professional viewers, allowing users to execute program control operations from the same source editor used to enter C++ source code or to make corrections to source code right in the debugging viewer.

The debugger allows a programmer to debug multiple programs simultaneously, including multiple threads in each program. Figure 46 shows a typical arrangement of debugger viewers in a browser window. Debugger viewers can be organized in panes and wired together just like any other *cp*Professional viewers. Standard debugger viewers include source code with breakpoints and execution indicator, disassembly, stack frames, registers, memory, symbols, and the like. It's also possible to initiate the debugger after a program crashes and obtain useful information about the crash even if the program wasn't running "within" the debugger at the time of the crash.

Team programming

The source control system uses the *cp*Professional project database to provide support for parallel development by teams of programmers. Most source control systems manage versions at the file level. Because the project database stores code at the granularity of member functions and data members, it provides a much more flexible paradigm for parallel development.

FIGURE 46
SOURCE LEVEL
DEBUGGER

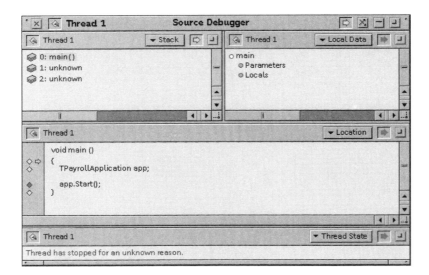

For example, the *cp*Professional development environment doesn't require team members to check program elements in and out. Instead, using a paradigm sometimes called "optimistic configuration management," a programmer gets a copy of a particular program element. When the programmer checks the updated element back in, the system determines whether there are any conflicts, whether someone else has checked out the same element, and so on, and provides tools to help the programmer merge the code with the project.

The merging process is automated, with the exception of conflict resolution. Like the build system, the merge tools use the project database to keep track of the precise dependencies related to any change, so merging occurs at a much finer resolution than classes and files. Conflicts are less likely than with traditional development systems, because it's less common for two different people to touch the same member function at the same time than to touch different member functions in the same file at the same time. The range of the merging process is tightly restricted to the range of changes and their dependencies.

*cp*Professional browsers allow programmers to view project history information in much the same way that they view information about other elements of a project. For example, Figure 47 shows a browser that displays both the implementation and the history of the EmployeeSatisfaction class.

FIGURE 47
PROJECT
HISTORY

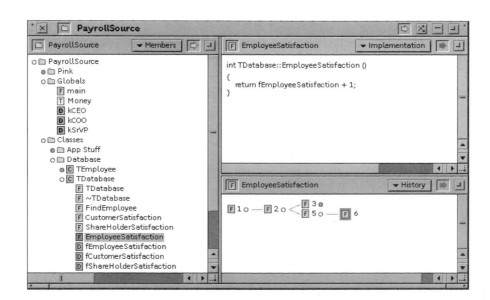

Importing and exporting source code

The *cp*Professional development environment can import source code from a variety of development environments and can also export code in a form suitable for use in those environments. When it imports source code, the *cp*Professional development environment works out all dependencies and converts the files correctly even if they don't include make files. When it exports CommonPoint source code, it reproduces the project database as a set of standard source files with corresponding make files for use in the external development system. These capabilities facilitate both the reuse of existing source code written for non-CommonPoint systems such as OS/2 or Windows NT and the conversion of CommonPoint source code to code suitable for those systems.

cpProfessional extensibility

Future versions of the *cp*Professional development environment will expose some of its internal frameworks for use by third-party tool developers. Figure 48 shows some of the APIs that Taligent plans to expose:

- **The Viewer framework** supports *cp*Professional editors, debuggers, and customizable browsers and viewers provided by Taligent and third parties. APIs for the debug engine and object-oriented project database will also be exposed for third-party development efforts.

- **The Tool framework** supports tools that are used for batch processing large amounts of data in the object-oriented project database to produce new or modified program elements. These can include search engines, style checkers, analysis and design tools, and so on.

- **The Language framework** can be extended to support assembly language and other languages for use directly with the *cp*Professional development environment. While C++ or a language with equivalent OOP capabilities is necessary to exploit the CommonPoint application system to the fullest, other languages can play a useful role in constructing CommonPoint programs. Support for a variety of languages can also help developers use existing code in their CommonPoint applications.

Plans for future versions of the *cp*Professional development environment include cross-platform tools, support for large distributed teams, support for distributed client/server application development, and dynamic representations of the flow of control within CommonPoint frameworks.

FIGURE 48
EXTENSIBLE *cp*PROFESSIONAL
FRAMEWORKS

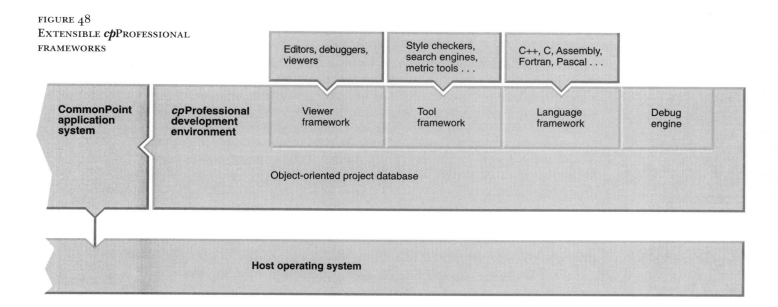

cpCONSTRUCTOR

The *cp*Constructor user interface builder streamlines the creation and layout of visual interface elements such as buttons, text fields, windows, dialog boxes, and menus; enables rapid user interface prototyping; and greatly simplifies localization of CommonPoint applications. The *cp*Constructor user interface builder is itself a CommonPoint application running directly on the CommonPoint system, so it doesn't need the *cp*Professional development environment to work. It is useful for all CommonPoint applications, including those created with host development tools or non-*cp*Professional tools hosted on the CommonPoint system.

Working with the *cp*Constructor user interface builder is similar to working with a drawing program. The user interface designer can copy and paste visual elements, modify them, and arrange them on the screen, then export them to a *cp*Constructor archive.

An archive is usually associated with a shared library, and contains all the localized versions of the visual interface elements used by that library. Code in an application or in frameworks used by an application reads the elements from an archive as necessary. To change user interface elements, the designer modifies the corresponding *cp*Constructor document and re-exports the archive.

This arrangement not only facilitates rapid visual interface prototyping and development but also simplifies the process of creating localized versions of an application for use in different parts of the world. The *cp*Constructor user interface builder uses the locale mechanism (introduced on page 301) to organize localized versions of interface elements. Instead of having to provide a different application file and different resources for each localized version of an application, a developer can provide just one file with one *cp*Constructor archive containing all the localized versions of the visual interface that the developer wants to support. The locale mechanism determines which version to use according to the locale currently specified by the machine on which the application is running.

The figures that follow illustrate how the *cp*Constructor user interface builder works. Figure 49 shows the *gallery viewer* for a new *cp*Constructor document on the left and the *parts palette* on the right.

FIGURE 49
GALLERY
VIEWER AND
PARTS
PALETTE

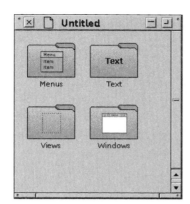

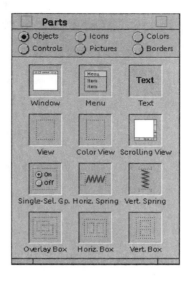

The parts palette in Figure 49 contains icons for various kinds of interface elements, including windows, controls, buttons, icons, and colors, that user interface designers can drag into various *cp*Constructor viewers and editors to create new user interface elements. The gallery viewer displays thumbnails for the categories of interface objects that can be dropped into it, such as windows and text objects. Double-clicking a thumbnail reveals a list of individual objects in each category, and each object in the list can be opened, edited, previewed, and tested.

The interface elements for a *cp*Constructor document can also be viewed from an *archive viewer* like the one shown in Figure 50. The archive viewer displays the entire locale hierarchy and allows the designer to create and examine interface objects associated with a particular locale. When an application uses an archive, it searches for archived objects only in the current locale and in locales that are ancestors of the current locale. Localizers work with the archive viewer to create localized versions of strings and other interface elements for various locales.

FIGURE 50
ARCHIVE
VIEWER

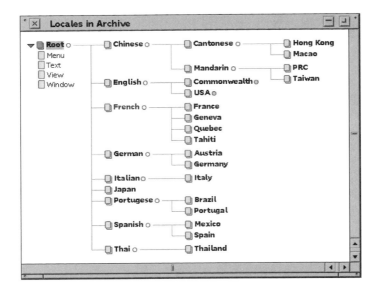

Two *cp*Constructor user interface builder menus are especially worth noting. The Archive menu facilitates exporting the document as an archive. The Viewers menu provides access to three kinds of viewers for examining and editing any interface object: an editor, an inspector, and a previewer.

Figure 51 shows a typical *cp*Constructor *editor* for a calculator user interface. The editor is being used with the Colors portion of the control palette. An editor can be opened for any interface object to examine the menus, buttons, and other elements associated with it and change their layout and appearance.

FIGURE 51
*cp*CONSTRUCTOR
EDITOR

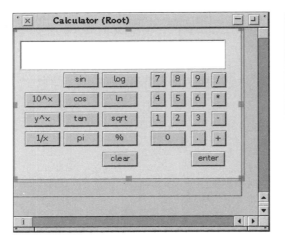

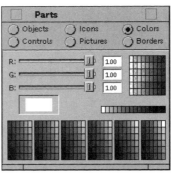

Figure 52 shows an *inspector.* The inspector for any object permits viewing and editing of detailed characteristics of any interface object, such as its size, its name, any action associated with it, and visual characteristics, whereas an editor permits only visual editing and layout. (Actions are basically text strings used to communicate a user action, such as selecting a radio button, to a handler provided by your application that processes the action. For more information about actions, see "Controls," which begins on page 207.)

FIGURE 52
*cp*CONSTRUCTOR
INSPECTOR

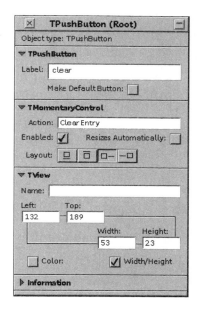

Figure 53 shows the *previewer* and *action monitor* windows. Opening a previewer for the currently selected object displays it as it will appear in the application and permits preliminary testing. This supports prototyping without the need for coding.

FIGURE 53
*cp*CONSTRUCTOR
PREVIEWER
AND ACTION
MONITOR

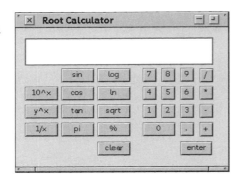
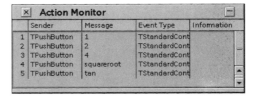

The previewer shows a CommonPoint user interface object executing as it will in the actual application, not a facsimile. Its appearance in the *cp*Constructor user interface builder exactly matches its appearance in the application.

Once satisfied with the visual interface elements for an application, a user interface designer can export them as an archive for use by the application at runtime. Because a *cp*Constructor archive is completely independent of the code that uses it, it's possible to set up an application so that the designer can modify its visual interface in the corresponding *cp*Constructor document, re-export the archive, and see the resulting changes while the application is running. This greatly simplifies the process of testing and modifying an application's visual interface.

Taligent plans to add features to future versions of the *cp*Constructor user interface builder that provide access to its capabilities from within the *cp*Professional development environment and simplify the layout process.

GETTING STARTED AS A TALIGENT DEVELOPER

This section summarizes some of the steps you can take to get started with OOP and CommonPoint software development.

Adopting object-oriented technology

Hundreds of books and magazines are devoted to various aspects of OOP. The major sources Taligent recommends are listed in the Bibliography, which begins on page 455. If you're completely new to OOP, books on object-oriented analysis and design are a good place to begin. The journals and magazines listed in the Bibliography include descriptions of conferences, classes, and other sources of information.

Another important step is to learn C++, which is becoming an industry standard for OOP. Knowledge of C++ is currently a requirement for developing CommonPoint software. Some knowledge of frameworks is also helpful if you are considering adopting Taligent technology. The framework concepts that underlie the CommonPoint system are similar to the concepts that underlie other framework-based products, so experience with MacApp, Microsoft Foundation Classes (MFC), or any other application framework is useful preparation for CommonPoint development. The Bibliography lists some books and articles about frameworks that Taligent references in its own training programs. Taligent's book *The Power of Frameworks* (1995) is especially useful for Windows programmers who want to learn basic framework concepts by working with a simple framework that runs in the Windows environment.

Perhaps most important, start thinking about the kinds of applications you'd like to create that are difficult, impossible, or not economical to build within traditional operating systems. Taligent presents a significant opportunity for developers with innovative ideas to turn their ideas into products with long-term market potential.

**Lessons learned
by early adopters**

When Taligent was first formed, it conducted several studies of companies that were engaged in significant object-based application development. One of these studies is summarized in the Taligent white paper *Early Adopters of Object Technology* (1992). This section summarizes the major lessons learned by the companies that participated in that study, including American Airlines, American Express, CIGNA, Eastman Kodak, Federal Express, Liberty Mutual, and Texas Instruments.

**Secure support and set
conservative expectations**

1. **Educate management.** Object technology involves a paradigm shift. Don't expect executives to grasp it in a half-day seminar. Be prepared for organizational resistance and cultural barriers to new ways of thinking and working.

2. **Recruit a high-level sponsor.** Secure executive sponsorship early from a sponsor who is technology literate or keenly interested in technology as a strategic asset.

3. **Set expectations appropriately.** Initial OOP projects are likely to be more difficult, expensive, and time-consuming than anticipated. Be conservative about short-term payback and emphasize that shortened delivery cycles will occur only after a solid base of experience has been established.

Don't reinvent the wheel

4. **Learn from experienced peers.** This can include seeking out companies engaged in business-critical object technology projects, attending object-oriented conferences that feature "user" speakers, and asking vendors and associations for introductions to object-experienced peers.

5. **Recruit and carefully manage outside experts.** Identify vendors and consultants with successful track records in large-scale object technology implementation. Make sure the internal team owns the project, and plan carefully for skills transfer.

6. **Target developers based on personal motivation.** Personal curiosity and intellectual curiosity are far more important than specific programming experience.

**Build small,
flexible teams**

7. **Work in small, geographically close teams.** Teams of about five people are ideal for the intensive communication object-oriented development requires. Large teams should be broken up into smaller subteams.

8. **Plan for new roles and skills.** New roles can include evangelists who act as mentors and educators, object analysts and designers, architects responsible for the overall object model, librarians who keep track of class libraries, and assemblers who create applications from existing libraries of objects.

9. **Target object-based projects wisely.** Appropriate targets can include small, business-critical applications; complex, interactive applications that can benefit from object modeling; families of closely related applications; and projects that require multiple or continuous rounds of user input.

10. **Invest heavily in training.** OOP concepts present the greatest difficulty for newcomers. Learning new development environments and languages is by comparison a more moderate challenge. Strategic investment in training will pay off many times during development.

Develop appropriate methodologies

11. **Recognize that analysis and design are difficult.** Qualified outside consulting help is essential for initial analysis and design. No single method is dominant; just pick one and stick with it. It can take a year or more to develop internal staff with expertise in this area.

12. **Consider building an enterprise model.** An enterprise model simulates companywide business processes. Building an enterprise model can help a company identify common sets of objects and decide which ones to develop first.

13. **Choose an object-oriented language carefully.** Current languages have strengths and weaknesses. C++ is dominant, but many newcomers to objects have had better success starting with Smalltalk because of its pure approach and then moving on to other more powerful languages once the concepts are clear.

Let applications evolve

14. **Evolve prototypes into production systems.** OOP is well-suited to an iterative approach to application development. Developers can work side by side with users in an ongoing code-and-test process.

15. **Conduct regular design and code reviews.** Regular reviews ensure appropriate modeling and consistency among classes. Because team members stay better informed about each other's activities, regular reviews also encourage code reuse.

16. **Focus early on performance.** Object programmers can and should focus on performance at every step of the development process. It should not be left to last-minute tweaking.

Be realistic about reuse

17. **Position reuse as a long-term benefit.** Short-term benefits of OOP include increased flexibility, lower maintenance, and business-modeling capabilities. Analysis and design reuse come later, and code reuse is not likely until a company has completed at least two or three large-scale projects.

18. **Put organization structures in place.** Reuse can't occur unless some form of library is accessible, well-promoted, and easy to use, with appropriate assistance available as necessary.

19. **Create new incentives.** Programmers should be encouraged to create and use reusable code, not to write large quantities of code.

20. **Develop object-oriented metrics.** These can include predictive metrics such as time required, resources required, risk of failure, and business impact; structural metrics such as the number and size of classes; and productivity metrics such as costs, team size, and reuse achieved.

**Documentation,
training, and
technical support**

Taligent provides new CommonPoint developers with a series of developer guides that cover frameworks and services and include code examples. Taligent also provides a programming tutorial, sample code, documented sample applications, human interface guidelines, white papers, on-line documentation, and a variety of other resources.

Taligent has developed training courses based on feedback from participants in pre-beta developer programs. The resulting courseware targets commercial developers, corporate clients, and investors. Taligent is working with various investor training organizations to qualify trainers, discuss and plan future training deliverables, and tailor courseware to investor curricula. In addition to training opportunities provided through the investors, Taligent provides its own training program for strategic partners.

Taligent is also working closely with its investors to provide technical support for corporate and higher education developers, commercial developers, value-added resellers (VARs), and system integrators (SIs) via the existing investor support and service infrastructures, the Internet, and on-line services such as CompuServe.

For more information

If you have access to the Internet, the easiest way to get current information about Taligent, including product information, white papers, investor information, developer support programs, developer profiles, press releases, and job postings, is to go to Taligent's home page in the World Wide Web:

`http://www.taligent.com`

To obtain current information about the programs that Taligent and Taligent's investors provide for commercial developers, send a request to this address:

`isvdev_request@taligent.com`

For general information, you can also call 1 800 288-5545.

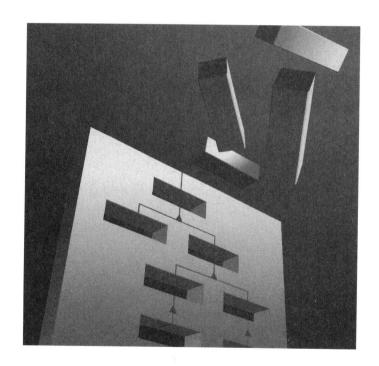

PART II

COMMONPOINT
SYSTEM ARCHITECTURE

CommonPoint application system

Application frameworks				
Embeddable Data Types	**Graphics Editing framework**	**Text Editing framework**	**Document Data Access framework**	**Time Media User Interface framework**
Desktop frameworks	**Workspace frameworks . . .**	**Presentation framework**	**Document frameworks . . .**	**User Interface frameworks . . .**
Application Services	**Interoperability Services . . .**	**Printing . . .**	**Scanning**	**Time Media . . .**
	Localization Services . . .	**Text . . .**	**Graphics . . .**	

System Services

Enterprise Services	**Data Access framework**	**Caucus framework**	**System Management . . .**	**Messaging Services**
	Concurrency Control and Recovery	**Remote Object Call Services**		

Foundation Services	**Notification**	**Identifiers . . .**	**Object Storage . . .**	**Testing . . .**	**Math and Language Libraries . . .**

OS Services	**Communications . . .**	**File System**	**Time Services**	**Object Runtime Services . . .**	**Microkernel Services . . .**

Host operating system

CHAPTER 6

INTRODUCTION TO THE COMMONPOINT APPLICATION SYSTEM

This chapter introduces the CommonPoint system architecture and the notation conventions used in later chapters to show relationships among classes.

The rest of the chapters in Part II introduce each group of frameworks in the system. These chapters constitute a reference for experienced programmers who want overviews of CommonPoint capabilities in specific areas. They focus on basic concepts and architecture and are not intended as a guide to CommonPoint programming. In some places, however, some implementation details and code examples are included to help programmers understand the capabilities of a particular framework.

Detailed programming information and sample code is beyond the scope of this book. The CommonPoint developer guides and related documentation provide the technical information required to program the system.

COMMONPOINT OVERVIEW

The figure on the opposite page shows the two major groups of frameworks in the CommonPoint application system:

- **Application frameworks** implement the core Taligent programming model for application development. They provide high-level building blocks that developers can use as is, extend, or customize to design innovative interactive applications of all kinds. These include frameworks that support user interfaces, compound documents, text, graphics, multimedia, interoperability with host systems, printing, and many other features.
- **System Services** provide the foundation for building distributed solutions with the Application frameworks. Available services include enterprise services such as data access, collaboration, and system administration; low-level foundation services that support identifiers, data structures, object storage, numerics, testing, and other basic programming needs; and the OS Services, which give CommonPoint applications access to low-level host services such as communications and file systems.

This chapter briefly introduces the major frameworks and object services within each of these groups. Roughly speaking, the "lower" a framework is within the CommonPoint taxonomy, the closer it is to hardware, and the "higher" it is, the closer it is to the user. However, the layers in the figure don't represent a strict hierarchy of dependencies. Rather, they are functional groupings that reflect the taxonomy of the CommonPoint system as it is viewed from within *cp*Professional browsers and viewers.

Applications don't sit on top of all this structure as in conventional operating systems. Instead, as explained in Chapter 2, an application is an ensemble of pieces of code that use or extend frameworks at various levels of the system in different ways. An application can call a framework directly no matter where it's located in the system, and it can also call its own frameworks, if it has any, in exactly the same way. Similarly, frameworks call each other's APIs to reuse design or to request services.

Basic system statistics

The first release of the CommonPoint application system includes about 100 integrated frameworks and object services, about 1,900 classes, and about 27,000 member functions, of which about 7,000 are constructors used by other functions. Most developers need to learn only a fraction of these classes and functions—just those parts of the system that are relevant to their own application domains. Nevertheless, these totals give some indication of the breadth of extensible capabilities provided by the system.

Even though it provides comprehensive support for many different application domains, the beta release of the entire CommonPoint system comprises only about 850,000 lines (nonblank, noncomment) of code, of which about 150,000 are headers and other declarations. Thus, the beta release includes only about 700,000 executable lines of code. This number will grow over time as new features are supported, but it is still remarkably small compared with today's operating systems.

The relatively small size of the CommonPoint system demonstrates the power of framework programming. CommonPoint frameworks reuse a significant amount of each others' code, and all applications built from them benefit from reuse in the same fashion.

The size of the CommonPoint system on disk varies from one host to another, but in general it occupies about as much disk space as a single large host application, such as a full-featured layout, presentation, or spreadsheet program and its associated files. Similarly, the CommonPoint system's RAM footprint is approximately equivalent to that of a large host application.

Because of the degree of code reuse among CommonPoint frameworks and applications, Taligent expects that CommonPoint applications will tend to take up less room on disk and in RAM than similar applications running on traditional systems. Therefore, for typical users the CommonPoint system and its applications should add up to be about the same size as or even smaller than the equivalent applications running directly on the host operating system.

Application frameworks

The Application frameworks are divided into three broad groups: Embeddable Data Types, Desktop frameworks, and Application Services.

Most CommonPoint developers begin programming with the Desktop frameworks, which implement the heart of the Taligent programming model. The Embeddable Data Types, a group of frameworks that in turn use both Desktop frameworks and Application Services frameworks, provide ready-made embeddable data types for creating graphics, text, data access, and time media components and related objects. The Application Services frameworks provide underlying support for text, graphics, and other application-programming domains.

Embeddable Data Types

The Embeddable Data Types frameworks (the top row of the figure on page 158) provide ready-made embeddable data types for specific application domains. These frameworks make extensive use of both the Desktop frameworks and the Application Services frameworks.

Chapter 8 introduces the Embeddable Data Types frameworks:

- **The Graphics Editing framework** provides classes based on the Presentation framework that developers can use with some of the 2-D Graphics classes to assemble a range of graphics-editing elements, from simple drawing components to CAD programs and other specialized drawing applications.

- **The Text Editing framework** provides classes based on the Desktop frameworks and the text system that developers can use to assemble a range of text-editing elements, from simple text boxes and controls to simple word-processing applications.

- **The Document Data Access framework** provides a high-level interface that allows developers to create database access documents (DADs) rapidly for users who are familiar with Structured Query Language (SQL). The first version of this framework supports SQL queries only. Plans for future versions include supporting higher-level C++ abstractions of SQL objects for users who aren't familiar with SQL.

- **The Time Media User Interface framework** provides classes for creating lightweight embeddable components that play and record a media sequence such as a movie, MIDI sequence, or audio clip. The first version of this framework supports playing and recording only. Plans for future versions include supporting editing of different media types in ways that parallel the editing capabilities of the Text Editing and Graphics Editing frameworks.

Desktop frameworks

The Desktop frameworks (the second row of the figure on page 158) are designed for creating embeddable components such as those provided by Embeddable Data Types. Learning to use the Desktop frameworks is a prerequisite for most forms of CommonPoint application development.

Chapter 7 introduces the Desktop frameworks:

- **The Workspace frameworks** allow developers to create new Workspace stationery, set attributes of Workspace elements, create appliances, and perform other basic tasks involving the Workspace. Future versions of the CommonPoint system will build on this foundation to support the customization of Place objects, the presentation of People objects within Place environments, behavior associated with adding People and Things objects to Place environments, and so on.

- **The Presentation framework** combines the embedded data concepts provided by the Document frameworks with user interface elements provided by the User Interface frameworks. It provides the generic presentation capabilities typical of interactive applications, and it is the CommonPoint framework that most closely resembles traditional application frameworks such as MacApp.

- **The Document frameworks** consist of the Shared Document, Compound Document, and Basic Document frameworks. They provide the basic capabilities of embeddable components.

- **The User Interface (UI) frameworks** support user interface elements such as controls, windows, palettes, and buttons. The UI frameworks also include the Views and Input frameworks, which control the display and input of data, respectively.

Application Services

Application Services provide services in seven application domains. Chapters 9 through 12 provide an overview of these services:

- **The Graphics system** supports 2-D and 3-D graphics, graphics device drivers, colors, and fonts. Key features include high-level curve geometries defined by nonuniform rational B-splines (NURBS), device-independent 2-D and 3-D coordinate systems, integrated 2-D and 3-D graphics, a uniform interface for accessing all kinds of fonts, a rich set of color spaces, and color matching.

  The Graphics system also provides low-level support for sprites, pixel buffers, and displays.

  Chapter 9 introduces the Graphics system.

- **The Text system** supports the storage, manipulation, and display of multilingual text based on the Unicode character-encoding standard. Multiple script systems can be combined wherever text can be displayed. All text in the CommonPoint system can be styled, including menu items, labels, and editable fields in dialog boxes as text in text components.

Chapter 10 introduces the Text system.

■ **The Time Media frameworks** provide classes that developers can use to play, record, and synchronize a variety of audio, MIDI, and video data types. These frameworks also include classes that provide programmatic support for telephony, allowing CommonPoint applications to control a voice telephone line.

Chapter 11 introduces the Time Media frameworks.

■ **Interoperability Services** support compound document standards such as OpenDoc and OLE. These services also support the conversion of CommonPoint data types to non-CommonPoint data types by using Graphics Converters, Text Converters, and the Data Translation framework.

Chapter 12 introduces Interoperability Services, beginning on page 284.

■ **The Printing frameworks** support printing for all applications based on the Document frameworks. They can also be extended to support specialized printing requirements and the CommonPoint equivalent of printer drivers.

Chapter 12 introduces the Printing frameworks, beginning on page 289.

■ **The Scanning framework**, which is planned for future versions of the CommonPoint system, manages scanning applications and scanner handlers.

Chapter 12 introduces the Scanning framework, beginning on page 300.

■ **Localization Services** support multilingual text input and output, localization of system and application interfaces, text analysis, and text scanning and formatting.

Chapter 10 introduces multilingual text input, beginning on page 261. Chapter 12 introduces the other Localization Services, beginning on page 301.

System Services

The System Services frameworks are divided into three broad groups: Enterprise Services, Foundation Services, and OS Services.

Enterprise Services

Enterprise Services provide high-level distributed services that support key enterprise capabilities such as data access, collaboration, system management, and messaging. These services in turn rely on the underlying transport mechanisms provided by the Communications frameworks (see OS Services on page 166).

Chapter 13 introduces Enterprise Services:

- **The Data Access framework** handles communication among applications, connectivity software, and databases.
- **The Caucus framework** provides multicast transport facilities for the Shared Document framework and collaborative applications.
- **The System Management frameworks** support administrative tasks such as software installation, licensing, configuration, maintenance, and authentication. The first release of the CommonPoint system includes the Licensing Services frameworks, and future releases will support additional services.
- **Messaging Services**, which are planned for future CommonPoint releases, provide object abstractions for store-and-forward messaging that shield CommonPoint developers from the details of host messaging protocols.
- **The Concurrency Control and Recovery framework** provides basic local transaction-processing capabilities that ensure logical consistency of data that can be modified by multiple tasks at the same time. Future CommonPoint releases will provide more extensive transaction-processing support.
- **Remote Object Call (ROC) Services** allow applications to invoke remote Commonpoint services running on various hosts. ROC Services also provide the basis for Taligent's long-term support for CORBA and distributed objects, which will allow CommonPoint applications to invoke remote non-CommonPoint services.

The initial absence of some Enterprise Services capabilities (such as software installation or Messaging Services) doesn't prevent the use of equivalent services provided by the host. Developers can use host libraries directly to implement such services in much the same way that they would implement them for any application developed for today's host operating systems. Applications that use this strategy won't be portable, but the host-specific code can be isolated and replaced when the CommonPoint service becomes available.

Foundation Services

Foundation Services provide basic services for use by all CommonPoint applications and frameworks. Chapter 14 introduces these services:

- **The Notification framework** provides a systemwide mechanism for the propagation of change information among objects.
- **Identifiers** support three ways of associating a name with data:
  - **Properties** are used for keeping track of small collections of heterogeneous instances when type safety is important. The Properties classes also include a mechanism for querying collections of objects that have associated properties.
  - **Attributes** are used when a specific name is always associated with a corresponding type.
  - **Tokens** provide lightweight wrappers for static text identifiers that don't need to be displayed or edited by the user.
- **The Object Storage classes** support persistent storage of objects and their structure in memory:
  - **Archives** support the storage and retrieval of persistent objects as individual units within a larger entity, much like entries in a simple database or dictionary.
  - **Data Structures and Collections** represent a flexible alternative to traditional computer science data structures, eliminating the need for application-specific implementations of arrays, linked lists, and tables.
  - **Streams and Persistence** support streaming, the process used by most CommonPoint applications to flatten objects into a byte-encoded stream, store them to disk or send them across a network to a different CommonPoint program running on a different host, and read them back into memory.
- **The Testing frameworks** provide tools and services for testing objects. The first release of the CommonPoint system includes the Test framework, which provides a uniform protocol for automating test execution.
- **The Math and Language libraries** include the Numerics libraries for floating point calculations and the standard C and C++ libraries.

OS Services

OS Services provide CommonPoint object abstractions for low-level services performed by the host operating system. Chapter 15 introduces these services, including some of Taligent's plans for TalOS Technologies:

- **The Communications frameworks** facilitate both local and remote communication between threads:
  - **Directory Services** provide a homogeneous view of non-Taligent namespaces, including DNS, X.500, AOCE™, and DCE CDS.
  - **Service Access** provides a mechanism for identifying and accessing services available on a network.
  - **Message Streams** provide a uniform API for handling physical communication between threads at all levels, within the same task or in different tasks on different machines.
  - **Protocols** are intended to support standard communications protocols, including TCP/IP, AppleTalk®, and Novell. Protocols will be part of TalOS technologies and don't have an API in the CommonPoint application system.
- **The File System interface** provides object abstractions for manipulating files, directories, and volumes that reside on hardware or on virtual devices.
- **Time Services** provide a hardware-independent model for timing support.
- **Object Runtime Services** support heap management, exceptions, shared libraries, and metadata services.
- **Microkernel Services** support tasking, scheduling, synchronization, and system shutdown.
- **The Object-Oriented Device Driver Model (OODDM) frameworks** will provide input-output services for use by hardware-independent device drivers. The OODDM will be part of TalOS technologies, which Taligent plans to make available to Taligent's investors. The OODDM doesn't have an API in the CommonPoint application system.

OS Services (excluding Protocols and the OODDM) are available to all CommonPoint applications on all host operating systems. They provide the lowest-level APIs that all CommonPoint applications and frameworks use to communicate with the host.

HOST REQUIREMENTS

The CommonPoint application system can run on any modern 32-bit operating system that supports these features:

- Tasks and threads
- Semaphores
- Monitors/conditions
- Memory-mapped files
- Shared memory
- Interprocess communication
- Input device access
- Copy on write
- Extended file attributes
- Loadable shared libraries with metadata

If a potential host doesn't support all of these capabilities, it is sometimes possible to support them within the CommonPoint application system in a way that augments the features the host does provide. For example, monitors and conditions can be implemented on semaphores, and a pthread package can be added if kernel-level threads aren't supported.

Taligent's investors plan to ship versions of the CommonPoint system that run on AIX, HP-UX, Mac OS, and OS/2. Taligent plans to ship versions that run on Windows NT, Windows 95, and other platforms. For more information about Taligent market development, see Chapter 4.

TALIGENT CONVENTIONS

This section briefly introduces some of the principles that underlie Taligent's approach to C++ and summarizes the notation used for class diagrams in the chapters that follow.

Using C++ to write Taligent software

For detailed guidelines on using C++ to write Taligent software, see *Taligent's Guide to Designing Programs: Well-Mannered Object-Oriented Design in C++* (1994). It includes a discussion of the object-oriented design principles that underlie the CommonPoint system architecture:

- **All interfaces are expressed through objects.** CommonPoint objects are defined in terms not of the implementation but of the abstraction presented to the client. In general, conventional data structures such as structs are not used as arguments in CommonPoint functions. Instead, arguments are either objects or built-in data types such as long.

- **Commonality is managed through inheritance.** Base classes provide successively more refined points of commonality, and objects can inherit from multiple base classes.

- **Objects are leveraged wherever possible.** Using an existing object is better than inventing or reinventing one. Less code means a smaller memory footprint, less for developers to learn, fewer bugs, and a more robust system.

- **Frameworks provide the foundation.** Frameworks provide an infrastructure that decreases the amount of code that a programmer must develop, test, and debug and makes a comprehensive system easier to learn.

- **Let resources find you.** Assumptions about where resources come from aren't built into objects that don't need to know. Instead, resources are described as objects, enabling the polymorphic substitution of equivalent resource objects later on.

Taligent's Guide to Designing Programs discusses these and other rules that Taligent engineers follow, including C++ programming conventions, CommonPoint programming conventions, class template standards, and other tips and techniques. It is required reading for all CommonPoint programmers.

Reading class diagrams

The class diagrams in Part II show classes and relationships selectively and generally do not include all classes in a subsystem. The diagrams appear only when they illustrate basic structural concepts. For more detailed information about CommonPoint class relationships, see the CommonPoint developer guides and the online documentation provided with the *cp*Professional development environment.

Taligent uses these naming conventions (described in *Taligent's Guide to Designing Programs*) for all classes:

Prefix	Example	Indicates
A	ADocRefType	Template arguments
E	EExceptionType	Enumerated type names
f	fUniqueId	Data members
fg	fgClassSemaphore	Nonconstant static data members
k	kEmbeddedModelAdded	Constants (including those of enumerated type)
M	MEventHandler	Mixin classes
T	TGrafEditSelection	Standard classes
V	VInitialize	Virtual base classes

Taligent class diagrams use the following notation conventions to depict classes and their relationships:

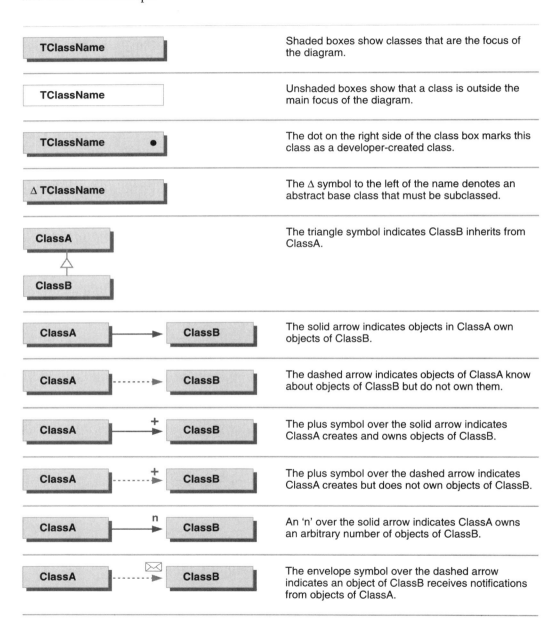

Shaded boxes show classes that are the focus of the diagram.

Unshaded boxes show that a class is outside the main focus of the diagram.

The dot on the right side of the class box marks this class as a developer-created class.

The Δ symbol to the left of the name denotes an abstract base class that must be subclassed.

The triangle symbol indicates ClassB inherits from ClassA.

The solid arrow indicates objects in ClassA own objects of ClassB.

The dashed arrow indicates objects of ClassA know about objects of ClassB but do not own them.

The plus symbol over the solid arrow indicates ClassA creates and owns objects of ClassB.

The plus symbol over the dashed arrow indicates ClassA creates but does not own objects of ClassB.

An 'n' over the solid arrow indicates ClassA owns an arbitrary number of objects of ClassB.

The envelope symbol over the dashed arrow indicates an object of ClassB receives notifications from objects of ClassA.

Class diagrams can also include examples of the member functions for a class. In such cases the class generally includes additional functions that aren't shown:

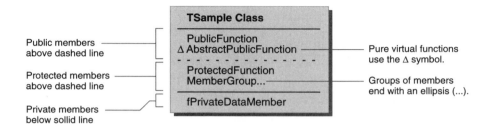

This class diagram provides an example of the notation in use:

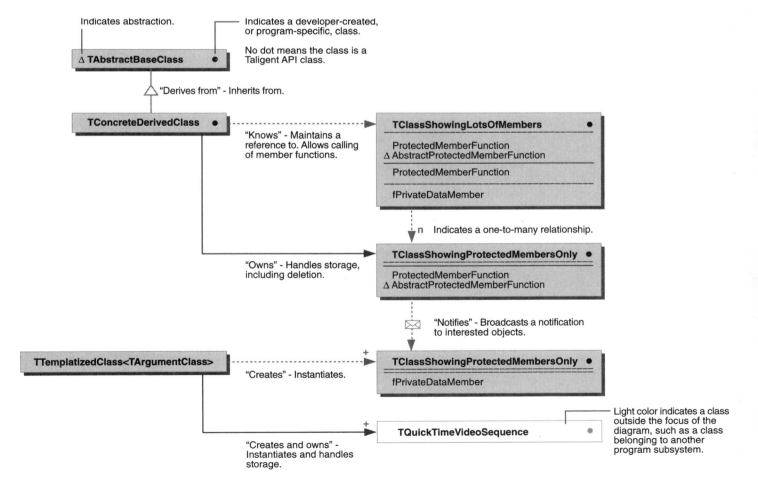

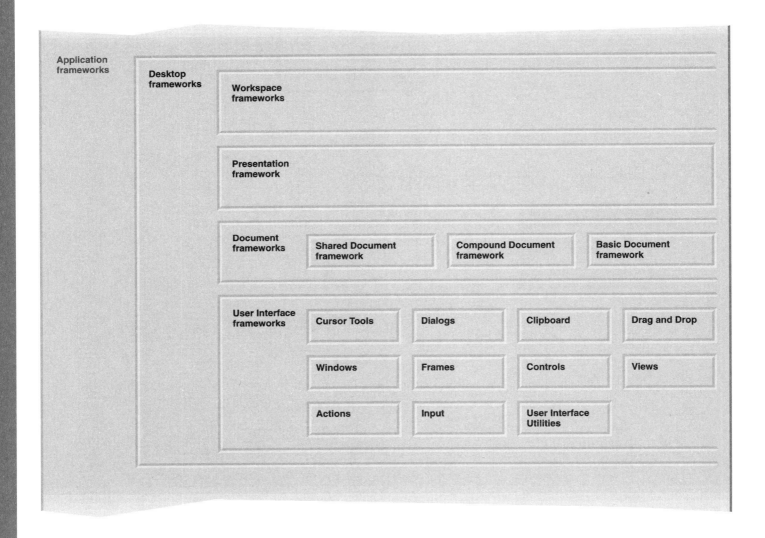

Application frameworks

Desktop frameworks

Workspace frameworks

Presentation framework

Document frameworks

Shared Document framework

Compound Document framework

Basic Document framework

User Interface frameworks

Cursor Tools

Dialogs

Clipboard

Drag and Drop

Windows

Frames

Controls

Views

Actions

Input

User Interface Utilities

CHAPTER 7

DESKTOP FRAMEWORKS

The Desktop frameworks are designed for creating embeddable components. Learning to use them is a prerequisite for most CommonPoint application development. After learning to use the Desktop frameworks to create a functioning component, a developer needs to learn only the additional frameworks that are relevant to the problem domain of the application under development.

Applications created with the Desktop frameworks share code that provides a rich set of ready-to-use features. "Embeddable components," which begins on page 68, introduces Taligent's approach to embeddable components and the features that such components have in common.

The figure on the opposite page summarizes the Desktop frameworks. Note that the Document frameworks are completely separate from the User Interface frameworks, which include the Views framework. This reflects the fact that it's possible to create CommonPoint documents that are completely independent from any representation on the screen. The Presentation framework ties documents and their user interfaces together, providing working menus and other standard CommonPoint features that can be used by instantiation and extended by subclassing.

This chapter begins with a brief overview of the major Desktop frameworks. The rest of the chapter introduces the basic programming concepts that underlie these frameworks, including the representation and manipulation of data, connection of and navigation among components, and presentation of data to the user.

Before reading this chapter, you should understand the concepts described in Chapter 2, "The Taligent programming model."

OVERVIEW OF THE DESKTOP FRAMEWORKS

"The four questions," beginning on page 71, introduces the four questions a programmer must answer to create an interactive, embeddable component:

1. What is the structure of the data?

2. What can the user select?

3. What can the user do to the data?

4. How is the data to be presented?

The Compound Document framework and the Presentation framework provide a mechanism for answering these questions. The other Desktop frameworks provide standard user interface elements and the underlying support for the component and its connections with the rest of the system.

This section introduces the roles played by the major Desktop frameworks.

Document frameworks

The Document frameworks support the basic capabilities of documents in the CommonPoint system.

Compound Document framework

The Compound Document framework provides a set of abstractions that support standard embedded components. However, these abstractions are not tied to the user interface or to any other medium, because they deal only with the way a document stores and manipulates data.

The Compound Document framework manages the relationships among three basic kinds of objects—objects that answer the first three of the four questions listed above:

- **A model** encapsulates the structure of a component's data.
  (Question 1: What is the structure of the data?)
- **A selection** identifies a discrete portion of a model's data.
  (Question 2: What can the user select?)
- **A command** performs an action on a selection.
  (Question 3: What can the user do to the data?)

These are the essential objects for a working embeddable component, which can be presented to the user in a variety of ways. It's also possible to create a server with these objects that has no presentation.

Components created with the Compound Document framework inherit a rich set of integrated capabilities, including copy/cut/paste, embedding, linking, drag-and-drop, continuously "live" frames, editing in place, and OpenDoc/OLE interoperability. The Compound Document's built-in streaming and logging mechanisms also support multiple undo/redo, saveless operation, scriptability, and collaboration across a network.

Basic Document framework

The Basic Document framework takes care of data storage for Compound Document components and provides other basic elements needed by all applications managed by the Workspace frameworks. Because it provides only the minimum support required for documents, most application developers use the higher-level Compound Document and Presentation frameworks.

Shared Document framework

The Shared Document framework supports collaboration capabilities for all Compound Document components. For more information about the Shared Document framework and the high-level collaboration capabilities it supports, see "CSpace—a collaborative space," which begins on page 105.

Presentation framework

The Presentation framework combines the embedded document data concepts provided by the Compound Document framework with user interface elements such as controls, windows, palettes, and buttons provided by the User Interface frameworks. It also provides additional abstractions needed to implement the Taligent human interface guidelines.

Developers can use Presentation framework classes to answer the last of the four questions listed at the top of page 174:

- **A presentation** represents how a model's data is displayed and interacted with. (Question 4: How is the data to be presented?)

The Presentation framework has the following key responsibilities:

- Bring up and manage a component's presentation, or user interface, which can include both visual elements (such as a main content view, menus, dialog boxes, and palettes) and nonvisual elements (such as sounds).
- Activate and deactivate the presentation
- Maintain the current selection

It also provides support and convenience classes that facilitate application development:

- Additional stationery classes that simplify the creation of documents
- Support for simple embedding of components
- Frames that manage an embedded presentation's activation
- Implementations of many of the abstractions provided by lower-level Desktop frameworks

User Interface frameworks

The User Interface frameworks include classes for creating and using interactive user interface elements such as windows and controls. These classes can be used to implement any human interface policy. The Presentation framework uses them to implement the Taligent human interface guidelines.

For most developers, the Views and Input frameworks are the most important of the User Interface frameworks listed here.

Views

Views are objects that can draw themselves on a display device such as a computer monitor or a printer. They provide the areas within which an application draws its data. Applications organize views into hierarchies that determine which views are drawn in front of other views.

The Views framework manages views and connects them to display devices. It uses features of the Input framework to distribute mouse and keyboard events to the views it displays.

The Views framework provides three basic services for any view:

- A port, called a GrafPort, to which an application can draw images
- A way to distribute and handle events
- A way to combine views into hierarchies

By displaying views on the screen and receiving user input, the Views framework provides basic user interface features. Other User Interface frameworks build on the Views framework to provide an extensible set of standard user interface elements.

Input

The Input framework solves the generic problem of delivering user input (for example, mouse or keyboard actions) to an application and provides the application with basic tools for interpreting that input. Input device drivers use streams to communicate input event information to representatives of the device in a target application.

When an embeddable component launches, it receives a complete list of input devices. As input devices are added to or removed from the system, applications receive information for updating the list. The Input framework delivers a given application's input events to the application in the order in which the Input framework received them.

The set of possible event types is not constrained by the Input framework, so it is possible to derive frameworks for new kinds of input devices. The CommonPoint application system includes specialized support for two kinds of input devices: keyboards and mice.

The Input framework has two kinds of clients: devices and applications. Devices send input events, and applications receive them. Designers of frameworks for new kinds of input devices use the Input framework as a foundation on which to build device-specific support.

Cursor Tools   The Cursor Tools framework facilitates the creation of cursor tools that allow
users to manipulate a variety of data types directly.

Dialogs   The Dialogs framework is used to group user interface elements such as views
and buttons together in a dialog box.

Clipboard   The Clipboard framework provides a mechanism for copying and pasting data
within or among applications.

Drag and Drop   The Drag and Drop framework provides a low-level protocol for direct
manipulation of user interface objects.

Windows   The Windows framework provides a set of basic window types and handles
common window management operations, including resizing, zooming,
and moving.

Frames   The Frames framework manages a selectable frame around a view.

Controls   The Controls framework manages a variety of interactive user interface elements,
such as check boxes, toggle buttons, menus, and scroll bars.

Actions   The Actions framework supports the use of actions and action handlers to
manage multiple user options—in a dialog box, for example.

User Interface Utilities   The User Interface Utilities provide miscellaneous services for creating user
interface elements such as labels and decorations.

Workspace frameworks

The first release of the Workspace frameworks supports the creation and management of documents in ways analogous to the Mac OS Finder™ or the Workplace Shell™ in OS/2, allowing developers to create desktop objects that are integrated seamlessly with host desktops. It also provides a suite of development tools that allow a developer to create new Workspace stationery, set attributes of Workspace elements, create appliances, and perform other basic tasks involving the Workspace.

Taligent plans to extend and add to these Workspace frameworks as the CommonPoint system evolves:

Containable frameworks

The Containable frameworks support the representation of desktop objects that can be collected in containers such as folders, participate in drag-and-drop operations, be used with appliances, enumerate their children, and so on.

Workspace Drag-and-Drop frameworks

These frameworks allow developers to add specific drag-and-drop behavior to Workspace representations of their objects. For example, the Printing Devices framework uses the Workspace Drag-and-Drop frameworks to support printer appliances.

Appliance frameworks

The Appliance frameworks facilitate the creation of lightweight source and acceptor objects that can be attached to containables and used to provide extensible capabilities for Workspace drag-and-drop operations. These frameworks support the appliance capabilities described on page 100. The Appliance frameworks and the Workspace Drag-and-Drop frameworks are the key frameworks used by developers to create Things objects.

Viewers framework

This framework supports viewers, or presentations of Workspace data types, that allow new layouts and views to be added or extended easily. Viewers can display a flexible set of data in standard formats, such as icon views, tree views, outline views, property inspectors, and so on. These are distinct from lower-level Views framework entities used for clipping, layering, and screen drawing.

Other Workspace frameworks

Other Workspace frameworks under development will support extensible Place and People objects, allowing developers to customize Place software, the presentation of People elements in Place environments, behavior associated with adding People and Things objects to Place environments, and so on. For more information about Taligent's long-term approach to the People, Places, and Things metaphor, see Chapter 3.

For current information about the Workspace frameworks, see the CommonPoint developer guides.

REPRESENTING DATA

The Basic Document framework establishes the concept of a basic document that can present and modify its self-contained data. The Compound Document framework expands this paradigm to provide support for embedding different types of data in a single *compound document.* Compound documents use embeddable components as containers for this heterogeneous data.

Chapter 2, "The Taligent programming model," introduces the role of embeddable components in Taligent programs. When a component is displayed on the screen, it is associated with a *presentation,* or user interface, that determines how the data is displayed and how the user can manipulate it.

A particular component's presentation is not saved with the component. It depends on the human interface policy defined by the Presentation framework and objects provided by the User Interface frameworks. As Figure 54 suggests, a component's presentation mediates between a component's data and the user.

A component's data is contained by a *model* (based on class TModel) that encapsulates its data and provides the rest of the system with the means for accessing the data. This strict separation between a model and its presentation (similar to the model-view-controller separation first used in Smalltalk) allows the use of more than one presentation for the same model. For example, an address book might have a graphical user interface for use when you're at your desk and a telephone interface for use remotely from a telephone. Both interfaces could work with the same model.

This arrangement also reinforces the primacy of data in the CommonPoint application system. If you design your program well, you can change a model's presentation without touching the model itself or the data it contains. Presentations don't need to be visual. For example, a set of numbers could be presented as notes on a piano keyboard or valve settings in a factory.

FIGURE 54
USERS INTERACT WITH A
COMPONENT'S DATA VIA
ITS PRESENTATION

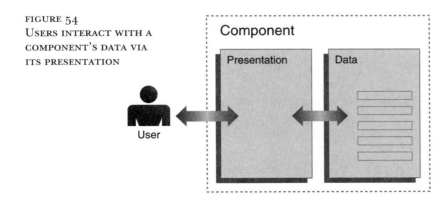

Usually the data encapsulated by a model is further encapsulated within one or more data-specific objects with their own data access member functions. For example, the model for a spreadsheet component encapsulates the rows and columns of cells, the contents of each cell, the formula in each cell, and the dependencies among the cells. The model for a word-processing component encapsulates the characters, lines, paragraphs, and styles for the text. The model for a time-management system encapsulates information about days, months, and appointments. The model provides the protocol that relates its data objects to the surrounding framework.

Compound documents

A compound document consists of a hierarchy of embedded components. Conceptually this is equivalent to a hierarchy of models within models. The structure of the hierarchy of models corresponds to their embedding relationships on the screen, as illustrated by Figure 55.

FIGURE 55
MAPPING
STRUCTURE TO
APPEARANCE

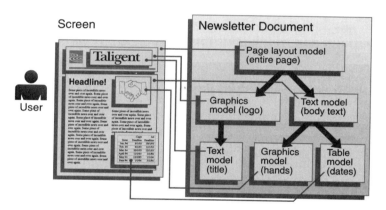

Persistence of the data

The data represented by models can be either persistent or transient:

- **Persistent data** is stored for future use. For example, entries in an address book that can be added to and edited each time the address book is opened are persistent data.

- **Transient data** is generated on demand. For example, a model might be designed to represent the current temperature in a given location. When queried for the data, the model retrieves the temperature from a thermal sensor in real time and immediately discards the data.

Location of the data

A model must provide the interface to its data for the rest of the system, but the data doesn't necessarily have to be located inside the model. In some cases it may be more convenient to keep it elsewhere, such as in a remote database.

If the data is simple, it makes sense to keep it in the model. For example, you might locate the data for a simple phone list component inside the model as a list of name records that the model owns and manages, as shown in Figure 56.

FIGURE 56
A MODEL
THAT
CONTAINS
ITS DATA

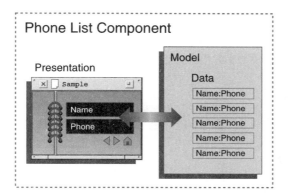

For more complex data or for large amounts of data, it makes more sense for the model to provide only an interface to the data, which is actually stored elsewhere. A model for a database access component, for example, might provide only a query front end for the actual database, which the model would access by using client-server mechanisms provided by the Data Access framework. Figure 57 illustrates this arrangement. The model encapsulates (hides) the actual means by which it handles the job for which it is responsible.

FIGURE 57
A MODEL
THAT
PROVIDES AN
INTERFACE
FOR DATA
STORED
ELSEWHERE

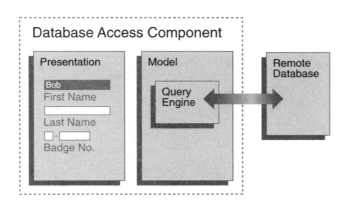

Like many other design decisions, deciding whether to locate the data inside or outside the model involves trade-offs. Locating the data inside the model typically makes the model much easier to implement. If the storage overhead is low and the data isn't shared, it's generally preferable to locate the data inside the model.

However, locating the data outside the model has several advantages:

- **Rapid saving and restoring.** The resulting model is lightweight and can be saved and restored quickly. It may even be possible to save or restore only those parts of the data that have changed rather than the entire model.

- **Code reuse.** You can build many different models from the same underlying classes and libraries. In contrast, if each of several models contains and manages all its data, similar data needs might require multiple implementations—one for each model.

- **Interoperability with non-CommonPoint data.** The model can be used to perform any necessary translations between CommonPoint data and host data or data managed by other operating systems running on various hardware platforms connected over a network.

- **Data sharing.** Many lightweight models can provide simultaneous access to the same data, as shown in Figure 58.

FIGURE 58
KEEPING DATA
OUTSIDE THE
MODEL
SUPPORTS DATA
SHARING

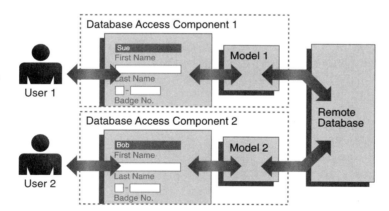

Preserving the data

The CommonPoint application system provides two mechanisms to store data permanently on storage media such as hard disks: streaming and filing.

Streaming

Streaming is the process of saving objects from memory to permanent storage and restoring them in the opposite direction. Streaming converts an object to a flat byte-encoded stream before transmitting it to storage. The stream includes anchors, links, the current selection, and other information about its presentation and current state as well as the embedded model. Streamed data can also be sent to another process, another model, or another machine. Interprocess communication (IPC) and remote object calls (ROC) both use streaming as their transmission medium. All objects in the CommonPoint application system must know how to stream themselves.

The streaming mechanism also supports several key features of embeddable components, including multiple undo and redo, saveless operation, and collaboration. See "Streaming of selections and commands" on page 188 for details. For information about the streaming mechanism itself, see "Streams and Persistence," beginning on page 351.

Filing

Filing is different from streaming, although in some cases filing and streaming mechanisms can share some code. Streaming operators flatten everything in a model, including anchors, links, and embedded models. The filing operators, however, are capable of streaming subsets of the information in a model, such as just the data. Filing also allows you to save data in a form that can be read by a non-Taligent file system. Unlike streaming, which converts objects to a flat byte-encoded stream that can be restored only within the CommonPoint system, filing allows you to store data in whatever generic data format is convenient for a particular purpose.

The Compound Document framework includes a separate subframework for reading and writing models and their attributes, including a default implementation for clients who don't need to customize the format or location of the stored data. The filing mechanism is in turn built from Archives classes, which are introduced on page 356.

CHANGING DATA

Any operation on data involves specifying first the data to be acted on and then the action to be performed. Selections and commands are the CommonPoint objects that encapsulate this information.

This section introduces selections and commands and describes how you can use them to modify or exchange data. You can perform other data operations in a similar fashion.

Selections and commands

You specify data by defining selections. A *selection* designates a specific set of data in the model on which an action can be performed, as shown in Figure 60. Valid selections include all the data in a model, such as an entire image or document; contiguous or noncontiguous parts of the data, such as a range of characters within a text component or a set of graphics objects within a diagram; and no data at all, such as an insertion point in text. Selections may be established interactively (such as by using the mouse and keyboard) or programmatically (such as by choosing objects that meet test criteria).

FIGURE 59
A SELECTION
THAT SPECIFIES
A REGION OF A
BITMAP

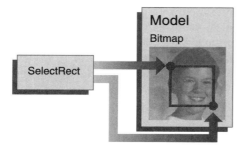

In a bitmap-editing component a selection might specify a particular rectangular region of the bitmap.

You modify the data specified by selections with commands. A *command* is a programming construct that you apply to a selection to change data. It might be invoked when the user chooses a menu item, clicks a button, or makes a gesture, or it could be invoked programmatically.

FIGURE 60
A COMMAND
THAT DARKENS
THE SELECTED
REGION

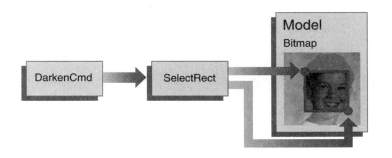

In a bitmap-editing component a command might be used to darken a washed-out region of the bitmap specified by a selection.

For a model to work properly with the rest of the Compound Document framework, you must perform all modifications of the model's data solely by means of commands acting on selections. If you change a model's data directly by using the model's own data access member functions, your component won't conform to the rest of the CommonPoint application system.

Thus, selections and commands mediate between a model and the rest of the system. They provide the interface to the model. As shown in Figure 61, a command calls a selection's member functions, and only the selection calls the model's member functions.

FIGURE 61
THE INTERFACE
FOR A MODEL HAS
TWO LAYERS

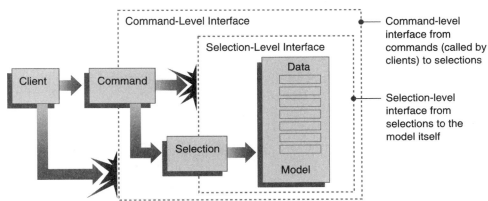

Command-level interface from commands (called by clients) to selections

Selection-level interface from selections to the model itself

**Advantages of a
two-layer interface**

Using selections and commands as intermediaries between a model's data and the rest of the system has several advantages:

- **Predictability.** Selections and commands provide a standard interface for all designers of models and of clients of models. This allows the various CommonPoint frameworks to interact with models added to the system by third parties. You must follow the selection and command protocols strictly, or your software won't work properly with the rest of the system.

- **Extensibility.** You can easily extend the capabilities of a component by creating new selections and commands. You can often do this without making changes to the model or to preexisting selections and commands. For example, suppose you have a text model, and you want to add the ability to randomize the letters in a selected range of text—that is, to create an anagram. As shown in Figure 62, you can implement this new capability inside a new command that operates on an existing selection. You don't have to change any existing code for models, presentations, selections, or other commands.

- **Isolation from changes.** Because clients operate on a model's data through selections and commands, clients require no additional knowledge of the data in the model. This design isolates clients from changes to the implementation of the model. Only the implementations of the selections and commands are affected. Even significant changes to the underlying model, such as changing the location of the data from inside to outside the model, can be concealed from clients.

FIGURE 62
YOU CAN ADD A
NEW COMMAND
WITHOUT
CHANGING THE
WAY A SELECTION
WORKS

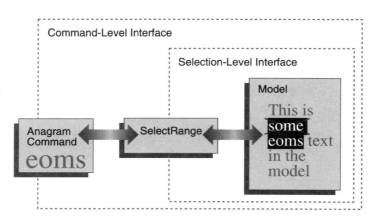

**Independence of
selections and
commands**

Figure 63 shows how the Presentation framework keeps commands and selections separate from the various ways in which a user can perceive data, establish selections, and invoke commands.

The presentation determines how the user perceives the data, such as visually (in a window) or aurally (listening to a sound). This aspect of the presentation involves direct read-only access to the data, because it involves perception only, not manipulation.

The presentation also allows the user to establish exactly the same selection of data in various different ways. For example, a selection of a range of text can be established by using a mouse, the keyboard, a menu item, a search begun by a server, or a test driver. The selection is identical in all cases.

Similarly, different ways of invoking a command and applying it to a particular selection produce exactly the same result. For example, you can invoke a command to italicize a selected range of text by using a mouse, the keyboard, a menu item, a response to a dialog box, a button, a command line, a server, a test driver, or a script.

The strict separation of selections and commands from the way they are established and invoked means that you can drive exactly the same set of selections and commands with any number of different user interfaces, servers, and test drivers without changing any of the existing code for the selections and commands. This design allows for rapid prototyping and testing of new user interfaces and input devices against stable and trusted data models. It also facilitates reuse of existing data models in different application domains.

FIGURE 63
SELECTIONS
AND COMMANDS
ARE INDEPEND-
ENT FROM THE
WAY THEY ARE
ESTABLISHED
AND INVOKED

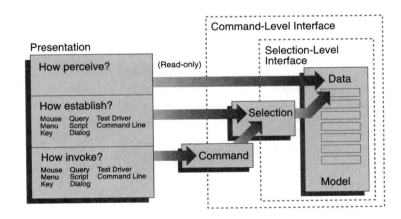

Streaming of selections and commands

When an embeddable component is first opened, the Compound Document framework streams in the data from storage (such as a hard disk). From that point on, as each command completes, the Compound Document framework streams the command and the selection on which it operates into a *command log*. The command log contains a sequential record of the command history for the component.

When the model receives notification that a document is closing, it streams itself out to storage. The framework deletes the command log whenever the entire persistent state of the document is committed to storage.

This streaming of commands and selections supports several key features of embeddable components:

- **Multiple undo/redo.** Multiple undo is simply a matter of starting at the current location in the command log and undoing successive commands until you have reached the desired previous state. Multiple redo is based on the same principle, except in the other direction.

- **Saveless operation.** Changes to a component are saved continuously in the command log. If the system crashes and later restarts, it uses the command log to bring the document into the same state it was in just before the crash. This eliminates the need for users to perform periodic saves. The autosave mechanism provided by the command log is much faster than conventional autosave mechanisms, because only a command-selection pair is saved each time, not the actual data.

- **Scriptability.** Commands and selections can be recorded and played back later to cause a sequence of actions to take place. Because all Desktop applications and the CommonPoint application system itself are built with commands, all CommonPoint applications automatically support any scripting language created for the CommonPoint system.

- **Collaboration.** The CommonPoint application system supports real-time network collaboration by streaming commands and selections and applying them to copies of documents on remote machines or to a shared document on a server. A network locking protocol ensures that users take turns "owning" the document on which they collaborate, so that only one user makes changes to the document at a time and the document stays synchronized on all collaborator machines. For more information about the collaborative capabilities of CommonPoint software, see "CSpace—a collaborative space," beginning on page 105.

Address-space
independence

The way in which a selection specifies its corresponding data must be independent of any particular address space. Otherwise, the selection might not refer to the same data after the data has been streamed to the command log and restored in a different part of memory or after it has been streamed to a different machine.

For example, Figure 64 shows the selection of a rectangular portion of a bitmapped image. The selection refers to the data it selects by means of coordinates, the x–y pairs for the upper-left and lower-right corners of the rectangular area within the image. Only when the selection is actually applied to the data are these abstractions resolved into address-space-dependent offsets.

FIGURE 64
THE IMPLEMEN-
TATION OF A
SELECTION
MUST BE
ADDRESS-SPACE
INDEPENDENT

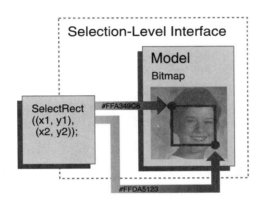

Incremental commands

An *incremental command* is a command that goes through a number of intermediate states before arriving at the final result. Incremental commands are often used to provide smoother feedback to the user than is possible with a command that is executed all at once.

Figure 65 shows how an incremental command in a graphics component can be used to drag shapes. When the user first starts to drag the mouse, the command starts executing; as the shape is moved, the command updates the shape's position in the model. The model then notifies the user interface, which updates its display. When the user releases the mouse button, the command finalizes the position of the shape and terminates.

FIGURE 65
INCREMENTAL
COMMANDS ARE
OFTEN USED FOR
CONTINUOUS
OPERATIONS SUCH
AS DRAGGING AN
OBJECT

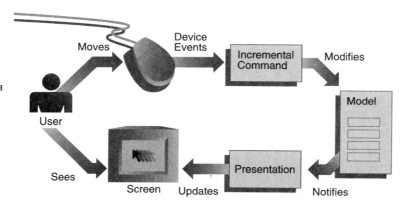

EXCHANGING DATA

In some cases, commands understand the data types on which they operate. In Figure 60 on page 185, for example, the darkening command knew how to call the darkening member function provided by the selection to darken the bitmap.

This isn't always necessary. Generic commands, for example, often need to manipulate data without knowing anything about the data itself.

Consider what the system must do to execute a simple copy-and-paste sequence:

1. The Copy command must make a copy of the data specified by an arbitrary selection on an arbitrary model (including a model added to the system by a third party).

2. The system clipboard must store the copied data.

3. The Paste command must remove the copied data from the clipboard and paste it onto an arbitrary selection on an arbitrary model.

To accomplish this sequence, the system must be able to move chunks of data around without knowing anything specific about the data. The CommonPoint data exchange protocol fulfills this need. It's like a mail transport system that sends and receives messages without having to read their contents.

The data exchange protocol is based on the exchange of models between selections and commands. Data is never exchanged directly—it is always contained within a model.

A copy-and-paste scenario

Figure 66 shows how the data exchange protocol supports a copy-and-paste sequence:

1. The Copy command receives from the selection a model containing a copy of the data specified by the selection

2. The System clipboard (which is itself a document) embeds the copied model.

3. The Paste command removes the copied model from the clipboard and sends it to the selection on which it is to be pasted.

4. The selection extracts the data from the copied model and adds it to its own associated model as appropriate.

The selections in this scenario know how to create the models to exchange and know details about the models, such as how to extract data from models they receive. However, the commands in this scenario know nothing about the models other than how to move them from selection to selection.

FIGURE 66
A COPY-
AND-PASTE
SCENARIO

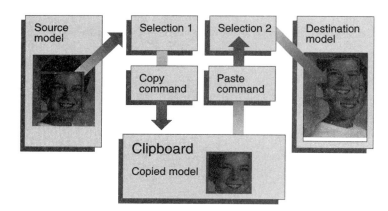

Supplying multiple types of models

For data replacement to work properly, the model containing the exchanged data must be of a type that both the sender and the receiver understand.

Selections and commands are designed to exchange more than one type of model. For example, as shown in Figure 67, a selection for a graphics model might provide data either in a graphics model (complete with complex internal data structures) or in a simple bitmap model that contains a pixel image of the graphic information in a standard format like TIFF, EPS, or PICT. (The Data Translation framework, which is described briefly on page 287, helps automate translation of standard data types.)

Providing multiple formats increases the chances that a command or selection will understand at least one of the available formats, particularly if the options include standard formats such as Unicode or TIFF. To support this capability, selections and commands use a mechanism called *type negotiation* to determine which of several possible formats to use. The default type negotiation attempts to find a type the destination selection understands so that the model's data is absorbed as native data. If type negotiation doesn't produce a type that the destination selection understands, embedding is always possible. It's also possible to implement a special paste command that overrides the default type negotiation and forces embedding even when absorption is possible. (The distinction between embedding and absorption is explained on page 70.)

FIGURE 67
A SELECTION
CAN PROVIDE
DATA IN MORE
THAN ONE
FORMAT

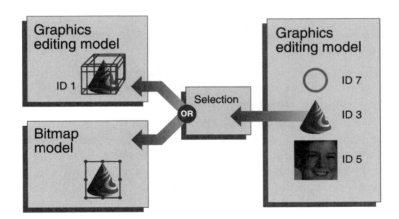

CONNECTING AND NAVIGATING AMONG COMPONENTS

The Compound Document framework supports data synchronization and navigation among embeddable components via links and anchors. A *link* is a connection between two selections called anchors. An *anchor* is a selection of data that can be joined to another selection of data by means of a link.

There are two kinds of links: data links and reference links. A *data link* is a bidirectional communication channel that keeps the data specified by two anchors synchronized. In some systems, a data link has a direction in the sense that one end is a master copy and the other end is a slave copy; only the master can be changed, and the changes propagate to the slave. In the CommonPoint system, all data links are bidirectional and symmetric by default, so changes can be made and propagated from either end.

Anchors and data links also support access control. A particular anchor can be read-only, or it can support editing of its contents. An anchor can also be set to allow or disallow navigation to the originating document.

A *reference link* uses anchors to connect different objects so that a user can navigate between them by clicking a button or performing some other action. In this case the anchors establish the beginning and end of a particular path.

Using links and anchors

Data links, reference links, and anchors can be used to create a complex web of connections among different components on the same machine or over a network, through which data is freely and continuously exchanged and over which users can navigate.

For example, a user might establish a data link from a spreadsheet in one document to a business report in another document, as illustrated by Figure 68. Whenever the state of the spreadsheet changes, the link automatically updates the business report.

By design, the user interface for setting, updating, viewing, and manipulating data links, reference links, and anchors closely resembles the OpenDoc user interface for similar capabilities. Developers can also choose to present links in other ways, depending on the data type and context.

FIGURE 68
LINKS
PROVIDE LIVE
UPDATING
BETWEEN
TWO
DOCUMENTS

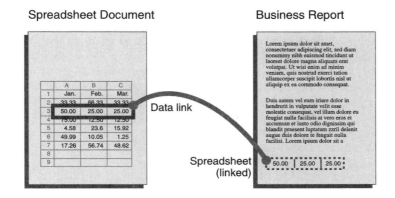

Both links and anchors are subclasses of selections. The connected models shown in Figure 69 can be in the same or different components, including components located on different machines.

FIGURE 69
DATA LINKS
CONNECT
MODELS

The same anchor can be an endpoint for more than one data link. This makes it possible, for example, for a common data source to update several documents, as shown in Figure 70.

FIGURE 70
ONE ANCHOR
CAN BE THE
ENDPOINT
FOR MORE
THAN ONE
DATA LINK

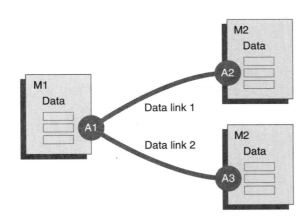

Because anchors are a form of selection, anything you can select in the CommonPoint application system can support linking. You can make the anchors at the end of each link visible to the user, or you can make them strictly an internal implementation detail. You can even design a model that gets data only indirectly via links to other models. For example, you can design a simple graphing utility with anchors labeled x and y to which you can attach links from any two sources of numerical data.

Concurrency

Links automatically handle concurrency issues. For example, the models at both ends of a link are automatically locked during data transfer to ensure consistent results.

Persistence and referential integrity of anchors

Anchors maintain referential integrity despite changes to their surrounding context. You can think of them as "sticky" selections. This means you always know what data will be sent down a link from the source and where the data will appear at the destination.

An anchor can be either static or dynamic. A static anchor tracks (stays with) static data across editing changes and location changes. For example, a text anchor marks a range of characters in a text model and moves as necessary with the data.

A dynamic anchor marks different data at different times, depending on some conditions. For example, a maximum value anchor in a spreadsheet might indicate a cell with the maximum value in a range of cells. As the maximum value changes, so would the actual cell associated with the anchor.

Anchors preserve their referential integrity despite relocation, even across machines. For example, if you send a copy of an anchor to a different machine on the network, the anchor attempts to reestablish its connection to the model at the other end of the original link.

PRESENTATIONS

A presentation determines how the user perceives, selects, and performs actions on data. It also translates events generated by the user into selections and commands that have meaning in your program.

Figure 71 illustrates some of the roles a presentation can play. Presentations need not be visual. The Desktop frameworks support any kind of presentation, including audio and nonvisual interfaces associated with specialized input or output devices.

A presentation takes care of most of the work involved in tracking the mouse, drawing windows, playing sounds, handling scrollbars, and so on. It also activates and deactivates menus and menu entries, displays tool palettes, handles dialog boxes, negotiates overlapping elements on the screen, and manages all other aspects of the user's interaction with the data in the model.

The Presentation framework takes care of most of this behavior. You need to supply only the presentation details that are specific to your program. The sections that follow introduce the basic mechanisms the Desktop frameworks provide to support a typical visual presentation.

FIGURE 71
ROLE OF A TYPICAL
PRESENTATION

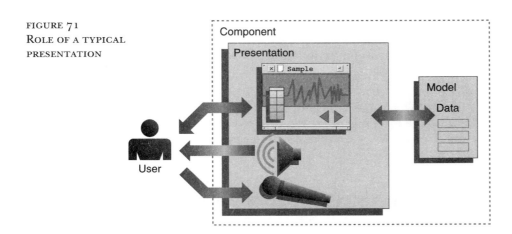

**Views and the
Views framework**

A *view* is an object that can draw itself on a display device such as a computer monitor or a printer. It provides the area within which you draw your program's data. A view doesn't necessarily have to appear on the screen. For example, a printer test program could instruct a view to draw a test pattern onto a page without displaying it on the screen.

The Views framework provides these capabilities for any view:

- **Clipping.** Views clip their contents. For example, if a graphic element extends beyond the bounds of the view, the view truncates it at the view boundary.
- **Transformations.** Views and their contents can be rotated, scaled, and so on.
- **Relative coordinate system.** Locations within a view are specified according to the view's coordinates.
- **Grouping.** Views can group their contents so that all objects within a view can be treated as a single unit for transformations.
- **Buffering.** You can double-buffer views so they redraw without flicker.
- **Hit detection.** The Views framework (with the Input framework) can detect the locations of mouse clicks and similar pointing-device events and distribute them to the views on the screen.

Your program normally needs to provide only the code that draws an image and handles input events. The Views framework takes care of the rest.

View hierarchies

A view can contain one or more other views, forming a *view hierarchy*. When one view contains another view, they are said to have a parent-child relationship: the containing view is the parent and the contained view is a child of the parent.

Figure 72 illustrates the relationship between a view hierarchy and the way the Views framework displays it. The left side of the figure shows a view hierarchy containing four views. View A has two children, view B and view C. View B has a single child, view D. The right side of the figure shows how the view hierarchy might appear on a display device. Note that parent views contain their children.

FIGURE 72
THE
STRUCTURE
OF A VIEW
HIERARCHY IS
RELATED TO
THE WAY THE
VIEWS
FRAMEWORK
DISPLAYS IT

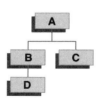

A view hierarchy

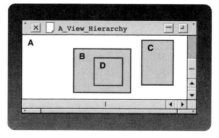

How the view hierarchy might
appear on a display device

A view becomes the child of another view when the parent adopts (takes control of) the child. This means that the parent view doesn't merely contain the child; it also manages its storage. Until it orphans (releases control of) the child, the parent owns the child. This ownership paradigm not only makes code less prone to error but also prevents lexical cycles—situations in which a parent and a child refer to each other either directly or indirectly.

Drawing

To render an image inside a view when the Views framework displays it, you override the view's DrawContents member function with one that draws the image. This takes care of both the initial drawing and the later refreshing of the image.

A view's Draw and DrawContents member functions provide the general mechanism for rendering a view. Draw calls DrawContents, then calls every child's Draw; they in turn call their children's Draw functions, and so on, as shown in Figure 73.

The Views framework uses this mechanism to render the view when it's first displayed. Objects outside the Views framework can also draw a view. For refreshing a view after it's first displayed, the Views framework provides a similar mechanism that also ends up calling DrawContents.

For most uses of the Views framework, the rule for drawing is (as for any framework): "Don't call us, we'll call you." You never initiate a drawing cycle. Instead, you tell the Views framework that part or all of your view is invalid or needs to be redrawn. The Views framework adds areas that you couldn't know are invalid, such as a corner of your view that is exposed when another view moves, and then redraws all the invalid areas.

FIGURE 73
THE DEFAULT
BEHAVIOR OF THE
DRAW MEMBER
FUNCTION

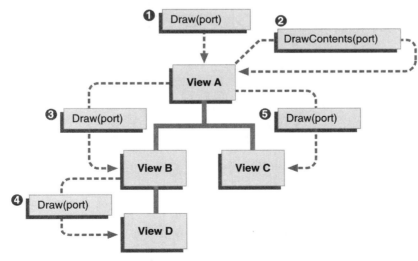

This approach to redrawing has several advantages:

- **Simplicity.** You don't need to determine the appropriate time to draw. If you mark areas invalid, you can count on them being redrawn at the correct time.
- **Efficiency.** The Views framework reduces the number of redrawing cycles by combining the redrawing of the areas you invalidate with the redrawing of areas that become invalid for other reasons. It redraws each area just once.
- **Robustness.** The Views framework reliably redraws every view that needs redrawing. It is difficult for an individual view to manage that process itself. The system can also prioritize drawing against other operations, thereby maintaining overall system performance.

You don't need to invalidate an area except when you change something that needs to be updated on the display. The Views framework automatically draws your view during standard operations such as moving, exposing and hiding, scrolling, or resizing.

Event handling

The high-level Desktop frameworks handle most user input automatically. However, it's easy to handle user input yourself by using the Views framework directly.

The Views framework provides the simplicity of single-threaded programming within a multithreaded environment (see page 408 for an introduction to the Taligent tasking model). This greatly simplifies the programmer's job. Events automatically arrive in the order they should be received, so the programmer doesn't have to keep track of what's happening in multiple threads or handle synchronization, locking, or concurrency.

The Views framework supports the illusion of single-threaded programming by encapsulating function calls from objects outside a view's thread of execution into packages called requests and putting these requests into a request queue. A request handler removes one request from the queue at a time.

A *request* is an object with only one important member function: Do. A request encapsulates a target object and a call on one of the target object's member functions. When you execute the Do function, the request makes the call on the target object. This allows a client object in another thread to build a request that is later executed in the target object's thread.

A *request queue* is a first-in, first-out queue of requests with a very simple interface that allows you to add and remove requests. Request queues can safely receive requests from clients in multiple concurrent threads.

A *request handler* removes the next request from a request queue and executes the request's Do member function. This process of removing and executing a request is called dispatching the request.

Figure 74 illustrates how this works. The box labeled theView at the bottom of the figure represents a view object in a thread whose boundary is represented by the large dashed box. Client1 and Client2 are clients of the view in other threads. Rather than call theView's member functions directly, the clients package the function calls into requests (Request1 and Request2) and then post the requests to the request queue associated with theView's thread. The request handler in theView's thread dispatches requests one at a time, eventually dispatching the requests to their target, theView. The higher-level Desktop frameworks set up most of the details of this for you. The process of handling user input is similar for both mouse and keyboard events.

The Input framework (including the event receiver in your task) and the request handler manage the process up to the last step. With the default behavior, all you have to do to handle input events is provide member functions to handle the function call generated in the last step. The Views framework takes care of distributing events through the view hierarchy to the appropriate views.

FIGURE 74
REQUEST
QUEUES AND
REQUEST
HANDLERS
SHIELD VIEWS
FROM CONCUR-
RENCY ISSUES

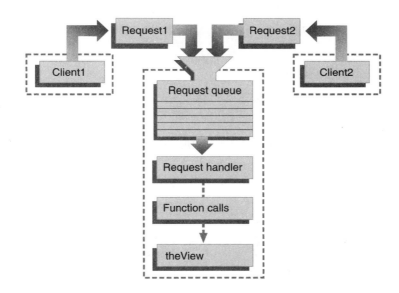

Background drawing   While a thread is drawing your view, it can't do anything else. The entire view hierarchy that shares the thread is also frozen while your view is drawing. If you need to perform a drawing operation that's inherently slow or CPU-intensive (for example, an animation with a high frame rate or 3-D rendering), you should do the computations or even the rendering in a different thread of execution.

Avoiding deadlock   An important requirement of this single-threaded concurrency model is that a view doesn't directly access its parent in a view hierarchy. Giving the parent view ultimate control over its children helps prevent deadlock situations and ensure data integrity.

Notifications   Whenever the state of the data in a model changes, any views opened on the model that the change affects need to be informed so that the views can present the change to the user. The user can also request updates. For example, in a spreadsheet component the user interface can update the display whenever the model completes a recalculation requested by the user.

To keep changes consistent across views, the CommonPoint application system includes a Notification framework that supports the propagation of change information from a source to any clients interested in the change. This framework allows any number of client objects to maintain a consistent state with respect to a particular source.

To use the Notification framework, the source defines a publicly visible notification token, called an *interest,* that's specific to a particular kind of notification. Any number of clients can then express interest in receiving that particular notification by registering as clients of the interest.

FIGURE 75
CLIENTS OF
THE SOURCE
REGISTER TO
RECEIVE
NOTIFICATION

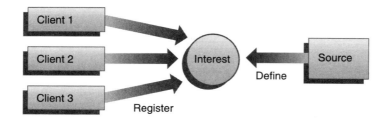

As part of the registration process, clients provide a member function to be called by the notification mechanism when the required change occurs.

FIGURE 76
NOTIFICATION
FRAMEWORK
CALLS CLIENT
MEMBER
FUNCTION
WHEN SOURCE
CHANGES

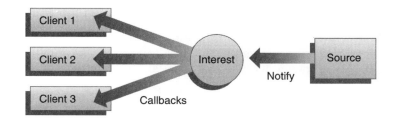

This approach isolates the source from the details of its clients. A source has no information about who its clients are, how many clients it has, or even if it has any clients. Providing notification can best be described as a blind broadcast. Receipt of the notification is not assured; the receiver must be expecting it.

✅ NOTE   The Notification framework deals with any change that occurs in a model right up to the point at which your program needs to make a decision. It then calls your code to obtain that decision. This is another concrete example of the principle summarized by "Don't call us, we'll call you." When examining the flow of control from a debugger, you would see something similar to the bottom part of Figure 15 on page 59: a series of calls to the framework interspersed with calls to your code.

Because the client supplies the member function called by the Notification framework, the result on the client side is completely customizable by the client's author. As a Taligent software designer, you must provide notification of changes to the state of your model. When and how often you choose to do so are design issues.

Notification works across address spaces, including address spaces on different machines. For more information see "Notification framework," beginning on page 328.

Interactions

The Presentation framework uses notifications, models, and views to handle basic interactions between the elements of your program. Commands act on selections, which modify a model's data. The Notification framework conveys the new information back to the presentation, which updates the view. You could write a small program that responds to a menu command by making a simple change to a view, such as changing its color, just by using the Presentation framework, the Views framework, and the Notification framework.

Generally, of course, user interactions are much more complicated, and you need to learn something about the way the Desktop frameworks deal with interactions to write a program that does anything more substantial.

For example, consider the user gesture illustrated by Figure 77. First, the user positions the pointer over an icon representing a document and holds down the mouse button. This selects the file. Next, the user moves the pointer into the autoscroll areas of the folder's window, causing the window to scroll, first horizontally and then vertically. Finally, still holding down the mouse button, the user moves the pointer across the window boundary into another window and releases the mouse button, thus completing the gesture. The end result is the movement of a selected file from one folder to another.

FIGURE 77
AN EXAMPLE OF
A USER GESTURE

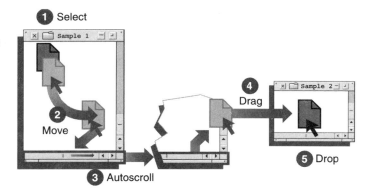

Interaction states

The gesture illustrated in Figure 77 involves some complex interactions. As Figure 78 shows, it can be broken down into five states (Select, Move, Autoscroll, Drag, and Done) and the possible transitions between those states (Mouse Down, Mouse Move, Enter Autoscroll Boundary, Enter Main Area, Cross Window Boundary, Drag, and Mouse Up).

The Select state in Figure 78 receives the initial Mouse Down event. The next event in the gesture is a Mouse Move, so the Select state sends the Mouse Move event to the Move state. The Move state handles further mouse movement until the pointer crosses the autoscroll boundary, at which point the Move state passes control to the Autoscroll state. The Autoscroll state handles further mouse movement until the pointer reenters the main area or crosses the window boundary or a Mouse Up event occurs, and other states take control in turn until the gesture comes to an end.

FIGURE 78
STATE
TRANSITIONS

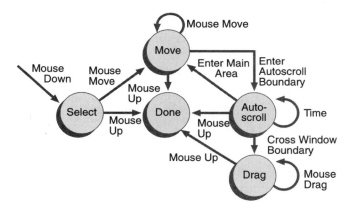

Fortunately, the Presentation framework takes care of parsing these kinds of interactions for you. A presentation translates the syntax of incoming events into the semantics of selections and commands that have meaning for your program, as shown in Figure 79.

FIGURE 79
TRANSLATING
THE SYNTAX OF
EVENTS INTO
THE SEMANTICS
OF SELECTIONS
AND COMMANDS

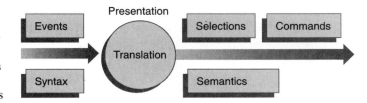

To carry out this translation process for a visual presentation, the Desktop frameworks provide ready-made interactors, controls, and cursor tools that you can use as is or extend as necessary to meet your program's needs. Figure 80 illustrates the role of these states in binding a visual presentation to data.

FIGURE 80
BINDING A
PRESENTATION
TO DATA

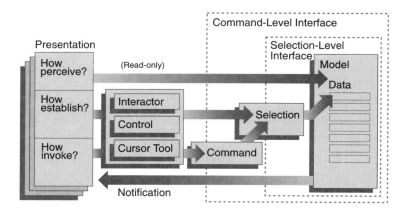

As Figure 80 shows, interactors and controls mediate the binding of a presentation to a selection; cursor tools mediate the binding of a presentation to a command; and notifications communicate changes in the state of the data. The sections that follow describe these concepts.

Interactors

An *interactor* provides a means of breaking down complex user gestures into a set of states that form a structure (like that shown Figure 77) capable of responding to a stream of events. Once this structure is created, the Input framework can send events to the interactor, which handles transitions among the states.

An interactor takes care of everything associated with a given state except for the command provided by your application. Figure 81 illustrates how this works. The interactor is provided by the framework. Its job is to parse events as they arrive. The interactor knows when to go into and out of states in response to events. While a given state, such as a Move state, is in effect, something is supposed to happen, which is where your code comes in. For example, each time the Move state inside the interactor in Figure 78 (page 205) receives a Mouse Move event, it calls the Move command, which handles the incremental movement.

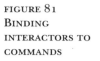

FIGURE 81
BINDING
INTERACTORS TO
COMMANDS

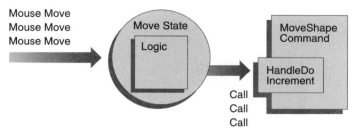

> ✅ NOTE   This is yet another concrete example of the principle summarized by "Don't call us, we'll call you." The interactor calls your code only to determine what to do when the initial transition occurs, what action to take while the state is continuing, and what to do when the state ends. As in the earlier notification example, when examining the flow of control from a debugger, you would see something similar to Figure 15 on page 59: a series of calls to the framework (in this case, the Presentation framework) interspersed with calls to your code.

Controls

Direct manipulation is usually the most obvious way to manipulate an onscreen object. For example, to move an object, you drag it from one place to another. However, many actions require more specialized choices than mouse gestures can accommodate. Controls provide a way for users to make such choices.

A *control* is an onscreen object that sends messages to other objects when a user manipulates it. A control recognizes a specific set of mouse gestures and translates those gestures into the semantics of the object it controls. The User Interface frameworks provide classes that implement standard controls such as check boxes, buttons, menus, sliders, and scrollbars.

A control consists of a view and an associated interactor. The view for a control establishes the appearance of the control to a user. The interactor for a control handles the user's interaction with the control, converting the user's event stream into commands or actions.

Controls that
generate commands

Figure 82 shows a slider control that triggers a command that sets temperature. When the user drags the slider to a new position and releases the mouse button, the interactor triggers the HandleDo handler of the SetTemperature command, which sets the temperature.

FIGURE 82
A CONTROL THAT
GENERATES A COMMAND

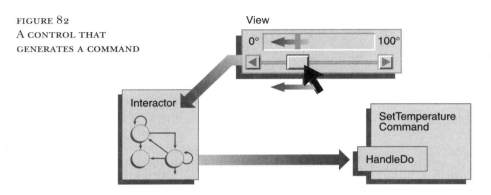

Controls that
generate actions

In many situations, such as a dialog box that presents multiple options, it may not be desirable to trigger a command immediately when a user changes a control setting. Instead, the User Interface frameworks allow interactors to generate actions as well as commands. An *action* is a semantic token that gets sent to an action handler provided by a view, as shown in Figure 83. If a particular view doesn't have a handler for a particular action, the action continues up the view hierarchy until it finds a view that does include a handler for it. If no view in the hierarchy contains a handler for the action, the Presentation framework handles it.

FIGURE 83
A CONTROL
THAT GENERATES
AN ACTION

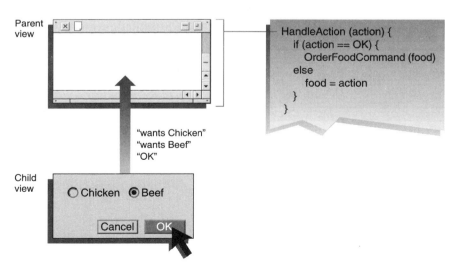

An action handler collects the results of actions until it's appropriate to apply them in some way. It provides an intermediate level between the syntax of events and the semantics of commands and selections.

Figure 83 shows how this works. Suppose a user first clicks Beef. This generates an action, which delivers the string "wants Beef" to the action handler. The action handler sets the food variable to "wants Beef," but doesn't do anything else. The user then clicks "Chicken," and the action again delivers a string, "wants Chicken," to the action handler, which sets its food variable accordingly. The user can keep clicking around like this as long as necessary, sending off actions with the appropriate strings, until he or she clicks the OK button. At that point, the handler generates a command that takes the most recent setting for the food variable as a parameter and applies that setting.

This mechanism makes it possible to keep controls completely separate from the code that handles a series of actions. Figure 84 shows this separation schematically. Because actions are strings, not code, you can easily modify controls without touching the code that implements their behavior. For example, the *cp*Constructor user interface builder allows you to create, edit, and manipulate controls without affecting the logic of your program. For more information about the *cp*Constructor user interface builder, see page 146.

FIGURE 84
ACTION
HANDLERS
PROVIDE AN
INTERMEDIATE
TRANSLATION
BETWEEN
SYNTAX AND
SEMANTICS

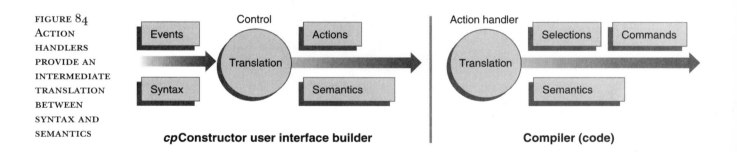

Cursor tools

From the user's point of view, a *cursor tool* is an icon that the pointer changes to when a particular tool is selected in a tool palette and the pointer is over an area of the screen on which that tool can operate.

For example, suppose an eraser tool can erase text and bitmaps, but not individual graphic objects. When the user selects the eraser tool and moves the pointer over a text or bitmap view in the active presentation, the pointer changes to the eraser tool icon. When the pointer passes over any other view in the active presentation, over the space between documents, or over any inactive document, it reverts to the default arrow tool icon, as shown in Figure 85. (Note that there is a difference between the current tool, which is the one the user selected, and the active tool, which is the one that's actually available at a particular time.)

FIGURE 85
USING A CURSOR TOOL

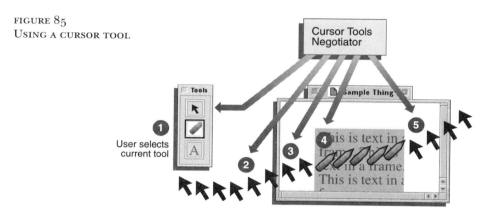

Cursor tools, like controls, depend on views and interactors. The Cursor Tools framework (one of the User Interface frameworks) provides a cursor tools negotiator that performs most of the housekeeping involved in using a cursor tool. Along with additional information you provide via other cursor tool classes, the cursor tool negotiator controls the following aspects of cursor tool operation:

- Detecting when the cursor has crossed into or out of a view in an active presentation

- Overseeing type negotiation between the cursor tool and the active selection in a view to determine whether the current tool is applicable to that type.

- Changing the cursor tool icon as appropriate, depending on whether the current tool is applicable

- Starting an interactor of the appropriate type when a Mouse Down event occurs in a valid view.

Cursor tools themselves need to provide only a list of the types they understand, an interactor for each specified type, and the icon used to identify the tool in a palette. By providing multiple interactors, you can create a cursor tool that works across a wide variety of types. For example, the eraser tool illustrated in Figure 85 might have one interactor for erasing text, another for erasing bitmaps, and so on.

Flow of control

Figure 86 summarizes the flow of control among events, requests, actions, notifications, commands, and selections. Events generate requests, which the Views framework directs to the appropriate view in a presentation, which in turn translates the request into appropriate selections and commands or actions. Changes in the model's data caused by actions or commands are conveyed back to the presentation by means of notifications.

FIGURE 86
FLOW OF
CONTROL
THROUGH A
PRESENTATION

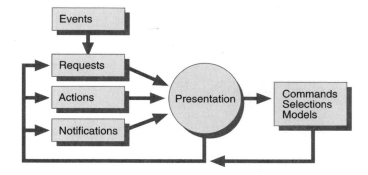

For example, Figure 82 on page 208 shows how a slider control generates a command. When the user releases the mouse button, that event generates a request, which the Views framework directs to the slider's view, whose interactor generates a SetTemperature command, which (by modifying the model) generates a notification back to the slider's view.

Similarly, Figure 83 on page 208 shows how buttons in a dialog box generate actions. When the user clicks OK, that event generates a request, which the Views framework directs to the radio button. The radio button generates an action that travels up the view hierarchy until it reaches its action handler, which generates an appropriate command.

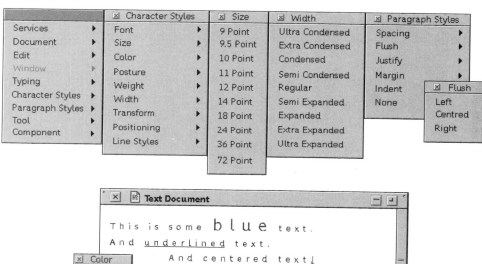

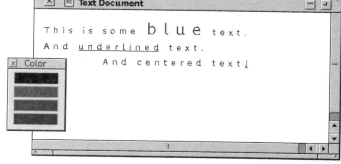

The default text-editing application provided by the Text Editing framework.
For an overview of its features, see page 216.

CHAPTER 8

EMBEDDABLE DATA TYPES

The Presentation framework, which is introduced in Chapter 7, provides the elements of a generic application, including working menus, windows, controls, and so on. In this sense it resembles traditional application frameworks such as MacApp or Microsoft Foundation Classes. Unlike those frameworks, however, the Presentation framework ties together several distinct frameworks (the Desktop frameworks) that can all be extended in interesting ways. It also provides a rich set of default features, especially in the area of collaboration, and highly flexible programming structures that ensure integrated and reliable behavior for all applications derived from it.

Taligent and its investors and developers can use the Presentation framework to create more specialized frameworks that support embeddable data types for specific application domains. This chapter introduces the Text Editing and Graphics Editing frameworks, the first two such frameworks provided by Taligent. They include classes for creating menus, windows, tools, and other data types specifically designed for editing text and graphics. Developers can use these ready-made data types as is or by subclassing to assemble components like those introduced in "Embeddable components," beginning on page 68.

The Embeddable Data Types frameworks can be thought of either as traditional application frameworks for specific types of applications (such as applications for editing text or graphics) or as collections of building blocks to be used in more specialized applications (such as a text field for an order entry application or graphics tools for a project management application).

This chapter also briefly describes the Time Media User Interface framework and the Document Data Access framework, which provide embeddable data types for presenting or recording time media and querying a database. Plans for future releases of the CommonPoint system include extending these frameworks to support fully editable data types like those provided by the Text Editing and Graphics Editing frameworks.

TEXT EDITING FRAMEWORK

The Text Editing framework includes classes that developers can use to assemble a wide range of text elements, from simple text boxes and controls to embeddable components for editing text. It integrates the generic application capabilities of the Presentation framework; the text storage, style, and layout capabilities of the Line Layout framework and Basic Text Services; and the multilingual text input capabilities of Localization Services. Figure 87 illustrates these relationships.

Basic Text Services support Unicode characters, text and style storage formats, and text and paragraph styles. The Line Layout framework displays a line at a time of styled text. The Text Editing framework provides a *text formatter* that fits lines of text displayed by the Line Layout framework into text panels on the basis of line-breaking algorithms and high-level paragraph and page styles.

Localization Services, which include Text Input and Output, support multi-lingual text input and software localization throughout the CommonPoint application system. *Typing interactors* (provided by the Text Editing framework) convert keystrokes into character data on the basis of information from a *typing configuration* (provided by Text Input and Output), which encapsulates language-specific information about keyboard layout, character combinations, and (optionally) input methods for entering ideographic text from nonideographic keyboards.

FIGURE 87
TEXT EDITING
FRAMEWORK

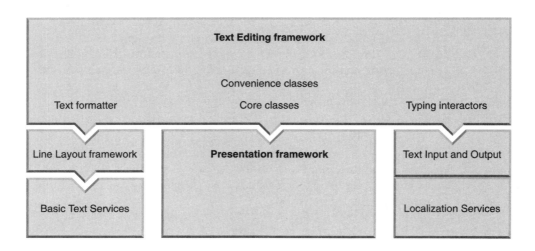

The Text Editing convenience classes, which are intended to be instantiated and used as is, provide specific high-level capabilities such as text highlighter tools and menu support. The core Text Editing classes use the Presentation framework to define basic text selection and interaction capabilities. The core classes are designed to be subclassed by developers who need more specialized text objects than those provided by the convenience classes. For example, the convenience classes themselves are constructed from the core classes in this way.

It's also possible to create simple text-editing elements without using the infrastructure provided by the Presentation and Compound Document frameworks. The classes for text formatters, typing interactors, typing commands, and other specialized objects for working with text can be used to create simple elements, such as text box controls in dialog boxes, that aren't part of a compound document.

The sections that follow briefly summarize some of the capabilities of the Text Editing framework. For detailed information about Basic Text Services and Text Input and Output, see Chapter 10.

Standard Text Editing document

The Text Editing framework includes a convenience class that developers can instantiate to create text-editing stationery for a full-blown text document like the one shown on page 212. Documents based on this and related Text Editing framework classes are derived from the Compound Document framework and therefore share all the characteristics of Compound Document components, including the ability to embed or be embedded in other components.

The classes that underlie the standard Text Editing document are derived from a set of abstract classes that define the protocol needed for handling text data. For example, the class representing the data model for an editable text component is derived (via multiple inheritance) from both the Compound Document framework class TModel and the Text Editing framework class MTextRepresentation.

TModel defines the protocol for handling any data model within a compound document, and MTextRepresentation defines the protocol for manipulating character and style data. This separation gives developers a lot of flexibility in deciding which behaviors to inherit when subclassing from the Text Editing framework.

Standard Text Editing features

The standard text component provides the default capabilities listed here. All of these features can also be implemented independently of the Compound Document framework in simple non-document-based text elements of various kinds:

- Multilingual text handling, including input and display
- Cursor placement and text selection by clicking and dragging the mouse
- Word selection by double-clicking and sentence selection by triple-clicking
- Extension of selections by clicking and dragging the mouse with the Shift key pressed
- Automatic font substitution for all text input
- Cutting, copying, and pasting of text selections within a document or between documents
- Selection or deletion of all text currently in the document
- Free intermixing of characters from any script by changing the active typing configuration
- Application of different combinations of character styles from character to character
- Application of paragraph styles such as line spacing and margins
- Autopositioning (scrolling to keep cursor in view during typing)
- Basic printing capabilities, including pagination and imposition.

Future versions of the Text Editing framework will provide additional features, such as device-independent line wrapping, device-dependent spacing, and multicolumn formatting.

Standard Text Editing menus

The default text-editing document includes a menu of commands used for text editing. It's possible to extend or replace any of these commands or submenus. The standard commands can be used for the following operations:

- **General editing commands.** The user can undo and redo text changes; cut, copy, and paste text selections; select all text currently in the document; and delete selected text.

- **Changing the typing configuration.** The user can activate any currently installed typing configuration. In future releases, users will be able to toggle typing configurations by using keyboard commands. (Typing configurations control text input. They are introduced in Chapter 10, beginning on page 261.)

- **Applying character styles.** The user can apply a variety of styles to characters, including:
  - Fonts
  - Point size
  - Color
  - Posture—italicizing text
  - Weight—creating bold or light text
  - Width—condensing or expanding text
  - Transformations—skewing, stretching, and rotating text
  - Position—subscripting or superscripting text or controlling the letter spacing
  - Line styles—underlining or striking through text

- **Specifying paragraph formatting.** The user can apply paragraph styles, including:
  - Line spacing between and within paragraphs
  - Flush left, right, or center
  - Justification
  - Leading and trailing margin widths
  - Indentation

- **Using text cursor tools.** The user can select from a number of text cursor tools, including highlighters, markers, and a style eraser.

- **Changing the appearance of the presentation.** The user can set the text margins relative to the panel size and set colors for the presentation background, the selection highlighting, and the insertion point caret.

GRAPHICS EDITING FRAMEWORK

The Graphics Editing framework provides classes that developers can instantiate or extend to create embeddable components for editing graphics. These can range from relatively simple components for use within larger desktop publishing, charting, or presentation applications to dedicated drawing or CAD applications.

The Graphics Editing framework integrates the generic application capabilities of the Presentation framework with the graphics capabilities of the 2-D Graphics framework. Plans for future versions of the CommonPoint system include a 3-D equivalent of the Graphics Editing framework based on the 3-D Graphics framework.

Figure 88 shows the high-level Graphics Editing architecture. The shaded boxes in the figure show that the framework consists of Standard Graphics Editing and Basic Graphics Editing. The other boxes represent the Graphics system (specifically, the 2-D Graphics framework and related classes) and some of the Desktop frameworks.

Standard Graphics Editing is built on the Presentation framework and assumes the use of the standard Compound Document model (TModel) to store graphics data. It includes a variety of convenience classes that developers can instantiate to create standard menus; standard tools for drawing lines, rectangles, polygons,

FIGURE 88
THE
GRAPHICS
EDITING
FRAMEWORK

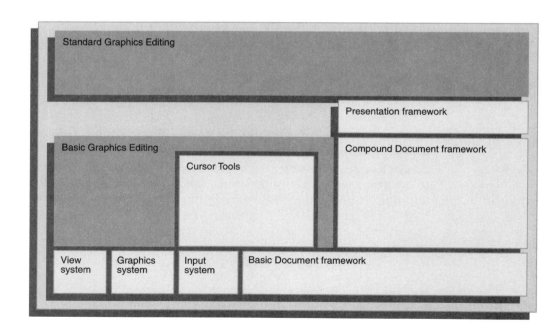

curves, and text; and so on. The graphics objects created by these tools can be selected, dragged, scaled, rotated, manipulated, and edited. Plans for future releases of the CommonPoint system include supporting additional features, such as grouping and ungrouping objects and snapping to an underlying grid.

Developers who are writing sophisticated drawing programs might want to modify or replace some of the underlying code provided by Standard Graphics Editing. Developers who just want to include a generic set of drawing tools in an application without spending a lot of development time can use the convenience classes with little or no modification.

Basic Graphics Editing doesn't use the Presentation or Compound Document frameworks and doesn't assume the use of a standard model to store graphics data. Developers who wish to create specialized graphics tools or capabilities that aren't supported by Standard Graphics Editing can still take advantage of the basic drawing and selection mechanism provided by Basic Graphics Editing while supplying their own model.

The Graphics Editing framework and the Desktop frameworks

As explained in Chapter 7, components based on the Compound Document framework need a model to manage their data, a view to display their data, and (optionally) an interface for the user that consists of menus, tools, and controls. Developers can create the data model, view, and user interface for a graphics component in three ways:

- Use the Standard Graphics Editing classes of the Graphics Editing framework (which in turn use the Desktop frameworks) and the appropriate Graphics classes.
- Use the Basic Graphics Editing classes of the Graphics Editing framework for basic drawing and selection capabilities, the Desktop frameworks for the data model and user interface, and the appropriate Graphics classes.
- Use the Desktop frameworks and the appropriate Graphics classes to build a custom graphics component.

The Graphics Editing framework provides the working elements of a graphics-editing component that developers can assemble according to their own needs. Using Standard Graphics Editing requires the least amount of code and provides the most default capabilities but the least amount of flexibility. Using Basic Graphics Editing involves writing more code but provides additional flexibility. Using the Desktop frameworks directly requires the most code but provides the most flexibility.

It's also possible to use the Graphics system directly without creating a component; for example, to draw arbitrary 2-D or 3-D graphics directly in a window. The Graphics frameworks and classes are described in Chapter 9.

A typical graphics-editing document

This section describes a sample application called Mars, illustrated in Figure 89, that's based on the Graphics Editing framework. This application, which consists of 126 lines of code, illustrates some of the features supported by the Graphics Editing framework. It has a tool menu that contains tools for drawing lines, rectangles, polygons, curves, text, and so on. The user can create multiple objects, select them, drag them around the screen, scale and rotate them, change their colors, and perform other standard editing tasks. If a developer wants to change some aspect of that code—for example, to indicate selections by a moving dashed line ("marching ants") instead of the solid outline provided by the default CommonPoint implementation—it's easy to override the functions involved.

Mars supports standard graphics data types, including points, lines, rectangles, and curves, without any further modification. To add new graphics primitives, a developer subclasses from the corresponding Graphics Editing classes, thereby inheriting all the standard behavior (drawing, selecting, rotating, and so on). This can be useful for creating specialized drawing programs such as a CAD package that draws transistors, resistors, and diodes instead of points, lines, rectangles, and curves. No matter what new primitives may be required, hooks are in place that permit manipulation of the resulting objects without having to reinvent the editing functions.

FIGURE 89
MARS
DRAWING
PROGRAM

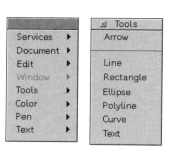
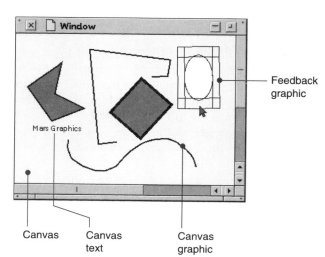

Mars also supports copying and pasting, multilevel undo and redo, printing, saving, and some of the other default capabilities provided by the Compound Document framework. The menus and windows are fully functional, and all user interface elements not only look and act like the same elements in other programs based on the Desktop frameworks but also are controlled by exactly the same code.

The basic capabilities of Mars, which are briefly summarized in the sections that follow, illustrate the kinds of features that the Graphics Editing framework provides for use by any application.

Menus

Mars lets a user draw, edit, and manipulate graphic shapes on a drawing surface called a canvas. It includes a menu of commands used for graphics editing, any of which can be extended or replaced.

Edit menu

The standard Edit menu commands work on the currently selected canvas graphic or graphics. They let the user undo and redo changes, select all canvas graphics currently in the document, delete selected canvas graphics, and cut, copy, and paste.

Tool menu

The Tool menu commands let the user draw graphics on the canvas. The User Interface frameworks also include classes developers can use to implement these capabilities with a tool palette rather than menus.

The tools in the Tool menu work much like the equivalent tools in traditional graphics applications. To draw a canvas graphic, the user first chooses a creation tool from the Tool menu, which changes the cursor to a crosshair for a line, rectangle, ellipse, polyline, or polygon, to an I-beam for text, and to a pencil for a curve. The user can then drag the tool on the canvas to create the corresponding shape. Graphics added to the canvas are placed on top of any existing graphics. The Arrow tool allows the user to select, transform, and drag any graphic.

Color menu

Graphics are initially drawn with a black 1-point frame and a white fill. The Color menu lets the user select a red, green, or blue frame combined with a red, green, or blue fill. Although Mars is a sample program that supports only these simple choices, it's also possible to use the Graphics Editing framework to support the selection of arbitrary colors.

Pen menu

Graphics are initially drawn with a 1-point frame. The Lines menu lets the user select from possible line widths. The line widths are in the standard graphics world coordinate units, where one unit equals 1/72 of an inch.

Selecting canvas graphics

To select a canvas graphic, the user chooses the Arrow tool from the Tool menu and does one of the following:

- Clicks on an edge or filled interior of a canvas graphic
- Drags a selection box around all canvas graphics the user wants to select
- Adds a selection to the currently selected canvas graphics by pressing the Shift key and clicking the new graphic
- Adds multiple selections to the currently selected canvas graphics by pressing the Shift key and dragging a selection box around the new graphics
- Uses the Select All item on the Edit menu to select all canvas graphics

All selected canvas graphics in Mars display a feedback graphic like the one shown in Figure 90. Once a canvas graphic is selected, the user can change its colors or pen width. The feedback graphic also lets the user manipulate the selected graphic with the Arrow tool. The feedback graphic provides scale, rotation, and translation (SRT) feedback with four lines that mark out four corners for scaling (stretching), four sides for rotating, and a center for translating (moving).

The Graphics Editing framework supports other feedback mechanisms, such as handles similar to those used with MacDraw, and developers can also subclass to create their own mechanisms.

FIGURE 90
USING THE
FEEDBACK
GRAPHIC TO
MANIPULATE
A SELECTED
OBJECT

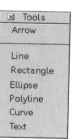
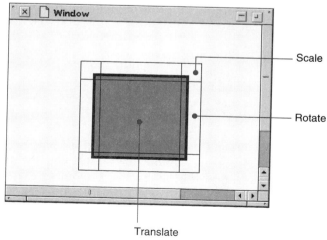

TIME MEDIA USER INTERFACE FRAMEWORK

The Time Media User Interface (UI) framework provides classes for creating lightweight embeddable components that play and record a media sequence such as a QuickTime™ movie, MIDI file, or audio clip. The framework allows a developer to perform any of these tasks:

- Embed a media presentation in a view
- Embed a media presentation in a document
- Embed multiple media presentations in a single document
- Provide custom control panels for time media presentations

Embedding a media presentation in a view is the easiest way to support time media in a CommonPoint program. The Time Media frameworks include player classes (TSound, TMIDI, and TMovie) that can play audio, MIDI, and video sequences for presentation by a *media presenter* provided by the Time Media UI framework. The media presenter acts as a bridge between the Time Media frameworks and the Document framework. It can be used to play or record a media sequence from within a Compound Document component or from within a simple lightweight view that doesn't inherit all the characteristics of embeddable components.

Once embedded in a compound document, a media presentation provides standard windows and controls like those shown in Figure 91 for loading, playing, recording, stopping, seeking, or adjusting the volume of a media sequence.

FIGURE 91
STANDARD
WINDOWS AND
CONTROLS FOR
PRESENTING
A VIDEO
SEQUENCE

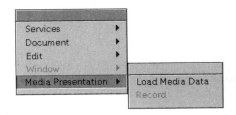

The player controls shown in Figure 91, which are built from standard elements provided by the User Interface frameworks, resemble those found on a typical audiocassette or videotape player. They allow the user to play or record a single media sequence. The Time Media UI framework also includes a set of media stationery classes that can be used programmatically or, in the form of stationery pads, by a user to create media presentations that import and play audio, MIDI, or video sequences.

Programmers who are creating full-fledged time media applications can use the Time Media frameworks directly. They are introduced in Chapter 11.

Plans for future releases of the CommonPoint system include extending the Time Media UI framework to support editing of different media types in ways that parallel the editing support provided by the Text Editing and Graphics Editing frameworks.

DOCUMENT DATA ACCESS FRAMEWORK

The Document Data Access framework provides a high-level interface, based on the Compound Document framework, that allows developers to create database access documents (DADs) rapidly for users who are familiar with Structured Query Language (SQL). SQL is an industry standard for accessing relational databases such as IBM's DB2® or Oracle or Sybase databases.

Figure 92 shows a typical DAD displaying tabular multirecord, multifield data retrieved from a relational database. DADs are compatible with other components based on the Compound Document framework.

The Document Data Access framework builds on services provided by the Data Access framework. For a description of the Document Data Access framework in the context of the Data Access framework, see the section beginning on page 308.

Plans for future releases of the CommonPoint system include extending the Document Data Access framework to support additional capabilities. The Object Access framework, a new framework Taligent plans to build on top of the Document Data Access framework, will provide higher-level C++ abstractions of SQL objects for use by database administrators and others who need to create custom database objects but aren't familiar with SQL.

FIGURE 92
A TYPICAL
DATABASE
ACCESS
DOCUMENT

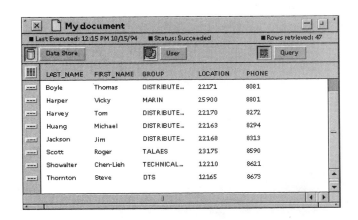

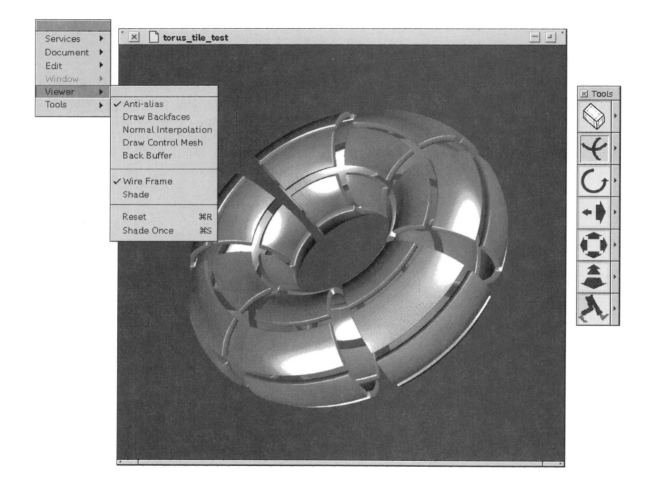

The piece of code used to draw this 3-D graphic consists of 29 lines (for details, see "Creating a more complex graphic," beginning on page 249*). From top to bottom, the tools in the tool palette support a virtual 3-D box with handles for 3-D rotation, simple 3-D rotation, simple 2-D rotation, scaling, 2-D translaton, 3-D translation, and a walk-through mode that can be used to navigate through 3-D graphics scenes.*

CHAPTER 9

GRAPHICS

The Graphics system is a self-contained collection of frameworks and classes for creating and displaying 2-D and 3-D graphics. Developers can use the Graphics system to add graphics capabilities to any CommonPoint program.

To create a graphics application or add a graphics component to an application, developers typically use Graphics classes, either with the Graphics Editing framework (which in turn uses the Desktop frameworks) or with the Desktop frameworks directly to create editable graphics components. The Graphics Editing framework, which is described in Chapter 8 beginning on page 218, provides default editing capabilities and user interface elements for editable graphics components. It's also possible to use Graphics classes directly without creating a component; for example, to draw arbitrary 2-D and 3-D graphics directly to a window.

Developers can use the client interfaces of the Graphics system simply by instantiating classes and calling the applicable member functions. However, because the Graphics system is itself built from several closely related frameworks and class libraries, many Graphics classes can also be customized, permitting developers to create their own classes for specialized graphics needs. Although the Graphics system is mathematically quite sophisticated, developers don't need any knowledge of linear algebra or other advanced math to use it effectively.

Because computer graphics are important for nearly all interactive applications, this chapter describes the Graphics system in considerable technical detail. Readers who aren't familiar with computer graphics terminology should consult a standard graphics textbook such as Foley et al. (1994).

GRAPHICS ARCHITECTURE

In most graphics systems, shapes such as lines, rectangles, and circles are tightly coupled with attributes such as color, patterns, and line thickness. This approach works if you want to draw standard shapes with standard attributes but makes it difficult to create graphics with specialized shapes or attributes. For example, if you want to create a unique shape and fill it with a gradient of color that changes smoothly across the spectrum, you must usually provide all the code that performs that task (if it can be done at all) with little or no help from the system.

The CommonPoint graphics system allows you to create specialized objects and effects with much less effort. A graphic's modeling, attributes, and geometry are all controlled by separate objects. A *graphic object* can draw, print, and stream itself. It has an associated *attribute bundle* that specifies attributes such as color and thickness, and a *geometry* that provides the mathematical abstractions for the lines, curves, shapes, fonts, surfaces, and so on used to define the object.

Because the modeling, attributes, and geometry of a graphic object are abstracted and separated in this way, any aspect of the object can be extended without changing the way it works with the other classes and frameworks in the system. For example, you can add transparency or gradient fill to a graphic object's attribute bundle without changing the graphic object or its geometry.

Displaying a graphic object involves drawing it to a *drawing port,* which in turn invokes the rendering operations of a particular graphics device. *Graphics devices* provide graphical imaging services for a particular category of output device, such as a frame buffer of a particular size and bit depth, a PostScript device, or a vector plotter.

These are the major frameworks and classes in the Graphics system:

- **The 2-D Graphics and 3-D Graphics frameworks** manage individual graphic objects. They provide a default set of classes for creating and drawing various kinds of lines and shapes and allow you to derive custom graphic objects. All 2-D and 3-D Graphics classes are subclassed from the same abstract class, MDrawable, and they all know how to draw, print, and stream themselves and perform hit detection. They also include transformation functions for translating, rotating, and scaling graphic objects.
- **The 2-D and 3-D Attribute Bundle classes** manage graphic objects' attributes, such as color, pattern, and thickness. Classes derived from the abstract class TGrafBundle maintain a list of visual properties, including fill color, frame color, pen pattern, dithering, end caps, joints, and properties that determine image sampling when an image is enlarged or reduced. Developers can define additional subclasses that implement new attributes and still interact predictably with other programs and other parts of the system.
- **The 2-D and 3-D Geometry classes** provide the mathematical abstractions (lines, curves, and so on) used to define graphic objects. Unlike graphic objects, geometries are pure abstractions, not drawable objects. The Geometry

classes have no parent classes because they don't share any behavior and aren't intended to be subclassed and customized. To add capabilities or create complex shapes, you derive from the basic 2-D and 3-D graphic object classes and override or add functions as necessary.

- **The 2-D and 3-D Transform classes,** TGrafMatrix and TGrafMatrix3D, allow you to apply custom algebraic operations to the set of coordinate points that define a 2-D or 3-D graphic object. Such operations involve multiplying a coordinate vector by a *transformation matrix,* resulting in new transformed coordinates. This can be used for a variety of purposes, including changing coordinate systems, rotating and scaling graphics, placing them in a specific location on the screen, perspective, and so on.

- **The Drawing Port classes** define the ports to which graphic objects are drawn. A drawing port is an abstraction for a drawing channel to a particular device or "piece of paper" that displays a graphic. The actual device might be a monitor of a specific bit depth, a printer, a graphics accelerator board, a fax machine, an offscreen bitmap, or just about anything else that can present an image. All port classes are derived from TGrafPort, which provides the basic capabilities for a multitasking port that allows multiple threads to draw to it simultaneously without interference.

- **The TImage class** is a specialized 2-D graphics class. It's possible to obtain a port for drawing to an image object in much the same way that you obtain a port for drawing to a graphics device driver. Each image object has an associated pixel buffer that can be used for various purposes, such as back buffering (used for drawing to an offscreen image, then drawing the whole image to the screen) or drawing an image prior to saving it in a particular file format.

- **The Graphics Devices framework** provides basic capabilities for graphics device drivers, such as rasterization, device transformations, color maps, and dithering. It not only simplifies the writing of device drivers for new hardware but also supports application functions. For example, the CommonPoint system includes a bounding box device driver that doesn't display anything. Instead, it accumulates the bounds of all the primitives drawn to it and returns the total bounds for all of them.

- **Font Support** provides an integrated, uniform interface for accessing all kinds of fonts, including fonts from different manufacturers, fonts stored and displayed using different formats (including outline fonts), and large ideographic fonts.

- **The Color frameworks** provide an extensive set of color spaces with an optional color-matching mechanism. Color spaces available include RGB color, printing color spaces such as Lab color, and television color spaces such as YIQ color. Color matching is useful for tasks such as matching the colors of displayed graphics to the best colors available on the printer when the display monitor and the printer do not support exactly the same colors.

The Graphics system also provides low-level support for sprites, pixel buffers, and abstract display screens.

2-D AND 3-D GRAPHICS FEATURES

This section summarizes the features provided by the 2-D and 3-D Graphics frameworks and related classes. For an introduction to the Graphics Device framework, see page 243. For an introduction to the CommonPoint font system and color frameworks, see page 244 and page 245, respectively.

High-level geometries

The 2-D and 3-D curve and surface geometries are defined by nonuniform rational B-splines (NURBS). *Nonuniform* means that the parameterization of the curve or surface can be changed to allow kinks, gaps, and smooth joins. *Rational* means that rational polynomials are used to allow exact representations of circles, ellipses, and other conic sections. *B-spline* stands for basis spline, a spline curve similar to the Bézier curve except that it facilitates better curve fitting and modeling. For more information about NURBS and other computer graphics concepts, see Beatty, Barsky, and Bartels (1987) and Farin (1993).

IEEE double precision (64-bit) floating point arithmetic

The floating point capabilities described in "Numerics," which begins on page 366, support fine resolution and high accuracy in a variety of media using a global coordinate system rather than screen coordinates. Combined with the sophisticated modeling capabilities of the 3-D Graphics classes, double precision of up to 16 decimal places allows the use of CommonPoint data structures not only for displaying complex models on the screen but also for CAD and manufacturing purposes. For example, the same data structures used to model automobile engine parts on the screen are precise enough to be used directly for manufacturing specifications.

Device-independent coordinate systems

The Graphics system is not pixel based. Instead, it uses a coordinate unit of 1/72 of an inch, or 1 point. A line with a length of 72 coordinate units is always 1 inch long regardless of the resolution of the device. Any CommonPoint program can draw graphics directly to any screen or printer without writing extra code to accommodate different resolutions.

The Graphics system's use of coordinate units allows graphics programs to run any hardware driven by a graphics device driver based on the Graphics Devices framework. The 2-D Geometry classes use these coordinate units for *x*- and *y*-axes, and the 3-D Geometry classes use them for *x*-, *y*-, and *z*-axes.

As shown in Figure 93 and Figure 94, the 2-D coordinate system is left-handed (y-axis going down), and the 3-D coordinate system is right-handed (y-axis going up). These arrangements reflect customary ways of measuring 2-D and 3-D space. The left-handed 2-D coordinate system matches a standard document page that starts at the top left and extends downward and to the right. The right-handed 3-D coordinate system is oriented around a central origin identified as the point (0,0,0).

It's possible to transform the 2-D and 3-D coordinate systems to represent a particular application's modeling and viewing needs. For example, to make the 3-D y-axis point in the same direction as in the 2-D coordinate system, you can move the 3-D camera 180 degrees so that the y-axis points down. (The 3-D camera is described beginning on page 233.) Similarly, you can use modeling transforms to match the coordinate spaces used for a particular problem domain—anything from angstrom units to light years.

Two-dimensional coordinates

Figure 93 shows the x- and y- axes for a 2-D coordinate system. The positive coordinate units along the x-axis lie to the right of the origin, and the positive coordinate units along the y-axis lie below the origin. The grid lines represent where points in coordinate units lie. For example, the point (5,3) is five grid lines in the positive x direction and three lines in the positive y direction. The pixels are positioned in the spaces between the grid lines. For example, each space contains one pixel on a 72-dot-per-inch (dpi) monitor, or four pixels on a 144-dpi monitor.

FIGURE 93
TWO-
DIMENSIONAL
COORDINATE
UNITS

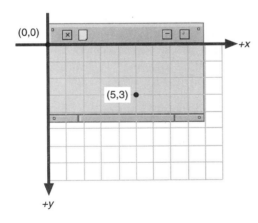

Three-dimensional coordinates

By default, positive coordinate units along the *x*-axis lie to the right of the origin; positive coordinate units along the *y*-axis lie above the origin; and positive coordinate units along the *z*-axis lie "out from the screen" from the origin toward the viewer. By default, the position of the origin is the middle of the view. Figure 94 illustrates these relationships.

FIGURE 94
THREE-DIMENSIONAL
COORDINATE UNITS

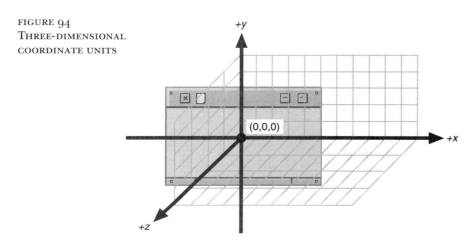

Graphics and geometry classes

The Graphics system provides graphics and geometry classes that can be used for every area of graphics programming. These include classes for creating 2-D and 3-D shapes and curves, defining and shading surfaces, grouping graphic objects while still permitting them to be transformed individually (useful for animation), and creating arbitrary 2-D shapes with Constructive Area Geometry (CAG). The most important of these classes are listed in "2-D and 3-D Graphics classes" and "2-D and 3-D Geometry classes," beginning on page 234.

**Integrated 2-D
and 3-D graphics**

To draw a graphic, you create it and call its Draw function. The Draw function takes a drawing port as a parameter. You can draw 2-D and 3-D graphics into the same drawing port. When drawing 3-D graphics or when drawing 2-D and 3-D graphics together, you set three attributes—camera, light, and atmosphere—that determine the appearance of all graphic objects in the scene.

The camera attribute determines a near clipping plane, a projection plane, a far clipping plane, and other aspects of the way a 3-D graphic looks when it is projected. If you think of a person holding a camera, that person decides where to stand in relation to the subject (the reference point), which direction to aim the camera (center of interest), and whether to hold the camera parallel to the horizon or to rotate it left or right (tilt angle). Likewise, the camera attribute allows you to set the reference point, center of interest, and tilt angle.

Any 2-D or 3-D graphic created in one CommonPoint program can be copied and pasted into any other CommonPoint program. It makes no difference which program created the graphic. Most transferred graphics can be added to, deleted from, and otherwise manipulated in the programs to which they have been transferred.

To use 2-D and 3-D graphics together, you use the 2-D coordinate system to specify the points of a 2-D graphic and the 3-D coordinate system to specify the points of a 3-D graphic. The camera attribute makes it possible to extract 2-D coordinates from a 3-D scene, so that a particular point in a 3-D graphic can be projected onto a 2-D screen. It's also possible to place a 2-D graphic on a 3-D graphic (such as a 2-D sign on a 3-D building). When you move the camera, the 2-D graphic is translated appropriately, remains on the 3-D graphic, and looks right.

The 3-D curve geometry takes any 3-D geometry in its constructor, plus a 2-D curve geometry. This design makes it possible to convert any 2-D geometry to a 3-D geometry.

2-D AND 3-D GRAPHICS CLASSES

The 2-D and 3-D Graphics classes inherit from MDrawable, which specifies the minimal protocol for drawing, printing, and streaming a 2-D or 3-D graphic object. Each concrete class derived from MDrawable provides its own Draw member function for drawing a line, rectangle, polygon, and so on.

As shown in Figure 95, MGraphic and MGraphic3D derive from MDrawable. MGraphic provides basic 2-D graphic capabilities, and MGraphic3D provides basic 3-D graphics capabilities.

FIGURE 95
MDRAWABLE,
MGRAPHIC,
AND
MGRAPHIC3D

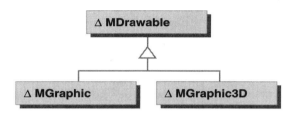

MGraphic provides the protocol common to all 2-D graphics—obtaining attribute bundle information, transforming the graphic, finding the bounds of the graphic, and detecting whether the graphic has been selected by the user (hit detection). Figure 96 shows the basic class relationships for MGraphic, which are nearly identical for MGraphic3D.

FIGURE 96
CLASS
RELATIONSHIPS
FOR MGRAPHIC

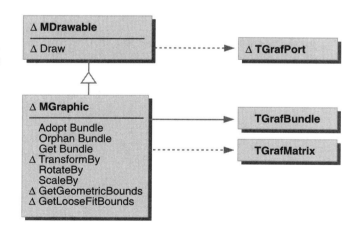

MGraphic and MGraphic3D use three other classes as parameters:

- **TGrafPort** (for both 2-D and 3-D) provides a drawing port.
- **TGrafBundle** (or TGrafBundle3D) provides the graphic's attribute bundle.
- **TGrafMatrix** (or TGrafMatrix3D) provides the graphic's custom transformation matrix, if any.

All classes derived from MGraphic can draw themselves. Drawing information for a graphic (its geometric shape and attributes such as color and line style) is passed to the drawing port when the Draw function of the graphic is called.

The 2-D and 3-D Graphics classes whose names include a geometry (TLine, TCurve, TEllipse, and so on) are derived from MGraphic and MGraphic3D. As shown in Figure 97, a Graphics class (such as TLine) has one or more Geometry classes (such as TGLine) that provide the mathematical description for the graphic object. A graphics class has public functions specific to that graphic that allow interaction with its referenced geometry.

FIGURE 97
TLINE
AND ITS
REFERENCED
GEOMETRY

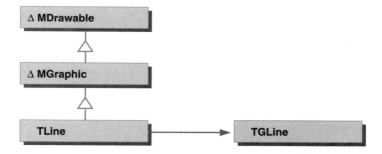

You can customize the Graphics classes to add capabilities or to create your own custom graphic objects, such as a triangle, an automobile, or a human figure. This is done by deriving from the basic Graphics classes and overriding the public and protected functions to change the behavior or add shapes. Because a complex graphic is actually a combination of basic Geometry classes, the drawing port can draw it because it knows all of the basic Geometry classes.

Graphics naming conventions

The names of Graphics classes are distinguished from the names of Geometry classes and the names of 2-D classes are distinguished from the names of 3-D classes as follows:

- Graphics class names begin with the letter "T" followed by the name of the geometry (for example, TLine).
- Geometry class names begin with the letters "TG" followed by the name of the geometry (for example, TGLine).
- All 3-D geometry and Graphics classes end with the letters "3D" (for example, TGLine3D and TLine3D).

2-D Graphics classes

Figure 98 shows the standard classes derived from MGraphic.

The relationships between the classes shown in Figure 98 and the basic 2-D Geometry classes are shown on page 239. You can use the 2-D Graphics classes as follows:

- **TView.** Although derived from MGraphic, TView is the abstract base class for the View framework. A view defines the portion of the display device to which a program can draw. See "Views and the Views framework," beginning on page 198, for more information.
- **TPicture.** Lets you create a system of references to a collection of individual 2-D graphic objects that are treated as a unit.
- **TCachedGraphic.** Lets you cache graphic objects to improve performance. (This class will be implemented in future versions of the CommonPoint system.)
- **TGraphicHierarchy.** Parent to TGraphicGroup, which lets you create a hierarchy of references to a collection of 2-D graphic objects that can be individually transformed.

FIGURE 98
CLASSES DERIVED FROM MGRAPHIC

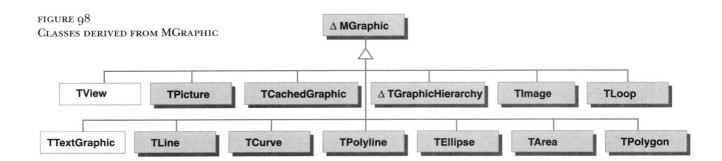

- **TImage.** Defines a pixel-based image that is appropriately filtered (enlarged or compressed) so the image is the same size in inches on any monitor and aliasing is less visible.
- **TTextGraphic.** Encapsulates a text instance and treats it like a graphic object. TTextGraphic objects can be transformed just like any other graphic objects.
- **TArea.** Supports the use of Constructive Area Geometry (CAG) to create arbitrary shapes by performing Boolean operations on 2-D geometries.
- **TLoop, TLine, TCurve, TPolyline, TEllipse, and TPolygon.** Basic 2-D Graphics classes.

Taligent plans to support these additional capabilities in future versions of the CommonPoint system:

- **2-D deformations.** Classes that facilitate distorted visual effects such as text displayed along a curve or in an elliptical shape
- **2-D cached graphics.** Classes that improve the drawing speed of 2-D graphics by saving information from previous uses.

3-D Graphics classes

Figure 99 and Figure 100 show the standard classes derived from MGraphic3D.

The classes shown in Figure 99 play the following roles:

- **TLine3D, TCurve3D, and TPolyline3D.** Basic 3-D Graphics classes.
- **TSurface3D.** Implements smoothly curved surfaces used to model cones, cylinders, spheres, and so on. The 3-D Sweeps classes shown in Figure 100 can also be used to model such surfaces. Using TSurface3D requires a technical understanding of the creation of quadratic shapes.
- **TGraphicHierarchy3D.** Parent to TGraphicGroup3D, which lets you create a hierarchy of references to a collection of 3-D graphic graphics that can be transformed individually.

FIGURE 99
SOME CLASSES DERIVED FROM
MGRAPHIC3D

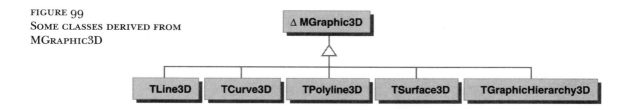

Figure 100 shows the 3-D classes used to create swept surfaces by moving 2-D objects through 3-D space; for example, by rotating a circle to make a torus or by extruding 2-D text into 3-D block letters.

FIGURE 100

3-D SWEEPS

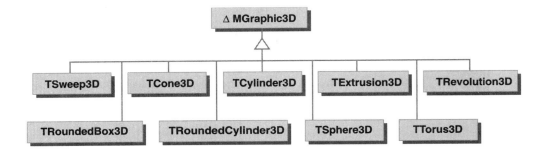

The 3-D Graphics framework does not currently supply the following features:

- **Traditional volumetric rendering.** Used to show the interior of a solid 3-D graphic. However, it is possible for experienced graphics programmers to use the sampled surface geometry to do volumetric rendering by converting the surface into triangles.

- **Constructive Solid Geometry (CSG).** Used for operations such as adding portions to or subtracting portions from a 3-D graphic object.

- **Global illumination methods.** These require the Graphics system to have access to an entire scene at a time. Examples include radiosity and ray tracing.

2-D AND 3-D GEOMETRY CLASSES

The Geometry classes provide geometric shapes that are used by the Graphics classes. Every basic graphics class owns at least one basic geometry class that is created or deleted when the graphic is created or deleted.

The 2-D and 3-D Graphics classes are constructed from their corresponding Geometry classes. Most of the Geometry classes have overloaded constructors that let you create the geometries from points, point arrays, or other basic 2-D Geometry classes. For example, a rectangle is a four-sided polygon. You can construct a rectangular TGPolygon from four TGPoints or from a TGRect. The TGPolygon can be used to construct a TGPolyline, TGCurve, or TGLoop, which can then be passed to the constructor of the corresponding graphic (TPolyline, TCurve, or TLoop).

These are the 2-D Geometry classes and the corresponding 2-D Graphics classes:

Shape	2-D Geometry class	Description	Corresponding 2-D Graphics class
●	TGPoint	2-D point	None
●	TGRPoint	Rational (homogeneous) 2-D points	None
●●●	TGPointArray	An extensible array of 2-D points	None
●●●	TGRPointArray	An extensible array of 2-D rational (homogeneous) points	None
◄—►	TGInfiniteLine	Basic building block for other classes	None
▭	TGRect	Basic building block for other classes	TPolygon, TEllipse
—	TGLine	Line segment	TLine
∧∧	TGPolyline	Set of points connected by line segments	TPolyline
⊃	TGCurve	Free-form curve, arc, and path geometry	TCurve
◯	TGEllipse	Elliptical shapes including circles	TEllipse
◖	TGLoop	Closed curve that can be filled and framed	TLoop
◁	TGPolygon	Closed polyline that can be filled and framed	TPolygon
⇨	TGArea	Arbitrary shape created from Boolean operations on one or more 2-D geometries	TArea
ABC	TGGlyphRun	For local text layout	None
	TGImage	Pixel-based graphic	TImage

These are the 3-D Geometry classes and the corresponding 3-D Graphics classes:

Shape	Basic 3-D Geometry classes	Description	Corresponding 3-D Graphics classes
	TGPoint3D	3-D point	None
	TGRPoint3D	Rational (homogeneous) 3-D points	None
	TGPointArray3D	An extensible array of 3-D points	None
	TGRPointArray3D	An extensible array of rational (homogeneous) 3-D points	None
	TGBox3D	Basic building block for other classes	None
	TGLine3D	Line segment defined in 3-D space by two endpoints	TLine3D
	TGPolyline3D	Set of points in 3-D space connected by straight lines	TPolyline3D
	TGCurve3D	Free-form 3-D curve, arc, and path geometry	TCurve3D, TSweep3D, TRevolution3D, TExtrusion3D
	TGSurface3D	Common quadratic shapes such as cones, cylinders, spheres, tori, and so on	TSurface3D, TSweep3D, TCone3D, TCylinder3D, TExtrusion3D, TSphere3D, TTorus3D, TRevolution3D, TRoundedCylinder3D, TBox3D

A special 3-D Geometry class, TSampledSurface3D, is used to to model complex shapes such as digitized or scanned data, fractal surfaces, and fluid flow. For example, a 3-D laser rangefinder produces data that basically consists of row after row of points ("heights") stored in a data structure.

DRAWING PORTS

A drawing port is an abstraction for channeling graphics to a graphics device such as a monitor or a printer or anywhere else you like. To draw a particular graphic, you pass information about the graphic, its attribute bundle, its geometry, and any transformations to a drawing port for a particular device. The drawing port has a set of Draw functions that correspond to the Render functions of the graphics device. This arrangement keeps the drawing port separate from the graphics device it controls, so that drawing operations are completely independent of the devices doing the actual drawing.

Similarly, the separation between the low-level geometry used by the port and the higher-level graphic object being drawn permits developers to use graphics for their own purposes without having to translate back and forth between Graphics system data structures and their own application formats. For example, if an application requires a grid object, it could define it as a group of TLine graphic objects and then assign colors and other attributes to the lines. But a more efficient way to do this would be to specify a grid object as geometries for x horizontal units and y vertical units and then construct the lines on the fly when actually drawing the object, thus avoiding any need to store the lines individually.

It's possible to call the Draw function for any class derived from MGraphic and pass it a drawing port. This corresponds to the traditional "object.Draw" approach taught in introductory OOP textbooks. However, it's also possible to draw some geometries by calling the port's Draw function directly. This separation of the Draw function from the graphic object makes it possible to create graphic objects without regard for the devices on which they are eventually displayed.

In both cases, the drawing port receives the following information:

- The geometries provide the drawing shapes.
- The graphic state describes the graphic and scene attributes, model and view transformations, and a clipping region.
- The graphics device determines the method by which the drawing occurs: for example, via a frame buffer, PostScript, plotter, video, or screen device.

These relationships are illustrated in Figure 101.

FIGURE 101
DRAWING PORT DEPENDENCIES

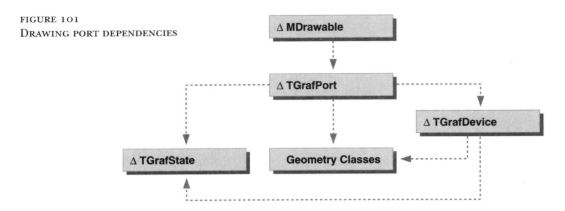

Figure 102 shows the drawing port class architecture.

FIGURE 102
DRAWING PORT CLASS
ARCHITECTURE

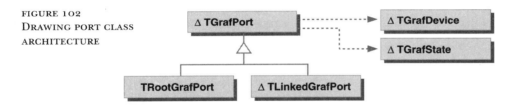

TGrafPort is the drawing port. Every TGrafPort knows about a graphics device (TGrafDevice) and a graphic state (TGrafState).

A graphic state describes the attributes of the graphic and the scene, the model and view transformations, and the clipping region. When a program calls the MDrawable::Draw function, the graphic concatenates its graphic state with the TGrafState instance. If a program supplies a TGrafBundle and TGrafMatrix when it calls the TGrafPort::Draw function, their data is also concatenated with the TGrafState instance.

TLinkedGrafPort is an abstract base class for concatenating graphic attributes to the graphic state of the parent. Because the graphic state is separate from the drawing port and has no knowledge of the graphics device, the graphic state is available in the system outside the context of drawing a graphic.

The 2-D and 3-D attribute classes provide a default graphic state in case the Draw call doesn't have all the necessary information. The TRootGrafPort provides this default graphic state, which consists of identity transform matrices, an infinite clipping region, and attributes defined by root graphic state classes.

GRAPHICS DEVICES FRAMEWORK

The Graphics Devices framework supports the basic capabilities of a graphics device driver, such as rasterization for drawing shapes, device transformations for working with different sizes and resolutions, color maps, and dithering. Depending on the kind of graphics device driver you want to write, you can use parts of the framework code as is and extend other parts to provide specialized graphics capabilities.

For example, if you're writing a graphics accelerator, you might want to override framework code that draws 2-D lines with code that calls your accelerator hardware to draw the line. This kind of selective subclassing is typical of the Graphics Devices framework. In addition to supporting a standard set of calling APIs, it provides a very dense and carefully designed subclassing API that allows you to override just those details that you want your hardware to take care of and leave everything else alone.

Graphics device drivers can also drive printers. A printer handler based on the Printing Devices framework (introduced on page 299) is normally associated with a graphic device driver that converts Taligent graphics primitives into whatever form a particular printer requires, such as PostScript or Hewlett-Packard's Page Control Language.

The Graphics Devices framework not only simplifies the writing of device drivers for new hardware but can also be used to support application functions. For example, the CommonPoint system includes a bounding box device driver. A program can get a port to the bounding box device driver just as it can for any other device, but the driver doesn't display anything. Instead, it accumulates the geometric bounds of all the primitives drawn to it, taking care of any transformations and so on like any other device driver. The bounding box device driver can be used for tasks such as laying out pages that require the calculation of bounds for multiple graphic objects. Logical device drivers of this sort can be used for a wide variety of programmatic tasks.

Taligent provides standard graphics device drivers that support 8-bit, 24-bit, and many other standard graphics devices.

FONT SUPPORT

Font Support provides an integrated, uniform interface for accessing all kinds of fonts, including fonts from different manufacturers, fonts stored and displayed using different formats, large ideographic fonts, and so on. It also includes a mechanism for device-dependent character spacing in any font, so that text is spaced suitably both in print and on screen without reformatting.

Font services are provided by a font server that is always running as a separate process and can be shared by any other processes. The font server makes use of a global cache that stores bitmaps for individual characters of particular sizes as they are used and makes them available to all processes. The font server and its global cache thus provide very fast and efficient systemwide support for font rendering.

Font support is automatic and transparent for programs based on the Desktop frameworks. Even programs that don't use the Desktop frameworks can easily provide font support without dealing directly with the font server. Developers of font-intensive applications such as font design and typesetting packages may need to modify some aspects of the font server itself.

The font server supports various kinds of font formats by means of a font handler that takes care of interpreting the contents of font files, rendering, and other font-specific tasks. The first version of the CommonPoint system includes a font handler for TrueType® 1.0 fonts as well as a base set of TrueType fonts. Taligent and third parties can create additional font handlers to support other font formats such as TrueType 2.0, Adobe Type Set I, or Bitstream. The font server provides a uniform interface for a variety of font handlers.

If a requested font is missing, the first release of the CommonPoint system substitutes the system font. Plans for future versions of the system include support for font matching, which means that the font server will substitute the available font most closely matching the original if the original font isn't available on a particular machine. Individual applications can override the default font-matching mechanism with their own mechanisms.

Plans for future versions of the system also include support for the development of custom font servers and multiple distributed font servers.

COLOR

This section introduces the Color Model framework and the Color Matcher framework, which support the application of color to objects throughout the CommonPoint system. The Color Model framework supports color specification in different *color spaces,* or self-consistent coordinate systems for assigning scalar values to colors. The Color Matcher framework manages *color matchers* used to match colors when a specified color isn't available on a particular output device.

Color instances created from color space classes are passed to the fill and frame colors for 2-D attribute bundles, to the outside and inside colors and shaders for 3-D attribute bundles, and to the ambient light for scene bundles.

Colors and color profiles

All color space classes descend from TColor. The following common properties and requirements are present in all classes derived from TColor:

- Every color can typecast itself into a TRGBColor or TXYZColor.
- Every color is defined in relation to a color space.
- All colors are calibrated (device independent).
- Every graphics device knows the colors it can produce and record.
- Each graphics device can characterize itself relative to an ideal device.
- Every color can return itself through the TColor assignment operator.

Figure 103 shows the the relationship between the abstract base class TColor and the class TColorProfile. Every color object has a reference to a *color profile.* In the first release of the CommonPoint system, color profiles are based on the profile format developed by the International Color Consortium (ICC), of which Taligent is a founding member. Plans for future releases include supporting additional formats. Regardless of the format, every color and every image in the CommonPoint system has an associated color profile containing device-specific information about the device for which the color or image was originally defined. Color profiles are transparent to programmers and users, but they are fully integrated in the CommonPoint system and make it possible to support color matching for a wide variety of display devices.

FIGURE 103
COLORS AND COLOR PROFILES

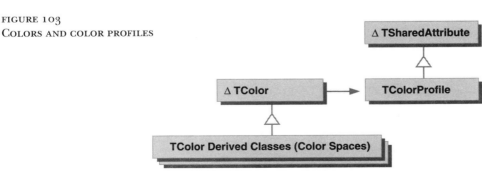

Color space classes

Every class derived from TColor represents a three-dimensional color space. All 3-D color spaces except HSL, HSV, and spectral are orthogonal.

Table 1 lists each color class with its corresponding color space and purpose.

TABLE 1
COLOR SPACE
CLASSES

Class	Color space	Definition	Purpose
TRGBColor	RGB	Red, green, blue	Color monitors and drawing programs.
TXYZColor	XYZ	Tristimulus color space	Basic space that defines all visible colors. X, Y, and Z roughly correspond to red, green, and blue.
TxyYColor	xyY	Chromaticity and luminance	Closely related to XYZ.
TLabColor	Lab	Color and brightness	Color printers.
TLuvColor	Luv	Color and intensity	Calibrated monitors.
TGrayColor	Gray	Shades of gray	Black-and-white monitors.
THSVColor	HSV	Hue, saturation, value	Paint programs.
THSLColor	HSL	Hue, saturation, lightness	Paint programs.
TCMYKColor	CMYK	Cyan, magenta, yellow, black	Four-color printers.
TCMYColor	CMY	Cyan, magenta, yellow	Three-color printers.
TSpectralColor	Spectral	Pure color with light of one wavelength	High-quality rendering in drawing programs.
TYIQColor	YIQ	Luminance, in-phase signal, quadrature	Television.
TYuvColor	Yuv	Luminance and intensity	European television (PAL, SECAM)

RGB is an uncalibrated (device-independent) red, green, and blue color space. XYZ, xyY, Lab, and Luv are calibrated red, green, and blue color spaces that use the Commission Internationale de l'Eclairage (CIE) tristimulus color system. The remaining color spaces are uncalibrated, but can be transformed into and out of the XYZ and RGB color spaces to achieve device independence.

It's possible to represent other color spaces by deriving from TColor and implementing its virtual functions and transformation functions.

Color matching

Color matching is the process of transforming a color on a source device to a color on an output device. Color matching may be necessary when the color specified on a source device isn't available on the output device. For example, some colors can be displayed on a monitor but cannot be displayed on a printer, and vice versa.

Users typically turn color matching on or off from a control panel. When color matching is turned on, the user can select from one of the following default color-matching schemes, each of which corresponds to a concrete color matcher class provided by the Color Matcher framework:

- **Colorimetric.** Matching colors by equalizing spectral chromatics and finding relative luminances.
- **Appearance.** Matching colors by performing a deformation between the source and target gamuts so that the color or image appears correct.
- **Exact.** Matching colors by equalizing spectral chromatics and finding absolute luminances.

It's possible to subclass from the Color Matcher classes to support additional color-matching schemes.

3-D GRAPHICS CODE EXAMPLES

The code examples that follow demonstrate how to draw a torus, rotate it, and fill it with a color. The last example shows the code that generated the sectioned torus shown on page 226.

Drawing a torus

The sweep classes make it easy to create shapes such as spheres, cones, tori, and cylinders in a few lines of code without any knowledge of math or NURBS. For example, these lines of code draw the torus shown in Figure 104:

```
TTorus3D torus(100, 25);
torus.Draw(thePort);
```

The big radius of a torus is the distance from the center of the torus to the center of the tube, and the small radius is the distance from the outer edge of the torus to the center of the tube. The torus drawn on screen by this code example has a big radius of 100 coordinate units and a small radius of 25 coordinate units. (The actual size of the image reproduced here differs from the original image on screen.)

FIGURE 104
DRAWING
A TORUS

Transforming a torus

Because a torus is derived from MGraphic3D, you can use the MGraphic3D transformation functions to alter every point in a graphic to resize (scale), reorient (rotate), or move (translate) the torus without using a matrix and getting into the intricacies of matrix multiplication.

The code example that follows first translates the torus 100 coordinate units to the right, then rotates the torus 50 degrees around the x-axis. Figure 105 shows the original torus on the left, and the same torus after the translation and rotation on the right.

```
torus.TranslateBy(TGPoint3D(150, 0, 0));
torus.RotateBy(50, TGrafMatrix3D::kAboutXAxis);
```

FIGURE 105
ROTATING
A TORUS

Coloring a torus

Colors for a graphic object are defined by its associated attribute bundle. The classes derived from TColor provide support for a variety of color spaces that can also be specified in the attribute bundle.

This code example creates an attribute bundle that defines a red fill in the red, green, blue (RGB) color space and then uses the fill bundle to draw the torus:

```
TFillBundle fillBundle(TRGBColor(1,0,0)); //Create a red fill bundle

TTorus3D torus(100,25);                    //Create the torus
torus.Draw(thePort, new TGrafBundle(fillBundle));   //Draw the torus using the
                                           //red fill bundle
```

It's also easy to transform a color from one color space to another, as shown in this example:

```
TRGBColor anRGBColor(1,0,0);      //Create a red color in RGB space.
THSVColor hsvColor(anRGBColor);   //Create the same color in HSV space by
                                  //transforming the RGB color
TFillBundle fillBundle(hsvColor); //Create a fill bundle using the HSV red.
```

Creating a more complex graphic

The code example that follows draws the sectioned torus shown on page 226. This example doesn't include the code for the menus and tool palette or for shading the graphic after it's drawn. It just computes the tiled surface once. In the context of a program, it would normally be desirable to cache each surface once in the constructor and recompute only when the generative data is modified.

```
void TTiledTorus3D::Draw( TGrafPort& port ) const
{
    long i, j;

    // Gap between tiles, as fraction of tile size
    GCoordinate kGap = 0.2;
    // Amount to round tiles by
    GCoordinate kEdgeRoundness = fTileThickness / 5.0;

    // Convert the base class torus into a TGSurface3D
    TSweep3D *torusSweep = CreateSweepSurface();
    TGSurface3D outerTorus = *torusSweep->GetSurface();
    delete torusSweep;

    // Create another surface representing the "inside" of the tiles
    torusSweep=TTorus3D(GetOuterRadius(),
                      GetTubeRadius()-fTileThickness).CreateSweepSurface();
    TGSurface3D innerTorus = *torusSweep->GetSurface();
    delete torusSweep;

    // Compute the parametric steps from which the tiles will be formed
    GParametric ustep = outerTorus.GetMaxParameter( TGSurface3D::kuDirection )
        / fNumSegments;
    GParametric vstep = outerTorus.GetMaxParameter( TGSurface3D::kvDirection )
        / fNumSegments;
    GParametric ugap = ustep * kGap;
    GParametric vgap = vstep * kGap;

    for ( i = 0; i < fNumSegments; i++)
        for ( j = 0; j < fNumSegments; j++)
        {
            // Step through the parameter space.  For each tile, extract
            // a top and bottom subsection, then construct an edge surface
            // between them.

            TGSurface3D topSection;
            TGSurface3D botSection;
            outerTorus.GetSectionOfSurface( ustep * i, ustep * (i + 1) - ugap,
                                            vstep * j, vstep * (j + 1) - vgap,
                                            topSection );
            innerTorus.GetSectionOfSurface( ustep * i, ustep * (i + 1) - ugap,
                                            vstep * j, vstep * (j + 1) - vgap,
                                            botSection );

            TGSurface3D sideSection( topSection, botSection,
                                     kEdgeRoundness, kEdgeRoundness );
            port.Draw( topSection );
            port.Draw( sideSection );

            // Reverse the inside section so that it faces in.
            botSection.ReverseDirection( TGSurface3D::kuDirection );
            port.Draw( botSection );
        }
}
```

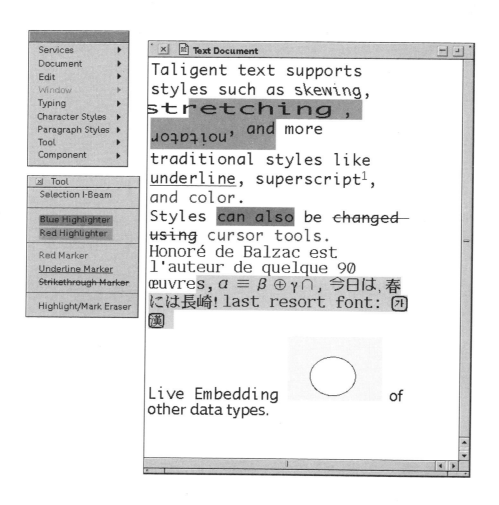

The Text frameworks and classes support multilingual text throughout the CommonPoint application system.

CHAPTER 10

TEXT

The Text system supports the input, storage, manipulation, and display of multilingual text. The figure on the opposite page illustrates some of the default text features available to all CommonPoint applications:

- **Lines 2–7.** Text can be arbitrarily styled, and styling is maintained during cutting and pasting anywhere in the system. Styles include graphic transforms such as skewing, stretching, and rotation as well as more traditional styles such as italic and bold. Characters can be arbitrarily positioned, including superscripting, subscripting, and manual kerning. These can be specified absolutely, relative to the point size, or by a combination of the two.

- **Lines 8–9.** Text cursor tools can apply color, strikethrough, or other styles directly to text just by selecting it. The styles are also very flexible; for example, it's possible to specify the absolute or relative height and thickness of the line used for a strikethrough.

- **Lines 10–13.** The text system provides full support for Unicode, including systemwide support for multiple scripts and input methods in a single line. It also provides multiple methods for typing accented characters.

- **Lines 11–12.** Users can type characters directly or use typing configurations to identify symbols by name—for example, typing "intersection%" to get the symbol ∩ or "identical to%" to get the symbol ≡. Automatic font styling ensures that characters are always displayed in an appropriate font. Changing fonts never causes spurious boxes and garbage characters to appear.

- **Lines 13–14.** Whenever the system doesn't have a font for particular characters, it always displays a meaningful representation of the character that can't be displayed, so the user knows what kind of character it is and what kind of font it requires.

- **Lines 15–16.** The Text system supports live embedding of other data types, such as graphics, among Unicode characters.

This chapter introduces the frameworks that provide the underlying support for all CommonPoint text:

- **Line Layout** displays lines of styled text.
- **Basic Text Services** comprise the following:
  - **Paragraph Styles** handle indentation, line spacing, and other characteristics of paragraphs.
  - **Text Styles** handle font, size, color, positioning, and other characteristics of individual characters or ranges of characters.
  - **Text and Style Storage Management** handles storage of textual information, including styles, ranges, and positions.
  - **Character Sets** manage Unicode characters and conversion between Unicode and other character-encoding standards.

The relationships among these frameworks and the Text Editing framework are illustrated in Figure 106.

This chapter also describes the Text Input and Output framework, which is part of Localization Services. It is described here because it supports all aspects of multilingual text input and works closely with the Text system.

The high-level Text Editing framework provides a quick way of creating editable text components and simple text elements that take full advantage of all the frameworks described in this chapter. Chapter 8 introduces the Text Editing framework, beginning on page 214.

FIGURE 106
TEXT ARCHITECTURE

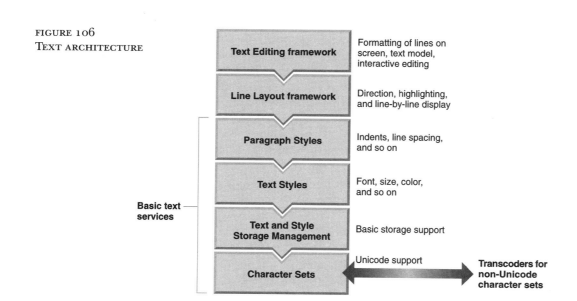

BASIC TEXT SERVICES AND LINE LAYOUT

Figure 106 shows the layers of text support provided by Basic Text Services, the Line Layout framework, and the Text Editing framework.

The CommonPoint storage mechanism for all character data is based on the 16-bit Unicode character-encoding standard, which provides the basis for all multilingual text. The Character Sets framework manages Unicode characters and supports conversion between Unicode and other character-encoding systems via transcoders for non-Unicode character sets. (Transcoders are described in more detail later in this chapter.)

Text and Style Storage Management provides classes that support the storage of style and character data in the same text instance. Unlike traditional system software, which frequently loses styling information during cut, copy, and paste operations, the CommonPoint system allows users to cut and copy styled text and move it freely anywhere without losing any styling information. Character and style data can also be manipulated separately.

Text and Style Storage Management also includes classes for indicating specific positions or ranges in text, iterating through character and style data, and other string manipulation functions.

Paragraph Styles and Text Styles provide a rich set of extensible styles. All text in the CommonPoint application system can be styled, including menu items, labels, editable fields in dialog boxes, and spreadsheet cells, as well as text in text components.

The Line Layout framework displays a line at a time of styled text. It can handle multiple languages in a single document, transparently changing direction and transliterating characters (that is, mapping one character sequence to another) appropriately as the input changes from one language to another. The Line Layout framework also maps the user's clicking and dragging and highlights the corresponding characters; for example, it automatically slants the highlighting or insertion point for italicized text.

The Text Editing framework, which is introduced beginning on page 214, takes the lines displayed by the Line Layout framework and arranges them on the screen. It provides a default text model based on the Presentation framework for creating text documents and text components and provides basic interactive editing capabilities. Developers with standard multilingual word-processing requirements, for example for an email application or an order entry system, can use the Text Editing framework almost exclusively. Developers creating dedicated word-processing or page layout applications are more likely to use the Basic Text Services frameworks directly along with the text model provided by the Text Editing framework.

Storing and manipulating multilingual text data

Unicode, part of the internationally recognized standard ISO 10646, is a fixed-width 16-bit character-encoding system that provides a code for every character in every major writing system, along with an extensive set of symbols, punctuation, and control characters. Unicode currently supports these writing systems, or *scripts*:

Arabic	Greek	Kana	Oriya
Armenian	Gujarati	Kannada	Tamil
Bengali	Gurmukhi	Lao	Telugu
Cyrillic	Han	Latin	Thai
Devanagari	Hangul	Malayam	Zhuyinfuhao
Georgian	Hebrew	Mongolian	

The character set for each script is independent; that is, even if a character appears in multiple scripts, it has a separate code in each. For example, the Latin, Greek, and Cyrillic scripts all contain the character "A," but Unicode contains a different code for the character "A" in each script.

In addition to the script name, Unicode associates other information with each character in the form of character properties. Character properties identify information such as the following:

- Upper-, lower-, or noncased characters
- Diacritical marks
- Characters used to represent digits
- Punctuation marks
- Symbols
- Control characters

The CommonPoint implementation of Unicode characters provides access to all character property information.

Because all text is stored using the Unicode character-encoding system, any text instance can contain freely intermixed characters from any language. Text can have any orientation: left-to-right, right-to-left, bidirectional, or vertical.

Some operating systems allow you to build multilingual capabilities into your programs by using tools like the Mac OS Script Manager or by manipulating multiple code pages. The CommonPoint text storage mechanism provides multilingual capabilities for all CommonPoint applications transparently with no additional programming effort.

For more information about Unicode design and usage, see *The Unicode Standard, Version 1.0* (1991) and *Unicode Technical Report #4* (1993). The latter describes the amendments to Unicode 1.0 included with Unicode 1.1, the version implemented by Taligent.

Transcoding text data

Any text imported from or exported to a system that uses a character-encoding system other than Unicode must be *transcoded,* or converted to or from the Unicode character set, as shown in Figure 107. The text system includes classes that manage the conversion of unstyled text data between Unicode and other character sets—for example, the ASCII (ISO 8859/1) or Mac OS character encodings. These transcoders are useful for programs such as networking services or electronic mail applications that need to handle non-Unicode data.

FIGURE 107
TRANSCODERS CONVERT CHARACTER DATA BETWEEN UNICODE AND OTHER ENCODING SYSTEMS

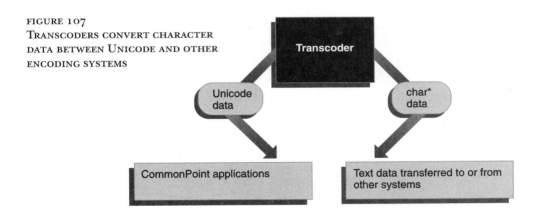

Creating and managing styled text

Text and Style Storage Management provides a set of classes, shown in Figure 108, that take care of the housekeeping involved in storing and manipulating sequences of Unicode characters. These classes provide the lowest-level protocols for creating a string and adding styles to it, but they don't provide a display mechanism. The Line Layout and Text Editing frameworks provide higher-level interfaces that allow the user to display text and use menu commands to apply styles to selections.

TText is an abstract base class that provides the standard protocol for accessing character data, inserting and deleting characters, and accessing and modifying style information. TStandardText provides a default implementation of TText that is appropriate for most text needs. A TStandardText object can store a string up to two billion characters long, and it can have any number of TStyleSet objects associated with particular ranges of characters. Each TStyleSet object in turn can have any number of individual TStyle objects associated with it. Each style is defined as a style object containing the style name and the current value—for example, the style name "Point size" and the value 14.

TStyle is derived from TAttribute, an abstract base class included among the Foundation classes. For information about attributes, see page 340.

The Text and Styles Storage framework includes a complete set of standard character style classes for style categories, including these:

- Character appearance, such as font, point size, and color
- Lining features, such as underlines and strikethroughs
- Positioning, such as kerning and superscripting
- Paragraph layout styles, such as margins and tabulation

The examples that follow show how to create a text instance, create and apply styles, and change a style.

FIGURE 108
CLASSES FOR
CREATING AND
MANAGING
STYLED TEXT

Applying style data
to text

This example demonstrates how to instantiate an instance of TStandardText, instantiate an empty TStyleSet object, add styles to the TStyleSet object, and apply the style set to a range of text.

```
// Create an instance of text.
TStandardText text ("Hello, world!");

// Create a style set, add styles, and apply the style set to the text.
TStyleSet textStyleSet;
TToken helveticaFontName("TaligentSans");
textStyleSet.Add(TFontIdentifierStyle(TaligentSansFontName));
textStyleSet.Add(TFontPointSizeStyle:GetDefaultFontPointSizeStyle());
textStyleSet.Add(TTextColorStyle::GetRed());

text.AddStyles(textStyleSet, TTextRange::GetMaximumRange());

// Text is currently red, 12 point (or the current default),
// and in the TaligentSans font.
```

Modifying style data

This example demonstrates how to instantiate a new style object, assign it a new value, and apply the new style object to a range of text.

```
TTextRange partialTextRange(12,TTextCount(1));
styledText.AddStyles(TFontPointSizeStyle(24), partialTextRange);

// Text in the range partialTextRange is now red, 24 point,
// and in the TaligentSans font.
```

Displaying static text

The Line Layout framework includes two classes for displaying static text strings:

- **TTextDisplay** encapsulates a text instance and provides a Draw function that displays the text on a single line. TTextDisplay permits specification of a font, point size, and color for the text.
- **TTextGraphic** provides an easy way to create static text and treat it as if it were a graphic. TTextGraphic objects can be transformed just like any other Taligent graphic objects.

These classes are used for creating simple static text elements such as labels and buttons.

Displaying editable text

The Text Editing framework works with the Line Layout framework to display multilingual text:

- A *text formatter* provided by the Text Editing framework provides line-breaking algorithms and high-level paragraph layout.
- The Line Layout framework displays individual lines, transparently changing direction if necessary as the text changes from one language to another.

The standard text formatter lays out text by fitting it into text panels on the basis of the current paragraph and character styles. The Text Editing framework also provides abstract text formatter classes to facilitate the creation of custom text formatters.

The Line Layout framework takes both character and style data into account when laying out a line. For example, the character's script determines the direction in which the character is displayed, and style data determines font, color, line spacing, and so on. Line layout capabilities are built into all applications created with the Text Editing framework. It's also possible to use the Line Layout classes directly to customize text layout behavior.

Font Support

As shown in the preceding examples, style objects can include font information. The Font Support system, which is briefly described on page 244, handles all fonts (including large ideographic fonts) in the same way. Developers don't have to build support for different types of fonts into their applications. The system includes a mechanism for device-dependent character spacing in any font, so that text is spaced suitably both in print and on screen without any need for reformatting.

The Line Layout framework also supports font substitution. When enabled, the font substitution mechanism performs contextual analysis to find the best substitution for a character that has no equivalent in the current font. The user never gets a meaningless display when entering characters, changing fonts, or importing text from another system. The system includes a missing glyph font that shows the origin of characters that cannot be represented by any available font.

Tokens

Foundation Services, which are described in Chapter 14, include classes for creating *tokens,* which are objects that encapsulate unstyled Unicode character arrays for internal manipulation of text strings that do not need to be displayed. Token instances can also be shared among programs. For more information, see "Tokens," beginning on page 346.

TEXT INPUT AND OUTPUT

This section describes the support provided by the Text Input and Output framework for multilingual text input. For information about other Localization Services, including the locale mechanism, text analysis services such as collating and pattern matching, and conversion of dates, times, and other text formats, see page 301.

The default editable text component provided by the Text Editing framework uses the Text Input and Output framework to support multilingual text input. The primary mechanism for controlling text input is the typing configuration. A *typing configuration* identifies a virtual keyboard and, optionally, text modifiers and an input method:

- A *virtual keyboard* maps the characters in the script to the keyboard. Virtual keyboards support keyboard layouts for different countries and alternative layouts such as the Dvorak keyboard.
- *Text modifiers* include transliterators and lexical tools. *Transliterators* map one sequence of characters to another—for example, mapping a letter and a diacritical mark into a single accented character, or providing phonetic transcription between two scripts. *Lexical tools* perform operations on words; examples include spelling and grammar checkers.
- An *input method* allows users to input ideographic characters from a nonideographic keyboard.

In addition, each typing configuration is associated with a particular natural language such as English or French. Typing configurations provided by the text system include the following:

- Standard U.S.
- Japanese
- Greek
- Unicode
- Symbols

The Symbols typing configuration allows a user to enter the name of a Unicode symbol and have it transliterated to the actual character. For example, "infinity%" is transliterated to "∞."

In the user environment one typing configuration is active globally at any one time. Users can switch freely among typing configurations, using multiple configurations in the course of creating or editing a single document. When a user clicks in a particular input area again after using a different typing configuration in another part of the document, the system automatically activates the correct configuration for the original input.

All the installed configurations are available to the user at any time through the standard text-editing menu, thus avoiding the use of escape-key sequences to toggle between virtual keyboards.

Developers can create virtual keyboards, text modifiers, and input methods for specific user requirements.

How the typing configuration handles typing input

The Text Editing framework uses the typing configuration mechanism to process user typing input. It accesses the typing configuration as shown in Figure 109 via a *typing interactor,* which is an object that converts keystrokes into character data according to information specified by the typing configuration.

The typing interactor chooses the most appropriate typing configuration for the current selection in the text input area. For example, if the user is using a global configuration for English but clicks within Japanese text, the typing interactor switches to the Japanese typing configuration (which includes the Japanese input method for ideographic text entry). The typing interactor selects a configuration based on the language of the character immediately preceding the selection and the user's preferred configuration for that language. If no text precedes the selection, the interactor selects the global configuration.

For a brief introduction to the role of interactors in binding presentations to data, see "Interactions," which begins on page 204.

For a brief introduction to the role of interactors in binding presentations to data, see "Interactions," which begins on page 204.

FIGURE 109
PROCESSING
TYPING INPUT

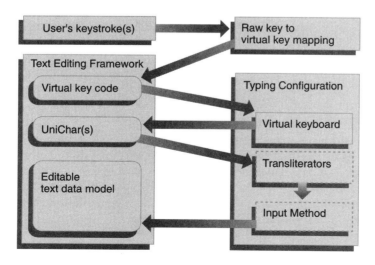

If the configuration does not contain an input method, the UniChars are written to the model by the last transliterator in the chain.

Virtual keyboards

A *virtual keyboard* maintains a set of mapping rules between a virtual key code, or a combination of modifier keys and a virtual key code, to either a single Unicode character or multiple Unicode characters. These mappings are independent of the layout of the physical keyboard and can be used for a variety of purposes, including alternative layouts such as the Dvorak keyboard. Virtual keyboards also support keyboard layouts for different countries and can have localizable names for use with the locale mechanism.

The virtual keyboard classes provide a foundation for creating virtual keyboard editors. Such editors allow users to view, modify, and create virtual keyboards for their own purposes. Plans for future versions of the CommonPoint system include a virtual keyboard editor, and third parties can create more specialized editors.

Transliterators

Transliterators are used to perform transformations on text input based on a specific algorithm or set of rules. They differ from transcoders in that they convert Unicode characters into other Unicode characters, not to an external character set.

These are some of the ways you can use transliterators:

- Accent composition, such as combining the key sequence "a" - """ into the character "ä".
- Changing the case of certain letters, such as changing lowercase to uppercase or capitalizing the first letter of each word.
- Enabling smart quotes, so that straight quotes (") are replaced with opening and closing quotes (" ").
- Phonetic transcription between scripts, such as converting from a Latin "s" to a Cyrillic "c" or (as shown in Figure 110) from a Latin "a" to a Greek "α". Phonetic transcription allows the user to enter text in a script different from the keyboard script.

FIGURE 110
TEXT INPUT
TRANS
LITERATION

Transliterators are also used to create input methods for ideographic languages. See "Input Method framework" on page 265 for an overview of input methods.

Users can select transliterators to include in a typing configuration and can chain them to process typing input in a specific way. Plans for future versions of the CommonPoint application system include providing an interface that allows users to manipulate transliterators directly.

Available transliterators

The text system includes the following rule-based transliterators:

- An extended Latin transliterator providing accent composition, smart quotes, and smart spacing (eliminates double spaces). This is the default transliterator for the system.
- A capitalization transliterator providing capitalization for the Latin script.
- Phonetic transliterators from the Latin script to Japanese. Transliterators for other scripts are planned for future versions of the CommonPoint system.

How transliterators work

A transliterator takes a text instance and processes it according to the transliterator's algorithm or set of rules. This text instance typically represents typing input and is passed to the transliterator by the typing configuration. It's also possible to pass a text instance to a transliterator programmatically. The transliterator either returns the translated text in a separate text instance or directly modifies the input text.

When the typing configuration contains several transliterators chained together, the modified text produced by one transliterator is the input text to the next transliterator in the chain.

Input Method framework

The Input Method framework provides a mechanism for inline ideographic text entry. It provides a small number of classes that a text-editing application must support to provide this capability for all text input. Users can enter text directly into documents, and the input method converts it in place rather than in a separate window. Users can also employ multiple input methods within the same document.

The Input Method framework currently provides an input method for Japanese that allows users to type Japanese in any Text Editing document, dialog box, or text field. Chinese and Korean input methods will be added in future releases.

Ideographic text input

Input methods typically work like this:

- The user types in text phonetically using an entirely different script (for example, Latin).
- A keyboard transliterator transcribes the input into phonetic symbols for the target language (for example, hiragana or katakana for Japanese or hangul for Korean).
- The input method converts the phonetic transcriptions into the appropriate ideograms (for example, Kanji for Japanese).

Because this process occurs entirely inline in the input method's active input area, text in any of the three stages may appear on screen. The user can manually adjust the ideograms produced by the input method and confirm the translation when the result is satisfactory.

Input method dictionaries

Input methods use dictionaries to translate text. These dictionaries typically contain entries that map component keys, or groups of phonetic characters, to resulting ideographic characters. Each entry has associated grammatical information that helps the input method choose the most appropriate result for the current context. When more than one translation is possible, the set of matches from the dictionary can be presented to the user for selection of alternatives to the default choice.

An input method can use one or more user dictionaries in addition to the main dictionary. The Input Method framework allows users to edit their personal dictionaries and use them with multiple input methods.

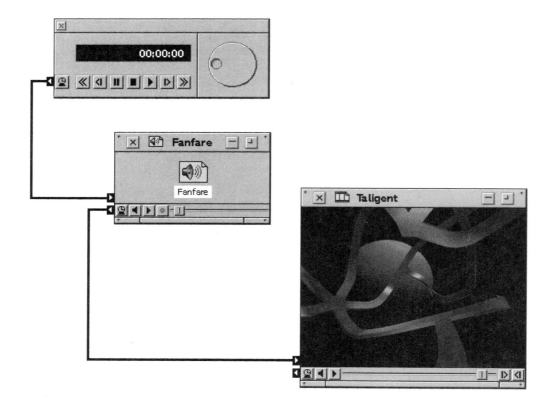

The Time Media frameworks allow CommonPoint applications to play, record, and synchronize time-based media. In this example, a video sequence (named Taligent) is synchronized to a sound (named Fanfare), which is in turn synchronized to a controller that includes a jog/shuttle knob and other standard controls.

CHAPTER 11

TIME MEDIA

Time media are forms of data that change meaningfully with respect to time. Audio, Musical Instrument Digital Interface (MIDI), and video are examples of time media that CommonPoint users can manipulate in sophisticated ways.

If developers just need to embed a movie, a sound, or a MIDI sequence in a view or a document, they typically use the Time Media UI framework (introduced on page 223). The Time Media UI framework provides user interface abstractions for creating lightweight embeddable components that allow users to play or record time media sequences.

Time Media player classes can also be used programmatically to play or record a sound, a MIDI sequence, or a movie. For example, a programmer can use a TSound player to play a particular sound when a user performs an action or to accompany a visual effect.

The Common Time Media framework provides the basic mechanism for storing, recording, playing, and synchronizing any kind of time media data. The Audio, MIDI, and Video frameworks are subclassed from the Common Time Media framework to implement these services for their respective data types, as suggested by Figure 111.

Although not directly based on them, the Telephony framework is closely linked to the other Time Media frameworks. Plans for future releases of the Telephony framework include support for playing and recording any kind of time media over a telephone line.

This chapter introduces basic Time Media concepts and the Audio, MIDI, Video, and Telephony frameworks.

FIGURE 111
TIME MEDIA
FRAMEWORKS

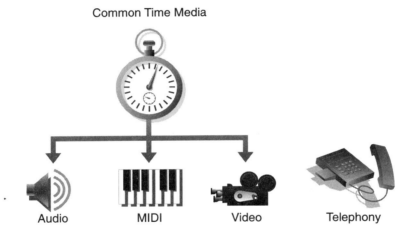

Common Time Media

Audio   MIDI   Video   Telephony

TIME MEDIA CONCEPTS

The Common Time Media framework defines two fundamental abstractions used by the Time Media frameworks:

- **Media players** are analogous to playing and recording devices such as tape recorders and VCRs. Media players are used to play, record, and synchronize media data.

- **Media sequences** represent the data played by media players, much the way an audiotape is played by a tape deck. These data files or streams of media data can contain clips of audio, video, or MIDI data.

These abstractions closely model the use of audio, MIDI, and video in the real world. Media sequences that resemble videotapes, CDs, audiotapes, and so on are loaded into players that support functions such as play, record, stop, and seek.

FIGURE 112
MEDIA PLAYER
CLASS ARCHITECTURE

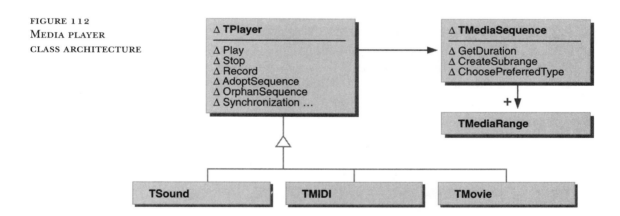

Media players and media sequences

Media players are instances of classes derived from TPlayer. In addition to TPlayer, the Time Media frameworks include three subclasses for audio, MIDI, and video players, as shown in Figure 112.

These classes play the following roles:

- **TPlayer,** a special type of media component, is the abstract base class from which all types of media players are derived. Media players play, record, and synchronize media data.
- **TMediaSequence** is the abstract base class from which all types of media sequences are derived. Media sequences are the media data streams played by media players.
- **TMediaRange** represents a subrange within a media sequence. It facilitates editing operations.

A player owns a media sequence. Players and media sequences are separate, so that players can be reused; you can play one sequence and then load and play a new sequence using the same player. A player is characterized by the duration of its sequence and the current position within the sequence. Both the duration and current position are represented as TTime values.

A player's start time is always zero, and its duration is the duration of its sequence. The current position in the sequence is always greater than or equal to the player's start time (0) and less than or equal to its duration, as suggested by Figure 113.

When you call Play, the player plays the sequence from the current position and continues until you call Stop, the end of the sequence is reached, or an error occurs.

When you call Record, the new data overwrites any existing data, starting at the current position. Recording continues until you call Stop or an error occurs. Recording also stops if the TPlayer's clock is synchronized to an external clock and that clock stops or moves backward.

Plans for future releases of the CommonPoint system include supporting the use of media players to represent and control external playing and recording devices such as videodisc machines, videotape recorders, and digital frame stores.

FIGURE 113
CURRENT
POSITION OF
A PLAYER

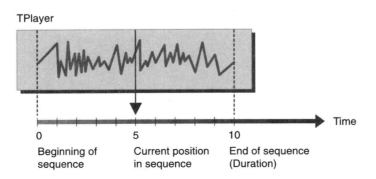

Synchronizing media players

The Common Time Media framework provides a mechanism for coordinating the playback and recording of multiple media streams. Because each media player has an internal syncable clock, you can force one media stream to follow the time behavior of another.

Each player's internal clock determines how fast and in what direction it plays. Ordinarily this clock is synchronized to a default clock, such as a real-time clock based on hardware. Using the synchronization support provided by TPlayer, you can also synchronize a player to other clocks, such as the internal clock of another player. When you synchronize two clocks, you can also reset the time on the clock you are synchronizing. For more information about timing services and syncable clocks, see "Time Services," beginning on page 393.

The current position of a player is controlled by its clock time. However, the current position is bounded by zero and the duration of the loaded sequence. The player will not play unless the time of its internal clock is between zero and the sequence duration.

For example, suppose you want to play the sound of a gong 10 seconds after a movie starts playing. Figure 114 shows how this might work. The synchronization rate between the audio player's clock and the movie player's clock is set to 1.0. The audio player's clock is set ten seconds behind the movie player's clock. If the movie player's clock starts at 0, the audio player's clock reads –10. If you call the sound player's Play function at this point, the gong doesn't sound until the movie player's clock reads 10, at which point the audio player's clock reads 0.

The Common Time Media framework provides a set of TTime subclasses that implement Society of Motion Picture and Television Engineers (SMPTE) time codes. These classes support conversion between the different SMPTE frame rates and other TTime subclasses. They use a floating point value to extend the SMPTE format to fractional frames.

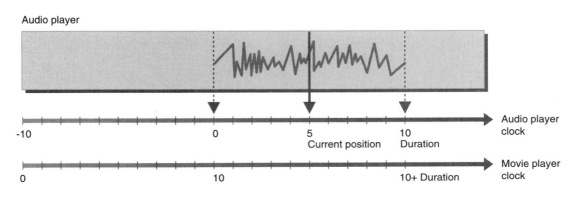

FIGURE 114
AUDIO PLAYER
SYNCHRONIZED
TO MOVIE
PLAYER
RATE = 1.0,
OFFSET = –10.

AUDIO

The Audio framework provides the developer of audio, music, or multimedia applications with a hardware-independent interface for a variety of audio functions. Audio classes support digital recording, playback, processing, and storage of audio data.

Figure 115 shows the two main classes provided by the Audio framework: TSound and TAudioSequence.

FIGURE 115
AUDIO
CLASSES

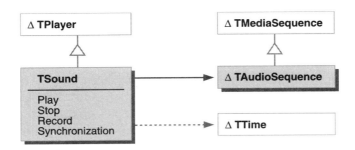

Audio players

TSound represents a media player that's used to play, record, and synchronize audio data. It corresponds to a real-world tape recorder. Because TSound is derived from TPlayer, it's possible to synchronize multiple TSound objects or synchronize a TSound object with another kind of player.

TSound also provides features such as pitch and gain controls. For example, you can adjust the playing or recording level by calling TSound::SetOutputGain or TSound::SetInputGain before you play or record a sound.

Audio sequences

TAudioSequence is an abstract base class derived from TMediaSequence that represents the audio data streams played by audio players. Audio sequences correspond to real-world cassette tapes. Only one audio sequence can be loaded into a player at a time.

You can derive new classes from TAudioSequence to wrap different sound file formats or create new synthesized sounds. Sound file formats supported by the Audio framework include Audio Interchange File Format (AIFF), QuickTime, and sine wave.

Audio types

Each audio sequence supports one or more of the audio types shown in Table 2. Audio types specify the format of the audio data.

TABLE 2
AUDIO TYPES

Audio type	Sample rate (samples/sec)	Sample width (bits)	Description
16-bit linear	44100	16	Compact disc quality. Two's complement integer samples.
8-bit linear	22050	8	Medium quality. Two's complement integer samples.
Offset binary	22050	8	Medium quality. Offset binary samples.
µ-Law	8000	8	North American telephone standard. Log-companded samples.

MIDI

Musical Instrument Digital Interface (MIDI) is the industry standard for exchanging information between electronic musical instruments, computers, sequencers, lighting controllers, mixers, and recording equipment. MIDI is used for studio recording, live performance, automated control, audio/video production, and composition. It plays an integral role in the use of computers for multimedia communications.

The MIDI framework provides a hardware-independent interface for communicating with MIDI devices, manipulating MIDI data, and reading and writing standard MIDI files. Manufacturers of MIDI devices, such as serial-to-MIDI converters or internal MIDI cards, can derive their own MIDI subclasses to provide specialized support for that hardware.

MIDI framework services include the following:

- Time-stamped MIDI messages
- MIDI protocol support with derived classes for message types
- Support for MIDI time code as a time source
- Recording and playback of MIDI sequences, including standard MIDI files
- Synchronization of MIDI sequences with other media sequences

Figure 116 shows the main types of MIDI classes.

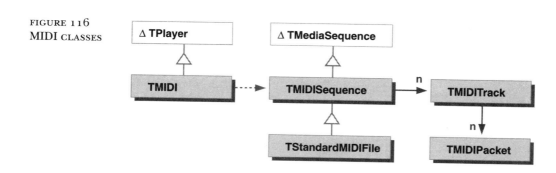

FIGURE 116
MIDI CLASSES

MIDI players

TMIDI represents a media player derived from TPlayer that's used to play, record, and synchronize MIDI sequences. As with all types of media players, you can synchronize MIDI players to external time sources, including the internal clocks of other types of players.

MIDI sequences

TMIDISequence represents the logical cassette played by a TMIDI player. It encapsulates MIDI events and timing information for playing prearranged performances and recording new ones. Each TMIDISequence contains a tempo track and one or more music tracks. The tempo track is used for the metrical format only and can be empty.

As shown in Figure 116, a MIDI track represents a collection of MIDI packets:

- **TMIDITrack** represents the individual data tracks that make up a MIDI sequence. Each MIDI track contains a time-ordered sequence of MIDI packets.

- **TMIDIPacket** encapsulates all of the MIDI message types and structures. Each MIDI packet contains a MIDI message, a time stamp, and a status byte that identifies the purposes of the data bytes that follow, thus allowing each message to be read individually.

The MIDI framework supports three time formats:

- **Metrical.** Time is measured in terms of rhythmic meter, determined by the tempo and the resolution. The resolution is expressed as the number of MIDI ticks per quarter note.

- **SMPTE.** The time code developed by the Society of Motion Picture and Television Engineers, expressed as Hours:Minutes:Seconds:Frames. The SMPTE resolution is expressed as the number of MIDI ticks per frame. The MIDI framework supports three SMPTE frame rates: 24fps, 25fps, 30fpsDropFrame, and 30fps.

- **Real time.**

Classes derived from TMIDISequence encapsulate specific file formats for use by TMIDI. For example, TStandardMIDIFile can be used to access files that use Standard MIDI File formats 0 and 1.

VIDEO

The Video framework provides a hardware-independent interface for recording, playing, and manipulating any graphical information that can be sequenced with respect to time, such as video or animations. It supports the following features:

- File-based digital video
- Video compression and decompression
- Interleaved recording of audio and video

The Video framework uses the TTime subclasses described on page 271 for working with SMPTE time code. Figure 117 shows the main types of video classes.

FIGURE 117
VIDEO CLASSES

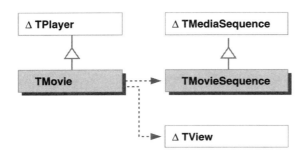

Movie players

TMovie represents a special type of media player derived from TPlayer that's used to play a movie sequence (containing synchronized video and sound, for example) represented by the class TMovieSequence.

Like all classes derived from TPlayer, TMovie can be synchronized to external clocks, so you can synchronize movie sequences with any other type of media sequence.

Developers who need to implement new compression algorithms for digital video or support specialized video hardware devices can subclass from TMovie.

Movie sequences

TMovieSequence represents a collection of media sequences, including video, sequences of other kinds of graphic objects, and sounds. For example, you can use TMovieSequence to represent a sequence of video images or a frame-based animation. You can also derive new classes to create a new type of time graphic to support time-dependent rendering of 3-D graphics.

TQuickTimeMovie is a subclass of TMovieSequence that allows CommonPoint applications to play, record, and synchronize QuickTime movie files. A QuickTime movie file includes one or more tracks as well as information about the movie.

TELEPHONY

Computer-based telephony allows a computer to control a voice telephone line. It makes complex telephony systems easier to use and makes large lists of telephone numbers easier to retrieve and maintain. Eventually the Telephony framework will be able to play and record any kind of time media over a telephone line.

The Telephony framework supports computer-based telephony by providing a hardware-independent interface for voice-oriented telephone functions. It insulates application-level code from differences in telephony hardware and can be extended to support new features. It also accommodates unique combinations of telephone sets, local hardware and software platforms, network types, and switch-signaling protocols.

In the real world, the most common telephony object is the single-line telephone handset that you connect to a telephone line by plugging it into a wall jack. This connection makes the phone line accessible through the handset. The fact that there is an enormous network of wire, fiber, switches, and central offices behind the wall jack doesn't enter the consciousness of the average user. What's important is that a specific line is now accessible via a specific handset.

The correspondence between handsets and lines need not be one-to-one. A single line may be split into several extensions, each with its own handset; or a single handset may provide sequential access to several lines. The former case is typical of residential installations. The multiline handset is typical of business installations; for example, an administrative assistant who supports three executives has one handset that can access all three lines via push buttons.

For computer-based telephony, the computer is connected to the line through an internal or external device, such as a modem or telephone interface. The handset no longer connects directly to the line; it connects to the same device as the computer. In some cases, this allows the computer to query or control the handset.

The *telephone line* classes provided by the Telephony framework model real telephone lines, and the *telephone handset* classes model real handsets. In addition, *telephone call* classes model the creation, placing, and answering of telephone calls, and *telephone line feature* classes model specific features of telephone lines such as conference calls and call forwarding.

The sections that follow describe these four groups of classes in more detail.

Telephone lines

The Telephony framework treats the telephone line as a system resource that can be shared among voice-oriented programs (unless the line has been reserved for data communication). You don't need to know how the physical phone line is connected to the computer to access it through the Telephony framework.

Figure 118 shows the telephone line classes. TTelephoneLine represents a telephone line and provides a low-level interface to simple telephone network capabilities. You can modify the state of the telephone line through a TTelephoneLineHandle, which provides member functions for initiating telephone call connections, determining the hook status of the line, and accessing telephone feature types. TTelephoneLineConfiguration uniquely identifies a telephone line and specifies its numbers and features.

You can create multiple instances of TTelephoneLineHandle for the same line and distribute them across task boundaries. This allows a user to run multiple programs that use the same line, such as an answering machine application and an autodial application.

FIGURE 118
TELEPHONE
LINE CLASSES

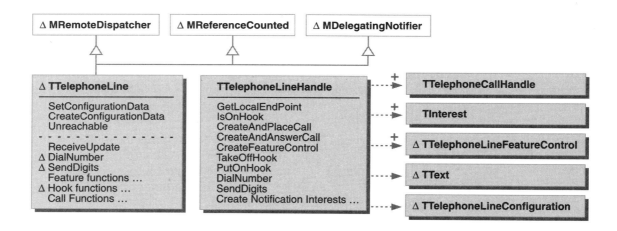

Telephone calls

A call represents an ongoing telephone connection, which progresses through a series of conditions or states. In many cases, a single line can support multiple, simultaneous calls. For example, one call might be on hold while another is active, or a call might be added to an existing connection for a conference call.

You access information about a call through a TTelephoneCallHandle created by the TTelephoneLine, as shown in Figure 119.

The Telephony framework allows the computer to monitor the progress of a call. In the real world, call status feedback is communicated audibly. For example a continuous dial tone indicates that a call can be placed, and an intermittent tone indicates that the destination line is busy. The Telephony framework provides status constants that indicate the current call status. These status constants represent all of the states indicated by the familiar audible signals as well as more detailed information.

FIGURE 119
TELEPHONE
CALL
HANDLES

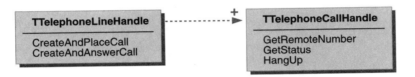

Telephone line features   In addition to supporting the standard phone controls that permit calls to be placed, answered, and ended, the Telephony framework supports advanced features through a set of classes derived from the abstract class TTelephoneLineFeature. Figure 120 summarizes these classes.

> ✅ NOTE   The availability of features depends not only on what the telephony hardware platform is potentially capable of providing but also on the features to which the user has actually subscribed.

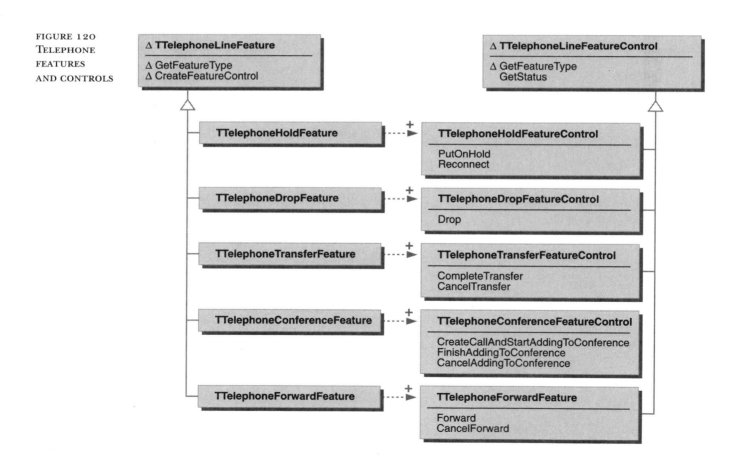

FIGURE 120
TELEPHONE
FEATURES
AND CONTROLS

The classes derived from TTelephoneLineFeature support several common telephone features:

- **TTelephoneHoldFeature** allows you to put one call on hold and answer another.
- **TTelephoneDropFeature** allows you to disconnect one participant from a conference call.
- **TTelephoneTransferFeature** allows you to transfer a call to another endpoint.
- **TTelephoneConferenceFeature** allows you to set up a conference call.
- **TTelephoneForwardFeature** allows you to pass a call through to another endpoint.

You control these advanced features through a set of classes derived from the abstract class TTelephoneLineFeatureControl. These feature control classes inherit the functions you use to get the feature type and status from the corresponding feature class.

Handsets

A physical telephone handset provides manual control for a telephone line or set of lines. In the Telephony framework, physical handsets are represented by TTelephoneHandset, which is shown in Figure 121.

You use TTelephoneHandsetHandle to monitor the hook status and access the I/O capabilities of the handset. It represents the physical telephone device (such as the telephone sitting on your desk), not the telephone line (which you connect to the handset through the phone jack in the wall). For handsets with special features, you can create new types of handles that perform additional monitor and control functions.

TTelephoneHandsetHandle makes use of information about the handset's configuration provided by TTelephoneHandsetConfigurationData, which also specifies the telephone lines to which the handset can be connected.

FIGURE 121
TELEPHONE
HANDSETS

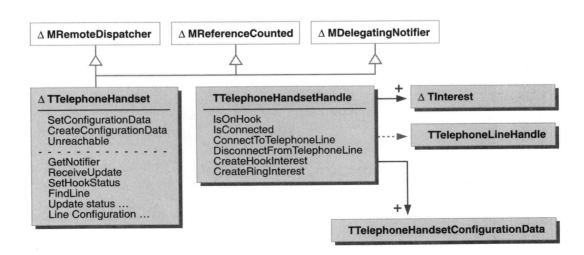

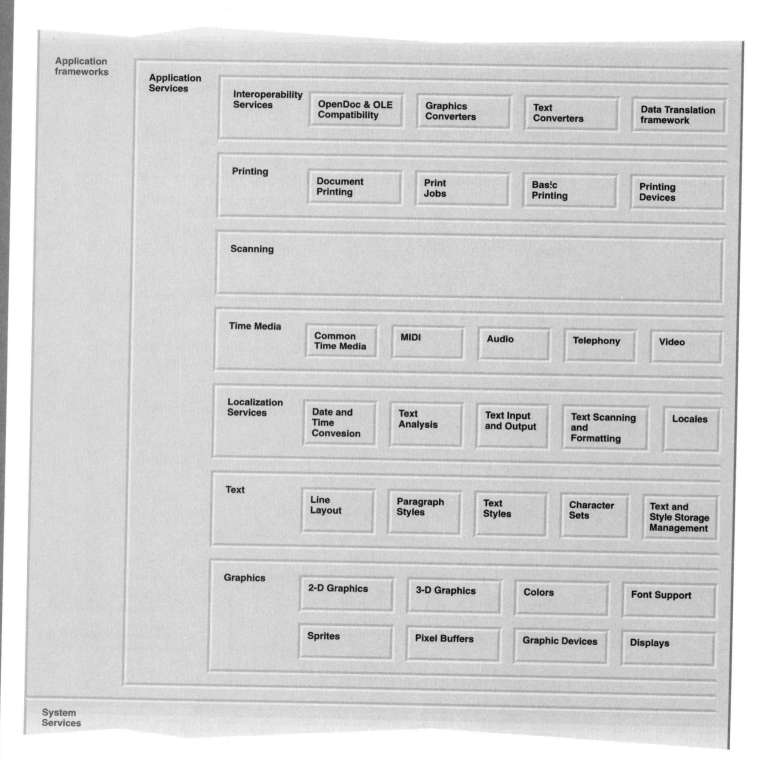

Application frameworks

Application Services

Interoperability Services

| OpenDoc & OLE Compatibility | Graphics Converters | Text Converters | Data Translation framework |

Printing

| Document Printing | Print Jobs | Basic Printing | Printing Devices |

Scanning

Time Media

| Common Time Media | MIDI | Audio | Telephony | Video |

Localization Services

| Date and Time Convesion | Text Analysis | Text Input and Output | Text Scanning and Formatting | Locales |

Text

| Line Layout | Paragraph Styles | Text Styles | Character Sets | Text and Style Storage Management |

Graphics

| 2-D Graphics | 3-D Graphics | Colors | Font Support |
| Sprites | Pixel Buffers | Graphic Devices | Displays |

System Services

CHAPTER 12

OTHER APPLICATION SERVICES

Application Services include the Graphics, Text, and Time Media frameworks described in previous chapters. Application Services also include Interoperability Services, the Printing and Scanning frameworks, and Localization Services, which are all introduced in this chapter.

Interoperability Services support OpenDoc and OLE and, via the Data Translation framework, the conversion of CommonPoint data types to non-CommonPoint data types.

The Printing and Scanning frameworks provide imaging services:

- **Document Printing** provides basic printing capabilities for all objects based on the Compound Document framework.
- **The Basic Printing framework** manages page folios and spools print jobs to disk.
- **The Print Jobs framework** manages print jobs, which combine information from the document being printed with information about the printer.
- **The Printing Devices framework** prints files spooled by the Basic Printing framework. It supports the CommonPoint equivalent of printer drivers.
- **The Scanning framework,** which is planned for future versions of the CommonPoint system, manages scanning applications and scanner handlers.

Localization Services support multilingual, localizable user interface elements and text:

- **The Text Input and Output framework** supports multilingual text input. It is described in Chapter 10 beginning on page 261.
- **The Locales framework** simplifies the localization of both the system interface and application interfaces.
- **The Text Analysis framework** manages collating, pattern matching, and boundary analysis of multilingual text.
- **The Text Scanning and Formatting framework** supports language-sensitive conversion of textual data.
- **The Date and Time Conversion framework** supports language-sensitive conversion of dates and times.

Interoperability Services

In general, Interoperability Services support whatever basic cooperation the host system requires between its own applications. Depending on the host, this can include support for copying and pasting, drag and drop, proprietary networking and file system formats, file translation, OpenDoc and OLE compound document standards, and other industry standards. In this sense the CommonPoint application system is itself an application running on the host operating system, just like any other host application.

The degree of interoperability between CommonPoint applications and host applications varies depending on the host and will increase as the CommonPoint application system matures. Taligent's goals for host interoperability can be summarized as follows:

- **Clipboard.** For pasting host data into a CommonPoint application, the rule is to "absorb if possible." This involves converting the data to the best Taligent equivalent; if that's not possible, the system embeds the host data as an object that the user can edit with a host application or part editor. For pasting CommonPoint data into a foreign clipboard, the Taligent data will be converted to the best host equivalent. The Taligent human interface allows users to control the way these operations work in both directions.

- **Dragging and dropping data selections.** Dragging and dropping objects between host and CommonPoint applications works much the same way as copying and pasting.

- **Host file system.** CommonPoint files are fully integrated with the host file system and can be manipulated from within the host environment by using host utilities for file and directory navigation, renaming, moving, launching, deleting, and so on. As support for the People, Places, and Things metaphor matures in future releases, it will also be possible to manipulate both host files and CommonPoint files from within CommonPoint Place environments.

- **File translation.** Taligent will provide appliances that import and convert host files and export and convert CommonPoint files. The Data Translation framework supports data conversion between the CommonPoint application system and host systems.

The sections that follow briefly introduce Taligent's approach to OpenDoc and OLE compatibility and the role of the Data Translation framework in supporting data converters.

OpenDoc and OLE compatibility

OpenDoc and OLE are key technologies that push the boundaries of conventional operating systems in the right direction: that is, away from an application-centered programming model and toward a document-centered model that allows a user to get work done without constantly switching layers, menus, and tools. OpenDoc achieves this by means of *parts,* which represent the data that can be embedded as one portion of a compound document, and *part handlers,* which consist of code a developer writes that allows users to view and edit the data presented in parts. OLE uses a similar mechanism.

OpenDoc and OLE provide two new APIs on top of procedural operating systems. These APIs are basically new sets of rules that must be learned and supported in addition to all the other layers of APIs that those systems require. As long as developers interpret the rules the same way, their code will interoperate successfully with other developers' code in compound documents.

It may take some time for compound documents to be universally used on the platforms that support OLE or OpenDoc. In the long run Taligent's own component-based system architecture provides the most useful and robust implementation of compound documents for all CommonPoint developers—not by requiring additional coding on their part, but by allowing them to inherit common design and implementation from the underlying frameworks. However, Taligent also needs to support interoperability for developers whose products run on CommonPoint host platforms. Therefore, Taligent provides several kinds of support for OpenDoc and OLE.

OpenDoc

From a developer's point of view, supporting OpenDoc on host operating systems such as OS/2 or Mac OS involves supporting several interrelated standards, including these:

- **OpenDoc API**, used by a developers to write their own implementations of OpenDoc parts and part handlers
- **Bento**, a data file interchange format
- **OpenDoc human interface policies**, which govern the way users interact with OpenDoc parts
- **System Object Model (SOM)**, a mechanism for calling objects in one program from another program that may be written in a different language
- **Open Scripting Architecture (OSA)**, a cross-platform architecture developed by Apple and used by a variety of scripting languages, including AppleScript™ and IBM's REXX.

A detailed discussion of these standards and their significance for OpenDoc developers is beyond the scope of this book. To achieve interoperability with OpenDoc on the host platforms on which it runs, Taligent plans to provide support in these areas:

- **Bento.** Taligent plans to facilitate developer use of the Bento format by providing subclasses based on the Compound Document framework that reduce the amount of code that a CommonPoint developer has to write.
- **OpenDoc human interface policies.** The Taligent human interface policies for embeddable components are based on the OpenDoc human interface policies, so users can work the same way with CommonPoint and OpenDoc documents.
- **SOM.** Taligent plans to support SOM for communication among different kinds of components.
- **OSA.** Taligent plans to support OSA-compliant scripting systems.

The CommonPoint system doesn't need to support the OpenDoc API, because it provides its own object-oriented, framework-based method for creating components with basic OpenDoc compound document capabilities as well as features like collaboration and multilevel undo.

Taligent's support for OpenDoc will take several different forms as the CommonPoint application system matures, all of which are ultimately directed to the same end. CommonPoint users should be able to:

- Drag and drop OpenDoc parts between any host application that supports OpenDoc and any CommonPoint application that supports OpenDoc, resulting in mutual embeddability for both kinds of compound documents.
- View and manipulate OpenDoc parts with part viewers and part editors within their own CommonPoint frames in the same way users do in the host environment.

Taligent is a founding member of Component Integration Laboratories (CI Labs), the independent organization formed to develop and promote OpenDoc. This allows Taligent to use OpenDoc technology to facilitate the development of both its own human interface policies for compound documents and CommonPoint interoperability with OpenDoc parts. In addition, Taligent's investors can use Taligent technologies and programming APIs to enhance the further development of OpenDoc-compatible software and tools and ensure a greater synergy and compatibility between CommonPoint applications and OpenDoc.

Writing CommonPoint part handlers for OpenDoc parts will become easier for a developer as the CommonPoint application system matures. Taligent also plans to allow a part and its part handler running in the host environment to appear and work within a Taligent document window without the CommonPoint developer writing any additional CommonPoint code.

OLE

OpenDoc is being developed for Windows as well as other operating systems, so it supports interoperability with OLE and OLE-based Windows applications. Because Taligent supports interoperability with OpenDoc, it can take advantage of OpenDoc's interoperability with OLE. In addition, if necessary, Taligent can extend the Compound Document framework to support OLE directly, including support for OLE Structured Storage (comparable to the way Taligent plans to support Bento), the Component Object Model (COM, comparable to SOM), and OLE Automation (comparable to the OSA).

Data Translation framework

The Data Translation framework supports the conversion of data to and from another operating system or file format. In most cases, the non-CommonPoint operating system is the host for the CommonPoint system. For example, a user might wish to convert a Windows word-processing file into a CommonPoint text document or vice versa; drag components from a CommonPoint document to a non-CommonPoint application; or copy and paste data between the CommonPoint system and the host operating system.

The Data Translation framework provides the low-level support required for converting data from a non-CommonPoint format to a CommonPoint format and back. Translation to and from a specific external format is handled by converters that can be added to the CommonPoint system as necessary.

Text and graphics converters

Taligent provides text and graphics data converters for some basic data formats, and third parties can use the Data Translation framework to write new converters. Developers creating their own custom model types may want to provide one or more converters to convert those models to or from other application data formats, especially if a developer already has an application that runs on the host operating system. For example, a developer who has an existing word-processing application for Windows and wants to writes a word-processing component for the CommonPoint system will probably also want to write a converter that can handle both formats.

PRINTING AND SCANNING

The first release of the CommonPoint system includes the Printing frameworks, which provide basic support for printing. Plans for future releases of the system include the Scanning framework, which will make it possible to write scanning applications that transfer images directly from a scanner into any CommonPoint component.

FIGURE 122
OVERVIEW OF THE PRINTING PROCESS

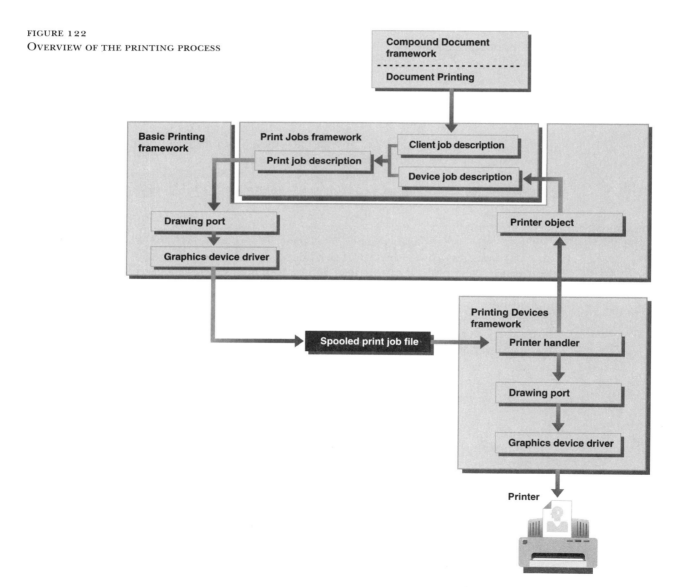

Overview of the printing process

Figure 122 shows the flow of data among the four main elements of the CommonPoint printing architecture. All printing is ultimately handled by the Basic Printing framework, the Print Jobs framework, and the Printing Devices framework. The other element of the printing architecture, Document Printing, provides a default printing implementation, based on the Basic Printing framework, for any document derived from the Compound Document framework. Such documents inherit a broad range of capabilities from Document Printing without any additional programming. Programmers need to use the Basic Printing framework directly only if they want to provide additional capabilities that aren't part of Document Printing.

Printing occurs in two stages. The Basic Printing and Print Jobs frameworks (near the center of Figure 122) are primarily responsible for stage 1: from the time printing is initiated to the time the print job is spooled to disk. The Printing Devices framework (near the bottom right of Figure 122) is primarily responsible for stage 2: from the time the print job is spooled to disk to the time it is actually printed. Stage 2 is completely independent of the application from which printing was initiated in stage 1.

Stage 1

When the user of a document based on the Compound Document framework initiates printing, the Basic Printing framework uses the Print Jobs framework to create a print job description. A *print job description* encapsulates a client job description and a device job description.

A *client job description* encapsulates information about the document being printed, such as the content to print, the number of copies the user wants, the page range, the kind of paper to use, and so on. This information is provided by the document that generates the printing request. A *device job description* encapsulates information about the actual printer, such as the media types it can use, the kinds of pages it can print, and other hardware details. This information is supplied by a *printer object* that represents the currently selected printer.

The Basic Printing framework uses the Graphics system to pass the print job description to a graphics device driver (subclassed from TGrafDevice) via a drawing port (subclassed from TGrafPort). The Graphics system uses these objects to draw the image, just as it would if it were drawing to the screen. Basic Printing then converts the graphics primitives to objects and streams them to disk as a spooled print job file, which the system associates with a queue for the printer specified by the printer object. (For a discussion of streams and persistence, see page 351.)

Stage 2

Next, but possibly at a later time, the Printing Devices framework (at the bottom right of Figure 122) and low-level portions of the system that support printing take control of the spooled print job description. A *printer handler,* which is usually represented on the screen by a printer appliance icon, prepares a spooled print job for a particular printer. Users can double-click a printer appliance icon to view that printer's current queue, reorder their print jobs, set a print time, delete a print job, or (if more than one printer is available) drag icons representing print jobs from one printer's queue to another.

To print a spooled print job, the printer handler resurrects the streamed data and uses the Graphics system to send it to the printer via a drawing port and graphics device driver. The graphics device driver converts the graphics primitives into whatever form is appropriate for the printer. The printer handler maintains a connection to its printer over the network or via one of the computer's ports and provides printer objects when needed for print job descriptions. In some ways a printer handler is equivalent to a printer driver for the Mac OS, although it works at a higher level and is much easier to write.

Notice that the entire printing process involves using the Graphics system twice: once in stage 1 to draw the image in a form that can be spooled to disk, and again in stage 2 to draw the spooled image to a graphics device and thence to the printer. The Graphics system uses floating point arithmetic and can take full advantage of any display device's capabilities, whether it's a 72-dpi screen or a high-resolution color printer. Because the Graphics system takes care of all drawing into graphics device drivers for the Printing frameworks, documents always print optimally for a printer's resolution and other characteristics. (For more information about graphics device drivers, see page 243.)

Document Printing

Document Printing implements the following default features for all applications based on the Compound Document framework:

- Precise graphic imaging to the highest level possible for any given display device—What You Want Is What You Get (WYWIWYG)
- Color matching (can be switched on or off)
- Automatic pagination
- Printing ranges of pages
- Imposition (printing a multipage folio on a large sheet of paper)
- Printing compound documents
- n-up composition

Plans for future versions of the CommonPoint system include supporting the following Document Printing capabilities for Compound Document applications:

- Label making
- Printing envelopes and letterhead
- Adornments such as borders and page numbers
- Color separations and page sorting.

Developers who wish to provide more specialized printing capabilities can use the Basic Printing framework directly to implement variations on the standard Document Printing features or add new features. For example, the Text Editing framework uses this approach to provide pagination specifically tailored to word-processing needs. Developers can also use Basic Printing to implement custom pagination schemes and other features, such as specialized preprocessing for print jobs.

Basic Printing

In the simplest cases, printing requires just three objects: a folio of pages, a printer object, and a print job description. The Basic Printing framework manages folios and printer objects and provides classes for composing completed pages. The Print Jobs framework manages print job descriptions.

Folios

A *folio* represents the document or collection of *pages* to be printed. Access to the pages within a folio is provided by a page iterator created by the folio. The page iterator also establishes the order of the pages.

All folios have two important properties: they can print and they can create page iterators. The system provides several kinds of folios, and developers can also define their own. The Basic Printing framework currently supports three types of folios:

- **A compound page folio** encapsulates a collection of folios. Compound page folios represent documents that have more than one format per sheet of output, such as letters and envelopes, transparencies and plain paper, or 1-up and 2-up variations. Any compound page folio can contain any folio, including other compound page folios, with no limit to the number of nested folios.
- **A paginated page folio** encapsulates a large canvas area partitioned into pages. It contains page-sized tiles arranged in a two-dimensional array with optional borders and gaps. A paginated page folio can be used as a pagination aid when pagination is required in a model presentation, but it doesn't handle widowed or orphaned text or reflow the document.
- **A book page folio** is a type of paginated page folio that divides a given work area into book pages with appropriate margins or gaps between pages. Word processors commonly use this approach.

Every folio has a page iterator that accepts page ranges:

- **A page iterator** provides access to the pages in a folio, establishes page order, and typically prints the pages. Unlike a regular collection iterator, a page iterator owns its contents and can accept page ranges, and each iterated page is valid only while it is being iterated.

- **A page range** accepts a page number and determines whether that page is in the range. When a page iterator is iterating over pages in the folio, it automatically skips pages that are not in the range. A page range also returns first and last page limits of the range, but page ranges do not have to be continuous. For example, page ranges that specify only odd or only even pages are quite useful.

A page iterator can parse all of the pages of the folio that created it, but it cannot parse other folios. It can parse pages in random or sequential order, both forward and backward. One page folio can create several page iterators that operate independently. As long as the folio contents are not altered, a folio and any of its iterators can be printed simultaneously, provided they are multithread-safe. Once a folio is deleted, its iterators are no longer valid.

MPageFolio and related classes

Figure 123 shows the major classes the Basic Printing framework provides for managing folios, page iterators, and page ranges.

These classes play the following roles:

- **MPrintable** standardizes calling conventions associated with printable objects. When mixed in with any class, it allows any object of that class to print itself. It provides two key functions: Print and PrintAndCreateJobHandle, which returns a job handle for tracking the print job.

- **MPageFolio** represents a collection of printable pages and defines the structure and content of a printable folio. To extend or modify the default Document Printing capabilities, a developer must override Document Printing's implementation of the MPageFolio function CreatePageIterator, which defines each page's characteristics. The Basic Printing framework provides three kinds of page folios:

  - **TCompoundPageFolio** represents an arbitrary collection of MPageFolio objects. TCompoundPageFolio creates iterators that are instances of TCompoundPageIterator.

  - **TPaginatedPageFolio** represents an area partitioned into pages. It creates iterators that are instances of TPaginatedPageIterator.

  - **TBookPageFolio** represents a paginated page folio for books. As a subclass of TPaginatedPageFolio, it creates iterators that are instances of TPaginatedPageIterator.

- **TPageIterator** provides access to the pages in a folio. A TPageIterator object returns objects of type TPage, which mixes in MDrawable. The Printing frameworks use the drawing capabilities inherited from MDrawable to draw TPage objects.

The Basic Printing framework provides two types of page iterators that can print the pages they iterate. These iterators must be sequenced to a valid page when they draw a page, and they can draw only one page at a time:

- **TCompoundPageIterator** is an iterator for compound page folios, used to access the documents that make up the compound folio or individual pages.
- **TPaginatedPageIterator** is an iterator for paginated page folios, including instances of TBookPageFolio.

- **TPageRange** defines specific page groups or selections in a page folio. A TPageRange object allows any combination of pages to be included or excluded during printing. Every page iterator has a page range; the default page range is the entire document. The Printing Services framework provides three types of page ranges:

  - **TStandardPageRange** is a general-purpose page range class that can be set and modified to emulate virtually any set of pages. It obeys the rules of set operations such as Union, Intersection, Difference, and ExclusiveOr. The Not operation excludes the pages specified by the range.
  - **TEvenPageRange** includes only the even pages of a folio.
  - **TOddPageRange** includes only the odd pages of a folio.

FIGURE 123
FOLIOS, PAGE ITERATORS, AND PAGE RANGES

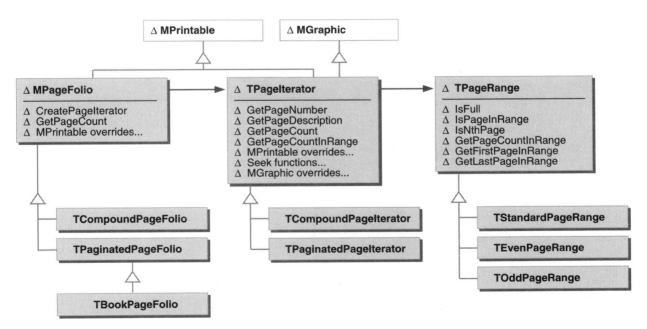

Page descriptions

A page typically consists of a sheet of paper, but printers can also use other media such as film or transparencies. A page is characterized by its page description and media type.

A *page description* describes the media and page metrics for every page in a printable folio. Page descriptions are represented by classes derived from the TPageDescription class shown in Figure 124. They encapsulate information for the folio such as the page bounds, duplex capability, mismatch options, page orientation, and media sources and destinations on the target printer. Developers using the Compound Document framework need to know how page descriptions work if they wish to customize the way their applications define pages.

Paper is an example of a common media type. A media type's characteristics include its material, color, texture, inherent thickness, and transparency. Instances of TPrintMedia indicate the preferred media for a page description. The default is to use the standard medium available on the printer. If no printer is specified, any medium can be used.

Every printable page must have a TPageDescription. It's possible to use a single page description if all of the pages in a folio are the same. TStandardPageDescription can be used for most pages.

Page descriptions usually come from printer objects, which contain collections of page descriptions that represent all the page types available on the printer. The user selects a printer and the page and media types.

Page descriptions are bound to the folio. If the page description bound to the folio does not match one of the printer page descriptions, the mismatch must be resolved. The folio is never reformatted to compensate for mismatches. Instead, the pages are scaled, tiled, or clipped. Users can specify defaults or choose to be notified when mismatches occur and select a mismatch option at print time. For example, if a particular printer prints on large pieces of paper and the page defined by the source document is relatively small, the user can specify that the source page should be positioned in the center of the printed piece of paper.

FIGURE 124
PAGE
DESCRIPTION
CLASSES

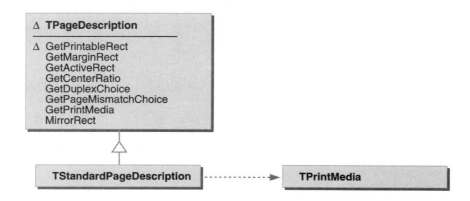

A page description describes the dimensions of the page by defining three
rectangular areas:

- **Physical rectangle.** The exterior dimensions of the print media.
  TPageDescription provides constants that represent standard page sizes,
  such as US Letter, US Legal, A4 Letter, and Business Envelope.
- **Printable rectangle.** The portion of the physical page on which a printer can
  print. The printable rectangle is used to map any given page onto the
  printable area of an actual printer. If there is a one-to-one mapping between
  the areas, the page is printed as is. If not, the page description printable area
  is mapped onto the printer printable area according to one of the page
  description mismatch options: Tile, Clip, or Scale.
- **Margin rectangle.** This area, also known as the user rectangle, can represent any
  area within the physical page—it is completely independent from the
  printable rectangle. The margin rectangle is not used by the Printing
  frameworks; it is reserved for application use, typically to mark the boundary
  of the printable area within the application.

Any one of these areas can be the *active rectangle,* the rectangle that indicates
which part of a page the printing system is to use for pagination, tiling, clipping,
or scaling. As shown in Figure 125, the origin for all of the page areas is the top
left corner of the physical page. The printable and margin rectangles are always
offset with respect to this origin.

FIGURE 125
PAGE ORIGIN
AND AXES

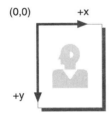

Printer objects

Figure 126 shows the class relationships for TPrinter. TPrinter instances represent actual printers. A printer object provides three things that are essential to printing:

- A collection of page descriptions that represent all the page types available on the printer, with at least one page description designated as the default for the printer
- A device job description (required for every print job)
- A list of all the available media types (provided by TPageDescription)

FIGURE 126
PRINTERS

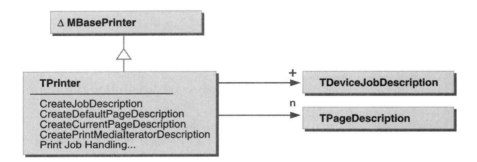

TPrinter also provides functions for canceling, deferring, adding, and removing print jobs from the printer queue.

The computer doesn't need to have access to an actual printer while a user is editing a document. The only printing resource needed is a page description, and the one associated with the folio is sufficient.

If a user attempts to print to a nonexistent printer, the Basic Printing framework throws an exception, looks for an alternative printer that matches the original printer in type or capabilities, and notifies the user, who can confirm the match or select another printer.

If there are no matches, no other printers available, and no selected alternative, the folio cannot be printed, but the user can continue editing. This is different from the Mac OS, for example, where the system printer is always used to print whether the document is matched to it or not.

Page composition

Page composition is the process of composing pages for a folio by using previously generated pages, adornments, and other page fragments. The Basic Printing framework takes care of page composition at printing time after generating a complete folio. Composition doesn't generate new pages; instead it operates on completed pages.

Page compositors provide extensions to printing without affecting preexisting folios. A page compositor can be used to do any kind of processing on a folio before spooling the print job to disk, including:

- Printing forms or templates
- Creating and placing labels automatically
- Adding adornments to a page without modifying it
- Making automatic production of 2-up, 4-up, or n-up compositions
- Automatically arranging pages in imposition form
- Converting pages into individual color separations and printing each separately

The main function of a page compositor is to create page iterators, which compose new pages out of old pages. Page compositors use the old pages as the basis for building the new page, which can contain information not included in the original pages.

The page iterators created by page compositors can be modified with page ranges, but they have no target folio. Instead, they use other page iterators as their target. Page compositors can be chained together to perform multiple complex operations on a single folio.

Composition and imposition

Automatic *n-up* composition prints *n* copies of a page image on a single sheet of paper. The sheet is cut to produce *n* finished pieces.

Automatic imposition prints a multipage folio on a single, large sheet of paper. The printed sheet is folded and cut so that all the pages are in the proper order and orientation.

Image

2-up on a single page

4-up on a single page

FIGURE 127
N-UP COMPOSITION

original pages

front of page   back of page

8-page booklet, trimmed at top

FIGURE 128
IMPOSITION

The Basic Printing framework provides the two types of page compositors shown in Figure 129:

■ **TNUpCompositor** creates variations of n-up printing. It places several target pages onto one destination page in a tiled format.

■ **TPageImpositor** is similar to TNUpCompositor. It composes several target pages onto a destination page, but it places the pages in an order and orientation that allows the printed sheet to be cut and folded so that the resulting booklet is already collated and ready for binding.

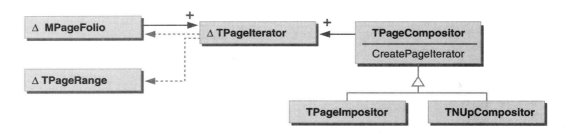

FIGURE 129
PAGE
COMPOSITORS

Print Jobs

The Print Jobs framework manages print job descriptions. TPrintJobDescription instances encapsulate information about the print job from the document that generates the printing request and from a printer object (TPrinter) that represents the printer the user wishes to use. This is another useful class for developers who are customizing the printing features provided by Document Printing. A program can create its own print job description, or it can allow a user to select options in a dialog box that the Basic Printing framework uses to generate a print job description automatically.

As shown in Figure 130, a print job description comprises a device job description associated with the printer object and a client job description associated with the folio.

FIGURE 130
PRINT JOB
DESCRIPTIONS

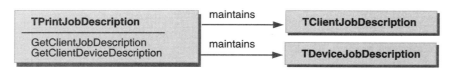

The client job description specifies the number of copies, cover page or end page, and page range. The device job description specifies the target printer object, type of document finishing (staples, collations, print quality), resolution, and paper tray selection.

The client job description and the device job description are independent, so application developers and printer handler developers can extend the print job description independently. Both have control over print-time customization, but their customizations don't conflict.

Printing Devices framework

The Printing Devices framework manages printer handlers. A printer handler can represent any kind of device to which a print job can be sent, including virtual devices, spoolers, server routers, and so on, as well as printers. Each printer available to a computer has a corresponding printer handler, which appears to the user as a printer appliance icon and provides information about its printer to applications and other parts of the system. "Overview of the printing process," beginning on page 289, describes the role of printer handlers in more detail.

Manufacturers of printing hardware and software can extend the Printing Devices framework to provide printer handlers for almost any kind of printing device. Specialized printer handlers can also be used to provide fax capabilities and plotter support.

Writers of printer handlers generally need to provide a graphics device driver for the printing device to use. The graphics device driver converts the graphics system primitives into whatever form is appropriate for the printer. The CommonPoint system provides at least four generic conversion engines that support these printing standards:

- PostScript
- Hewlett-Packard's Page Control Language (PCL®)
- The Hewlett-Packard Graphics Language (HPGL®), used for plotters and other vector devices
- Raster printing for "dumb" (bitmap) printers

Rather than writing a graphics device driver from scratch, developers who wish to support these standards can use the corresponding conversion engines as is or modify them.

Scanning framework

The Scanning framework, which is planned for future versions of the CommonPoint system, makes it possible to write scanning applications that use a scanning device to transfer images directly from a scanner into any component—unlike traditional scanning applications, which usually require the user to copy and paste a scanned image to its final destination.

Much like a printer handler, a scanner handler appears on the desktop as an appliance icon, provides information about a specific scanner to scanning applications and other parts of the system, and allows the user to adjust hardware settings or preferences. The Scanning framework cooperates with the Compound Document framework to support live links between any scanning application and any component, so that a scanned image appears directly wherever the user wants it.

Scanning devices conform to an API that all scanning applications can use. Scanning applications in turn conform to an API that suppliers of plug-in filters can use to support optical character recognition (OCR), feature reading, or other image-processing capabilities. Both scanning devices and plug-in filters support the Compound Document framework APIs.

Scanner manufacturers can use the Scanning framework to write scanning devices for their products. Scanning application developers can use the scanning framework to write scanning applications that work with any scanning device.

LOCALIZATION SERVICES

Localization Services support multilingual, localizable user interface elements and text. For information about multilingual text input, see "Text Input and Output," beginning on page 261. This section introduces Locales and language-sensitive text services.

Locales

A *locale* is a collection of archived resources that are localized for a particular geographic region. These resources might include:

- Formatting information for numbers, times, dates, currency units, and the like
- Regional information such as a country identifier or a time zone
- Collating rules for ordering and comparing ranges of text
- Styling information for text presentations, such as font information for specific elements within an interface
- Typing configuration preferences
- Localized user interface elements for individual applications

Locales are used in two ways:

- To identify the geographic regions for which objects need to be localized and organize them into a *locale hierarchy*. When you create localized objects, such as user interface elements, you can store them in an archive and associate them with that locale. Users within that locale then get localized user interface elements when they run your application.
- To store a group of objects commonly used by applications customized for a particular geographic region—for example, fonts, number formats, currency formats, and typing configuration preferences. Any CommonPoint class can access the objects stored in a given locale. Applications can therefore provide localized features without having to keep track of the contents of particular locales. It's also possible to develop applications that use more than one locale for multilingual processing within a single document.

Locale hierarchy

Locales are created and stored in a static hierarchy based on geographic relationships, descending from a single root locale (see Figure 131). The upper levels represent various world languages, and the lower levels correspond to increasingly subdivided geographic regions. Each locale represents a particular geographic region.

The lowest level of the locale hierarchy represents the largest geographic area within a country with common time and language characteristics. This allows for distinctions between, for example, the various time zones in the United States or the French-speaking and German-speaking regions of Switzerland.

This hierarchical approach allows developers to store only the information they need at each level. For example, many items need to be localized only at the English-speaking level, not at a country or time zone level. When a program uses the archive, it searches only for archived objects in the current locale and in locales that are ancestors of the current locale. In developing an application, you usually first create objects at the level for which they are the most appropriate—for example, "English" or "United States"—and then put additional objects in more specialized locales as necessary for the application's requirements.

Any object can be added to a locale to produce the correct behavior for that locale. Each object can also have a complete set of localized names—that is, the same object can have multiple names in different languages so that it can be identified by users in the language of their choice.

FIGURE 131
THE LOCALE
HIERARCHY

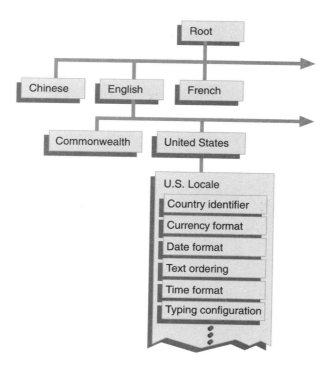

The initial release of the CommonPoint application system provides default locales for the United States, France, and Japan. Plans for future releases include locales for Great Britain, Canada, Germany, and Italy and support for the creation and installation of custom locales. The *cp*Constructor user interface builder makes it easy to associate user interface objects with particular locales; see the section beginning on page 146 for details.

Using locales

You can use the locale mechanism in several ways:

- For language- or region-sensitive features, such as number formatting or text collating, you can use resources from the current locale or a user-specified locale rather than providing for different languages or regions yourself. The system provides native language support transparently for both the user and the programmer.

- You can use *cp*Constructor to archive and retrieve user interfaces through locales. Localizers can create user interfaces in additional languages without having to access the source code or recompile the application, and users get a presentation in their preferred language whenever one is available.

- The locale hierarchy lets you attach multiple languages to a single object. This allows your application to translate a single presentation into multiple languages. When the program executes, it chooses a presentation based on the language of the current locale.

- You can archive your application's presentation at an appropriate level of the locale hierarchy, such as United States, and specify that level as the program's default locale. Localizers can create localized presentations at other levels. If no localized presentation exists for, say, a French user, the default presentation is used instead.

Language-sensitive support services	The Text Analysis, Text Scanning and Formatting, and Date and Time Conversion frameworks provide multilingual text analysis and formatting capabilities. Their classes use localized data to produce the correct text-processing behavior for particular languages or regions. These instances can be archived in the appropriate locale for use anywhere in the system.

Text Analysis

The Text Analysis framework provides language-sensitive behavior for:

- **Collation,** or algorithmic sorting and comparison of text strings
- **Pattern matching,** or searching for specific text patterns
- **Boundary analysis,** or boundary detection for text selection

Text-ordering classes

The text-ordering classes use tables of collation rules that define the ordering of characters for a particular language. These classes provide member functions for simple comparison operations on text strings. They also support custom sorting algorithms.

The text-ordering classes are useful for comparing text data according to the alphabetical ordering rules of a natural language rather than the byte values of the character-encoding set. For example, without language-sensitive collation, in the Latin script the letter "Z" would be ordered before the letter "a." Similarly, different languages involve different special ordering cases, such as the alphabetization of "McDonald" and "MacDonald" in English or special rules for languages such as Hebrew and Thai that cluster a principal character with secondary characters. It's also possible to customize collation sequences or merge them for multilingual text analysis. The CommonPoint application system provides language-sensitive ordering for a variety of languages, including English, French, Japanese, and Arabic.

Pattern iterator classes

The pattern iterator classes support language-sensitive pattern matching. Pattern iterator objects use a particular instance of a text-ordering class to provide language-sensitive searching capabilities for that language. They can be used to implement language-sensitive, case-insensitive searching.

Text chunk iterator classes

The text chunk iterator classes provide language-sensitive analysis for character, word, and sentence boundaries, providing the capability for language-sensitive text selection. For example, the letter "â" should typically be treated as a single character even though it may be stored as two characters (the base letter plus the accent). These classes also perform analysis to determine proper line-breaking behavior based on a table of word-break rules for each language.

Text Scanning and Formatting

The Text Scanning and Formatting framework provides classes for creating objects called formatters that can scan language-dependent text data to produce language-independent binary data or format binary data to produce text data. For example, a formatter can scan a date displayed in a standard Arabic date format to produce the binary equivalent, then format the binary data to produce the same date in a standard English format. Any text input to or output from a formatter can be styled. For example, negative numbers could be indicated by a red color style.

Text Scanning and Formatting includes default number formatters that provide a wide range of capabilities, including

- Normalization for numeric fields
- Decimal alignment
- Scientific notation
- Nondecimal formats such as Roman numerals and fractions

Text Scanning and Formatting also provides a string formatter that integrates text, number, and date and time formatting to facilitate the creation of text strings containing data in various formats. The string formatter is similar to the C `printf` function, except that it can also:

- Completely localize the message by:
    - Translating the string
    - Rearranging the parameters
    - Using localized formatters for each parameter
- Use subformatters based on the numeric value of a variable—for example, substituting month names for the values 1 through 12, or providing singular or plural noun and verb forms as appropriate.

Date and Time Conversion

The Date and Time Conversion framework provides date and time formatters that convert the internal system time into a meaningful expression for a particular locale. They do so by first converting the system time into the local time zone and then mapping the local time to the fields of a particular calendar. It's then possible to access individual fields of the calendar and create specific patterns of data. For example, the system representation of date and time can be formatted in any of these ways:

- Friday, January 25, 1999
- 1/25/99
- 25/1/99
- 12:01 A.M.

The CommonPoint application system supports the Gregorian calendar used in most parts of the world. Plans for future release include support for the Japanese and Arabic calendars. Developers can also create their own customized calendars.

Formatters can be combined for related scanning and formatting operations. For example, it's possible to use a Japanese number formatter within a Japanese date formatter.

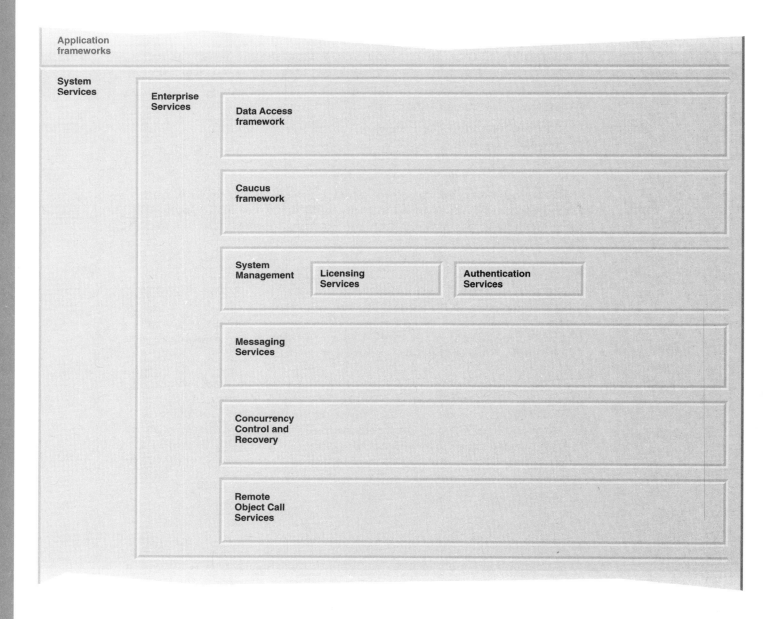

CHAPTER 13

ENTERPRISE SERVICES

The Enterprise Services frameworks provide specific services for distributed computing environments. They are built on top of the Communications frameworks, which provide low-level support for all data sharing and communication between different address spaces, whether on different computers or on a single computer running the CommonPoint system at the same time as the host system. The Communications frameworks are described in Chapter 15, beginning on page 376.

The Enterprise Services frameworks provide these services:

- **The Data Access framework** handles communication among applications, connectivity software, and databases.

- **The Concurrency Control and Recovery framework** provides local transaction-processing capabilities that ensure logical consistency of data that can be modified by multiple tasks at the same time.

- **The Caucus framework** provides multicast transport facilities for the Shared Document framework and collaborative user environments such as CSpace. (For an introduction to the Caucus framework in the context of the Communications frameworks, see "How the Communications frameworks work together," beginning on page 379.)

- **The System Management frameworks** support administrative tasks such as software installation, licensing, configuration, maintenance, security, and troubleshooting.

- **The Messaging Services framework** provides object abstractions for store-and-forward messaging that shield CommonPoint developers from the details of host messaging protocols.

- **The Remote Object Call (ROC) Services framework** allows applications to make remote procedure (member function) calls to Taligent services running on various hosts. It also provides the basis for Taligent's long-term CORBA and distributed objects strategy.

This chapter introduces Enterprise Services (except for the Caucus framework as noted above).

DATA ACCESS FRAMEWORK

The Data Access framework lets CommonPoint applications retrieve, create, or modify data stored in standard Structured Query Language (SQL) databases. Its primary purpose is to insulate applications from the complexities of SQL dialects and specific implementations of software modules such as ODBC, SQL*NET, and OpenClient that connect with SQL databases on multiple platforms.

Although many SQL dialects agree on basic retrieval protocols (SELECT commands), they differ in many other respects (table/column catalogs, table creation, index specification, data formats, and so on). This situation is being addressed by ANSI and other standards committees, but a complete solution is many years away and may be unattainable, given the desire of individual SQL vendors to distinguish their products with unique features.

Users of database services expect to be able to mix and match both SQL databases and connectivity software. The Data Access framework addresses this need by allowing the user to choose both elements at logon time and insulating the application software from particular server dependencies. At the same time, it permits custom use of specific database or connectivity features.

Figure 132 shows how applications and service providers use the Data Access framework. The Object Access and Document Data Access frameworks, introduced in Chapter 8, provide high-level abstractions of the Data Access framework's SQL capabilities. Data Access is a typical "middleware" framework in the sense that it provides both a client API for obtaining data access services and a customization API, the Provider API, for use by database providers, connectivity software vendors, and Taligent itself to support new connectivity modules.

The top of Figure 132 shows how three different kinds of applications can use the Object Access, Document Data Access, and Data Access frameworks:

- **Non-SQL-aware applications** use the Object Access framework, which maps C++ object abstractions to SQL abstractions provided by the Data Access framework. These applications interact with data from databases just as they would with any other Taligent data, using models, commands, and selections. They don't need to know where the data is stored or where it comes from.

- **SQL-aware applications** allow users who are familiar with SQL to work with SQL abstractions such as query documents and data documents to establish connections and make queries. These applications use the Document Data Access framework, which provides a high-level document-based SQL interface for database operations.

- **Sophisticated SQL-aware applications** tend to be written by specialized tool developers or corporate developers who want direct access to SQL capabilities for creating their own queries and data source documents. These applications interact with the Base Client API or the Extended Client API of the Data Access framework, depending on trade-offs among the simplicity, performance, and flexibility they require.

The Data Access framework uses a data transfer protocol defined by Record Source classes to transfer data among the objects it manages. A *record source* provides a streaming analog of a standard database table that can be used directly by client applications to handle data returned from a query.

The Data Access framework can be extended by third parties or by Taligent to support other protocols in addition to SQL.

FIGURE 132
DATA ACCESS
FRAMEWORKS

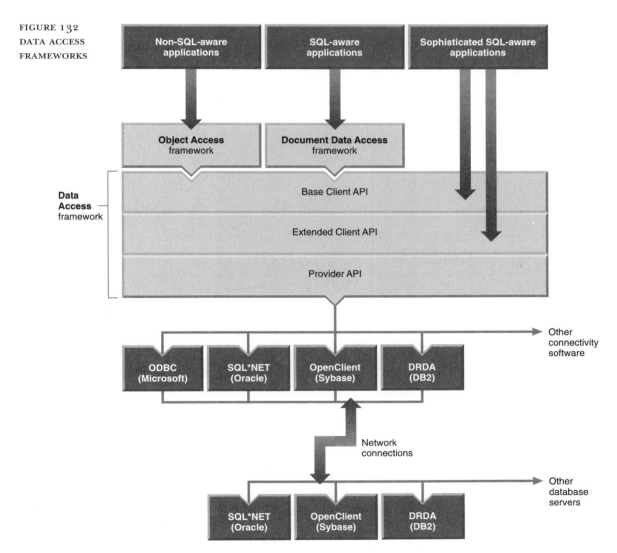

SQL Data Access class architecture

The Data Access framework provides two client APIs:

- The Base Client API provides access to a broad set of SQL commands with a minimal burden for the client application. This API focuses on simplicity rather than performance and flexibility. The Data Access framework parses Base Client SQL commands and translates them into the SQL dialect appropriate for the target database server/connection.

- The Extended Client API provides more extensive support for SQL commands, including queries that use SQL hints, custom logons, and column type specification. This API focuses on performance and flexibility. The Data Access framework doesn't parse Extended Client SQL commands. The client application must construct appropriate SQL statements by using SQL fragments provided by a parameter dictionary.

Figure 133 provides an overview of the basic classes provided by the Data Access framework.

A TSQLConnection object represents a connection between a client program and a data store via a database protocol. Connections may be active (connected) or inactive (disconnected).

FIGURE 133
SQL DATA
ACCESS CLASS
OVERVIEW

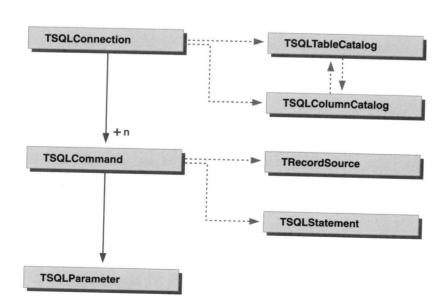

Each connection has one or more TSQLCommand objects associated with it that are responsible for executing individual SQL commands. Each TSQLCommand object embodies a parameterized and bound SQL statement and is associated with the code required to process that statement for a given database protocol server combination (such as SQL*Net to Oracle or ODBC to SQLServer). A TSQLCommand object is also associated with a TRecordSource object that embodies the data returned by the command.

Retrieving data from a data source with these objects typically involves four steps:

1. Establish a connection to a data store.

2. Use the connection to create a SQL command.

3. Execute the SQL command.

4. Display the retrieved data.

Record Sources

A record source consists of a read-only sequence of records, all of which have the same type structure (for example, long, long, real, string). Each record consists of individual fields that may have specific values or be null. Record source fields are arranged in columns, and each column is associated with a title, a data type, and so on.

The Record Source classes are part of the Base Client API. They provide a data transfer protocol that allows you to transfer records from arbitrary sources (such as the Data Access framework, spreadsheets, or databases) to arbitrary destinations. There are two kinds of record sources:

- Read-once record sources are meant to be read once. This constraint has several implications:
    - Record source providers need not worry about storage semantics or implementation.
    - Read-once record sources can be extremely lightweight and are therefore ideal for functional or data flow algorithms.
    - Read-once record sources can be of arbitrary length, because records can be retrieved on demand without prestoring them.
- Random-access record sources can be read more than once. They require more work to implement and may have very large storage requirements; however, they also have a much richer client interface.

To use record sources, objects that act as data sources must provide a member function that produces a record source, and objects that absorb record sources must provide a member function or set of member functions that accept a record source.

A live record source streamed from one application to another causes the creation of a record source at the destination that acts as a surrogate for the original, consuming records from the original as needed.

Document Data Access framework

The Document Data Access framework provides a high-level interface, based on the Compound Document framework, that allows developers to create database access documents (DADs) rapidly for use by sophisticated end users who are familiar with SQL. This interface includes extensible classes for creating query containers, assistance objects for getting connected, objects that represent data sources, objects representing users and their credentials, and so on. These are working objects that a programmer can easily instantiate and assemble into a stationery pad for database queries.

For example, a DAD user can perform the following operations

- Specify the address of a data store object by typing or by using the Directory Services mechanism. (For a brief description of the Directory Services framework, see page 380.)
- Designate a protocol type by dragging a protocol object into the data store document from a container that includes all the protocols available to the user.
- Select a data store type by dragging a data store object into the document from a container that includes all data stores available to the user.
- Create a SQL query with a standard query container, then drag and drop the query onto a particular data source object to execute it. The result comes back as a record source presented in a view that the user can select and manipulate.

DADs are often used to collect data from a data store either to be displayed immediately or to be passed on for processing or formatting. The Compound Document's support for links and anchors plays a key role in communication between DADs and other CommonPoint documents.

DADs can be used to support any operations supported by SQL statements, including the following:

- Browsing the data in a database table
- Executing a stored procedure
- Updating information in a data store
- Retrieving documents based on modification date

For an example of a DAD, see page 224.

| Object Access framework | In contrast to the Data Access framework, which requires getting and setting attributes and other programming tasks required to wrap up specific SQL information in DAD objects, the Object Access framework will provide higher-level C++ abstractions of SQL objects. These classes will allow a database administrator, for example, to create familiar business abstractions such as employee, organization, and project objects and connect them with the corresponding portions of a database without having to write a DAD. |

The Object Access framework is planned for future versions of the CommonPoint system.

CONCURRENCY CONTROL AND RECOVERY

When multiple tasks can modify the same data at the same time, system software must provide some form of concurrency control and recovery to ensure that the data remains logically consistent. The Concurrency Control and Recovery framework provides transaction-processing capabilities that address this need. Concurrency control allows multiple tasks to access data at the same time by making it appear that no sharing is occurring. Recovery addresses the problem of failures that leave data in an inconsistent state by making it appear that they never occurred.

This framework ensures data integrity by ensuring that all changes are serializable—that is, that they produce the same results as if they were executed serially. However, these capabilities are not automatic. Rather, the Concurrency Control and Recovery framework allows client applications to work with shared recoverable data by using transactions.

A *transaction* is a sequence of operations whose execution is:

- **Atomic.** Either all the operations take place or none do.
- **Consistent.** The same operations always produce the same results under the same conditions.
- **Isolated.** The operations appear to be the only ones occurring no matter how many other users may be performing operations against the same data.
- **Durable.** The results of the operations persist after the operations have been completed and committed.

In the first release of the CommonPoint system, the Concurrency Control and Recovery framework supports only local transactions (on the same machine). This means that a single transaction can't perform work across multiple machines. Plans for future versions of the CommonPoint application system include supporting more sophisticated transaction processing.

SYSTEM MANAGEMENT

The System Management frameworks provide integrated services that support a software infrastructure for packaging, promoting, distributing, selling, and supporting CommonPoint software products. The Licensing Services frameworks are the first such service provided with the CommonPoint system. Plans for future releases include parallel groups of frameworks for Software Distribution Services, Software Asset Management Services, Backup and Recovery Services, and other related services. Taligent also plans to expand the Software Administration framework, which will first be available in the context of Licensing Services, to provide service administration capabilities.

In addition to supporting a flexible software publishing infrastructure, as just mentioned, Taligent also intends to support monitoring and control services such as management agents, alarm reporting, and operations scheduling. Monitoring and control services are closely tied to the operating system that hosts the CommonPoint application system. Therefore, Taligent services in this area depend on certain key capabilities of the underlying host operating system.

The sections that follow introduce the Licensing Services frameworks, which are available in the first release of the CommonPoint system, and briefly describe Taligent's plans for security services, software distribution services, asset management services, and management agents in future releases.

Licensing Services

The Licensing Services frameworks provide a flexible licensing mechanism that allows users working on a network to mix and match products to suit their needs without depriving vendors of appropriate compensation. To use a particular product, a user purchases an activation key that encodes the terms and conditions of purchase.

Networked environments commonly include one or more license servers that support software licensing. A *license manager vendor* sells a licensing software package to a commercial software developer, who uses it to build licensing capabilities into a particular software product. The software developer can then distribute the product widely in a form that permits trial use for demonstration purposes. A customer (such as an in-house IS manager) who wants to purchase the product gives the software company some basic information about the customer's computing environment, pays for a license, and obtains an *activation key* that permits use of the software under the terms of the license. For the customer to install the activation key successfully, the license manager server for which the developer bought the original licensing package must be available on the customer's network.

This arrangement makes it possible for the software developer to distribute software over a network and receive compensation for licenses. However, a software company developing for multiple platforms has to deal with different kinds of license packages for different operating systems, each with its own interface for creating a licensed program and for minting new activation keys, and each requiring its own separate binary version of the software program. Similarly, the corporate customer has to deal with different kinds of interfaces for installing keys in programs. Both the software developer and the customer incur considerable overhead costs in supporting multiple licensing models.

The Licensing Services frameworks are designed to remove these and other barriers between software vendors and their potential customers. The purpose of these frameworks is to lower substantially the initial investment that commercial developers must make to distribute their products without risking unauthorized use. The Licensing Services frameworks decouple server dependencies and specific terms and conditions of use from the actual software product, making it possible for the software developer to distribute a single binary version to all its customers. The terms and conditions are encoded in the activation key, which the developer can mint and the user can install in the same way regardless of the license server involved.

There are three Licensing Services frameworks:

- **Licensing framework.** Provides a single client API called by software products at runtime to verify that an appropriate activation key has been purchased. The CommonPoint system includes a default license server that provides a minimum level of security, and other vendors can provide more sophisticated servers that use the Licensing framework to support the same client API.

- **Product Preparation framework.** Provides a single interface that software developers can use to mint activation keys for various kinds of license servers. Different keys can be used to activate a single binary version of a program under different licensing arrangements.

- **Software Administration framework.** Provides a single interface for use by system administrators to order and install activation keys, administer licensing resources, and manage different kinds of license servers.

Commercial software developers can use the Licensing and Product Preparation frameworks to support verification of activation keys that they create with the Product Preparation framework. Because the latter greatly simplifies minting of activation keys, developers can more easily sell their products via software publishers or system integrators, who can mint activation keys on the developer's behalf. The Licensing Services frameworks also make it easier for both software publishers and individual developers to use automated fulfillment mechanisms to distribute activation keys.

Customers can use a single interface provided by the Software Administration framework with a variety of license servers, greatly simplifying a complex system administration task.

License manager vendors can use all three frameworks to create license provider implementations, which are described in the next section.

License provider implementation

A *license provider implementation* created by a license manager vendor includes the following elements:

- Licensing framework implementation
- Product Preparation framework implementation
- System Administration framework implementation
- Associated license servers

Figure 134 shows how these elements work with the licensing frameworks. The Licensing framework implementation instantiates framework classes and calls member functions within the code of a Taligent software product. It communicates with the license server, sending a message containing a *challenge* and a request for license units. The server typically responds to this challenge by returning a message containing the license units. If the key data is satisfactory, the Licensing framework implementation allows the product to be used. If the framework cannot locate an acceptable key, it communicates that information to the product via an exception, and the product takes appropriate action.

The Product Preparation framework implementation provides access to key-minting capabilities for all license manager vendors' license servers via a single user interface. Similarly, the Software Administration implementation permits activation key installation and other licensing administration tasks for all license servers via a single user interface.

FIGURE 134
LICENSE
PROVIDER
IMPLEMENTATION

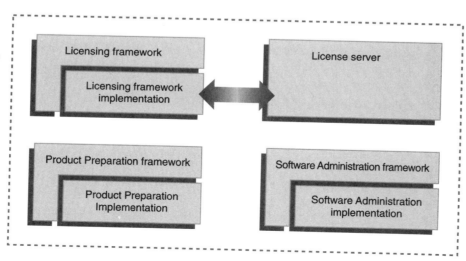

Operational model

Figure 135 illustrates how the three Licensing Services frameworks work together. The operational model described in the sections that follow assumes that the CommonPoint system is running on a non-Taligent host such as AIX or HP-UX and that the available license servers are running on non-Taligent systems or on the CommonPoint system. In the figure, "License Provider 1" and "License Provider 2" refer to implementations of the Licensing Services frameworks provided by different vendors of license server software.

Software developer
prepares product

The software developer incorporates code into a product that instantiates Licensing framework classes as needed. The construction and destruction of a TLicenseUse instance demarcate the use of a licensable user product. The former precedes the allocation of licensing units to use the product, and the latter releases them. When the product is ready for shipment, the developer uses the standard interface for the Product Preparation framework interactively to supply product data requested and mint an activation key for trial use.

The key format is determined by the license provider implementation of the Product Preparation framework the software vendor uses to generate the key. Trial use can permit operation of the software for a brief period of time, or with certain features (such as document saving) disabled until a long-term activation key is purchased. Alternatively, a key can consume license units each time the user launches the product, permitting "pay per use" instead of "pay for ownership" business models.

FIGURE 135
LICENSING
SERVICES
OPERATIONAL
MODEL

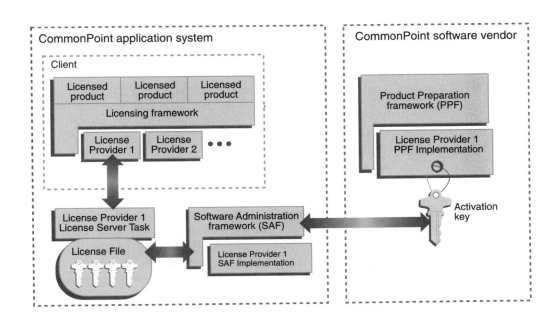

Customer installs
software

In early releases of the CommonPoint system, installation involves using a tool supplied by the license server vendor. When Software Distribution Services are available in future releases, the system administrator can use them to install the product for trial use by multiple users. (See page 320 for more information about Software Distribution Services.)

Customer buys
license units

After trial use of a product, a customer decides to buy a license for specific features, number of users, duration of use, upgrades, and so on. The customer contacts the software vendor (which can be the original developer or a software publisher or systems integrator acting on behalf of the developer) and provides information such as name, number of users, features wanted, list of license servers available at customer's site, and Taligent workstation identifier. The support person (or an automated fulfillment system) handling the call feeds product and customer data to the Product Preparation framework to produce an encrypted activation key that can be used by that customer only. The support person consults the licensing fee schedules and informs the customer of the number of license units required by the license and the price of the units. After confirming payment—with a credit card number, for example—the customer receives the key by telephone, fax, mail, or electronic mail. The customer then uses the standard Software Administration interface to install the key.

The customer experiences immediate access to the product for any user covered by the license without incidental purchase costs such as shipping and handling. The customer can purchase an expanded license at any time to include more users, features, workstations, and so on. The developer experiences the immediate completion of a sale, satisfaction of a customer, and guaranteed revenue from product use without sales costs such as shipment of media and documentation.

Floating licenses are among the many licensing options available under this arrangement. A floating license isn't tied to a particular user or machine but is shared by different people at different times. The customer can purchase a number of license units and dynamically allocate them among users, departments, projects, workstations, or LANs in response to changing needs.

Client-server operation

When a product is invoked by a user, it calls a framework function that issues a license verification challenge to the license server after negotiating a challenge protocol for the corresponding framework implementation. The server reads activation key data and confirms whether use of the product is within license parameters. If it is, the server subtracts license units from the current balance and calculates a challenge reply from key data. The client confirms the authenticity of the reply, authorizes withdrawal of the requested licensing units, and continues execution. When product use ends, the Licensing framework releases any unused license units back to the server implementation.

Challenge mechanism operation

The challenge mechanism helps to ensure that products are used only within licensing terms.

The Licensing framework defines the APIs that software developers use when developing CommonPoint products. The Licensing framework implementation provided by a specific license server vendor is dynamically loaded as a shared library into the application's address space. This allows CommonPoint products to be developed independently of the target license provider implementation and gives the user the option of selecting specific license server software.

This design could theoretically allow a sophisticated end user to replace the license provider implementation by building and installing an imposter shared library that satisfied all the interface requirements of the Licensing framework. The challenge mechanism deters this kind of attack by allowing the licensed product to authenticate the Licensing framework implementation and the activation key that was used to grant licensing rights. Although this mechanism is not guaranteed tamper proof, it does deter tampering. Any attempt at subverting the challenge mechanism requires an overt act of programming that is obvious and intentional.

The Licensing framework includes an abstract base class, ProviderOperation, that allows license provider implementations to subclass specialized challenge protocols of varying complexity and levels of security. The Licensing framework passes the ProviderOperation around as a polymorphic object that contains specific challenge data and operations. Typically the product creates the actual challenge, the license server answers it, and the product verifies the answer.

Each license provider implementation is expected to support a number of challenge protocols to provide customers with the required mix of security and flexibility. Each product can also be licensed under more than one license provider implementation without requiring separate binary versions of the product.

The first release of the CommonPoint system supplies one challenge protocol. License manager vendors can also supply proprietary challenge protocols that offer greater degrees of security and product differentiation.

**Authentication
Services**

Authentication Services, which are planned for future versions of the
CommonPoint system, are being designed to provide a uniform API for a
"reasonable first-line defense" against viruses and security attack on all
CommonPoint hosts. The design of these classes has been influenced by
government security definitions and recommendations for mainframe and
workstation security.

Authentication Services will provide basic protection against alteration or loss of
data, unauthorized disclosure of data, and denial of service. They can be used for
the following purposes:

- Identifying a user, determining whether an action is permitted for that user,
  and recording the action in a tamper-proof log
- Controlling access for users and programs
- Configuring the level of security
- Defining guest privileges
- Remotely administering security services
- Sharing files and other resources or keeping them private
- Using public key encryption

Each user must log on before performing any actions or accessing any system
resources. Authentication Services control access by means of user IDs and access
control lists (ACL) for each controlled object. They provide a common object
interface that uses the security mechanism of the host operating system to
perform these tasks. As a result, Authentication Services can only be as secure as
the security mechanisms of the host permit.

Authentication can't be turned off. However, it doesn't interfere with debugging
and program development. Many security measures are built into the system. For
example, creating new objects never exposes information from former objects.
Similarly, the strict isolation of application address spaces from each other helps
prevent unauthorized data access.

In the first release, before Authentication Services are available, the
CommonPoint system simply assumes that login and authentication occurred
at the host operating system level and relies on the host's file and resource
protections.

**Software Distribution
Services**

The Software Distribution Services frameworks, which are planned for future
releases of the CommonPoint system, support distribution and installation of
software products to large numbers of potential customers in networked
environments. These frameworks provide abstractions that allow one product
package to be installed and configured over a network on CommonPoint

systems running on a variety of hosts. Just as the Licensing Services frameworks support multiple vendors of license server software, the Software Distribution Services frameworks support a variety of existing distribution services via a uniform interface.

A software distribution agent performs most of the Software Distribution Services under the control of a system administrator working with an expanded version of the Software Administration framework. The software distribution agent can push or pull distributions, validate configuration constraints, recover from installation errors, and install, remove, upgrade, or build software. The software distribution agent also supports product browsing, selection, and test-driving; version control; and upgrade advertisement.

Software Asset Management Services

The Software Asset Management Services frameworks, which are planned for future releases of the CommonPoint system, support management of software assets in networked environments. These frameworks are designed to reduce costs associated with software asset management tasks such as auditing software assets, monitoring software usage, and managing software inventory. Just as the Licensing Services frameworks support multiple vendors of license server software, the Software Distribution Services frameworks support a variety of existing asset management services via a uniform interface.

Management Agent framework

The Management Agent framework, which is planned for future releases of the CommonPoint system, defines protocols for *management agents*—that is, CommonPoint programs that execute and reply to management protocol requests from a management station that may be running on a non-Taligent system. The Management Agent framework is the mechanism that allows CommonPoint systems to be managed in UNIX networks via protocols such as Simple Network Management Protocol (SNMP) or Desktop Management Task Force (DMTF). The objects managed can include applications, software components, network devices such as printers and CD-ROM drives, processes such as print jobs, and resources such as software licenses.

Master agents that implement specific management protocols plug in to the Management Agent framework in much the same way that license provider implementations plug into the Licensing framework (see Figure 135 on page 317). Developers of specific management interfaces for CommonPoint applications or system services create *subagents* that are clients of the Management Agent framework. Subagents are independent of particular management protocols. They can be used with all underlying master agents and implement the management interfaces of a particular application or service. Taligent plans to provide tools to help developers develop and test subagents rapidly.

MESSAGING SERVICES

Plans for future versions of the CommonPoint application system include the Messaging Services framework, which provides object abstractions for store-and-forward messaging. These abstractions shield CommonPoint developers from the details of host messaging implementations. The framework is primarily intended for use by developers of email applications or groupware applications that require the transport of documents and rich data types.

Unlike the Communications frameworks, which require a synchronous connection between two computers to transport data between them, the Messaging Services framework provides an asynchronous mechanism for sending messages to an application on another machine that may not currently be available. It uses the Communications frameworks to handle the actual transport of the messages it sends. It also provides subclasses based on the Desktop frameworks to simplify construction of user interface elements for messaging components.

The Messaging Services framework supports not only person-to-person messaging like that provided by existing email packages, but also program-to-program messaging. For example, the workflow between customer service representatives described in "A human interface scenario," beginning on page 76, relies heavily on the Messaging Services framework.

Support for existing standards

The computer industry supports many different messaging standards that use different protocols to package data and send it over a wire. It is not Taligent's intention to create yet another messaging protocol at this level. Instead, the Mail and Messaging Services framework provides a single API that developers can use to implement a range of support for existing protocols.

At the high end of the range, a uniform API for Taligent-to-Taligent messaging supports transport of rich data types among CommonPoint applications running on any combination of hosts. Messaging among CommonPoint applications and non-Taligent applications requires using a subset of this API that applies object abstractions to various non-object-oriented protocols. At the low end of the range, Taligent supports 7-bit ASCII, currently the lowest common denominator among industry protocols. Depending on the platforms and protocols involved, the degree of support for communication between Taligent and non-Taligent applications is likely to fall somewhere in the middle of the range.

For broad interoperability with non-Taligent applications, developers must restrict themselves to a subset of the Messaging Services API. For the greater freedom in sending rich data types from one Taligent application to another, they must sacrifice some degree of interoperability with non-Taligent applications.

Support for filtering agents

The Messaging Services framework uses the property query mechanism to provide filtering capabilities for incoming messages (see page 340 for a description of property queries). Developers can plug in programs that process incoming messages as they arrive and take action according to their properties or contents. These capabilities allow email applications or components to provide filtering capabilities for users. More importantly, message filtering gives workflow and other groupware applications a means of tagging messages so that incoming messages related to a particular application can be distinguished from other incoming messages.

REMOTE OBJECT CALL SERVICES

The Remote Object Call (ROC) Services framework allows applications to make member function calls (also called remote procedure calls, or RPC) to CommonPoint services via a uniform API that hides the low-level transport mechanisms, which vary from one CommonPoint host to another. The mechanism provided by the ROC Services framework and its interaction with the underlying Communications frameworks is described in more detail in Chapter 15, beginning on page 379. ROC Services allow CommonPoint objects on one host to communicate with CommonPoint objects on a different host. However, in the first version of the CommonPoint system ROC Services don't address the problem of communicating across address spaces between CommonPoint objects and non-CommonPoint services, which usually run on procedural operating systems.

The term *distributed objects* refers to both procedural and object-oriented software entities in different address spaces—running either on the same machine or on different machines connected via a network—and various ways of communicating between them. Object-oriented technology is particularly useful for dealing with distributed objects, because it simplifies the process of wrapping up mutually incompatible entities in a common protocol. Distributed objects are important not only for client-server interactions across large multiplatform networks but also for interactions between CommonPoint applications and applications running in the host environment on the same machine.

The computer industry has been attempting to solve the problem of distributed objects for a number of years, with mixed results. A wide array of standards, including Microsoft's Component Object Model (COM), IBM's Distributed System Object Model (DSOM), Hewlett-Packard's Distributed Object Management Facility (DOMF), Sun's Distributed Objects Everywhere (DOE), and NeXT's Portable Distributed Objects all promise to provide mechanisms for communication across address spaces. Many of these standards are in turn implementations of the Common Object Request Broker Architecture (CORBA) specified by the Object Management Group (OMG). Although CORBA-based standards support good distributed object services among machines from a single manufacturer, few of the initial implementations work very well with each other, if at all. Nevertheless, they are slowly improving and converging. Taligent is a member of OMG and is participating in this ongoing development process.

In the long term, as the efforts of OMG and other industry groups begin to pay off, Taligent plans to provide a CORBA-compliant Object Request Broker (ORB) framework, built on ROC Services, that will support a variety of standard APIs as well as different transport mechanisms. This will make it possible for a CommonPoint application to choose among several distributed object APIs to communicate via a variety of ROC protocols with non-Taligent entities in many different address spaces on the same or different machines. Any object service that can be specified with CORBA's Interface Definition Language (IDL) will be called from CommonPoint applications by using this mechanism.

Distributed objects provide a relatively coarse-grained approach to the problem of communication between address spaces. To use such mechanisms effectively, application developers must stick to a somewhat restricted API provided by a particular standard. The more an application relies on fine-grained implementation details of a single programming language or address space, the less chance it has of communicating effectively across address spaces among programs running on different operating systems.

In practical terms, developers face a trade-off between a product's need for platform-specific capabilities and its need for interoperability among different systems. As this new area of industrywide cooperation evolves, Taligent is committed to supporting distributed objects to the maximum extent possible, both between CommonPoint programs running on different hosts and between CommonPoint programs and programs running on other operating systems.

Implementing Enterprise Services
in early releases

The initial absence of a CommonPoint framework (such as Messaging Services) or of a particular implementation (such as support for remote object calls to non-Taligent systems) doesn't prevent the use of equivalent services provided by the host, since CommonPoint applications can always call host libraries directly. Applications that use this strategy won't be portable, but the host-specific code can be isolated and replaced when the CommonPoint service becomes available.

The direct use of host libraries also means that developers can't benefit from framework programming and reuse to facilitate writing those portions of their applications. In addition, CommonPoint frameworks generally map to multiple alternative standards, whereas developers of early CommonPoint applications will most likely code directly to the single standard supported by the host system. Despite these limitations, developers can implement any services they need for a CommonPoint application in much the same way that they would for any application developed for today's host operating systems.

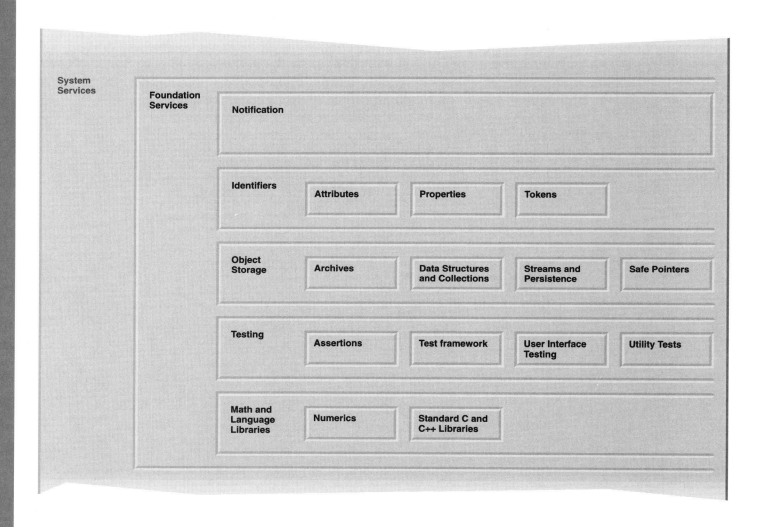

System
Services

Foundation
Services

Notification

Identifiers

Attributes

Properties

Tokens

**Object
Storage**

Archives

**Data Structures
and Collections**

**Streams and
Persistence**

Safe Pointers

Testing

Assertions

Test framework

**User Interface
Testing**

Utility Tests

**Math and
Language
Libraries**

Numerics

**Standard C and
C++ Libraries**

CHAPTER 14

FOUNDATION SERVICES

This chapter introduces Foundation Services, which provide basic OOP services used throughout the CommonPoint system:

- **The Notification framework** provides a systemwide mechanism for the propagation of change information among instances and functions.
- **Identifiers** support three ways to associate a name with data:
    - **Properties** provide a lightweight storage model for storing, retrieving, and querying small, independent collections of heterogeneous instances. It's possible to read properties even if the shared library on which they are based isn't available.
    - **Attributes** provide a mechanism for attaching a named wrapper, such as the "Font," to arbitrary, immutable data, such as the string "Helvetica."
    - **Tokens** provide lightweight wrappers for static text strings that don't need to be displayed to or edited by the user.
- **Object Storage** supports persistent storage of objects and the structuring of objects in memory:
    - **Archives** support the storage and retrieval of persistent objects as individual units within a larger entity, much like entries in a simple database or dictionary.
    - **Data Structures and Collections** provide a homogeneous interface for manipulating and processing collections of heterogeneous elements. They represent a flexible alternative to traditional computer science data structures, eliminating the need for application-specific implementations of arrays, linked lists, and tables.
    - **Streams and Persistence** support streaming, the process used by most CommonPoint applications to convert objects into a byte-encoded stream, store them on disk or send them across a network, and read them back into memory.
    - **Safe Pointers** provide wrapper classes that make using C++ pointers safer.

- **Testing frameworks** include the Test framework, which provides a uniform protocol for automating test execution.
- **The Math and Language Libraries** support numerics and C++:
  - **Numerics libraries** provide a robust environment for floating point calculations, including Taligent Numerics, based on Floating Point C Extensions (FPCE) and the standard FPCE and C interfaces.
  - **Standard C and C++ Libraries** are the ANSI function libraries commonly available for C and C++. They correspond to the current language standards and aren't described in this book.

NOTIFICATION FRAMEWORK

Any large object-oriented system involves many complex interdependencies among instances. For the CommonPoint application system to remain in a consistent state, instances constantly require new information about changes to other instances. The Notification framework provides a mechanism that supports the propagation of change information from an instance to other instances or functions interested in the change. This mechanism allows any number of client objects to maintain a consistent state with respect to a particular source.

Most software developers need to provide notification of changes to the state of their models. The Notification framework calls a member function supplied by a program to obtain information about changes the program needs to broadcast. The rest of the notification process is handled by the framework.

For an introduction to notifications in the context of the Desktop frameworks, see "Notifications," beginning on page 202.

Key elements of notification

These are the key elements of the notification mechanism:

- **Senders** are instances that notify other instances of changes to themselves; the sender decides exactly which changes. The sender defines an interest that's specific to the notification for a particular kind of change. Sender instances can perform the notification themselves, or they can share a *notifier* with other instances.

- **Receivers** register interest in and respond to notifications from senders. Receivers get notifications through a *connection*. Generally, each receiver owns a connection instance. Connections manage the link to the sender, while receivers implement the handling of the notifications.

- **Interests** identify a sender and an event. A sender defines an interest in each event about which it provides notification. A receiver uses this protocol to identify the events about which the sender should notify it.

- **Notifications** convey news of an event to receivers. When a sender receives an event for which it has defined an interest, it uses the appropriate interest, and possibly additional notification-specific data, to create a notification. The sender then sends the notification along to the receivers that want it.

Interests, notifications, and connections can all be subclassed to include additional information. The Notification framework takes care of most of the work. The developer simply plugs in versions of these three objects tailored to the needs of the application. Instances sending notification messages need to know nothing about the receivers of the notification; this includes the type of receiver (instance or function), the receiver's protocol, the number of receivers, or how the receivers respond to the notification. Connections and notifications are also entirely independent of the other elements' implementations, yet they work together reliably.

The Notification framework is used by many different parts of the CommonPoint system. For example, clients of a model (such as menus or content views) typically need to be notified of changes made to data in a model they depend on. In this situation, the model is the sender, and it defines the interests about which it can provide notification. Interested receivers register as clients of an interest by establishing a connection with the sender. After they have established such a connection, receivers automatically receive notifications from the sender of any changes specified by the interest.

Figure 136 summarizes these relationships.

In Figure 136, Model A (derived from the Compound Document framework class TModel) is the sender, and is therefore designed to export interests (such as AddedAnchor). The sender also creates the notifier. The receiver (a content view) creates the connection.

The numbers in Figure 136 correspond to these steps:

1. The receiver fetches an interest (TModelInterest) from the sender (Model A) and adds it to the connection object.

2. The connection object connects to the notifier (TNotifier) to establish a connection for notification. (The notifier is used by several different senders to provide notification of a particular event.)

3. The user adds an anchor to Model A, and the model creates a notification object (TModelAnchorNotification) that contains a reference to the model, a copy of the interest, and a reference to the anchor marker added. The model passes the notification to the notifier.

4. The notifier sends the notification object to all the connection objects that have registered with it as having an interest in this particular type of notification.

5. Each connection object takes the notification, looks up the member function it should call to handle that kind of notification (for example, HandleAddedAnchor), and passes the notification to that function.

The next section describes the notification classes involved in this example in more detail.

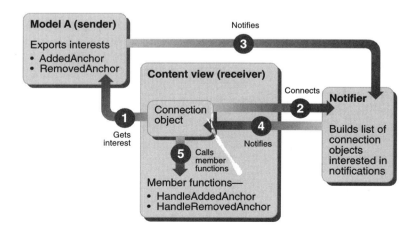

| **Notification classes** | This section summarizes the primary classes provided by the Notification framework, focusing on notification between instances in the same task. |

| **Notifier classes** | Senders use the notifier classes shown in Figure 137 for accepting connections and issuing notifications. MNotifier provides the basic protocols, and its subclasses form the basis for different implementations or "flavors" of notifiers. |

The notifier classes play the following roles:

- **MNotifier** provides the abstract protocol for accepting connections and for distributing notifications to them. MNotifier provides no implementation for this protocol. A class inherits directly from MNotifier if it provides a unique implementation for the notification protocol.

- **MDelegatingNotifier** supports the delegation of all notifier member functions to another notifier, thus allowing a single notifier instance to be shared among several MDelegatingNotifiers. The Compound Document framework uses this technique to share a single notifier among all the TModel instances in a document task.

- **TNotifier** is a concrete implementation of the protocol specified by MNotifier, based on a dictionary implementation. Interests are used as keys into the dictionary for looking up connections to notify. TNotifier sends notifications synchronously; that is, in the same thread as the caller of the Notify function.

- **TAsynchronousNotifier** is a concrete implementation of the protocol specified by MNotifier that delivers notifications asynchronously. You can provide a request processor for it to use, such as an instance of TSingleThreadRequestProcessor, or let it create a processor itself. TAsynchronousNotifier implements the MNotifier protocol by passing requests to the request processor and immediately returning.

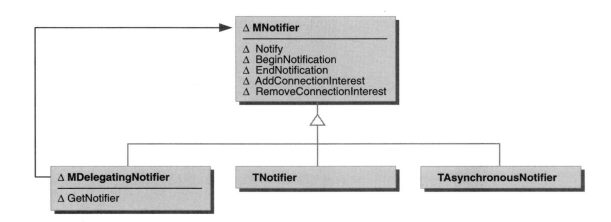

FIGURE 137
NOTIFIER
CLASSES

Connection classes

The connection classes shown in Figure 138 manage a receiver's set of interests and deliver corresponding notifications to the receiver. As with notifiers, these classes can be subclassed to create a variety of connection objects for use in different situations.

The connection classes shown in Figure 138 play the following roles:

- **TNotifierConnection** is an abstract base class for establishing connections between a sender and a receiver. It provides protocol and implementation for enabling and disabling the dispatching of notification in its Connect and Disconnect member functions, and for adding and removing interests in AddInterest and RemoveInterest member functions. Its Notify member function provides the protocol for dispatching notifications to the receiver.

- **TMemberFunctionConnectionTo<AReceiver>** provides notification dispatch to a receiver instance. The notifications are dispatched to the receiver by calling a member function on the receiver instance. You can specify an individual receiver function for each interest in the connection. You can also specify a default member function to handle notifications sent for interests that do not have an individual receiver function.

- **TFunctionConnection** provides notification dispatch to static member functions or global functions. As with TMemberFunctionConnectionTo, you can specify an individual receiver function for each interest in the connection. You can also specify a default member function to handle notifications sent for interests that do not have an individual receiver function.

FIGURE 138
CONNECTION CLASSES

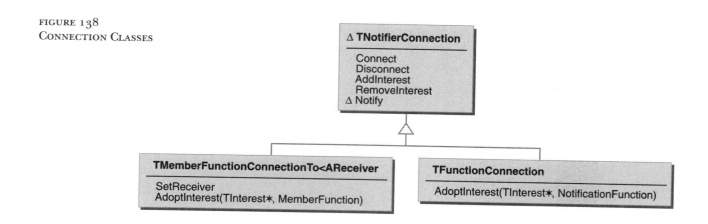

Interest classes

The TInterest class shown in Figure 139 identifies an interest as both the name of an event and a notifier (typically the sender). In many cases senders can simply use instances of TInterest. If needed, you can derive new classes to include additional information to refine the interest specification. For example, the Compound Document framework provides the subclass TModelInterest, which includes information about a specific change to a specific model. Figure 136 on page 330 illustrates the use of a TModelInterest object.

Both senders and receivers use TInterest objects. When senders generate a notification, they use a TInterest object to identify the sender and the event about which the notification is being sent. Receivers use TInterest objects to inform their connections which notifications to receive from which senders.

A sender must define for a receiver the interests the sender generates as well as the class of notification associated with each interest. Senders can export interests as TTokens, TInterests (or derived classes of TInterest), or member functions that create TInterests.

FIGURE 139
INTEREST
CLASSES

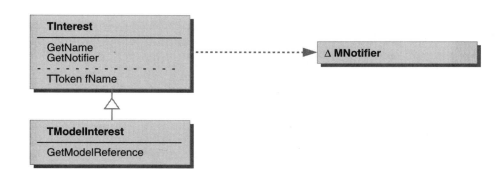

Notification classes

The Notification classes shown in Figure 140 deliver to receivers news of an event involving a sender. As with interests and connections, the Notification classes can be subclassed for specific purposes. For example, the Compound Document framework provides the subclass TModelAnchorNotification for notifying models of changes involving anchors. Figure 136 on page 330 illustrates the use of a TModelAnchorNotification object.

The notification classes shown in Figure 140 play the following roles:

- **TNotification** is the base class for transporting notification-specific information. TNotification contains a TInterest specifying the sender and the event about which notification is generated. You can derive from TNotification to add additional information for specific notifications. For example, the Compound Document framework defines a TSelectionNotification class that contains a selection. Receivers of this notification can then access the selection for their own purposes.

- **TBatchNotification** transports a group of notifications to a receiver as a single batched notification. The notifier typically generates it automatically; you do not generate it yourself. The next section describes how to use this class.

- **TModelAnchorNotification** is a typical subclass of TNotification. The Compound Document framework provides it for notifications involving anchors, and it contains a model anchor reference. Receivers of this notification can access the reference for their own purposes.

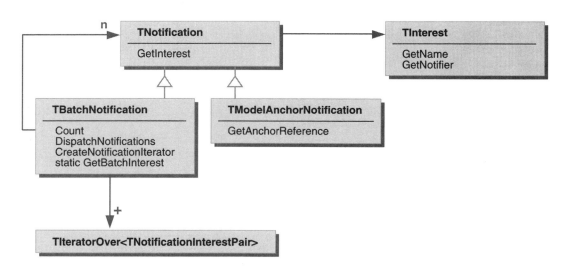

FIGURE 140
NOTIFICATION
CLASSES

Optimizing using batched notification

A single event often causes a sender to send several notifications. As a service to receivers, the sender can send these notifications in a batch; that is, as a single notification containing an ordered list of the individual notifications. This allows a receiver to optimize its response to the notifications. For example, a view on a Compound Document framework model might perform a single update for a user action, even though the action causes the model to issue several notifications.

For this to be effective, the sender has to batch notifications where appropriate, and the receiver has to request delivery of batched notifications.

Once a receiver has requested batched notifications, all notifications it receives are batched, whether or not the sender originally batched them. Conversely, a receiver that has not requested batched notifications always receives single notifications, regardless of how the sender sends them. This design allows you to modify the sender's code at a later time without breaking any receivers. Those designed to receive batched notifications still do so, and those that were not so designed still receive individual notifications.

Sharing a notifier implementation

To minimize the overhead associated with providing notification support, you can share a single notifier among many senders.

MDelegatingNotifier provides a straightforward approach to this (see page 331). A sender can derive from MDelegatingNotifier and provide it with a notifier implementation that is shared with other senders.

Because interests include a pointer to the original MDelegatingNotifier, no additional specialization of interests is necessary to distinguish between notifications from senders that share a common notifier implementation.

Synchronous versus asynchronous notification

You can send notifications synchronously or asynchronously, depending on the requirements of both the sender and the receivers. Some senders require that notifications be handled synchronously so that all notification processing is complete before returning to the sender.

Other senders, such as a file server, might require that notifications be delivered asynchronously so that they are not blocked for long periods of time waiting for receivers to complete notification handling.

The Notification framework provides two implementations of MNotifier that you can use depending on your needs. TNotifier provides a synchronous implementation, and TAsynchronousNotifier provides one that is asynchronous.

When you call TNotifier::Notify, the notifier calls the Notify member function of all the connections interested in that notification in the same thread in which TNotifier::Notify was called. When the call completes, the sender is assured that all receivers interested in the notification have received it. When they receive the notification, receivers also know that it reflects the current state of the sender as long as it has not somehow changed in the meantime.

When you call TAsynchronousNotifier::Notify, a request to perform the notification is passed to a request processor. The sender can then immediately continue to perform other work. When the request processor eventually delivers the notification, receivers cannot make any assumptions about the state of the sender (even that it still exists).

Remote notification

Two additional classes derived from TNotifier, TRemoteCallerNotifier, and TRemoteDispatcherNotifier, support sending notifications to receivers in different tasks. Once set up, you use the caller-dispatcher pair much as any other notifier—in particular, you do not need to modify the receivers or the protocol defined by senders even though the real sender instance actually lives in a different task.

Remote notifications are asynchronous.

IDENTIFIERS

The CommonPoint system supports three kinds of identifiers:

- **Properties** are used for keeping track of small collections of heterogeneous instances when type safety is important or for handling general-purpose objects that may originate on a different machine.
- **Attributes** are used in situations where you know the type associated with a given name.
- **Tokens** are used for static text identifiers that don't need to be displayed to or edited by the user.

Properties

Properties provide a lightweight, persistent instance storage model for storing and retrieving small collections (tens to hundreds, but not thousands) of heterogeneous instances. They aren't intended to replace a general-purpose database, but they can be useful for storing small collections when the format of the data to be stored isn't known in advance.

Properties also include classes for querying collections of objects with associated properties. A property query evaluates a Boolean expression against any collection of such objects to which the query is applied. For example, the File System interface mixes in Property classes to provide basic file manipulation and query capabilities.

Properties allow multiple, unrelated clients to access the same collection of instances, across tasks and across sessions, without interfering with each other. They ensure type safety and take care of memory management automatically.

Core Properties classes

Three classes provide the core capabilities of the Properties interface: TProperty, TPropertyID, and MPropertyStore.

TProperty instances encapsulate an identifier (an instance of TPropertyID) and the property value, as shown in Figure 141. However, TProperty does not handle the persistent store of the property; instead, it acts as a container for a specific type of property value to be read or written.

FIGURE 141
TPROPERTY
INSTANCE
ANATOMY

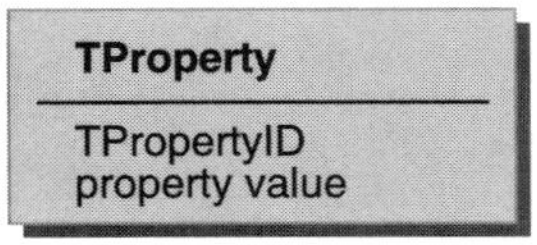

TProperty

TPropertyID
property value

TPropertyID instances act as names, or labels, for property containers, as shown in Figure 142.

MPropertyStore provides the read and write protocol for properties. Interfaces and frameworks that support properties—such as the File System interface—provide classes derived from MPropertyStore for accessing property values.

If a TProperty instance corresponds to a container, and the TPropertyID corresponds to the container's label, MPropertyStore assumes the role of a stock clerk in a warehouse. In the same way that a stock clerk manages inventory items, MPropertyStore manages property values. Its member functions can perform these tasks:

- Fill a container with an item from the store that corresponds to the label (ReadProperty)
- Store an item that you pass in a container (WriteProperty)
- Remove an item from the store (DeleteProperty)
- Tell you the number of items in stock (GetPropertiesCount)
- Return the amount of space that the items in stock take up (GetPropertiesSize)

Collections of MPropertyStore instances can also be queried by means of property query objects; see page 340 for details.

FIGURE 142
RELATIONSHIP
OF PROPERTIES
AND PROPERTY
IDENTIFIERS

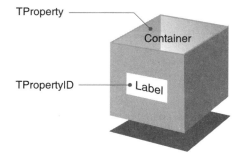

Managing a heterogeneous collection

Classes that mix in MPropertyStore often manage properties of different data types. For example, one MPropertyStore instance might store properties of types TTime, long, TText, Boolean, and TDoubleLong. Together, the properties managed by MPropertyStore form a heterogeneous collection.

Heterogeneous collections require type checking to avoid errors that can occur when retrieving a value or an instance of an incorrect type. To avoid these errors, the property classes use C++ templates for static type checking and for runtime checking where needed.

Property objects are used both for reading and for writing property values, and include constructors tailored to each use. A property object constructed for writing requires an initial value, while one constructed for reading does not:

```
TPropertyFor<double> prop1("myProperty",3.14);    // Make a property for writing.
aStore->WriteProperty(prop1);                      // Write it to the store.

TPropertyFor<double> prop2("myProperty");          // Make a property for reading.
aStore->ReadProperty(prop2);                        // Read it from the store.
```

Note that this example doesn't use identifiers; a name is passed instead. The constructors build the identifier automatically, and it may be extracted if necessary:

```
TPropertyIDFor<double>    myID = prop1.GetID();  // Make a property identifier.
```

Note also that prop2 is constructed without a value; the ReadProperty function uses the identifier contained within prop2 to retrieve the value, in this case 3.14.

This example highlights an important point about property objects: Functions that take a property as a "fill-in" (a function argument explicitly used as a return value) rather than a return parameter use the property for both input (identifier) and output (value). This means casting is not required when storing or retrieving properties.

Property collections

MPropertyStore contains the protocol for storing and retrieving properties individually or in batches. To facilitate batch operations, the Properties interface provides two collection classes: TPropertySet and TPropertyIDSet. TPropertySet collects TProperty instances and TPropertyIDSet collects TPropertyID instances.

Both of these collection classes include constructors that allow conversion to the other type of collection. For example, the TPropertyIDSet constructor allows conversion to TPropertySet. Both classes also have Add member functions that accept instances of either TPropertyID or TPropertySet as members.

Property and property identifier collections differ from other collection classes in that they do not use aliases. Instead of a set containing aliases to the actual properties or property identifiers, sets of this interface actually own copies of each of the members. This simplifies memory management.

Property queries

The Properties interface permits the construction of property queries to filter MPropertyStore instances that contain specific values. For example, the File System interface uses properties in association with file system entities (TDirectory, TVolume, and TFile instances). File system entities use MPropertyStore as a mixin to manage the properties associated with each entity. The File System interface also defines iterators for iterating through the file system entities in directories or volumes. Thus it's possible to use a property query with a directory iterator to filter file system entities with specified values.

This example shows how a property query might be used to select only files and directories whose modification date is greater than or equal to a given date:

```
TPropertyQuery qRecent = (TFileSystemEntity::kModificationDate
                         >= kTaligentStartDate);            // Make query.
TDirectoryIterator    iterator(aDirectory,qRecent);        // Make iterator w/ query.
```

In this example, kModificationDate is a TPropertyIDFor<TDateTime> object, and kTaligentStartDate is a TDateTime object; parentheses are for clarity only.

Query objects are created by comparing an identifier to a value. Evaluation of the query occurs later. Thus, the preceding example can be stated as follows: For each file or directory (MPropertyStore) to which this query is applied, fetch the modification date property and compare it to the supplied date. If the modification date is >= the supplied date, the query evaluates to true and the entity is returned; otherwise, the query evaluates to false.

Attributes

Attributes provide a mechanism for attaching a named wrapper called an *attribute* to arbitrary data. The Text system and the View system are the primary clients of Attributes. The Text system uses them to maintain information such as point size, font, style, and color.

Services provided by Attributes include the following:

- Creating and tracking specific attributes
- Sharing attribute data among several attributes
- Grouping attributes and managing the groups
- Relating attribute groups in a hierarchy to allow for dynamic inheritance from other groups

Properties vs. attributes Properties are different from attributes. Properties permit the use of overloaded names that may correspond to more than one type. If you know the name of an attribute, you should also know its type.

Table 3 summarizes the other major differences between properties and attributes.

	Properties	Attributes
TABLE 3 COMPARISON OF PROPERTIES AND ATTRIBUTES	Allow multiple, unrelated clients to access the same collection of instances, cross-task and cross-session—without interfering with each other.	Address issues related to storage management on a single task basis.
	Are mutable—you can change the value of a property as long as it is not defined by an interface that specifies the value as read-only.	Are immutable—once you establish the value of an attribute, you cannot change it.
	Allow storage of instances of almost any type without providing a special protocol.	Require inheritance from an attribute class to add an instance to an attribute collection.
	Provide a query mechanism for evaluating complex Boolean expressions against a collection of properties.	Don't provide a query mechanism.
	Use C++ templates for static type checking and runtime checking, thus avoiding the need for type casting.	Require downcasting to extract an individual attribute
	Don't support dynamic runtime inheritance.	Attribute groups support dynamic runtime inheritance

Attribute concepts

Attributes name arbitrary data. For example, the font size 24 can be associated with a range of text data as an attribute of that data. The attribute name would be `font size`, and the data it names would be the value 24. (Although styles such as font size are objects of class TStyle, the style classes inherit much of their behavior from the Attributes classes.)

Figure 143 illustrates this concept. An attribute's name simply provides the means to access the wrapped data. The name can be specific to the instance, shared by all instances of a class, or shared among instances of several related classes. The wrapping occurs dynamically when an attribute is instantiated. All attribute creation and deletion is performed at runtime.

FIGURE 143
AN ATTRIBUTE
IS A NAMED
WRAPPER FOR
ARBITRARY
DATA

The data portion of an attribute is completely arbitrary. None of the attribute classes include protocols that deal with attribute data. The assumption is that if you know enough to ask for a particular attribute, then you know the class of that attribute and the form of its data. Derived classes usually add their own protocol to access the wrapped data.

Attributes can be grouped

Attribute groups associate multiple attributes with a single data element. For example, font name and font size are both attributes that describe a range of text. Figure 144 shows two examples of attribute groups.

FIGURE 144
ATTRIBUTE
GROUPING

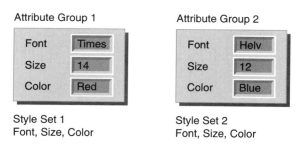

Within a group, no two attributes have the same name. Thus attribute groups may be thought of as sets of named values.

Attributes are immutable, groups are not

Once created, attributes are immutable; that is, they cannot be changed. Changing an attribute in an attribute group involves adding and removing attributes or changing their inheritance hierarchy. Figure 145 shows how this works. Attribute Group 1 contains a size attribute of 12. Changing the size to 14 involves creating a new size attribute, adding it to the group, and discarding the old size attribute of 12.

FIGURE 145
UPDATING
IMMUTABLE
ATTRIBUTES

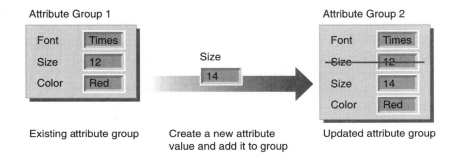

Attributes can share data

Attributes can share attribute data. The instance that holds the data is called an internal attribute, and the attributes that share this data are called shared attributes. The internal attribute can be accessed only via a shared attribute. The shared attributes point to one internal attribute, as shown in Figure 146.

FIGURE 146
SHARED
ATTRIBUTES

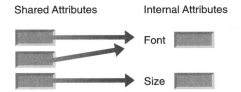

Groups can share attributes

Attribute groups can also be shared. The group that owns the attributes is called an internal group, and the groups that point to this group are called group handles. Many group handles can point to the same internal group, as shown in Figure 147.

FIGURE 147
SHARED
ATTRIBUTE
GROUPS

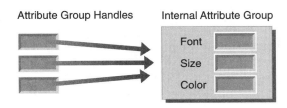

Attributes and groups have value semantics, group handles have reference semantics

Because attributes are immutable, even shared attributes have value semantics. Each instance of a shared attribute behaves as though it is unique. Simple groups own their attributes and therefore also have value semantics. Modifications to a group do not affect other groups.

Group handles, as the name implies, explicitly share their underlying groups and therefore have reference semantics. Modifications to a group handle can affect other group handles because change information is propagated to all of the related group handles.

Group attributes may be dynamically inherited from other groups

Groups can be organized in a hierarchy of inherited internal groups and group handles, providing for dynamic inheritance of attributes from parent groups. This feature makes it possible to query a group for an attribute and, if it is not found, automatically query the parent group, and so on recursively until the attribute is found or it is determined that a group has no parent.

A child group can override an inherited attribute if the child group includes an attribute with the same name. The parent of a group can change at any time.

Group changes provide notification

Because internal attribute groups can be changed, a special Attributes notification service informs the group's handles automatically whenever a change occurs. This is not necessary for shared attributes because, by definition, attributes do not change. The attributes notification service informs handles not only of changes to a single internal attribute group but also of changes to its ancestor groups and to the group hierarchy itself.

NOTE   The Attributes notification facility is unique to Attributes and is not related to the Notification framework.

The attribute model

Figure 148 illustrates the relationships among the principal Attributes classes at runtime.

TInternalAttribute instances are reference counted and stored together in a private format. No two internal attributes ever have the same name and value.

Each TSharedAttribute instance points to an internal attribute maintained elsewhere. Other TSharedAttribute instances with the same name and value share the same internal attribute.

A TSimpleAttributeGroup instance contains one or more TSharedAttribute instances. No two attributes within the group have the same name.

A TAttributeGroupHandle instance points to a sharedTInternalAttributeGroup instance. Other TAttributeGroupHandle instances might point to this same internal group. When the internal group changes, it calls NotifyChanged on each of its handles.

FIGURE 148
RUNTIME MODEL OF THE
ATTRIBUTE ARCHITECTURE

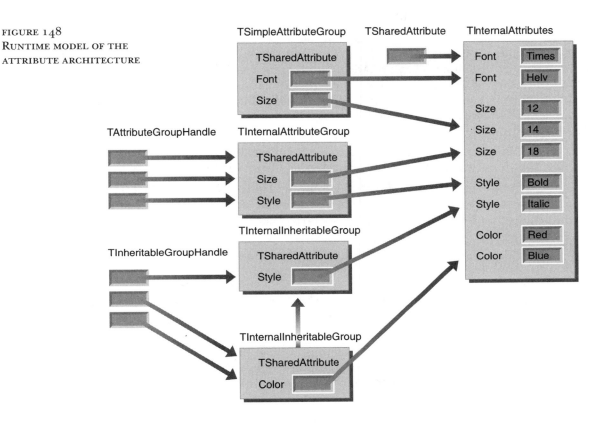

A TInheritableGroupHandle instance might be one of many such handles pointing to the same TInternalInheritableGroup instance. This shared group can have ancestors and children. When it changes, it calls NotifyChanged both on its own handles and on those of its children.

Note that the group handles point to the internal group (not the shared attributes) and that each shared attribute points to the internal attribute (not the data within it).

Tokens

Two concrete classes, TSimpleUnicodeArray and TToken, provide lightweight wrappers for text strings that don't need to be displayed for or edited by the user. They both inherit basic protocol for encapsulating nonstyled, nondisplayable strings of Unicode characters from the abstract class TUnicodeArray, as shown in Figure 149. The vast majority of text uses should be based on TText and TStandardText, which are introduced in Chapter 10, beginning on page 258.

TUnicodeArray provides abstract functions, implemented by TSimpleUnicodeArray and TToken, for getting the encapsulated string as either a Unicode or char array and for resetting the string after instantiation.

TSimpleUnicodeArray is useful for encapsulating a short string that is relatively static and has no styles, such as a key. It should be used carefully. Many natural languages require styles to represent text well.

TToken is useful for creating constant, low-overhead, frequently used strings, such as a static name for an object. Unlike a TSimpleUnicodeArray instance, the memory for a TToken instance, once assigned, is never recovered until the machine is restarted. One benefit of this is that non-deep-freeze streaming is very fast, because only a pointer needs to be streamed if the token will be streamed back in the same session. (See page 354 for information about freeze levels.)

TToken is useful only for strings that are frequently accessed during the normal functioning of the machine. Examples of appropriate uses include names of events or input devices, since these appear repeatedly in events. Examples of inappropriate uses of tokens include names of system resources that are fetched once, after which the name is not used again. Because of the memory requirements for TToken, you should use TStandardText rather than a token unless a string will get copied or streamed (non-deep-freeze) very many times.

FIGURE 149
TSIMPLEUNICODEARRAY
AND TTOKEN PROVIDE
LIGHTWEIGHT WRAPPERS
FOR TEXT STRINGS

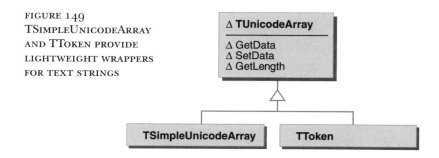

OBJECT STORAGE

Nearly all CommonPoint programmers need some form of persistent storage and structured memory and therefore need to use Object Storage services:

- **Data Structures and Collections** provide a flexible alternative to traditional computer science data structures.
- **Streams and Persistence** support streaming, a process used by most CommonPoint applications for persistent storage.
- **Archives** are used for random access persistent storage.
- **Safe Pointers** provide wrapper classes that make using C++ pointers safer.

Data Structures and Collections

A *collection* is a group of related objects. For example, components in a diagram editor or CAD program might manage collections of points and lines. The same program might also manage a set of views for a document as a collection.

Taligent collections provide flexible alternatives to traditional computer science data structures such as arrays, lists, and trees. CommonPoint collections are generally pointer based rather than value based and don't own their own storage. Deleting a collection won't delete the objects in the collection. Collections are therefore very fast; but the user of a collection must maintain ownership if necessary and document such ownership very clearly.

Types of collections

Taligent collections can be divided into two broad categories: ordered collections (sequences) and unordered collections (sets and dictionaries).

Ordered collections can be broken down further according to whether their ordering is internally (that is, automatically) or externally determined. A sorted collection or sequence, such as an alphabetical list of names, is an example of an internally determined ordering. Externally ordered collections include arrays, which provide random access to all elements, and stacks, queues, and deques, which provide different kinds of access to end elements.

Unordered collections include sets, which contain no duplicate elements, and dictionaries, which are unordered collections of elements identified by unique keys.

Figure 150 shows the inheritance hierarchy for Data Structures and Collections.

FIGURE 150
CLASS
HIERARCHY
FOR DATA
STRUCTURES
AND
COLLECTIONS

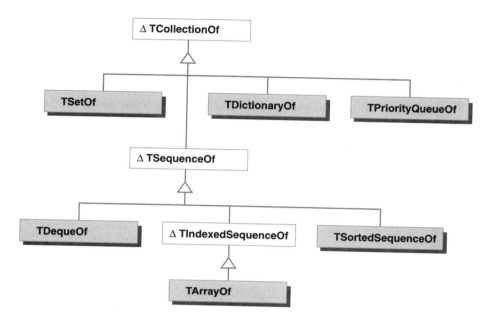

The table that follows summarizes the six basic collections classes, their ordering and duplication characteristics, and their hash function requirements. Stacks, queues, and deques are all implemented as deques. Priority queues are a special kind of sequence.

Type of collection	Ordered	Allows duplicates	Uses hash function
TSortedSequenceOf	Automatically	Yes	No
TArrayOf	By numeric index	Yes	No
TDequeOf	By insertion sequence	Yes	No
TPriorityQueueOf	Partially	Yes	No
TSetOf	No	No	Yes
TDictionaryOf	No	Keys no, values yes	Yes

TSetOf and TDictionaryOf collections (and also collections of properties, described on page 339) require a hash function. The hash function must be both persistent and portable: that is, it can't be altered, and it must return the same values on every platform. If no hash function is provided for TSetOf or

TDictionaryOf collections, or if it's not a well-distributed function (always returning the constant 0, for example), performance will suffer. For more information about writing portable hash functions, see *Taligent's Guide to Designing Programs* (1994).

All Taligent collections are parameterized using C++ templates and must be instantiated with an argument indicating the kinds of elements the collection is intended to manage. However, by specifying a class high enough in the inheritance hierarchy, a programmer can combine several related classes in a single collection. For example, an array of numbers could include both rational and irrational numbers.

Plans for future versions of the CommonPoint system include support for the recently adopted ANSI collection classes, which are based on Hewlett-Packard's Standard Template Library (STL) collection classes.

 NOTE   For historical reasons, many CommonPoint classes descend from MCollectible instead of using the Taligent extension macros and define the is-equal-to operator. This is an internal implementation detail and isn't required for any CommonPoint developer.

Sequences

A *sequence* is an ordered collection. Data Structures and Collections include three kinds of sequences: sorted sequences, arrays, and deques. Another kind of collection, called a priority queue, resembles a sequence conceptually although its implementation is different. Member functions for sequences generally support basic operations such as adding, extracting, deleting, iterating through, and comparing elements.

Sorted sequences

A *sorted sequence* is a sequence that's ordered automatically according to some lexical or numeric comparison such as alphabetical order. The class TSortedSequenceOf provides support for sorted sequences. Sorted sequences provide fast random access and fast sequential access.

Arrays

An *array* is a sequence that permits rapid random access by numeric key. The class TArrayOf provides basic array capabilities. Like any collection, an object of class TArrayOf can be polymorphic—that is, it can contain different classes of objects as long as they are all ultimately descended from the same class.

Arrays derived from TArrayOf differ subtly from arrays used in C and Pascal. For example, they can automatically grow to accommodate new elements when they become full, and they provide bounds checking and other safety features to protect clients that specify a collection element with an index value too small or too large for the collection. As with C arrays, indices for dynamic arrays start at 0. Array indices work much like keys for accessing elements of an array.

It's possible (but not particularly fast) to remove or delete elements in an array by value.

Deques

Stacks, queues, and *deques* are familiar data structures that support LIFO (Last In First Out), FIFO (First In First Out), and double-ended (add or remove elements at either end) queues, respectively. All of these can be implemented using the TDequeOf class, because the definition of a deque is general enough that it can function as any of the three. Using a deque as a stack involves using Push and Pop member functions to add and remove elements. Using it as a queue involves using Add and Remove functions to add elements at one end and remove them from the other.

Priority queues

A *priority queue* is ordered partly by an internal (automatic) sorting mechanism, and partly by external manipulation (that is, according to the order in which an element is added). The class TPriorityQueueOf provides support for priority queues.

In event-processing systems, it is sometimes useful to prioritize events according to their urgency. For example, a disk access may be given higher priority than a screen repaint. A system timer event would probably be given higher priority than a user menu command or keystroke. The events for such a prioritized queue would be sorted primarily by an internal mechanism (the rank of the event) and secondarily by external ordering (events of the same priority rank are processed in the order they arrive in the queue—that is, the order in which the events occur).

Dictionaries

A *dictionary* is an unordered collection of elements in which each element is identified by a unique key. Just as each word in a language dictionary is associated with a definition, each key in a dictionary collection is associated with a value. However, unlike words in a language dictionary, each key in a dictionary collection is unique and cannot be duplicated within the same collection.

Strings or symbols are often used as keys for dictionaries. For example, a compiler symbol table can be represented as a collection of pairs called key-value pairs. Pairs are two-element objects containing a lookup key and a value. In a symbol table, the key could be a string, and the value could be a structure containing type information and data associated with the key.

The class TDictionaryOf provides a mechanism for storing and looking up these kinds of key-value pairs. Each key in a dictionary must be unique, but the values associated with different keys may be identical. Assuming that it has a good hash function, TDictionaryOf provides fast random access, but sequential access is not predictable; that is, it's not possible to predict accurately the order in which key-value pairs are stored. The order will be the same for a single set, but another equal set may have a different order.

Sets

A *set* is an unordered collection that contains no duplicate members. Adding a duplicate member to a set simply replaces the original member. For example, to make a list of unique words used in a text document, a program could read through the words in a document and add each word to a set collection. If the same word is placed in a set twice, the second word replaces the first. Thus, each word appears only once in the set no matter how many times it's repeated in the original document.

The class TSetOf provides a mechanism for handling sets. Assuming that it has a good hash function, TSetOf provides fast random access, but sequential access is not predictable; that is, it's not possible to predict the order in which key-value pairs are stored. For example, two equal sets may store their key-value pairs in different order.

Streams and Persistence

Streams and Persistence support streaming, which is the process of converting objects to a byte-encoded stream or restoring them to their original condition (see Figure 151). The streaming mechanism supports several key features of components created with the Compound Document framework, including multiple undo and redo, scripting, saveless operation, and collaboration; for details, see "Streaming of selections and commands," beginning on page 188.

Streaming objects lets them outlive the immediate environment in which they are created. Most new classes for CommonPoint applications should support streaming, because CommonPoint instances that support streaming can be sent to other instances, written to disk, or sent across the network to another machine.

Unlike traditional approaches to storing data, streaming doesn't require complex specification of memory and file formats. Every CommonPoint object knows its type. Streaming operators use this knowledge to embed type information automatically along with data files and memory blocks.

The streaming mechanism doesn't address where instances are stored, how they are found, indexing into a database of instances, or garbage collection of persistent instances.

FIGURE 151
STREAMING
AN OBJECT
OUT TO AN
ARRAY OF
BYTES AND
RESTORING
IT AGAIN

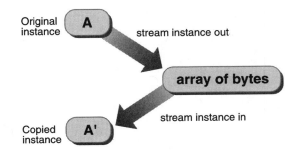

Original instance — A — stream instance out

array of bytes

Copied instance — A' — stream instance in

Contexts and streams

The streaming mechanism uses *contexts* to improve performance and maintain internal aliases. Contexts also save space and time for streamed objects of the same type even if no aliases are involved. For example, if an object being streamed out contains one or more identical subobjects, the streaming mechanism writes out the first subobject followed by a flag. Then, for each subsequent occurrence of the same object, the streaming mechanism writes another flag and the location within the stream of the first occurrence of the object. The context keeps track of these relationships and makes it possible to recreate the objects in their original configuration when they are streamed back into memory.

However, contexts make random access to individual objects within a given stream impossible unless you keep careful track of where things are and reset contexts as necessary. In general, streaming processes all objects and their subcomponents as a single unit, and they aren't accessed individually until the whole unit is resurrected. In this respect streams resemble a continuous magnetic tape or a sequence of bytes similar to a file stream or pipe in UNIX.

To store individual objects in a form that permits random access, you typically stream objects separately into a TDiskDictionaryOf object that manages key-value pairs and permits storage and retrieval of individual objects without disturbing other objects already in the dictionary (see "Archives," beginning on page 356). With streams, this random access to individual objects is possible but much more difficult.

Object streaming classes

Figure 152 shows the main object streaming classes and their primary member functions.

The abstract class TStream and the class TRandomAccess provide basic streaming protocols used by the other streaming classes. TFileStream provides protocols for streaming a file to disk for retrieval as a single unit.

There are two kinds of in-memory streams: chunky and contiguous. TChunkyStream and the related TChunkyGrowableStream (not shown in Figure 152) allocate memory in chunks, which facilitates memory management and growable memory. Chunky streams are faster than contiguous streams and are usually preferred for that reason.

TContiguousMemoryStream allocates a block of contiguous memory that is difficult to grow. Contiguous memory streams can be useful when you know the size of a stream and don't expect it to change.

FIGURE 152
PROTOCOL FOR OBJECT
STREAMING CLASSES

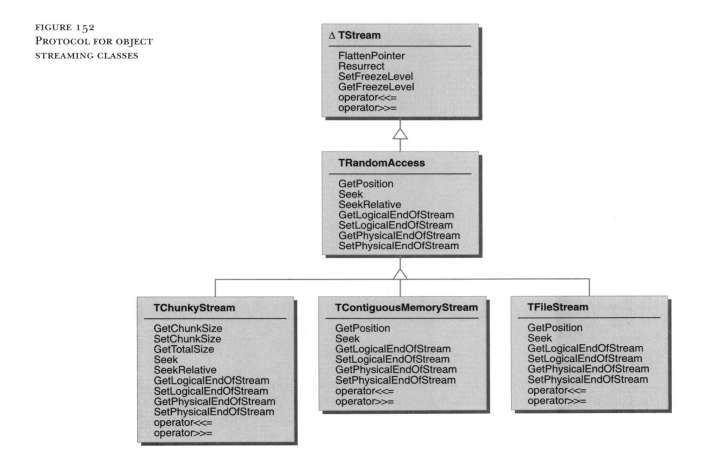

Monomorphic vs. polymorphic streaming	Streaming can be monomorphic or polymorphic. *Monomorphic streaming* involves calling an object's streaming operators directly and requires previous knowledge of the object's type. Monomorphic streaming can handle an object embedded within another object, but only if the type of the embedded object is known in advance. Monomorphic streaming is very fast.

Polymorphic streaming involves calling the FlattenPointer and Resurrect functions, which use Run-Time Type Identification (RTTI) to look up the object's shared library and type. Polymorphic streaming is useful for embedded objects or other objects whose type is not known; however, the lookup process slows performance.

To support polymorphic streaming, an object must either be derived from MCollectible or use the correct Taligent extension macros and be available in a shared library.

The function FlattenPointer, which is declared in the abstract class TStream, passes over the structure of an object as well as all objects referenced by its instance variables. This traversal of the object's structure, called *flattening*, continues recursively as individual object components are written out to the specified stream. The result is a linear (flattened) sequence of bytes representing the various components found in the original object. The flattened form of the object is a persistent representation that can span tasks, processes, sessions, and individual machines.

Reversing the flattening process is called *resurrecting* persistent objects. When a persistent object is resurrected, it is restored to a state in memory that is equal to its state at the time it was stored. The Resurrect member function defined in TStream takes a flattened persistent object and creates a new object as a result.

Instances that contain pointers to other instances (nested instances) can be written polymorphically and completely recreated when resurrected. Multiple references to the same instance are restored properly. Circular references are also correctly handled by the system. Sets of instances can be streamed out (written) and streamed in (read) together, keeping the correct relationships and data.

Polymorphic streaming permits efficient representations of flattened instances that are ephemeral or temporary (for example, a microkernel message) as well as efficient representations of flattened instances that persist. The flattening process considers the lifetime of a persistent stream when generating a flattened form for an object or set of objects.

Freeze levels	Using streaming involves making decisions about the amount of detail saved in the stream. Streaming an object can be thought of as freezing it in a given state. The streaming classes provide three levels of freezing, depending on the context in which the streaming is taking place. The deeper the freeze level, the more permanent the object. A deeper freeze level implies that more information must be written to the persistent stream, because less context will be available when objects are resurrected from the stream.

The three freeze levels are defined as follows:

- **kSameTeam.** A team is a collection of related threads associated with a task, all sharing a common address space. If objects saved as a persistent stream will be restored to the same address space, the kSameTeam freeze level makes it possible to save pointers to objects instead of the actual objects themselves.
- **kSameSession.** Objects streamed out at the kSameSession freeze level can only be resurrected inside a program or task before restarting or turn off the computer.
- **kDeepFreeze.** This the most permanent freeze level. It is required to store data on a hard disk in a form that can be resurrected after the computer is restarted or turned off. Deep freeze is also required for streams sent across a network to remote machines that share no common context with the source machine.

It's possible to design objects that check the freeze level and stream only enough information for that level. This can produce faster streaming within the same team or same session.

Making a class streamable

The CommonPoint developer guides provide complete instructions for writing streamers. To be streamable, a class must fulfill two basic requirements:

- **Write and read the version.** When streaming out, a class must write out its version using the utility routine WriteVersion. When streaming in, it must check the version using ReadVersion and make sure that the version is within the bounds of the available code.
- **Stream its immediate superclasses.** To ensure that the stream captures all relevant information, each class is responsible for streaming its immediate superclasses.

The ReadVersion utility throws an exception if the version it reads is out of bounds. The class is responsible for handling different versions correctly and for handling exceptions generated by ReadVersion. Writing and reading the version ensures that future changes to a class's streaming format introduced by new versions of a class library will be handled correctly.

As long as each class streams itself and its immediate superclass (or superclasses, if it uses multiple inheritance), streaming will always capture all the relevant information for a particular class. The streaming mechanism requires that all developers follow this rule.

The Test framework, which is introduced beginning on page 359, provides a utility test class called TWellBehavedObjectTestOf for testing the copying, flattening, resurrecting, and streaming of a class.

Archives

The streaming mechanism described in the preceding section makes it possible to flatten objects into a byte-encoded stream and restore them again, but random access to single objects within the byte stream is difficult. The Archive classes provide protocols for storing streamed objects separately in a disk dictionary in any order without disturbing other objects already in the dictionary.

Each developer must determine the most appropriate way to write out objects that need to be stored. It's generally desirable to have storage be as fine-grained as possible, which usually implies some form of dictionary-based storage. However, if a group of closely related objects will always be saved and restored as a unit, streaming the whole group at once may be appropriate, either as a separate file or as a single entry within a disk dictionary.

Dictionary-based storage

A *disk dictionary* associates key objects with value objects. Given a key, a disk dictionary returns the value (object) associated with the key or permits storage of a new object in the location associated with the key. Keys can be numerical data, such as integers or longs, or text (subclasses of TText). It's also possible to use other types for keys, but simple types provide optimal performance. The value object contains the data being stored and retrieved.

Two classes provide templatized disk dictionaries: TDiskDictionaryOf and THeterogenousDiskDictionaryOf. These classes can be extended to support many different access methods, and Taligent provides a default retrieval mechanism. They are related conceptually (but not in their implementation) to the Collections class TDictionaryOf, discussed on page 350.

TDiskDictionaryOf is templatized across both key and value, so all the keys must be instances of a single type (or of classes that are ultimately derived from the same class), and all the values must all be instances of a single (possibly different) type. In other words, both keys and objects are homogeneous. Within these limitations, TDiskDictionaryOf is relatively easy to use.

FIGURE 153
EMBEDDED
VALUES IN A
DOCUMENT

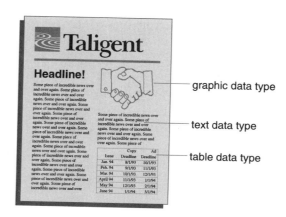

THeterogenousDiskDictionaryOf is templatized only on the key; its values can be of any mixture of classes, even if they're not ultimately derived from the same class. Thus, its keys are homogeneous but its values are heterogeneous. It is more complicated to use than TDiskDictionaryOf, but it provides more flexibility.

For example, all related data for a given document can be stored in a single THeterogenousDiskDictionaryOf instance, even if the document comprises many different kinds of objects. Figure 153 shows such a document. It includes a graphic (hands shaking), text, and a table. These objects can be stored together in the same THeterogenousDiskDictionaryOf instance, which indexes them by an index value it generates behind the scenes.

This is one possible mapping for the key-value pairs of a disk dictionary used to implement the document shown in Figure 153:

Key	Value
147	graphic
319	text
652	table

Creating and using a TDiskDictionaryOf object

TDiskDictionaryOf objects require two constructors: one used when the dictionary is created for the first time, and the other when an existing dictionary is opened. The creation constructor requires a comparator object for the key, a streamer for the key, and a streamer for the value. The open constructor uses the existing comparator and streamers as necessary. Both constructors require directory and text objects that provide the location and name of the disk dictionary to be created.

Here's an example that instantiates a TDiskDictionaryOf object:

```
myDictionary = new TDiskDictionaryOf<TCollectibleLong,TCollectibleLong>(
                        theDirectory, theDictionaryName, theComparator,
                        theKeyStreamer, theValueStreamer);
```

In this example, both the key and the value are TCollectibleLong objects. The other objects encapsulate the location and name of the new dictionary and its comparator, key streamer, and value streamer.

The next example shows how to add key-value pairs to this dictionary later in the same program:

```
myDictionary->Add(key1, value1);
myDictionary->Add(key2, value2);
myDictionary->Add(key3, value3);
```

The last example demonstrates how to retrieve a value given a specific key:

```
TCollectibleLong* someLong = myDictionary->Copy(TCollectibleLong(11));
qprintf("Value associated with key 11 is: %d\n", someLong->GetValue());
delete someLong;
```

Both keys and values in a disk dictionary are objects, and all parameters passed to TDiskDictionaryOf functions are objects. It's never necessary to revert back to base types. This is one important factor that permits the CommonPoint system to work the same way on multiple host operating systems.

Key objects can be fairly rich objects; for example, they may contain several different items. However, disk dictionaries aren't intended to provide a full-fledged database mechanism, and in most cases keys will be close to a base type.

Safe Pointers

Safe Pointers provide wrapper classes that support reference counting, automatic deletion upon exit from scope (including exit due to an exception), and nil dereference checking. Safe Pointers also make clear the intended semantics of a particular pointer via the name of the safe pointer's type. For example, TAliasTo indicates that the pointer does not own the object to which it points.

TESTING

The first release of the CommonPoint system supports testing in three areas:

- **The Test framework** supports execution, logging, and evaluation of tests.
- **Utility Tests** use the Test framework to implement standard tests.
- **Assertions** provide a mechanism for asserting invariants in a program and generating exceptions when these invariants aren't met.

This section focuses primarily on the Test framework.

Overview of the Test framework

The Test framework provides a consistent structure for running, maintaining, documenting, and reusing test code. Test code is not only separate from the code being tested but also completely independent of the user interface. This allows you to test objects that aren't affected by changes to the user interface early in the development process. The Test framework also provides convenience classes for testing standard CommonPoint behavior such as copying and streaming.

The Test framework makes it possible to link tests to specific parts of your code, as suggested by Figure 154, and run them with a testing utility provided by Taligent. The RunTest utility is used for this purpose with the CommonPoint reference release, which is hosted on AIX. Taligent plans to provide equivalent utilities for use with versions of CommonPoint that run on different hosts.

The TTest class, which is the core of the Test framework, provides a uniform protocol for

- Invoking tests
- Reporting test results
- Connecting tests to the class being tested
- Setting up tests and cleaning up afterward
- Combining tests
- Logging and timing

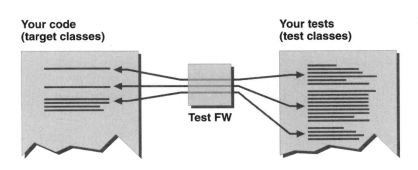

FIGURE 154
THE TEST
FRAMEWORK
PROVIDES A
CONSISTENT
INTERFACE
BETWEEN YOUR
CODE AND
YOUR TESTS

To use the Test framework, you write a test class derived from TTest that evaluates the behavior of the class you are testing, called the *target class*. When you run the test, the test class creates an instance of the target class and then compares its actual behavior with the expected behavior. If the results are the same, the test passes.

A *decision function* is the code you write that determines whether the code being tested is behaving as you expect. For example, if an object simply returns a value sent to it, a decision function might compare a value sent to the object with the value the object returns and make sure the two are equal.

Here is an example of a decision function that compares the value for a variable with an expected length:

```
if (maxlength != fExpectedLength)
   SetSuccess(false);
```

If the two values don't match, the function passes a value of `false` to SetSuccess, which means that the test failed.

A single TTest class can exercise a single decision function or can parse the input to select a subset of decision functions, as suggested by Figure 155.

You decide how much testing a single TTest class needs to perform. If a single TTest turns up several defects, the scope of the test is too large.

FIGURE 155
EACH OF YOUR
TEST CLASSES
CAN PERFORM
MULTIPLE
OPERATIONS

TMyClassTest performs several operations on TMyClass.

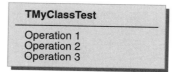

Each of the TMyClassTestXX classes perform a single operation.

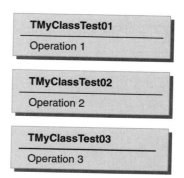

The Test framework makes it possible to organize decision functions into tests with standard interfaces that can be run repeatedly to create regression test suites. Such test suites can be run automatically and don't require special knowledge of the code being tested. The tests return information about the success or failure of the decision functions.

For example, you might find that for an instance of TSampleObject, which contains SetString and GetString functions, you can perform several different operations to test the functions. Each operation is cast as a decision: does the operation work correctly? The outcome of the test operation must be `true` or `false`, indicating the success of the associated test.

Test framework classes

TTest is an abstract base class. Figure 156 shows some of the TTest-derived classes provided by the Test framework.

TTest includes a Test member function that you must override with the code for a decision function. When you declare a derived class of TTest to be a friend (in C++) of the target class, the derived class can access all the private interfaces of the target class for internal testing purposes.

The sections that follow describe the roles of some of the classes derived from TTest.

FIGURE 156
TEST FRAMEWORK CLASS
HIERARCHY

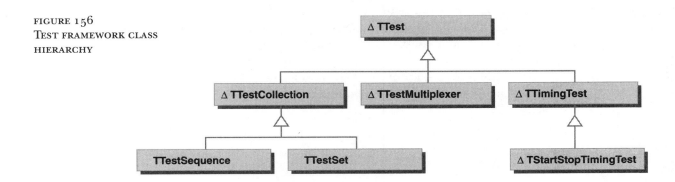

Test collection classes

The Test framework includes derived classes of TTest that allow you to group tests:

- **TTestCollection**, an abstract base class derived from TTest, contains a collection of TTest instances. The tests in the collection run sequentially to determine the success or failure of the entire group. TTestCollection has two concrete derived classes:

    - **TTestSequence** runs its subtests in a fixed sequence.
    - **TTestSet** contains an unordered set of subtests that can be shuffled to vary the order in which the subtests run.

- **TTestMultiplexer** derives from TTest and supports multiple decision functions applied to a single test target. It does so by means of a key-value dictionary in which each value is a decision function and the corresponding key is some text used to identify that function. TTestMultiplexer allows you to fill in the dictionary with appropriate key-value pairs. You can then specify keys from the command line when you run the text to invoke particular decision functions. This makes it possible to rerun a test by using different combinations of decision functions without having to recompile the test.

Timing tests

The Test framework provides two classes for timing tests:

- **TTimingTest** is an abstract base class that provides a basic guide for tests that measure the time a specific operation takes to complete.
- **TStartStopTimingTest** is an abstract base class derived from TTiming Test. It supports stopping and starting the timer several times.

Utility Tests

Utility Tests test an entire hierarchy of classes that share a common protocol. There are five concrete Utility Test classes:

- **TCopyTestOf** tests the copying of the target using the global Copy function.
- **TStreamTestOf** tests the streaming of the target.
- **TFlattenResurrectTestOf** uses the global Flatten and Resurrect functions to test the flattening and resurrecting of the target.
- **TPrimitiveComparisonTestOf** tests canonical member functions: the constructor, destructor, copy constructor, and assignment operator.
- **TWellBehavedObjectTestOf** tests the copying, flattening, and streaming of the target by creating TCopyTestOf, TStreamTestOf, and TFlattenResurrectTestOf tests for the target and running all of them.

Related classes

The Test framework uses several classes derived from TStandardText for buffering and logging purposes. All output from a test is buffered in the test object and, if the test is logged, in the log. TTieredText and TTieredTextBuffer allow you to organize test output in a hierarchy that makes it possible to control the level of detail displayed both during the test and when retrieving test output.

- **TTieredText** is the class of objects collected by TTieredTextBuffer. It is a derived class of TStandardText and allows you to define the relative importance of information in a test, from single-line headlines to debugging details. Once you have designed tiers for particular kinds of output, you can filter the level of information displayed as the test runs and when you retrieve the test output from a test log.

- **TTieredTextBuffer** behaves like the C++ ostream class. It contains << operators for all basic types. Unlike the ostream class, TTieredTextBuffer keeps a collection of all text sent to it. Other features of TTieredText include the following:

  - Echoing of text to a destination you specify
  - Filtering output so that detailed information is suppressed or displayed
  - Flushing text beyond a certain level of detail from the buffer.

  Each instance of TTest contains a TTieredTextBuffer to which derived classes can stream diagnostic text messages. TTest itself uses this mechanism to report progress and results.

- **TTextArgumentDictionary** parses a sequence of TText objects into pairs of keys and values. It allows you to parse the command line easily and quickly look up the arguments used by a particular test.

Creating a test

The simplest way to create a test class is to derive it directly from TTest, as suggested by Figure 157. In this example, TSampleObject is the target of the test.

FIGURE 157
TSAMPLEOBJECTLENGTHTEST CONTAINS CODE FOR TESTING TSAMPLEOBJECT

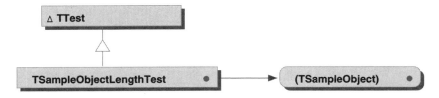

Figure 158 illustrates a more flexible approach that involves creating a base test class that contains common functions and data.

FIGURE 158
TSAMPLEOBJECTBASE CONTAINS CODE COMMON TO ALL TSAMPLEOBJECT TESTS

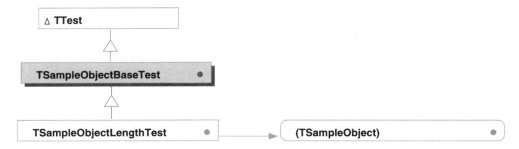

Each member function to be tested needs an instance of a TTest object, as shown by Figure 159. You can use a simple naming convention to clarify which test classes relate to the classes to be tested, such as TMyClassTest for TMyClass or TMyClassMyMethodTest for TMyClass::MyMethod.

FIGURE 159
EACH MEMBER
FUNCTION
THAT YOU
WANT TO TEST
NEEDS AN
INSTANCE OF A
TTEST OBJECT

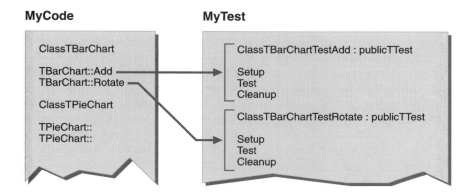

Combining tests

You can group tests in three ways:

- Combine tests that need to run together as a group into a suite. Each test suite has a script associated with it that runs all the tests.
- Create a derived class of TTestMultiplexer that contains multiple decision functions that can be applied selectively to a single test target.
- Use the TTestCollection derived classes TTestSet and TTestSequence to group related TTest classes in a single test. The resulting test passes only if all its subtests pass. This approach also allows you to use the same TTest classes individually.

TTestCollection derived classes allow you to:

- Define the order in which subtests execute
- Shuffle the subtests into a new random order
- Propagate inputs from the group to the subtests

You can also create tests that have different behavior depending on the outcome of other tests. For example, suppose TSecondTest works only if the system is in a state that is achieved only if TFirstTest is run and passes. If you place TFirstTest and then TSecondTest inside a TTestSequence, the subtests run in order when the TTestSequence executes. If a subtest fails, the remaining subtests do not run. This behavior can be switched on and off.

NUMERICS

The Numerics libraries support floating point calculations in the CommonPoint system. High-quality numerics are a business requirement for many of Taligent's target markets because of their importance for scientific and engineering computation, precision 2-D and 3-D modeling, advanced image rendering, visualization, and simulation. The Numerics libraries include numerical functions and classes that control the execution environment. Many features, such as the functions Sin, Cos, and Tan, are available on virtually all computers. Other, more esoteric features are peculiar to the IEEE floating point standards on which the Numerics classes are based.

The IEEE standards for floating point arithmetic describe the high-level environment in which numerical programmers work, but don't include specific language bindings. As a result, various companies have defined their own IEEE language extensions and libraries. Not surprisingly, lack of portability has impeded programming for these interfaces.

The recently approved Floating Point C Extensions (FPCE) standard provides a standard language binding for IEEE arithmetic. The Taligent numerics environment is broadly compatible with existing IEEE standards as well as with the FPCE standard. As a result, numerics code written for other operating systems can usually be ported to the CommonPoint system with little difficulty.

Numerics interfaces

The CommonPoint system includes three sets of header files that support the FPCE-based Taligent Numerics interfaces, the standard FPCE interfaces, and the standard C interfaces.

Taligent Numerics interfaces

The Taligent Numerics interfaces provide the CommonPoint implementation of FPCE. These interfaces include all the capabilities provided by the standard FPCE interfaces except that they follow the Taligent spelling conventions for global functions and are implemented by using typical Taligent classes and exception handling. They include the following header files:

- `Numerics.h`
- `FPEnvironment.h`

Taligent Numerics provide the broadest capabilities of the three sets of numerics header files and are recommended for all CommonPoint code that doesn't have to run directly in non-CommonPoint operating environments. Taligent Numerics include a consistent interface for all the operations in Standard C, all the operations recommended in FPCE, nearly all operations from the Apple SANE® standard, and other standard numerical functions from FORTRAN and Pascal. Most operations from other environments that are not directly supported by Taligent Numerics are easily obtainable from those it does provide.

All Taligent Numerics operations are as efficient as reasonably possible. In some cases, and within the bounds set by applicable standards, a small degree of accuracy or correct handling of side effects is sacrificed to maintain acceptable performance.

Although the Taligent Numerics interfaces don't currently support it, Taligent plans to support complex arithmetic in future releases.

FPCE interfaces

The Taligent header files `fp.h` and `fenv.h` support the generic FPCE standard and thus provide a superset of capabilities that includes those provided by the standard C header file.

Standard C interfaces

The standard C header file `math.h` (which is a small subset of the FPCE interfaces) provides the most broadly portable numerics interface. The use of this interface is described in standard C and C++ documentation.

The computational model

A single principle underlies Taligent's approach to floating point arithmetic and mathematical functions:

Compute each result as if with unbounded precision and exponent range; then coerce that mathematical result to the format of the destination.

Given the mathematical properties of the operations of interest, you can deduce the outcome of any computation.

Coercing a "mathematical result" can involve several operations:

- **Rounding** a (wide) result to the available precision entails adding or subtracting an amount beyond its least significant bit, effectively replacing the value by one of the two numbers that most closely bracket it from above and below. The system supports four kinds of rounding:

    a. To nearest. Ties go to the nearest value whose least significant bit is 0.

    b. Toward 0. Chop off all bits beyond the destination's precision.

    c. Toward ∞. Round to the nearest more positive neighbor.

    d. Toward –∞. Round to the nearest more negative neighbor.

- **Overflowing** a result too huge to represent to either ∞ or the largest representable number, depending on the rounding mode.

- **Underflowing** a result too tiny to represent, employing a class of tiny numbers called subnormal numbers that permit underflow to be graceful rather than abrupt.

- **Returning a NaN** (not-a-number) value, defined by the number system, when there is no meaningful mathematical result, as in the case of $0/0$.

Numerics concepts	Some concepts that underlie the Numerics classes are related to the problem of representing numbers and implementing algorithms on computer hardware and in software. The most important of these concepts are described here.
Correctly rounded results	Any arithmetic that stores its results in a fixed number of digits cannot accurately represent all real numbers. For instance, irrational values like $\sqrt{2}$ and π cannot be stored in a fixed number of digits. Converting numbers represented in one base, such as decimal, into another base, such as binary, can introduce additional imperfections. For instance, a simple value like $^1/_{10}$ cannot be represented exactly in a binary format.

$$^1/_{10} = 0.1_{10} = 0.000110011\ldots_2$$

The objective is to reach a correctly rounded result—in other words, a result that's accurate within the limitations of the result's storage type. For instance, $1.01010101010101010101011_2$ is a correctly rounded representation of $^4/_3$, rounded to the nearest binary value in the IEEE single-precision binary format.

The Taligent Numerics classes produce results that are correctly rounded for basic operations and, wherever efficiency allows, for other operations as well.

Exception flag handling	The IEEE floating point standards specify a base set of floating point exception flags: invalid, overflow, underflow, divide-by-zero, and inexact. These flags are directly supported in hardware on all CommonPoint hosts. For basic operations, these flags must be set according to specific rules. The Taligent Numerics classes follow the IEEE and FPCE standards for exception flag behavior where specified and attempt to follow their spirit for operations not covered by the standards.
Basic operations	Basic operations are those for which results are always correctly rounded and for which exception flags are set in specified ways. These are the basic operations for Taligent Numerics:

- +, −, *, /
- $\sqrt{}$
- Conversions between binary formats
- Remainder
- Conversions between binary and decimal formats

Within a specific expression evaluation method, and using the float and double data types, the Taligent interfaces deliver the same results for these operations on all platforms.

Special values

Special values are bit patterns that are not interpreted as normal binary numbers of their data type. To achieve closure in the computation model, the Taligent Numerics interfaces include these special values:

- NaN, or "not-a-number," results from operations such as $0/0$.
- $\pm\infty$ results from operations such as $\pm1/0$.
- Subnormal numbers are very tiny numbers that mitigate problems with underflow.
- Zeroes are treated like other binary numbers in that they have a sign, either positive or negative. This usually has no effect on calculations but can be useful in some contexts.

These special values are treated correctly where specified by IEEE standards or FPCE, and are treated consistently and predictably in other functions.

Taligent Numerics features

This section introduces the major features supported by Taligent Numerics.

Floating point functions

The CommonPoint application system is designed to support all functions supported by C, FPCE, and SANE, plus a few others. These are the groups into which floating point functions are divided and the functions in each group:

- **Trigonometric:** Cos, Sin, Tan, ArcCos, ArcSin, ArcTan
- **Hyperbolic:** Cosh, Sinh, Tanh, ArcCosh, ArcSinh, ArcTanh
- **Exponential:** Exp, Exp2, ExpMinus1
- **Logarithmic:** Log, Log2, Log10, Log1Plus
- **Power:** SquareRoot, Sqrt, Square, Hypotenuse, Hypot, Power
- **Financial:** Compound, Annuity
- **Nearest Integer:** Floating point return types: RoundIEEE, Rint, NearbyInt, AddHalfTruncate, Round, Truncate, Ceiling, Floor. Long integer return types: RoundToLongIEEE, RintToLong, AddHalfTruncateToLong, RoundToLong
- **Remainder:** Remainder
- **Auxiliary:** Abs, CopySign, NextLongDouble, NextAfter, NextFloat, NextDouble, Logb, Scalb
- **Inquiry:** IsFinite, IsInfinite, IsNormal, IsNaN, IsSignNegative, FPClassify
- **Special Values:** kInfinity, kPi, kNaN, kDegreesToRadians, kRadiansToDegrees, NaN
- **Max, Min, and Positive Difference:** Max, Min, PositiveDifference
- **Integer:** IntegerSquareRoot, IsPrime, NextPrimeAfter
- **Hash:** Hash

Floating point data types

There are three basic floating point data types built into standard C/C++ compilers used with the CommonPoint application system:

- `float`
- `double`
- `long double`

Two typedefs are defined to support efficient execution of code that runs on multiple platforms:

- `float_t`
- `double_t`

`Float` and `double` map directly to the IEEE single and double data formats. `Float_t`, `double_t`, and `long double` are mapped to different formats on different platforms.

Because all CommonPoint hosts use the IEEE binary floating point and radix-independent arithmetic standards, the C++ types `float` and `double` are precisely the single and double types of the arithmetic standards. Some CommonPoint hosts also support a `long double` type, which can be highly system dependent. Results that depend on `long double` or other host-dependent capabilities will be similar but not necessarily identical across hosts. Programmers must make tradeoffs between portability and efficiency on specific platforms.

In general, programmers should use `float` and `double` for data and `float_t` and `double_t` for intermediate calculations. In many cases requesting a `double_t` returns a `long double` when the host system provides one. It's not necessary to use `long double` explicitly unless absolutely necessary for additional range on a particular platform.

float and float_t

The `float` format, called "single" in IEEE Standards 754 and 854, is a 32-bit data format with precisely specified exponent, significand, and sign fields. It can express numbers in the range ±3.4E+38, and it has between 7 and 8 decimal digits of precision for normalized numbers.

The `float_t` typedef is provided to facilitate the writing of more efficient portable code. On any given machine, `float_t` is mapped to the most efficient data format at least as wide as `float`. (In some cases, `float` is significantly slower than a wider format.) Using a wider data type may offer improvements in performance, though at some cost in increased data storage space.

double and double_t

The `double` format is called "double" in both Standard C and the relevant IEEE standards. It is a 64-bit data format with precisely specified exponent, significand, and sign fields. It can express numbers in the range ±1.7E+308, and it has between 15 and 16 decimal digits of precision—more than twice the precision of `float`.

The `double_t` typedef is provided to facilitate the writing of more efficient portable code. On any given machine, `double_t` is mapped to the most efficient format at least as wide as `double`. For example, on the Intel family, an 80-bit extended format is most efficient, so `double_t` is mapped to it.

Long double, extended, and double double

The long double format is defined in the C and C++ standards and the FPCE draft standard. Taligent Numerics interfaces require that the compiler support long double with greater precision than double. A long double format used with Taligent Numerics should have the following characteristics:

- At least 64 bits of significance (same as IEEE extended type)
- At least 11 bits of exponent (at least as many bits as double)
- Results correctly rounded where long double is mapped to a format that meets the requirements for an IEEE double extended type
- Results not always correctly rounded where long double is mapped to a format that does not meet the requirements for an IEEE extended type

The long double format can be used for calculations that benefit from a wider-precision data type than double. It can be used within routines that have double operands or results to minimize rounding errors in multistep calculations.

Many hardware platforms have support for an extended format, which is recommended, but not required, in IEEE standards. Its format can vary across platforms as long as it has the following characteristics: a sign bit, at least 15 bits for the exponent, and at least 64 bits for the significand. On machines that support an extended format, long double is mapped to extended.

Some platforms, such as PowerPC, do not efficiently support any format that meets the requirements for extended. The PowerPC platform does have limited support for a format known as double double, which is a double plus a second double that adds length to the significand. The double double format has tremendous precision, but its range is no larger than that of double. On PowerPC, long double is mapped to double double.

For portability, either avoid the use of long double or depend only on its least common denominator characteristics. You cannot store long double data in shared data files or stream it to other machines; it is not readable by machines that use a different microprocessor.

Precision and magnitude summary

The table that follows shows the precision and magnitude of the numeric data types supported by Taligent Numerics. Magnitudes are given in a truncated two-digit decimal representation of the exact binary values.

	float	double	long double on PowerPC family	long double on Intel family
Decimal precision	7-8	15-16	≥32	19-20
Largest magnitude (approximate decimal)	3.4E+38	1.7E+308	1.7E+308	1.1E+4932

The floating point environment

The Taligent Numerics classes permit a high degree of control of the floating point environment. Each task starts with the default IEEE environment:

- Exception flags: clear
- Rounding direction: to nearest
- Rounding precision: results not narrowed in precision (cannot be changed)
- Trapping: disabled (cannot be changed)

FPCE-compliant compilers support #pragma fenv_access on, which must be placed in source code before using nondefault rounding or performing operations that set flags to be tested later. Numerics code that is compiled on non-FPCE-compliant compilers may not work in the CommonPoint system.

The computational model permits dynamic control of the means of rounding. The rounding direction can be set to nearest, upward, downward, or toward zero. Additionally, a set of flags under programmer control indicate whether any of various errors have occurred since the flags were last reset. Exception flags that can be tested, raised, or cleared are invalid, overflow, underflow, divide by zero, and inexact. Finally, a program can request a change in the flow of control depending on floating point exceptions.

Changes in the floating point environment can be scoped locally or globally. Exceptions can be handled by polling the exception flags or by using the C++ try-catch model. In the polling approach, the program checks the exception flags it is interested in after a computation, then takes appropriate action. In the try-catch model, the program creates an exception handler object that looks for specific exceptions that occur within its scope. When the exception handler goes out of scope, its destructor throws a C++ exception object corresponding to the highest-priority requested exception that occurred in its scope. Taligent Numerics interfaces don't support hardware trapping of floating point exceptions.

Portability and performance

This section summarizes some general considerations related to portability and performance of code written using Taligent Numerics.

Porting existing code to Taligent Numerics

Because the Taligent Numerics floating point environment is designed as a superset of other numerics environments, porting code from other numerics environments usually isn't difficult. Most standard C code can be ported transparently if you use the headers `float.h` and `math.h`. The only major area of difference between Standard C and Taligent Numerics is that Taligent Numerics do not support `errno`. If your code uses `errno`, you must rewrite it to use IEEE-style floating point exception flags instead.

If your code depends on details of any specific type wider than `double`, you must either rewrite it to eliminate these dependencies or run it only on platforms that support the desired type.

Writing portable code

To write code specifically for machines running the CommonPoint system, use the Taligent Numerics headers, but don't depend on details of the implementation of `long double`, which varies across platforms. Don't save or stream `long double` data, as not all platforms are able to read one another's `long double` data. Don't depend on absolutely identical results across platforms.

To write code that's portable among machines that support the proposed FPCE standard, including but not limited to machines running Taligent Numerics, use the FPCE-compliant headers `fp.h` and `fenv.h`. You can then use capabilities specified by FPCE, which are more extensive than those of standard C. Most functions in Taligent Numerics have analogs in FPCE; often only the capitalization of the names differs.

Performance

For best performance, avoid using types wider than the most efficient type on a given platform except where greater precision is required. When you do use a wider type, confine it to as few expressions as possible.

When you use the floating point environment, limit the access to a small scope. Turn on access to the environment just before the code in question and turn off access just after it. Use IEEE-style polling of exception flags to detect exceptions instead of using exception handler objects.

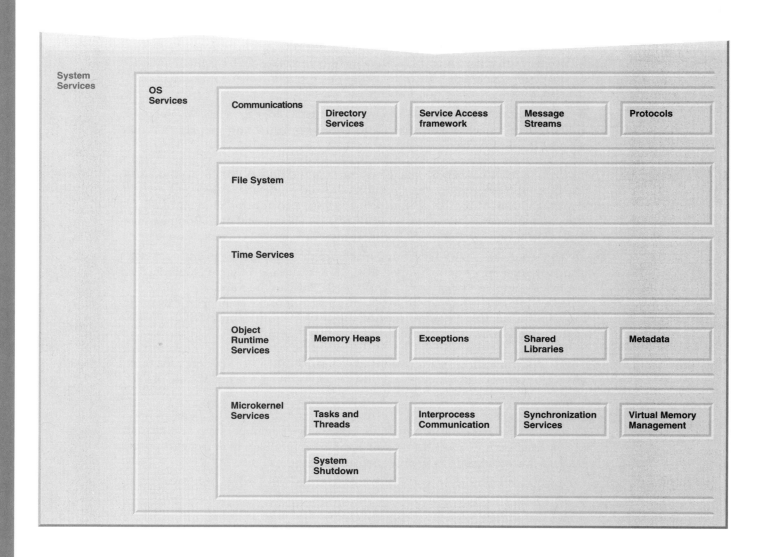

CHAPTER 15

OS SERVICES

OS Services provide CommonPoint object abstractions for low-level services performed by the host operating system. These abstractions are designed for use with modern microkernels such as Mach, but they also work equally well with equivalent services on non-microkernel-based hosts. OS Services work the same way no matter what host the CommonPoint system is running on.

OS Services include the following:

- **The Communications frameworks** facilitate both local and remote communication between threads. Message Streams permit the other Communications services areas, and in turn Remote Object Call (ROC) Services, to use any host operating system's underlying transport mechanisms via a uniform interface.
- **The File System interface** provides object abstractions for manipulating files, directories, and volumes that reside on hardware or virtual storage devices.
- **Time Services** provide a hardware-independent model for timing support.
- **Object Runtime Services** support heap management, exceptions, shared libraries, and metadata services.
- **Microkernel Services** support tasking, scheduling, synchronization, and system shutdown.

This chapter introduces OS Services. It also mentions some of the planned TalOS technologies that will complement OS Services. In particular, it introduces the Object-Oriented Device Driver Model (OODDM) frameworks, which will provide input/output (I/O) services for use by hardware-independent device drivers. Although the OODDM is currently not part of the CommonPoint application system, Taligent plans to make the underlying technology available to Taligent's investors and other licensees.

COMMUNICATIONS

The Communications frameworks facilitate communication between threads. The threads can be within the same task (address space), within different tasks on the same machine, on different machines running the CommonPoint application system, or on different machines where only one is running the CommonPoint application system.

These frameworks provide the foundation for all CommonPoint communications:

- **Directory Services** provide a homogeneous view of non-Taligent namespaces, including DNS, X.500, AOCE™, and DCE CDS.
- **Service Access** provides a mechanism for identifying and accessing network services.
- **Message Streams** provide a uniform API for handling physical communication between tasks at all levels, from tasks within the same thread to tasks in different threads on different machines, independently of the underlying protocols.
- **Protocols** are intended to support standard communications protocols, including TCP/IP, AppleTalk, and Novell. Protocols will be part of TalOS technologies and don't have an API in the CommonPoint application system.

The Remote Object Call (ROC) Services framework, which is considered part of Enterprise Services, works closely with the Communications frameworks to support remote calls to CommonPoint services. It also provides the basis for Taligent's long-term CORBA and distributed objects strategy. The ROC Services framework is introduced on page 323 and described in more detail in this chapter.

For the purposes of this book, *communication* is any data movement between threads. The Communications frameworks don't include interfaces that move data directly to or from devices. These services are provided by the underlying host operating system.

Communications features	This section summarizes the main features of the Communications frameworks and classes.
Destination transparency	The same APIs control all communications, no matter what kind of service is involved and regardless whether communication is within or outside the local task or takes place within the same machine or over a network.
Transport transparency	The client of a service doesn't need to know what kind of transport mechanism the communications interfaces use to move data to and from the service. Similarly, when defining a service, the service provider doesn't need to know what type of transports are available.

For example, a particular machine may have the Novell, AppleTalk, or Internet Protocol (IP) families installed. A service written using the Communications frameworks doesn't need to know which family is installed; it automatically takes advantage of whichever ones are available. If a fourth protocol family is introduced later, services can take advantage of it without having to change or rebuild any existing programs.

The only exception is for a client designed to work with a service running on a host operating system. Such a client is called an *interoperable client.* An interoperable client usually needs to look "behind the curtain" to tailor the communications techniques of another operating system to its particular needs.

Interoperability	The Communications frameworks are designed to work the same way with any host operating systems and protocols.
Synchronous communication	All Communications frameworks are synchronous. This doesn't mean that a client program must stop executing when a communications operation is outstanding. Only the thread making the request blocks; all other threads in the client task are unaffected and continue executing. A client can achieve concurrent behavior with multiple threads rather with than asynchronous interfaces. Asynchronous interfaces are necessary on older systems that don't support concurrent threads.

Communications models

The Communications frameworks currently support two communications models:

- The request-reply model involves an alternating exchange of messages between a source and a receiver. The source makes a request, and the receiver handles the request and returns a reply.
- The datastreams model resembles a telephone call: data flows both ways simultaneously. This model can also be used in a unidirectional mode.

Message Streams provide the underlying protocols for each model. In both cases, a service creates a *service definition* to publicize itself as available to clients, and a client creates a *service reference* to access the service through the service definition. The service reference encapsulates the contact information for a single service within a particular namespace and other information required to interact with the service. Each service has only one service definition, but any number of service references may interact with the same service, as shown in Figure 160.

FIGURE 160
SERVICE DEFINITIONS
AND SERVICE REFERENCES

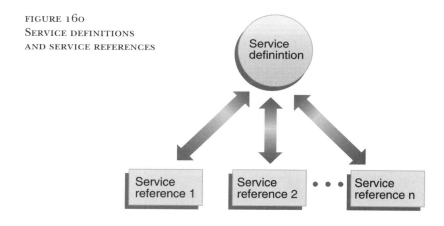

Communications architecture

The Communications frameworks support the Open Systems Interconnection (OSI) reference model as specified by the International Standards Organization (ISO). Adhering to this layered approach to structuring protocol levels makes the frameworks easier to understand, selectively modify, and extend to work with other communications interfaces.

The Presentation and Session layers in the OSI model roughly correspond to Message Streams, and the Application layer corresponds to ROC Services. The Communications frameworks support the OSI model, but not the OSI protocols.

How the Communications frameworks work together

Figure 161 shows the relationships among the Communications frameworks and between the Communications frameworks and the ROC Services framework.

The Service Access framework and Message Streams provide abstractions for use by other frameworks and by applications that need communications access. These service areas work closely together and translate as necessary between the CommonPoint application system and the host system's transport mechanisms. They are capable of transparently supporting TCP/IP, AppleTalk, SNA, and other networking protocols, and they provide the lowest level of communications access needed by most applications. Developers who wish to control very low-level networking protocols such as TCP settings can use the Protocols framework. In the meantime they can use the equivalent low-level APIs provided by other host operating systems.

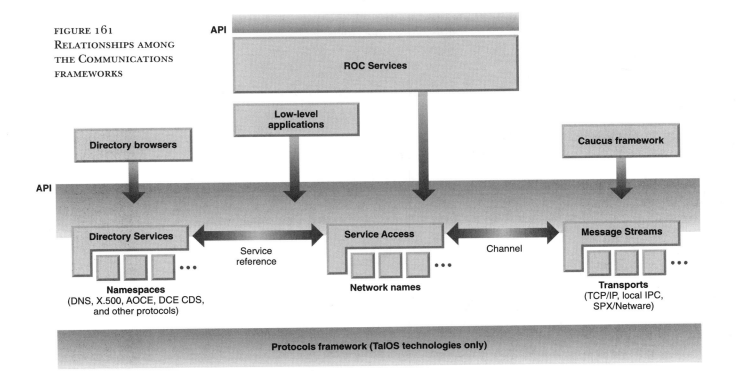

FIGURE 161
RELATIONSHIPS AMONG
THE COMMUNICATIONS
FRAMEWORKS

ROC Services framework

A *remote object call* is a member function call that spans tasks (address spaces). The ROC Services framework uses the Service Access framework and Message Streams to implement remote object calls to CommonPoint services. A member function called via ROC services might reside within another task on the same machine or on another machine on the network. Remote object calls are transparent—they appear as local calls even though they access remote functions.

As explained on page 323, the ROC Services framework also provides the basis for Taligent's implementation of the CORBA standard for distributed objects in heterogeneous environments. Applications dealing with non-CommonPoint services can also use Message Streams directly to assemble packets in known formats.

Caucus framework

The Caucus framework uses the communications access mechanism to provide multicast transport facilities for the Shared Document framework and collaborative user environments such as CSpace. (For more information about CSpace, see page 105.) Using the Caucus framework is like establishing a conference call. It establishes live connections among participants who are using different computers but doesn't specify what information they convey. It just establishes the connections and forwards packets of information to all participants as it receives them.

The Caucus framework can be used for other purposes besides real-time collaboration. The multicast transport mechanism it provides can also be used to replicate databases among several servers, or perform any other service that requires simultaneous connections among multiple machines.

Directory Services framework

The Directory Services framework will be available later than the other Communications frameworks. It provides a homogeneous view of both CommonPoint and non-CommonPoint namespaces, including DNS, X.500, AOCE, and DCE CDS. Taligent and third parties can extend the framework to support additional namespaces. Taligent provides a browser that allows users to look through available services in multiple namespaces, and third parties can use Directory Services to create additional browsers and viewers. When a user selects a particular service from a browser, the Directory Services framework returns a service reference for that service to the Service Access framework.

Service Access framework

The Service Access framework provides a mechanism for identifying and accessing services available on a network via service references. A service reference encapsulates information required to interact with a particular service. Extensions to the Service Access framework called *service adapters* encapsulate information about Taligent and non-Taligent services for use by the framework. Services can include virtually anything that is traditionally thought of as a "server," including naming services, database services, file servers, object transaction services, or World Wide Web servers.

Message Streams

Message Streams handle the basic communication between tasks. Taligent provides Message Streams transport implementations for all host systems, and Taligent and third parties can provide additional implementations. An application typically obtains a service reference from the Service Access framework and then uses Message Streams or ROC Services to obtain a channel for the communication itself.

Protocols framework

TalOS technologies include a Protocols framework that will extend the OSI reference model to the level of TCP/IP and other transport mechanisms. The Protocols framework sits between Message Streams and the transport mechanisms, exposing some of the transport infrastructure in a platform-independent manner. For example, the Protocols framework is expected to make it possible to set individual TCP/IP parameters the same way for any hardware on which it runs.

The Protocols framework accesses communications hardware as a client of the OODDM, which is introduced on page 411.

Local communications

In the simplest case, communication between two tasks on the same machine, a service first uses the Service Access framework to obtain a service definition. Clients can then use Message Streams or ROC Services to issue requests to the service via a service reference. Figure 162 shows this arrangement.

The client must know about basic Service Access, Message Streams, and (optionally) ROC Services instances. Transport mechanisms at the kernel level are completely hidden by these abstractions.

FIGURE 162
LOCAL
COMMUNICATIONS

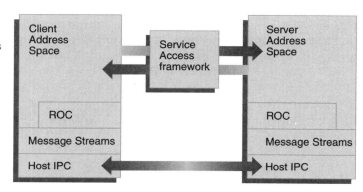

Communicating between machines

Communicating between threads on different machines differs only subtly from communicating between threads on a single machine. To establish a connection to a service, the client creates a network service reference and specifies the appropriate network name, then "opens a socket" (in UNIX terms) to listen for requests. Alternatively, the client can use the Directory Service framework to browse the network for the service the user wants and obtain a network service reference that way.

Using the optional ROC Services allows requests for a service to go directly to the remote object across the network, without the caller or remote implementation even being aware that a network is involved.

ROC Services

The ROC Services framework, which is introduced on page 323, uses the Service Access framework and the Message Streams request-reply interface to implement remote object calls to CommonPoint services.

Application developers most commonly create a remote object call to access data that is not local to the current task. For example, a local machine makes remote object calls to access files on a remote file server. A member function located on the local machine would not be able to access the remote files.

The local interface is known as the *caller,* and the remote interface is known as the *dispatcher.* A caller and dispatcher that work together to implement a remote request protocol are known as a *caller-dispatcher pair.*

A simple remote procedure call setup consists of:

- A caller instance
- A dispatcher instance
- An implementation instance containing the member functions you want to execute remotely

Figure 163 shows a simple caller-dispatcher pair model.

FIGURE 163
REMOTE
OBJECT CALLS

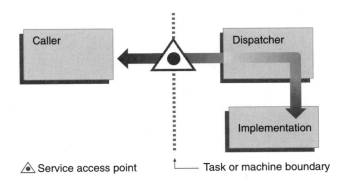

Service access point   Task or machine boundary

The caller resides in the local task in the local address space, while the dispatcher and implementation instances reside in the remote task. The caller sends function parameters to the remote task, where the dispatcher receives them and sends them on to the implementation, where the actual member function code executes. The member function returns results back to the dispatcher, and the dispatcher sends the results back to the caller.

Using a two-step process of dispatching keeps the member function implementation class independent of remote processing—the member functions don't need to know that they are being called remotely.

While the interaction of a caller-dispatcher pair uses a client-server model, callers and dispatchers are not the same as clients and servers. In general, clients and servers are more complex than a single caller-dispatcher pair. A client often has multiple callers, and a server might have one or more dispatchers. Also, a server usually has more structure than a dispatcher, including a tasking model, the transport mechanism, and resources that the server manages.

However, callers and dispatchers provide the building blocks for creating the CommonPoint equivalents of clients and servers. As Figure 164 illustrates, you can construct servers out of multiple caller-dispatcher pairs and their variations.

FIGURE 164
A CLIENT-
SERVER
CONFIGURATION
USING
MULTIPLE
CALLERS AND A
SINGLE
DISPATCHER

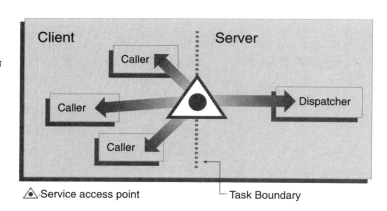

Service Access framework

The Service Access framework supports the following tasks:

- Defining service access definitions
- Creating service references to establish connections to services
- Making internal or external services available to network clients

Services advertise themselves as available by using service definitions, and clients that want to connect to a service obtain a service reference that corresponds to the name of a specific service within a particular namespace.

A service definition represents a point at which clients can connect to a service. The service reference acts as a pointer to that definition, providing the client with a handle through which the client can communicate to the service. This handle can lead directly to a local service or across a network or other communications service to another host.

Making an external service available to the CommonPoint application system via a network requires writing a service adapter. This adapter gives the framework the information it needs to translate the external service's naming structure, recognize its protocols, and make the service available to CommonPoint applications.

A service has only one service definition, and a client has only one service reference to a particular service. But because a service can have multiple clients, a single service can have many service references at one time.

For example, the service illustrated in Figure 165 has two clients on the same host (but in different address spaces) and one client on another host. As a result, three service references point to a single service.

FIGURE 165
SERVICE
REFERENCES
AND SERVICE
DEFINITIONS

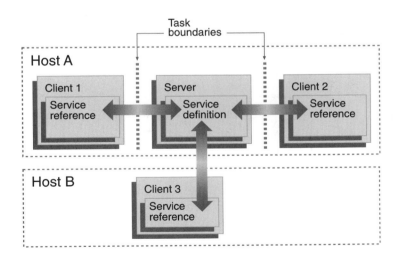

Message Streams

In general, application developers can use ROC Services for most communications needs. Direct use of the Message Streams instead of using ROC Services is necessary only for the following purposes:

- Defining an interoperable client
- Using datastreams for peer-to-peer communications
- Performing bulk data movement

Message Streams handle messaging the same way for communication between threads on the same machine, on different machines, and on different operating systems, hiding implementation details at all levels:

- Within the same task
- Within separate tasks on the same machine
- Between separate machines running the CommonPoint application system
- Between machines running the CommonPoint application system and machines running other operating systems

Figure 166 shows two tasks communicating across a task boundary. The Message Streams framework receives the message or request from Task 1 and transports this message across the task boundary by using host IPC services. On the other side of the task boundary, the Message Streams framework intercepts the message and sends it to Task 2.

Message Streams can be implemented with either the request-reply interface or the datastreams interface, which correspond to the request-reply and datastreams models introduced on page 378.

FIGURE 166
LOCAL
COMMUNICA-
TIONS USING
MESSAGE
STREAMS

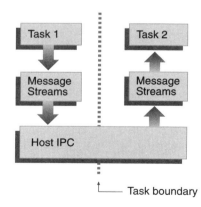

Request-reply interface   The request-reply interface implements a synchronous send-receive-reply model.
Request-reply communications use the following exchange (illustrated in
Figure 167):

1. The client sends a request to the server thread.

2. The server receives the client request and processes it.

3. The server formulates a reply and sends it back to the client.

4. The client receives the reply.

The request and reply are bound to a thread for the duration of the transaction.

Typical uses of the request-reply interface include:

- File servers that process each request independently
- Database query servers, where the server does not retain client information
  beyond a single request

The ROC Services framework uses the request-reply interface as the basis for
its communications.

FIGURE 167
REQUEST-REPLY
EXCHANGE

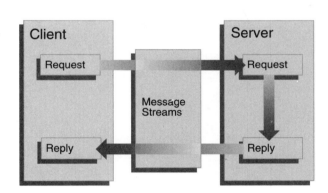

Datastreams interface

The datastreams interface implements a stream that can send and receive data in both directions simultaneously, as shown in Figure 168. Unidirectional and datagram models are also available.

Examples of the use of the datastreams interface include:

- Terminal emulators
- Application processes that funnel events

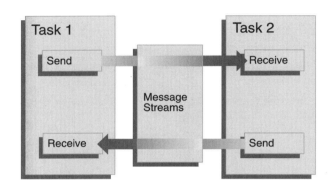

FIGURE 168
USING THE
DATASTREAMS
INTERFACE TO
EXCHANGE
MESSAGES

FILE SYSTEM

The File System interface consists of object abstractions for manipulating files, directories, and volumes that reside on hardware or virtual storage devices. These classes map directly to the low-level file system calls provided by the host operating system, and they are identical for all hosts.

This section introduces the primary File System classes and operations. Although the Compound Document framework takes care of many file-related operations, developers who wish to manipulate files directly need to understand both the File System interface and Streams and Persistence (described in Chapter 14, beginning on page 351).

File System classes

The File System interface provides classes that you can use to

- Access physical entities
- Access data
- Iterate through directories and volumes
- Copy and move file system instances

File System entities

Volumes, directories, and files are physical entities that reside on hardware or virtual devices. The File System interface provides access to these physical entities by means of surrogate instances called *file system entities,* as suggested by Figure 169.

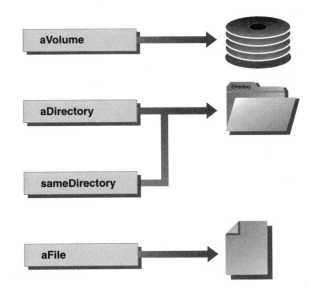

FIGURE 169
RELATION-
SHIP OF
SURROGATE
INSTANCES
TO PHYSICAL
OBJECTS

You use file system entities to:

- Locate physical entities
- Delete physical entities
- Initiate access
- Access the physical entity's properties

Figure 170 shows the standard classes for files system entities. TFileSystemEntity, an abstract base class, defines the common protocol for file system entities. TVolume, TDirectory, and TFile are the concrete classes that derive from TFileSystemEntity, implementing protocols specific to each kind of entity.

Each file system entity has properties associated with it. (Properties are introduced in Chapter 14, beginning on page 337.) For example, every volume, directory, or file has properties for its name, creation date, modification date, size, and file system entity type. Each file system entity also has properties specific to that type—for example, only files have end-of-file markers.

FIGURE 170
FILE SYSTEM
ENTITIES

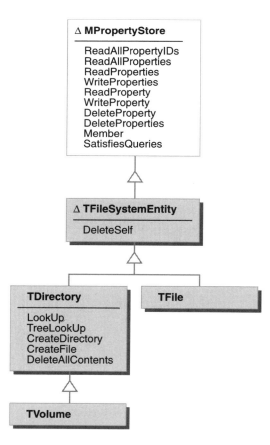

TFileSystemEntity implements the property store protocol of MPropertyStore to provide access to global file system properties, and TDirectory, TVolume, and TFile implement the protocol for properties specific to their corresponding physical entities. You can also define your own properties for file system entities.

Accessing data

A TFile instance is a reference to a physical file, but it doesn't provide access to the file's contents. To open a file for reading or writing, you first create an instance of TFileStream or TMappedFile, which both derive from MOpenFile as shown in Figure 171. Both TFileStream and TMappedFile take a TFile instance as a parameter and use it to establish file access.

TFileStream is a streaming class and is introduced on page 353. It provides a way to create a named, persistent stream from a TFile instance. To read the file, you stream from the TFileStream; to write the file, you stream into TFileStream. A Seek member function allows the read-write pointer to be positioned arbitrarily. TFileStream is particularly useful for streaming complex objects in and out.

TMappedFile provides a way to "map" the contents of a TFile instance into memory as part of an application's virtual memory address space. You can then treat the file as if you had copied its contents (or some specified portion of its contents) into a single buffer in memory, using pointers to access and store information. TMappedFile provides the buffer and copies in the data from the file. If changes are made to the buffer, they are automatically saved back to disk.

TMappedFile is particularly useful for frequent random access to file contents and for file sharing, because more than one process can have the same file mapped at the same time. It may be most useful with files whose contents were not originally created by streaming, such as documents created by non-CommonPoint applications.

Both TFileStream and TMappedFile are low-level constructs when compared with TDiskDictionaryOf archives (introduced on page 356), documents created with the Compound Document framework, and other high-level mechanisms for storing and accessing data in files. Neither TFileStream nor TMappedFile impose any structure on the files that they access. The client must supply all structure and formatting.

FIGURE 171
FILE ACCESS
CLASSES

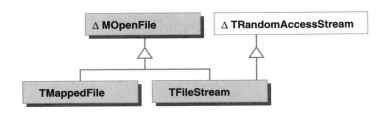

Iterating through volumes and directories

The File System interface includes iterator classes for use with the query mechanism provided by MPropertyStore. These classes allow you to iterate through volumes and directories and retrieve file entities with specific properties that have specific values:

- **TDirectoryIterator** iterates over the files and directories contained within a TDirectory instance. Instances of TDirectoryIterator do not iterate over subdirectories within the target directory.
- **TDirectoryTreeIterator** iterates over files and directories within a TDirectory instance and includes subdirectories. TDirectoryTreeIterator traverses subdirectories completely as it encounters them.
- **TVolumesIterator** iterates over all files and directories on all mounted volumes.

For an example of the use of TDirectoryIterator and the property query mechanism to select files and directories whose modification date is greater than or equal to a given date, see page 340.

Copying and moving files

TFileSystemCopier and TFileSystemMover provide the copy and move functions for files. TFileSystemCopier copies entities between directories on the same or different volumes. TFileSystemMover moves entities between directories on the same volume. To move entities between different volumes, you use TFileSystemCopier to copy them and then explicitly delete the source entities.

Flattening and resurrecting file system entities

Although you can flatten file system entities to a deep-freeze level and resurrect them again, they are not location-independent. You cannot stream a TFile instance alone to another machine and subsequently find the file to which the surrogate maps. You must wrap the file system entity with enough information to connect it to the proper file system server on the source machine.

When you resurrect a file system entity that has been flattened to a deep-freeze level, the file system attempts to reconnect the surrogate instance to the physical entity to which it refers. If the file system cannot make a connection, the surrogate is invalid and any file system operations on the surrogate generate an exception. However, non–file system operations performed on the surrogate, such as an equality comparison, are still legal operations and do not generate exceptions.

TIME SERVICES

The Time Services framework provides a consistent hardware-independent model that can be shared by all applications that require timing support. Services provided include:

- A convenient abstraction for representing time
- A clock architecture that represents timing dependencies
- Different time sources
- Control over the representation of time

Application developers commonly use the Time Services framework to get the current time or delay an action until a specific time. Applications with more specialized requirements can customize Time Services classes to provide sophisticated timing capabilities.

The Time Media frameworks, which are described in Chapter 11, use the Time Services framework extensively.

Time Services classes

The Time Services framework uses two fundamental abstractions: time and clocks. Together, time and clocks provide you with a convenient way to represent time and timing dependencies:

- *Time* is a quantity of picoseconds. Classes derived from TTime represent the common time units such as hours, minutes, and seconds.
- *Clocks* represent the passage of time and provide the interface for getting the current time and delaying until a specific time. A software clock derived from TClock starts at a particular time and keeps going, counting picoseconds, until it is turned off.

Time

A particular time is represented by an instance of a class derived from TTime. A time instance might represent a time on a particular clock, an elapsed time, or the duration for a delay. To know what a time instance represents, you need to know the context in which the time is being used and what clock it is being used with.

The Time Services framework provides TTime derivations for the common time units shown in Figure 172. Other parts of the system, such as the Time Media frameworks, provide other time units. TTime includes operators for arithmetic and comparison.

Time Services classes can be used to model anything from extremely small time intervals to intervals that represent millions of years. However, as the time range increases, the resolution decreases. For measurements on the order of years, the resolution is not accurate to a nanosecond. The system provides picosecond resolution up to about 1.25 hours, microsecond resolution up to about 142 years, and second resolution up to about 1.4281×10^8 years.

FIGURE 172
TIME UNITS

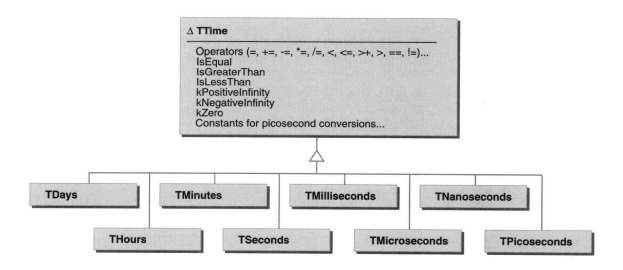

Clocks

Clocks provide the interface for the two main uses of Time Services: getting the current time and delaying until a specific time.

TClock is an abstract base class that defines the clock protocol for getting the time and setting delays on a software clock. As shown in Figure 173, a TClock object has a current time, represented by a TTime object, that is simply a floating point number that identifies a time in picoseconds. Time Services provides three standard clocks derived from TClock: TSystemClock, TDateTimeClock, and TSyncableClock. A related class, TStopwatch, is not a true clock but a convenience class provided for calculating elapsed times.

TSystemClock is a real time clock that counts time from system startup. It's used for standard timing operations, such as getting the current time and running time-dependent tasks.

TDateTimeClock is a persistent clock that represents the flow of time according to the international standard called Coordinated Universal Time (known by its French abbreviation UTC). It's used to get the time of day as a localizable value. For more information on localizing date values, see "Date and Time Conversion" on page 305.

It's also possible to use TDateTimeClock as a persistent clock. The date time clock counts time from 12:00 a.m. on March 1, 2000, so times returned from this clock are negative (until 12:00 a.m. on March 1, 2000).

TSyncableClock is a clock that can be synchronized with other clocks. Timing dependencies can be represented by setting up synchronization relationships between clocks. Syncable clocks are used extensively with time media.

FIGURE 173
CLOCK ARCHITECTURE

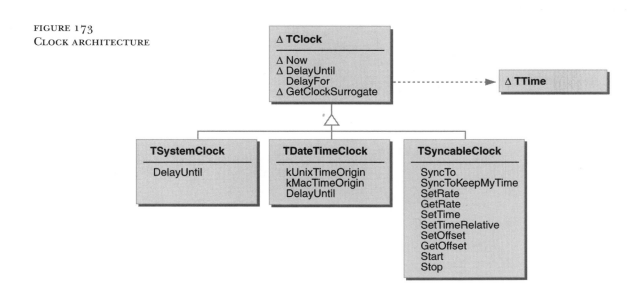

TStopwatch, shown in Figure 174, is a convenience class for calculating elapsed times—a stopwatch for timing intervals. An instance of TStopwatch starts running from time zero when it is created. Unless you specify another clock to use for timing, TStopwatch uses the system clock.

FIGURE 174
STOPWATCH

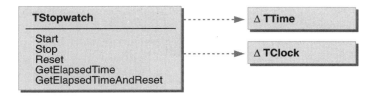

Syncable clocks

A *syncable clock,* represented by the TSyncableClock class shown in Figure 173, can be synchronized to another clock. When a clock is synchronized to another clock, its timing depends on that clock.

A syncable clock has two important properties, its rate and current time (clock time). A syncable clock gets its fundamental representation of the time flow from the clock that drives it, but it still controls its own time and rate.

Syncable clock surrogates, represented by the class TSyncableClockSurrogate, are used to synchronize one syncable clock to another. Surrogates can be passed across task boundaries to synchronize clocks that reside in separate tasks.

Rate

The rate of a syncable clock represents how fast its time is flowing with respect to the clock that drives it—for example, it might be going the same speed (rate = 1.0), twice as fast (rate = 2.0), or half as fast (rate = 0.5). The rate acts as a floating point multiplier for the amount of time that is flowing. The default rate is 1.0, but it can be changed.

You can implement tempo maps or shuttle knobs by changing the rate of a clock at different points in time. Tempo maps are commonly used in MIDI applications to specify changes in the playback rate of a sequence. Figure 175 shows a tempo map where the slope represents the rate. The points where the slope changes represent the rate changes.

FIGURE 175
TEMPO MAP

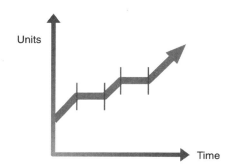

Clock times

Clock time is the current time on a clock. Several *slave clocks* can be synchronized to the same *master clock* and run at the same rate but still have different clock times because they count time from different points.

For example, as shown in Figure 176, different clocks can represent different time zones that are all synchronized to a clock representing Greenwich Mean Time (GMT). The clock that represents Pacific Standard Time (PST) and the clock that represents Eastern Standard Time (EST) have different clock times, but they are both driven by the GMT clock and run at the same rate.

✅ NOTE   This example illustrates the way master clocks work, but it doesn't illustrate the way time zones should normally be handled. The text scanning and formatting classes, which are introduced on page 305, take care of conversion between UTC time and local times.

This synchronization relationship is a simple clock hierarchy. You can change one of the slave clocks to represent a different time zone by simply resetting the time. One of the advantages of building clock hierarchies is that it is easy to change the relationships, as the next section explains.

FIGURE 176
CLOCK TIMES

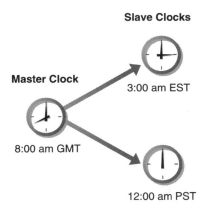

Slave Clocks

Master Clock

3:00 am EST

8:00 am GMT

12:00 am PST

**Representing timing
dependencies**

Syncable clocks can represent timing dependencies. Multiple clocks can be synchronized to the same master clock, which allows you to build clock hierarchies. The clock hierarchies determine the timing dependencies based on the clocks in the hierarchy. If you need to change the timing dependencies, you can change the clocks instead of recalculating time or delays.

For example, an animation might use a clock that indicates when each frame should display. By synchronizing the animation clock with another time source, you can play the animation in sync with sound, real time, or video.

The animation can control internal timing aspects by using different clocks. If the animation depicts a butterfly that flaps its wings as it moves across the horizon, the rate at which the wings flap might depend on how fast the butterfly moves. If you control the flapping rate with one clock, and the butterfly's speed with another, you can control the dependency by synchronizing the clocks as shown in Figure 177 and setting the desired rate.

It would also be possible to base the butterfly's speed on the video playback rate, and the flapping rate on the sound playback. To accomplish this, you would drive the butterfly speed clock with the video clock, and the flapping rate clock with the sound clock, as shown in Figure 178.

By using different clocks for each timing dependency and synchronizing the clocks, you can move the butterfly in sync with a video background and flap its wings to the beat of the sound track. The animation would still be synchronized with the real time clock.

FIGURE 177
CLOCK
HIERARCHY

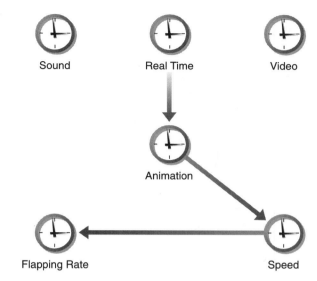

FIGURE 178
TIMING
DEPENDENCIES

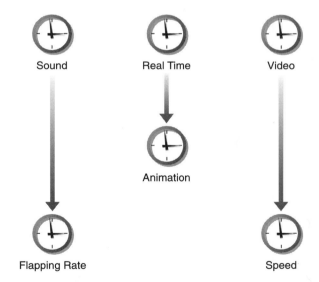

OBJECT RUNTIME SERVICES

The interfaces provided by Object Runtime Services support the following runtime capabilities:

- **Memory Heaps** provide a multithread-safe way to allocate memory.
- **Exceptions** provide runtime support for C++ exceptions and a set of common exception types for use by the CommonPoint application system.
- **Shared Libraries** provide a mechanism for packaging code and data into dynamically loadable shared libraries.
- **Metadata** provides a mechanism for accessing information about objects' types and allows dynamic instantiation of objects at runtime.

In the CommonPoint application system, Object Runtime Services consist of a uniform client API that supports these capabilities on all host systems. All application developers use Object Runtime Services, either directly or indirectly via the Desktop frameworks and other CommonPoint frameworks.

Heap management and storage allocation

A *memory segment* is a contiguous and usually rather large block of raw or unmanaged memory. All available memory is originally owned by the kernel, which returns memory segments to frameworks that allocate and deallocate memory.

A *heap* consists of one or more memory segments from which blocks of memory are allocated and freed. C++ instances created dynamically through operators such as new and delete are stored on a heap. C library memory functions such as malloc and free also allocate storage on heaps.

A task can contain one or more heaps. A primary or *default heap* is always associated with each task. Memory segments never overlap; this is true among all the heaps in a task and among the memory segments within each heap. Therefore, a given address can be contained in, at most, one heap, and a memory segment cannot be owned by more than one heap.

Object Runtime Services includes classes for all standard heap operations, including classes for local and shared heaps, user defined heaps, and iteration through blocks of memory.

Standard heap

Object Runtime Services provides an implementation of a standard heap (the default used by tasks) and additional management routines for heaps. You can derive your own special-purpose heaps from the standard heap.

The standard heap provides the following:

- The standard model for C++ to allocate and free nonrelocatable blocks—without compaction and without garbage collection
- Reentrancy and multithread safety (multithreaded applications need no special precautions when using the standard heap)
- High performance based on the host operating system's native capabilities
- Efficient management of huge heaps (given sufficient real memory)
- Simplified error handling, by ensuring that allocations of reasonable size always succeed (heaps grow automatically, if needed)

In addition, Object Runtime Services supports the following capabilities:

- Running tasks with multiple heaps
- Debugging for common problems such as double-deletion and uninitialized storage
- Iteration through the allocated or free blocks in a heap
- Allocation in shared memory, allowing instances to be shared among tasks
- Designing special-purpose allocators

You can use standard heap member functions when debugging to check a heap for possible corruption. You can detect common storage allocation problems, such as double deletion and uninitialized storage, by using an optional zapping mode that writes known values into allocated and freed blocks. You can also use a heap iterator to work through all the blocks in the heap, all the allocated blocks, or all the freed blocks.

TMemoryHeap

The standard heap is based on an abstract base class, TMemoryHeap, that provides the basic protocol for allocating and freeing blocks of memory. TMemoryHeap defines the interface through which applications invoke heap operations, but it does not supply any actual implementation. Implementations based on TMemoryHeap might or might not choose to use the host operating system's memory manager to obtain memory for suballocation. Object Runtime Services include two concrete classes derived from the standard heap, TLocalMemoryHeap and TSharedMemoryHeap, that do use the host operating system's memory manager.

Storage can be allocated directly by calling member functions of a TMemoryHeap instance (or its descendents), or indirectly by using the C++ operator new or the function malloc from the standard C library. Indirect allocations eventually reference an instance of a class derived from TMemoryHeap to perform the actual allocation.

In the CommonPoint implementations for most hosts, malloc uses a separate heap. Programs that conform to the CommonPoint API can make no assumptions about whether new and malloc allocate in the same or different heaps. Blocks of memory from new and malloc cannot be intermixed, and malloc blocks might not be from a TMemoryHeap at all.

TMemoryHeap provides virtual member functions for many of the basic heap operations. These functions must be implemented by the subclasses. TMemoryHeap includes functions that can:

- Identify the task's default heap and all other heaps
- Identify the heap in which a certain block is contained
- Allocate, free, and reallocate memory of any size
- Reset the heap to its initial conditions
- Obtain the size of all or any of the allocated blocks

A number of TMemoryHeap member functions are not required of all derived classes but are implemented for the TLocalMemoryHeap and TSharedMemoryHeap concrete classes. Operations performed by these functions include:

- Checking the heap for internal consistency
- Maintaining write protection for the heap
- Providing debugging aids
- Providing streaming operators for the heap information

TLocalMemoryHeap

TLocalMemoryHeap is the concrete storage allocator designed for use by a single task. A size constructor parameter to TLocalMemoryHeap specifies the initial size of the heap. TLocalMemoryHeap is the default heap for threads. You get it automatically: no explicit action is required. Unless specified otherwise, everything that you allocate, with either the C++ operator new or the C library function malloc, goes into a single default heap of this type. Most programs simply use the default heap (managed with C++ operators new and delete) without creating additional heaps.

A TLocalMemoryHeap generally grows enough to support the requests that it receives. The heap can dynamically grow larger than this initial size to satisfy requests. The growable heap feature allows you to eliminate checks for the return code of calls to new or malloc. You can assume that all reasonable memory requests will be satisfied. A TLocalMemoryHeap does not become exhausted unless it receives a request that it cannot satisfy with the amount of memory available from the system. If there is insufficient memory in the system to support the request, the TLocalMemoryHeap throws an exception.

TSharedMemoryHeap　　TSharedMemoryHeap provides a heap that can be shared across tasks; that is, across address spaces. To use a shared memory heap, a cooperating task must first create the heap and then stream the heap instance to another task. The other task then resurrects the heap instance from the stream. The heap instance is small because it does not contain the contents of the memory it represents. This mapping allows any number of cooperating tasks to read and write instances by using pointers.

A size constructor parameter specifies the size of a TSharedMemoryHeap. The storage for shared heaps is automatically mapped at some logical address in all tasks using the heap. A shared heap cannot grow larger than its initial size. Requests that cause the shared heap to become exhausted cause an exception to be thrown.

Features of shared heaps include the following:

- A shared heap appears at the same logical address in all tasks using it.
- Any task using the heap can perform any shared heap operation.
- The physical heap survives as long as any task is referencing it.
- A shared heap does not automatically grow if more memory is needed.

TSharedMemoryHeap also provides the write-protection member functions that allow one task to protect the contents of the heap from being modified by another task.

User-defined heaps　　Developers with special memory requirements can subclass from TMemoryHeap to support features such as the following:

- Heaps that support garbage collection
- Heaps in a constrained logical address space (such as on a peripheral board)
- Heaps that do not provide multithread synchronization (and are thus faster)
- Heaps optimized for specific usage patterns.

Exceptions

Exceptions occur at runtime and prevent threads from continuing to execute. They are also known as C++ exceptions. Examples include memory errors, such as "Heap Full," I/O errors, such as "Out of Disk Space," and bad parameters.

In contrast, processor faults occur within a processor's instruction set and prevent the processor from executing the next instruction. If a processor fault occurs, the running thread is immediately suspended, and the host operating system may take a system-specific action. Processor faults are host specific. Examples include bus errors, "Divide by zero," and "Privileged Instruction."

TStandardException

C++ exceptions are defined by the ANSI C++ language definition and provide the basic facilities for throwing and catching exceptions. C++ exceptions are raised by throw statements, caught by try-catch blocks, and thrown and caught within a single thread of execution. TStandardException and its derived classes represent specific categories of errors. When you raise a TStandardException (typically thrown with the C++ throw statement), it becomes a C++ exception.

Prior to execution, a TStandardException is just an ordinary instance. Not all C++ exceptions need to be TStandardExceptions. Any instance, or even primitive types such as int or char*, can be thrown as C++ exceptions.

TStandardException provides a standardized way of associating a specific error or message text with an exception. It defines the basic member functions for associating the parameters with the exception, providing the enum representing this particular exception, and throwing the exception to C++. In most cases you use one of the predefined concrete derived classes of TStandardException. Alternatively, you can define your own derived classes.

The set of possible error messages, TStandardException derived classes, and exception instances is not fixed. Each shared library can define its own, which become usable wherever and whenever the library is in use.

TExceptionFormatter

The error messages associated with exceptions are stored in an archive and accessed by TExceptionFormatter instances. Each library has an archive of message templates for error messages. A message template is selected based on the type (in the C++ sense) of the exception and the enum value obtained from TStandardException.

TExceptionFormatter is an abstract base class that serves two purposes: It provides an interface for custom formatters to override, and it provides two static member functions that make it easy to get messages without having to deal with anything else.

To create a custom formatter, you can subclass from TExceptionFormatter and override the Format method, which receives the exception that occurred, the archive corresponding to the shared library that contains the implementation of the exception that occurred, the current locale, and a reference to a TText object to fill in with the text of an error message.

For example, you could add other data members to an exception (such as filename, device name, volume, and so on) and format the data from the exception with a message retrieved from the archive to produce something like this: "A read error occurred on hard disk Alice while reading the file White Rabbit."

Message templates in archives are localizable.

Shared libraries

Taligent uses *library packages* to provide a host-independent API for loading shared libraries and reducing the name conflicts that can occur when streamed objects are dynamically loaded into a running program. A library package:

- Has the same name across all CommonPoint implementations and hosts.
- Contains a set of classes. Any given class is in the same package on all CommonPoint implementations that support that class.
- Belongs to, or is controlled by, a single vendor. This vendor is responsible for managing the class names within the package.
- Qualifies a class name in the streamed representation of a type. Class types on streams are represented by a package name and a class name.

The package mechanism also makes it possible to specify a package for a particular version of a shared library so that classes can be associated with the correct versions of the shared libraries from which they were derived. To keep binaries self-contained and easy to install, the package name is embedded in the library file itself.

Metadata

Metadata provides a means of representing the types of instances. True metadata provides a means of describing classes based on the following ANSI C++ extensions:

- **Checked casts** allow safe casting from a less derived type to a more derived type.
- **Casting from virtual bases** facilitates the casting of concrete classes from abstract base classes.
- **Run-Time Type Identification (RTTI)** allows enquiries about or comparisons of the types of most objects.

Taligent-specific capabilities

In addition to the ANSI C++ extensions, Taligent supports the following related capabilities:

- **Additional metadata information**, which includes the following:
  - The size of an instance of a class, in bytes (needed for resurrecting flattened objects from streams)
  - A shared library containing class definitions (needed for flattening and resurrecting objects from streams)
- **The Copy function**, which creates a copy of any object using the original object's copy constructor.
- **Dynamic instantiation** supports the creation of instances of dynamically identified classes (needed, for example, for resurrecting objects from streams).

Global functions

Global functions (that is, functions available for use at any point in a program) provided by metadata include FlattenPointer, ResurrectPointer, and Copy. FlattenPointer and ResurrectPointer are introduced in "Monomorphic vs. polymorphic streaming" on page 354.

Given a pointer to an instance, the Copy function makes a copy of the instance, either on the default heap or on a heap specified by the caller. It returns a pointer to the newly created instance. Copy operates by allocating storage for the new instance to the specified heap and then using the instance's copy constructor to copy the instance.

The Copy function is defined using global template functions:

```
template <class T> T *Copy(const T *sourcePointer);
template <class T> T *Copy(const T *sourcePointer, TMemoryHeap& whichHeap;
```

Its use is very straightforward:

```
class   Tx;
Tx  *ax, *bx;
. . .
bx = Copy(ax);
```

The Copy function can be used with any class type. It requires no additional declarations.

MICROKERNEL SERVICES

The interfaces provided by Microkernel Services support these services via object abstractions:

- **Tasks and Threads** manage executable entities called threads within separate address spaces called tasks.

- **Interprocess Communication (IPC)** provides a mechanism for sending messages to tasks and threads on the local machine. IPC is provided by the host operating system and doesn't have an API in the CommonPoint application system. Plans for TalOS technologies include extending Microkernel Services to an API for IPC.

- **Synchronization Services** support the use of reader-writer locks or counting semaphores to control access by threads to other threads in the same task or in different tasks.

- **Virtual Memory Management** facilitates the creation and management of virtual memory segments. Virtual memory management is provided by the host operating system and doesn't have an API in the CommonPoint application system. Plans for TalOS technologies include extending Microkernel Services to include a virtual memory API.

- **System Shutdown** shuts down the CommonPoint system in stages and returns the user to the host environment.

In the CommonPoint application system, Microkernel Services consist of a uniform client API that supports these capabilities on all host systems, including those with kernels rather than microkernels.

This section introduces only the services available to CommonPoint applications via the Microkernel Services client API. It doesn't cover hardware-specific aspects of Microkernel Services.

Tasking model

The CommonPoint tasking model exposes the multitasking capabilities of the underlying 32-bit operating system as a set of abstractions that work the same way on all host systems. This section introduces key aspects of the tasking model.

Tasks and threads

A *thread* is an individual unit of execution—a single series of instructions that execute in a logical sequence.

A *task* is a collection of one or more threads that share a single address space and, usually, a single purpose. The address space also contains various resources shared by the threads within the task, such as shared libraries, a default memory heap, library searchers, and global data. A task always starts executing with a main thread. Any thread in a task can start the execution of other threads. Threads can use a variety of mechanisms to communicate with each other.

CommonPoint threads are sometimes called *lightweight threads* because they are analogous to the "lightweight" processes of operating systems like newer versions of UNIX. Much of a thread's context is determined by the task and therefore doesn't need to be saved every time the thread is removed from its running state. As a result, switches between threads in the same task require minimal system resources and take less time than a context switch between two processes in a traditional operating system.

Microkernel Services support concurrency—that is, managing multiple threads of execution that share access to data and resources within a single task. The task manages the address space and other shared resources while allowing individual threads to execute at the same time. Concurrency can make applications more efficient, more responsive, and better suited to distributed systems.

Task lifetime and termination

Tasks are created and die. The lifetime of a task includes the duration of the main thread, plus the time it takes all remaining threads to terminate themselves according to a task's termination protocol.

Tasks die in one of three ways: when the main thread completes, when an exception is thrown and not handled, or when its owner kills it. The following five conditions must be satisfied for a task to die:

- The main thread completes normally or encounters an exception that is not handled.
- If the task contains one or more nonmain threads, each such thread eventually calls a blocking microkernel service.
- Thread creation in the task is disabled prior to cancelling subordinate threads.
- Each subordinate thread, upon receipt of a exception, either completes normally or doesn't handle the exception.
- Each static instance destructor completes normally or doesn't handle the exception.

Security

Microkernel Services do not violate the underlying security model of the host operating system.

Scheduling

Microkernel Services provide five scheduling classes that determine scheduling priorities for their associated threads. Threads associated with higher-priority scheduling classes are guaranteed to run and finish their tasks before threads associated with lower-priority scheduling classes.

In the CommonPoint system, the flow of control frequently passes between cooperating threads within a task, although on a single-processor platform there is still only one thread executing at any given time. However, the scheduling mechanism is preemptive, which means that any thread can be made to yield control of the CPU at any time. Because of this you cannot guarantee the order of execution of any given thread or how long any given thread executes before being preempted.

Synchronization

The CommonPoint system supports two paradigms for synchronizing threads between tasks or within the same task:

- **Reader-Writer locks** involve a single writer and multiple readers for a single piece of data. This mechanism locks out readers while the writer is writing and locks out the writer while readers are reading.
- **Counting semaphores** involves a producer-consumer relationship. If one thread is waiting to receive something from another thread, it just waits until it receives a signal to begin receiving.

System Shutdown framework

A user can choose a menu command that shuts down the CommonPoint application system. The System Shutdown framework shuts down the system in stages and returns the user to the host environment. Because the CommonPoint system isn't a typical layered operating system, the shutdown process must take account of many complex interdependencies. To participate in this process and ensure that it proceeds smoothly, developers subclass and instantiate shutdown handlers that perform shutdown processing, such as saving persistent data, for a particular client.

Each stage of the shutdown process shuts down a major area of the CommonPoint system. These stages progressively reduce dependences and system complexity. The completion of each stage marks the point in the shutdown process after which a large group of CommonPoint services should no longer be used. However, each stage is somewhat loosely defined, and the actual termination of each group of services is not enforced by the System Shutdown framework. Instead, shutdown proceeds cooperatively, with each service and component ensuring, via its own shutdown handlers, that it shuts down at the appropriate point.

The table that follows lists the services that are shut down during each stage.

Stage	Description
Pre-shutdown	Highest level components and services shut down first.
Desktop	Places, presentations, and documents are closed and the Workspace shuts down.
High-level services	High-level application frameworks (such as Text, Graphics, Time Media, and Printing) and the User Interface frameworks (including menus, dialogs, windows, and controls) shut down.
Low-level services	Communications, System Management (for example, Licensing Services), the File System Interface, and host-based I/O services shut down.
Final shutdown	Fundamental services such as Basic Text Services, the Notification framework, and Tokens shut down. This is the last stage accessible to clients before task termination.
Task termination	All remaining CommonPoint tasks are canceled.
Environment teardown	User returned to host environment

Clients of the System Shutdown framework subclass from the abstract class TShutdownHandler, which defines the protocol for all shutdown handlers, and instantiate and register their shutdown objects with the System Shutdown framework.

All public member functions of TShutdownHandler are intended to be overridden by clients and are called by the System Shutdown framework in the course of shutdown processing. These functions check whether uninterruptible operations are in progress, handle any necessary user interaction, save persistent data and perform other pre-shutdown operations, and perform actual shutdown operations such as releasing resources, deleting objects, and terminating threads and tasks.

OBJECT-ORIENTED DEVICE DRIVER MODEL (OODDM)

The OODDM and its associated frameworks bring the benefits of object-oriented technology to the realm of I/O services. The OODDM isn't part of the CommonPoint application system, but Taligent plans to include it in the TalOS technologies. The OODDM is available for use by Taligent's investors in their own system software and potentially by other vendors. It can be directly supported by a variety of hardware platforms and operating systems that don't necessarily support the CommonPoint application system.

OEMs and independent hardware vendors (IHVs) can use the OODDM to write device drivers for specialized hardware more quickly and easily than they can with traditional operating systems. The use of objects is especially appropriate for device drivers. Each hardware device is a physical object of a certain class that shares characteristics and behaviors with other devices of its class. Class hierarchies provide a powerful way to model both hardware and low-level software services.

Taligent's use of small, lightweight classes related by multiple inheritance makes for I/O frameworks that are highly flexible and easily maintained, because classes aren't forced into artificial or awkward inheritance relationships to achieve efficient code reuse.

This section provides an overview of the support the OODDM provides for device drivers. For information about printer drivers and graphics device drivers, which are implemented separately from the OODDM in the first versions of the CommonPoint application system, see page 299 and page 243, respectively.

A new approach to writing device drivers

You can write the OODDM equivalent of a device driver, called a *device ensemble,* by customizing device-specific OODDM frameworks. Each device-specific framework provides a reusable design for a particular I/O domain. For example, the Serial I/O framework provides a reusable design for serial devices. You can add or subclass the classes and member functions required for the hardware device for which you are writing a driver.

The OODDM clearly defines the tasks involved in developing any device ensemble and simplifies development, debugging, and maintenance. The sections that follow highlight its key features.

User focus

Traditional I/O architectures usually require users to learn arcane and time-consuming procedures for installing and configuring peripheral hardware, such as assigning an I/O memory range and an interrupt level to a hardware device or editing a configuration file.

To address these kinds of problems, the OODDM provides plug-and-play hardware installation for devices capable of using it and allows a device to continue functioning seamlessly after the device is physically moved from one hardware connector to another. The OODDM frameworks also keep track of the physical location of a device after the system restarts.

Broad-based compatibility

In traditional operating systems, you write a device driver not only for a specific device but also for a specific hardware platform and operating system. The OODDM allows developers to write device driver software that's source-code compatible with all operating systems that use the OODDM directly. The OODDM is expected to be supported by a variety of hardware platforms and operating systems provided by Taligent investors, including some that don't necessarily host the CommonPoint application system.

The OODDM supports this broad-based compatibility by defining two sets of interfaces for core services called *cocoons*. One cocoon executes in privileged mode, and the other in user mode. Developers can achieve the greatest compatibility and portability by using only the cocoon interfaces. As the CommonPoint system is revised, the cocoons are ported to each new version and I/O software can continue to rely on the same interfaces.

Flexible designs

Most operating systems require I/O software to adhere strictly to specific designs and standard implementations, leaving little room for innovation. One of the major goals of the OODDM is to support maximum design flexibility for I/O software.

This is especially true in the area of device access policies—the rules clients must follow to use devices. The OODDM defines no global device access policy itself. Instead, it allows each device-specific framework to define the most appropriate policy for the device, whether it's exclusive or multiple access, queued, or based on some other device-specific criteria. Traditional device interfaces tend to provide APIs that are limited to a set of basic operations such as open-close and read-write, forcing all devices into the same narrow mold. The OODDM's device-specific frameworks support a more varied range of capabilities for each kind of device.

You can run OODDM device ensembles in privileged mode, in user mode, or in both modes. This allows you to make intelligent trade-offs among performance, resource usage, and robustness.

The OODDM supports a wide variety of devices, including the following:

- Devices that support plug-and-play installation and those that don't
- Devices that issue interrupts at one or more levels and those that don't issue interrupts at all
- Devices that use direct memory access (DMA), programmed I/O, or channel processing
- Older devices that use narrow bus interfaces

Robust operation

In many traditional operating systems, device drivers run in privileged mode, and a severe I/O error can crash the entire system. The OODDM largely eliminates this problem by allowing most aspects of a device ensemble to run as user-mode tasks and by providing exception handling and recovery capabilities for code, such as interrupt handlers, that must run in privileged mode.

For example, if a severe error occurs in an interrupt handler, an exception-handling routine can gracefully unload the offending handler and notify any corresponding user-mode code.

An emphasis on services

The OODDM frameworks can be thought of as a collection of service providers interacting with service consumers. Hardware resources such as DMA channels and interrupt levels, as well as software services such as those that manage I/O buffers, can be understood generically as I/O resources.

Each resource is responsible for advertising its availability to the rest of the system. In other words, you "let resources find you." This approach turns out to be much more flexible than the traditional top-down resource searches that most operating systems use. For example, it's a very natural way to support intermittent connectivity for mobile (portable) computers.

Multiprocessor support

The OODDM fully supports symmetric multiprocessing (SMP) computers that use a uniform memory access model (UMA). The OODDM provides both privileged mode and user mode synchronization primitives that enable developers to protect data and optimize concurrent processing.

Overview of the OODDM architecture

OODDM software for a hardware device consists of several distinct parts. Collectively they perform all the tasks an ordinary device driver performs, but more reliably and with much greater flexibility. The I/O software for a particular hardware device is called a device ensemble to emphasize the collaborative nature of this new I/O software model. You create device ensembles by customizing or extending device-specific frameworks.

Device ensembles

The part of a device ensemble that executes in user mode is called a *device access manager*. A device access manager defines policies that determine how client software gains access to a hardware device. The part of a device driver that executes in privileged mode is called an *interrupt handler*. An interrupt handler processes hardware interrupts and reports back to an access manager.

A device ensemble also provides information used by a *configuration recorder* that works with the hardware configuration frameworks to configure the hardware device. The configuration recorder instantiates most of a device ensemble's objects at startup or when a hardware device is installed. For example, if a card contains two microprocessors, one to control SCSI connections and one to control a floppy drive, a configuration recorder for the card uses information provided by two device ensembles: one for the SCSI chip and one for the floppy drive chip.

FIGURE 179
A DEVICE ENSEMBLE

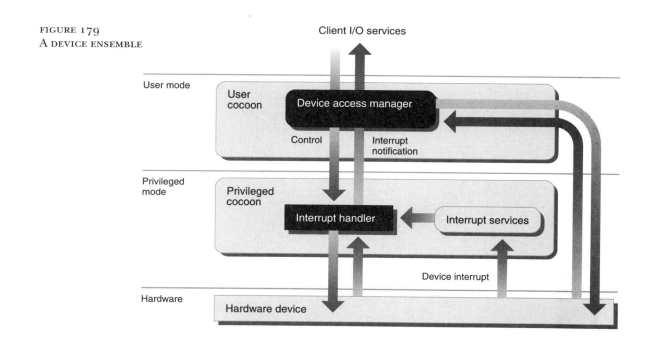

Figure 179 shows how a device access manager and an interrupt handler work together as a device ensemble. The OODDM interfaces available to device ensembles are defined by the *user cocoon* (for use by device access managers) and the *privileged cocoon* (for use by interrupt handlers). The privileged cocoon is further divided into interfaces that can be used during interrupt processing and those that cannot.

The cocoons shield the device ensemble from the underlying operating system. Although a device ensemble's interactions with OODDM frameworks and the microkernel are rich and complex, most of this complexity remains hidden behind the cocoon interfaces.

Device access managers

Device access managers manipulate hardware to handle I/O requests from clients. By running in user mode, they reduce the size of the microkernel and make the system more robust. Any error that occurs in an access manager is contained within the manager's user-mode task and doesn't threaten the integrity of the whole system.

An access manager for a device that uses interrupts receives a notification from its interrupt handler when the device issues an interrupt. This allows the access manager and interrupt handler to cooperate as necessary to handle the interrupt.

The OODDM doesn't impose rigid rules about which portion of a device ensemble's code should go in the access manager and which in the interrupt handler. However, an access manager should generally contain as much of the ensemble's code as possible to maximize reliability. A few devices, though, may have processing or performance needs that require most of the device ensemble's code to be implemented in the interrupt handler.

The OODDM doesn't impose rigid rules about which portion of a device ensemble's code should go in the access manager and which in the interrupt handler. However, an access manager should generally contain as much of the ensemble's code as possible to maximize reliability. A few devices, though, may have processing or performance needs that require most of the device ensemble's code to be implemented in the interrupt handler.

Interrupt handlers

An interrupt handler communicates directly with hardware to retrieve data, clear interrupt conditions, and perform any other programming the device requires at interrupt time. A single interrupt handler can manage several identical devices, such as two identical UART chips located on a single expansion card or on different cards.

To improve performance, an interrupt handler should generally do as little processing as possible while interrupts are disabled. This usually involves deferring some interrupt processing until after you have cleared the interrupt condition and reenabled interrupts.

Interrupt handlers are loaded dynamically into the microkernel at the request of access managers. They can be unloaded dynamically if an error occurs or if the device is removed from the system.

Configuring hardware devices

Hardware devices for modern computers can be attached in many different ways. Some are built into the motherboard, while others attach to expansion buses that in some cases can attach to other expansion boxes through adapters. Some devices, such as SCSI devices, are chained off a controller to form a virtual bus.

To keep track of complex hardware connections, the Hardware Configuration frameworks define a hierarchical software model that mirrors the computer's hierarchical hardware structure. This hierarchy is built and maintained dynamically as hardware devices are added to and removed from the system, thus providing support for plug-and-play connections. This model of the hardware configuration drives the rest of the OODDM, which relies on the model for all interactions with devices.

The configuration recorder works with the Hardware Configuration frameworks to configure the device. Some configuration recorders simply configure a predefined set of devices, while others must probe the hardware hierarchy to determine which devices to configure. Configuration recorders must be able to operate recursively.

OODDM frameworks

There are two kinds of OODDM frameworks:

- **Device-specific frameworks** provide interfaces to specific kinds of hardware devices, such as serial or SCSI devices.
- **General service frameworks** provide essential services such as interrupt handling and DMA for use by device-specific frameworks.

To write a device ensemble, you subclass from one of the device-specific frameworks, which shields you from the details of the general service frameworks. To create a new framework for a new kind of device ensemble, you use several of the general service frameworks to customize and extend one of the existing device-specific frameworks.

Device-specific frameworks

Each device-specific framework represents an efficient, appropriate design for a particular kind of device. When you customize or extend a device-specific framework, you are actually implementing a design. You can use the designs and partial implementations provided by the device-specific frameworks as the cornerstone of your own work.

Most device-dependent frameworks require little customization. They provide most of the code that most implementations need. You usually need to subclass only a few specific classes and override a few member functions to provide a complete framework implementation.

Device-specific OODDM frameworks currently under development include the following:

- Keyboard framework
- Pointing Device framework
- Serial I/O framework
- Parallel I/O framework
- Disk I/O framework
- Mass Storage framework
- SCSI framework
- Expansion bus frameworks:
    - ISA Expansion Bus framework
    - MCA Expansion Bus framework
    - PCI Expansion Bus framework
    - PCMCIA Bus framework

Taligent expects to add additional device-specific frameworks. It's also possible to create custom device-specific frameworks.

General service frameworks and classes

The general service OODDM frameworks and classes provide device ensembles with a versatile set of services that each run either in the user-level cocoon or the privileged cocoon. This section summarizes Taligent's plans for the services they will provide.

Hardware Configuration frameworks

The Hardware Configuration frameworks manage hardware configuration by maintaining a centralized software model of the computer's hardware structure, modifying the model as devices are added to and removed from the system. These frameworks:

- Maintain persistent configuration data for both autoconfigured and manually configured devices.
- Automatically assign or free hardware resources such as DMA channels or interrupt levels when a device is added to or removed from the system.
- Support a graphical user interface for configuring devices that must be configured manually.
- Provide clients with detailed device configuration data, specifying the type of every hardware resource in the system and the services that each can provide.
- Shield clients from the details of creating software services. For example, a client need not know whether a service is running locally or over a network.
- Allow clients to create software service stacks, such as those that implement network protocols, by specifying compact service descriptions that describe how to build service stacks.

Interrupt Services framework

The Interrupt Services framework provides services required by interrupt handlers, including handlers running on a symmetric multiprocessing (SMP) system that uses a uniform memory access (UMA) model.

The Interrupt Services framework:

- Dynamically installs interrupt handlers into the microkernel at any time at the request of device access managers.
- Allows each interrupt handler to address its hardware device in a location-independent way, regardless of how the device is physically connected to the system.
- Allows interrupt handlers to function well in both single-processor and multiprocessor architectures.
- Allows interrupt handlers to defer most interrupt processing until after interrupts have been reenabled.
- Can use an ROC-style control channel to pass synchronous requests from access managers to interrupt handlers.

- Allows interrupt handlers to notify access managers asynchronously when I/O requests are complete.
- Detects processor faults that occur in interrupt handlers, shuts down devices, frees resources, removes the interrupt handlers that caused the errors, and notifies the appropriate access managers. Interrupt handlers can also provide their own fault-handling mechanisms.

Conflict Resolver framework

To work with the OODDM frameworks, hardware devices need to use shared system resources such as I/O registers, I/O memory, interrupt sockets, and DMA channels. The Conflict Resolver framework manages resource contention in a way that's independent of bus architecture.

Device ensembles generally use the Conflict Resolver framework indirectly via other OODDM service frameworks, although it is also possible to use it directly.

The Conflict Resolver framework:

- Allows multiple clients to synchronize their use of I/O resources.
- Provides clients with detailed information about resource conflicts.
- Provides several bus-specific formats for use in specifying resource requirements and constraints, such as those traditionally specified by CFG configuration files for EISA and ISA devices.
- Allows clients to specify resource requirements for manually configured devices before the devices are physically installed. The Conflict Resolver framework tracks these resource requirements across system startups.
- Allows clients to override automatic resource assignments for autoconfigured devices.
- Allows clients to delete resource assignments.
- Automatically frees resources assigned to a device when the device generates a severe error or is disconnected from the system.

Programmed I/O framework

The Programmed I/O framework supports efficient programmed I/O (PIO) services that insulate device ensembles from the platform-specific details of device memory access. These services are available in both privileged mode and user mode. Ensemble code does not explicitly distinguish between memory-mapped and port I/O.

Buffer Services classes

The Buffer Services classes provide user-level and in-kernel clients with appropriately prepared buffers to use for I/O operations. I/O buffer services shield clients from having to understand the specific addressing constraints of physical memory or the details of the direct memory access. They are available in both privileged mode and user mode.

The Buffer Services classes:

- Allow you to write device access managers that are independent of DMA hardware
- Work around physical constraints imposed by the hardware
- Allow I/O buffers to stream data from one task address space to another
- Permit interrupt handlers to initiate queued I/O requests by using I/O buffers

DMA Services framework

The DMA Services framework implements efficient direct memory access (DMA) services that dynamically assign DMA channels, work with client I/O buffers, allow scattered read–gathered write (scatter-gather) operations, support narrow bus hardware, and work with third-party bus masters. These services are available in both privileged mode and user mode.

I/O Preferences framework

The I/O Preferences framework keeps track of hardware-related user preference information like that generated by personal computer control panels. It does so in a way that's independent of the host operating system.

The I/O Preferences framework:

- Can notify clients when I/O preferences change
- Can maintain separate preference information for each of several identical devices
- Provides I/O preference information needed during system startup, such as mouse tracking speed

422

GLOSSARY

A		

absorption

Merging data with the existing data in a model.

COMPARE   *embedding, enclosure*

action

A semantic token sent to an action handler provided by a view. An action handler collects the results of actions until it's appropriate to apply them in some way. For example, choices made by a user via dialog box are often represented as actions.

SEE ALSO   *command*

action monitor

A *cp*Constructor window that allows a designer to examine the sender, message, and other information associated with actions generated by objects displayed in a previewer.

SEE ALSO   *action, previewer*

activation key

In Licensing Services, a piece of encoded data that enables a CommonPoint product to be used under the encoded terms of a license agreement.

active rectangle

In the Basic Printing framework, the rectangle that designates which part of a page to use for pagination, tiling, clipping, or scaling.

address space

A range of accessible memory.

SEE ALSO   *task*

alias

A reference to another object.

SEE ALSO   *proxy*

anchor	A selection of data that can be joined to another selection of data by means of a data link or a reference link. SEE ALSO *data link, reference link*
appliance	An object that can perform some self-contained automated operation on data in other objects, typically initiated by dragging the icons for those objects over the appliance icon. For example, dragging a document icon over the icon for a printer appliance prints the document,
application framework	(1) A framework that provides preassembled generic application code that a developer can modify to create a real application. (2) In the CommonPoint system, one of the Application frameworks, a set of services that provide a rich feature set for developing interactive applications of all kinds. SEE ALSO *framework*
application program interface (API)	The classes, types, functions, and other programming constructs used by programmers to take advantage of the services provided by a particular operating system, subsystem, or other programming environment. SEE ALSO *calling API, client API, customization API, subclassing API*
application system	A comprehensive set of software services for building portable, adaptable application solutions for networked business environments.
archive viewer	A *cp*Constructor window that displays the entire locale hierarchy for a *cp*Constructor document and allows the designer to create and examine interface objects associated with a particular locale. SEE ALSO *editor, gallery viewer, inspector, parts palette*
array	A sequence that permits rapid random access to its elements by numeric key. SEE ALSO *sequence*
attribute	A named wrapper attached to arbitrary data. The attribute mechanism assumes that if you know the name of an attribute, you also know its type. COMPARE *property*
attribute bundle	In the Graphics system, the set of attributes for a graphic object. For example, the attribute bundle for a line might include a blue color attribute and a dashed line style attribute. SEE ALSO *graphic object*

B

base class	A class from which one or more other classes are obtained by subclassing; also known as a superclass. COMPARE *derived class, subclassing*
browser	In the *cp*Professional development environment, a window that can be subdivided into two or more panes containing different viewers, where selections in some viewers drive content shown in other viewers. SEE ALSO *viewer*

C

caller	The local interface making a remote object call. SEE ALSO *caller-dispatcher pair, dispatcher, remote object call*
caller-dispatcher pair	A caller (local interface) and dispatcher (remote interface) that work together to implement a remote request protocol. SEE ALSO *caller, dispatcher*
calling API	A framework API used much like the API for a class library: Programmers instantiate objects and call their member functions. SEE ALSO *client API, customization API, subclassing API*
challenge	A message, typically sent by a product to a license server, that's designed to obtain license units from the server so that a product may be used legally. SEE ALSO *license provider implementation*
class	A description of a structure, including data members and member functions, used as a "cookie cutter" for creating objects. COMPARE *data member, instantiate, member function, object*
class hierarchy	A hierarchical arrangement of classes that describes their patterns of inheritance. SEE ALSO *class, inheritance*
class library	A collection of one or more classes that implement related capabilities. Programmers use a class library by instantiating its objects and invoking their member functions. COMPARE *class, framework*

client	(1) In object-oriented programming, an instance of a class that uses the service of another unrelated instance. (2) In a client-server model, a program that uses services provided by one or more server programs. (3) In client-server architecture, a stand-alone personal computer connected via a LAN to a server computer. SEE ALSO *class, instance, service*
client API	A framework API employed by programmers who want to use the framework as it is intended to be used. Using a client API can in turn involve using both the calling and subclassing APIs, but without changing the fundamental internal operations of the framework. SEE ALSO *calling API, customization API, subclassing API*
client job description	An object maintained by a print job description that encapsulates information supplied by the document initiating the printing request, such as the objects to print, the number of copies the user wants, the page range, and the kind of paper to use. SEE ALSO *device job description, print job description*
clock	In Time Services, a clock represents the passage of time and provides the interface for getting the current time and delaying until a specific time. A clock starts at a particular point in time and keeps going, counting picoseconds, until it is turned off. SEE ALSO *time*
cocoon	SEE *user cocoon, privileged cocoon*
codec	Compressor-decompressor algorithm for video, audio, or other media.
collation	Algorithmic sorting and comparison of text strings; for example, for comparing text data according to the alphabetical ordering rules of a natural language rather than the byte values of the character-encoding set.
collection	A group of related objects; for example, a sorted sequence, array, deque, set, or dictionary. In the CommonPoint system, collections provide flexible alternatives to traditional computer science data structures such as arrays, lists, and trees. SEE ALSO *array, deque, dictionary, priority queue, queue, set, sorted sequence*
color matcher	An object that encapsulates information about the color-producing capabilities of an output device. The matcher has a built-in strategy for alternatives if the output device can't produce the input color.

color profile	An object that is associated with every color and every image in the CommonPoint system and contains device-specific information about the device for which the color or image was originally defined.
color space	In color display technology, a self-consistent coordinate system for assigning scalar values to colors. Most color spaces are 3-D and orthogonal. SEE ALSO *orthogonal color space*
command	A programming construct that can be applied to a selection to change the data specified by the selection. Commands are typically generated when a user chooses a menu item, clicks a button, or makes a gesture. They can also be generated programmatically. SEE ALSO *action, model, selection*
command log	A sequential record of the command history for an embeddable component from the time it is first opened. As each command completes, the Compound Document framework streams the command and the selection on which it operates into the command log. Command logs support several key features of embeddable components, including multiple undo-redo, automatic saving, scripting, and collaboration. SEE ALSO *command, selection*
commercial software developers	Developers who write and sell commercial software. Also known as shrink-wrapped software developers or independent software vendors (ISVs). COMPARE *corporate software developers*
communication	In the CommonPoint system, data transfer between two threads in the same task, two different tasks on the same machine, or two different tasks on different machines. SEE ALSO *task, thread*
component	Any discrete program element, including both embeddable components and more lightweight components such as buttons, controls, and other software building blocks, that can be assembled by interactive rather than programmatic means. SEE *component software, embeddable component*

component assemblers	Developers who use visual application builders such as Visual Basic or PowerBuilder to create applications from component software. Component assemblers are typically power users or corporate developers, although they can also include commercial developers. SEE *component builders, component software*
component builders	Developers who use third-generation programming languages such as C or C++ to create applications and component software. Component builders are typically commercial developers, although they can also include corporate developers. SEE *component assemblers, component software*
component software	Commercial or custom program elements, including both embeddable components and more lightweight components, that can be assembled and customized with visual programming tools, reducing or eliminating the need for handcrafted code. SEE ALSO *component, embeddable component*
compound document	A document that contains more than one embeddable component. For example, a report that contains text, a graphic, and a spreadsheet is a compound document. SEE ALSO *document, embeddable component*
compound page folio	In the Basic Printing framework, a collection of folios. SEE ALSO *folio*
configuration recorder	In the OODDM, an object that works with a device ensemble and the Hardware Configuration frameworks to configure a hardware device. The configuration recorder instantiates most of a device ensemble's objects at startup or when a hardware device is installed. For example, if a card contains two microprocessors—one to control SCSI connections and one to control a floppy drive—a configuration recorder for the card uses information provided by two device ensembles: one for the SCSI chip and one for the floppy drive chip. SEE ALSO *device ensemble*
connection	An object that connects to a notifier to establish a receiver's interest in the notifier's type of notification. SEE ALSO *interest, notification, notifier, receiver*

containable	Any object that has been explicitly implemented so that it can be placed in any container. Users can choose to filter the containables in a given container, such as a folder, so that only certain kinds are fully visible; the filtered containables are gathered together in a single icon until the user turns filtering off. Containers can also be programmed to act much like agents, performing actions on contained objects or retrieving objects from a variety of sources over a network based on the objects' attributes or content. SEE ALSO *container*
contained	An object is contained when it appears as an icon or a frame within a container. SEE ALSO *absorption, containable, container, embedding*
container	An object such as a folder or a document that can enclose other objects, including other containers. SEE ALSO *containable, contained, enclosure*
containment hierarchy	An arrangement of objects that describes which objects are contained by which other objects. COMPARE *inheritance hierarchy*
context	During streaming, a context keeps track of the locations of identical objects, thus making it possible to stream only the first occurrence of each. Contexts improve performance and save space. SEE ALSO *streaming*
control	An on-screen object that lets users initiate actions or make choices. Examples include buttons, check boxes, pop-up menus, scrolling lists, sliders, and text entry fields. SEE ALSO *action*
coordinate units	In the Graphics system, a device-independent system of measurement for 2-D or 3-D objects where one unit equals 1/72 of an inch.
corporate software developers	Developers who write software for in-house functions (such as inventory control) and developers who write software that is part of or closely tied to the goods and services sold by a corporation (such as the switching software used by telephone companies). In addition to corporations, a variety of other organizations include software developers with similar characteristics and concerns. COMPARE *commercial software developers*

cursor

A graphic symbol that can be moved around the screen by a pointing device such as a mouse.

SEE ALSO   *cursor tool, global tool*

cursor tool

A graphic symbol in a palette, representing a mode in which the user can create and modify a particular kind of data. To use a tool, the user first clicks the tool's icon to select it. Then the user applies the tool to the content area of a frame by moving the cursor over the frame and using it to manipulate the frame's data. The cursor typically changes shape whenever it's over a frame the selected cursor tool can act on.

SEE ALSO   *cursor*

customization API

A framework API employed by programmers who want to modify, enhance, or extend a framework's behavior. Using a framework's customization API usually involves using the subclassing API, but in more complex ways that end up changing some portion of the framework into something completely different. However, the customization API can also involve the calling API if customizing the framework requires the programmer to provide new calling API functions.

SEE ALSO   *calling API, client API, subclassing API*

D

data abstraction

The organization of data into small, independent objects that serve the specialized needs of a particular application or application domain.

SEE ALSO   *class, encapsulation, object*

data link

The live connection between data in two different locations. The data can be updated automatically when a change is made in either location, or it can be updated when specified by the user. The user can create a data link when pasting data.

COMPARE   *reference link*

data member

A data element defined by a particular class.

COMPARE   *member function*

datastreams interface

In Message Streams, an implementation of a communications model that works much like a phone call: data can flow in both directions simultaneously.

COMPARE   *request-reply interface*

decision function

In the Test framework, the code that determines whether the code being tested is behaving as it should.

default heap	The primary heap associated with a task. SEE ALSO *heap, task*
deque	A sequence that implements a double-ended queue, which can in turn be used to implement traditional stacks (LIFO)and queues (FIFO). SEE ALSO *queue, sequence, stack*
derived class	A class obtained by subclassing from a base class; also known as a subclass. COMPARE *base class, subclassing*
device access manager	In the OODDM, the part of a device ensemble that executes in user mode and defines policies that determine how client software gains access to a hardware device. SEE ALSO *configuration recorder, device ensemble, interrupt handler*
device ensemble	The OODDM equivalent of a device driver. The part of a device ensemble that executes in user mode is called a device access manager, and the part that executes in privileged mode is called an interrupt handler. SEE ALSO *configuration recorder, device access manager, interrupt handler*
device job description	An object maintained by a print job description that encapsulates information about a printer, such as the media types it can use, the kinds of pages it can print, and other hardware details. This information is supplied by the printer object that represents the currently selected printer. SEE ALSO *client job description, printer object, print job description*
dictionary	An unordered collection of elements that are each identified by a unique key. Just as words in a language dictionary are each associated with a definition, keys in a dictionary collection are each associated with a value. However, unlike words in a language dictionary, each key in a dictionary collection is unique and cannot be duplicated within the same collection. COMPARE *collection, sequence, set*
digitizer	In the Video framework, a video component that reads analog data from a source, converts it to digital data, and writes the digital video data to another video component such as a graphic view. SEE ALSO *effects processor, graphic view, media component*

disk dictionary

A dictionary used by Archives to associate key objects with value objects. Given a key, a disk dictionary returns the value (object) associated with the key or permits storage of a new object in the location associated with the key. Disk dictionaries are related conceptually (but not in their implementation) to dictionary collections.

COMPARE   *dictionary*

dispatcher

The remote interface called by a remote object call.

SEE ALSO   *caller, caller-dispatcher pair*

distributed objects

Software entities (both procedural and object-oriented) in different address spaces—running either on the same machine or on different machines connected via a network—and various ways of communicating between them.

document

A free-standing embeddable component that isn't embedded within any other component. A document can consist of a single component or of a potentially complex hierarchy of components.

SEE ALSO   *compound document, embeddable component, model*

drawing port

An object that channels graphic objects to a graphics device such as a monitor or printer.

SEE   *graphic object, graphics device, graphic state*

E

editor

A *cp*Constructor window that allows a designer to examine the elements of any user interface object, such as its menus, buttons, or controls, and change their layout and appearance.

SEE ALSO   *archive viewer, gallery viewer, inspector, parts palette*

effects processor

In the Video framework, a video component that reads video data from a source, alters the data, and writes it to another video component, such as a graphic view.

SEE ALSO   *digitizer, graphic view, media component*

embeddable component

In the Compound Document framework, an ensemble of code that constitutes a self-contained functional unit roughly equivalent to an application plus data. From a user's point of view, an embeddable component is similar in many respects to an OpenDoc part. Users can embed any embeddable component within any other embeddable component. Embeddable components are a form of component software.

SEE ALSO   *component software, compound document, document*

Embeddable Data Types	A group of CommonPoint frameworks for creating embeddable components and related objects for specific application domains. Examples include the Text Editing and Graphics Editing frameworks. SEE ALSO *embeddable component*
embedding	Incorporating one object into another within a frame so that the first object maintains its separate identity, including its own presentation. COMPARE *absorption, enclosure*
encapsulation	In OOP, the packaging of an object's data and the member functions that can act on it in a manner that protects the data from accidental or inappropriate changes. COMPARE *class, data abstraction, object*
enclosable icon	An icon that can be enclosed within an embeddable component while remaining a completely separate object. For example, a document icon is an enclosable icon. SEE ALSO *enclosure*
enclosure	A condition in which one document is contained inside another but still exists as a completely separate object. A document typically encloses other documents as a way of organizing them; for example, a folder usually contains related documents. A user can open an enclosed object in place (in a frame) or out of place (in a new window). COMPARE *absorption, embedding* SEE ALSO *containable, contained, container, enclosable icon*
ensemble	A group of application code fragments that "hang from" or are "nestled among" the frameworks provided by the system. The application code calls various frameworks, some of which it has customized, and some of which it uses as they were intended to be used. In framework programming, each application consists of an ensemble, and several applications running at the same time can use the same frameworks in very different ways without interfering with each other. SEE ALSO *application framework*
event	Information about some occurrence, such as a keystroke or mouse click, to which an application may need to respond. SEE ALSO *event loop*

event loop	The fundamental control structure in certain kinds of interactive applications, such as those written for Windows or Macintosh system software. It is a continuous loop that waits for user input, such as keystrokes or mouse clicks, and responds to those events. Also called the main event loop. SEE ALSO *event*
exception	Synchronous (time-based) notification of an error or abnormal condition, either in hardware or software, detected during program execution. In C++, when a function detects a problem, it "throws" an exception, and a function that can handle such a problem "catches" the exception.

F

file system entities	In the File System interface, objects that provide access to equivalent physical entities such as volumes, directories, and files.
filing	A high-level mechanism for persistent storage provided by the Compound Document framework. Unlike streaming, which converts objects to a flat, byte-encoded stream, filing permits storage of data in whatever data format is convenient for a particular purpose—for example, in a form that a non-Taligent file system can read. COMPARE *streaming*
flattening	Using the FlattenPointer member function defined in TStream to traverse an object's structure recursively and create a linear (flattened) sequence of bytes representing the various components found in the original object. The flattened form of the object is a persistent representation that can span tasks, processes, sessions, and individual machines. SEE ALSO *polymorphic streaming, resurrecting, streaming*
floating license	In Licensing Services, a license that isn't tied to a particular user or machine but is shared by different people at different times.
flow of control	The means by which executing software controls the interactions among objects or pieces of code.
folio	In the Basic Printing framework, a collection of pages to be printed. SEE ALSO *page, page description, page iterator*

frame	In CommonPoint documents, a way of representing an embedded component that can be selected and manipulated by a user. SEE ALSO *embedding*
framework	An extensible library of cooperating classes that make up a reusable design solution for a given problem domain. COMPARE *class library*

G

gallery viewer	A *cp*Constructor window that displays icons for various categories of user interface elements, such as windows, controls, buttons, icons, and colors, that a programmer has included in a *cp*Constructor document. SEE ALSO *archive viewer, editor, inspector, parts palette*
geometry	In the Graphics system, an object that provides the mathematical abstractions for lines, shapes, fonts, surfaces, and so on. SEE ALSO *attribute bundle, drawing port, graphic object*
global tool	A cursor tool that is separate from a specific embeddable component and is applicable across a variety of data types, to a single common data type, or only when components that support it are active. SEE ALSO *cursor tool*
graphic object	An object derived from MGraphic or MGraphic3D that can draw, print, and stream itself. A graphic object has an associated attribute bundle, which specifies attributes such as color and thickness, and a geometry, which provides the mathematical abstractions used to define the object. SEE ALSO *attribute bundle, drawing port, geometry, graphics device*
graphic player	A media player that records and plays graphic sequences, just as a VCR records and plays videotapes. SEE ALSO *media player*
graphics device	In the Graphics system, an object that represents a hardware device or any other destination that can render a graphic object. SEE ALSO *drawing port, graphic object*
graphic sequence	A media sequence containing any graphics that change with time; for example, a sequence of video frames. SEE ALSO *media sequence*

graphic state	In the Graphics system, the graphic state describes the local and global attributes, transformations, and clipping region for the drawing port. SEE ALSO *drawing port*
graphic view	In the Video framework, a video sink or destination. A graphic view typically displays video data on a monitor.

H

heap	One or more memory segments from which blocks of memory are allocated and freed. C++ instances created dynamically through operators such as new and delete are stored on a heap. C memory functions such as malloc and free also allocate storage on heaps. COMPARE *default heap, memory segment, stack*
hit detection	The process of determining whether an event from an input device has occurred within the bounds of a graphic object. SEE ALSO *event, graphic object*
human interface policies	A set of rules and conventions that govern the implementation of a user interface for a particular user environment. SEE ALSO *user interface*

I

incremental command	A command that goes through a number of intermediate states before arriving at the final result. Incremental commands are often used to provide smoother feedback to the user than is possible with a command that is executed all at once. SEE ALSO *command*
independent software vendor (ISV)	SEE *commercial developer*
inheritance	A mechanism that allows subclasses to make use of the members defined by classes above them in their branches of the class hierarchy. SEE ALSO *class hierarchy, multiple inheritance, polymorphism, subclassing*
in-house developer	SEE *corporate developer*
input method	A mechanism that allows users to input ideographic characters from a nonideographic keyboard. SEE ALSO *typing configuration*

inspector

A *cp*Constructor window that allows a designer to view and edit the detailed characteristics of any user interface object, such as its size, its name, any action associated with it, and its appearance.

SEE ALSO   *archive viewer, editor, gallery viewer, parts palette*

instance

An object created from a class.

SEE ALSO   *class, object*

instantiate

Create an instance of a class.

SEE ALSO   *class*

interactor

An object that breaks down complex user gestures into a set of states that form a structure capable of responding to a stream of related events.

SEE ALSO   *event*

interest

In the Notification framework, an object that identifies a sender and an event. A sender defines an interest in each event about which it provides notification. A receiver uses this protocol to identify the events about which the sender should notify it.

SEE ALSO   *connection, notification, receiver, sender*

interoperable client

A CommonPoint client designed to work with a service running on a host operating system. An interoperable client usually needs to "look behind the curtain" to deal directly with the host transport mechanism.

SEE ALSO   *client*

interrupt handler

The part of a device ensemble that executes in privileged mode, processing hardware interrupts and reporting back to a device access manager.

SEE ALSO   *device access manager, device ensemble*

L

lexical tool	A text modifier that performs operations on words. Examples include spelling and grammar checkers. SEE ALSO *text modifier*
library package	In Object Runtime Services, a mechanism that provides a host-independent API for loading shared libraries and reducing the name conflicts that can occur when streamed objects are dynamically loaded into a running program. SEE ALSO *streaming*
license key	SEE *activation key*
license manager vendor	A vendor of licensing software to commercial software developers. SEE ALSO *license provider implementation*
license provider implementation	Licensing software created by a license manager vendor that allows a product to send challenges and requests for license units to a license server. A license provider implementation includes Licensing framework, Product Preparation framework, and System Administration framework implementations and associated license servers. SEE ALSO *challenge, license manager vendor*
lightweight thread	In Microkernel Services, a thread that shares an address space with other threads of the same task and that can be created, maintained, and destroyed cheaply in terms of processor time and memory usage. Much of a thread's context is determined by the task and therefore doesn't need to be saved whenever the thread stops running. SEE ALSO *address space, task, thread*
link	A connection between anchors that allows a user to find related information or keep two selections of data synchronized. SEE ALSO *anchor, data link, reference link*
locale	A collection of archived resources that are localized for a particular geographic region. These resources can include formatting information for numbers and dates, regional information such as a time zone, collating rules for ordering and comparing ranges of text, typing information for text presentations, and localized human interface elements for individual applications. SEE ALSO *archive viewer*

locale hierarchy	A static hierarchy of locales based on geographic relationships, descending from a single root locale. The lowest level of the locale hierarchy represents the largest geographic area within a country with common time and language characteristics. This allows for distinctions among, for example, the various time zones in the United States or the French-speaking and German-speaking regions of Switzerland. SEE ALSO *archive viewer*

M

management agent	In System Management, a program that executes and replies to management protocol requests from a management station that may be running on a non-Taligent system. COMPARE *master agent, subagent*
master agent	In System Management, a program that implements a specific management protocol and plugs into the Management Agent framework. COMPARE *management agent, subagent*
master clock	In Time Services, a clock to which other clocks are synchronized. SEE ALSO *slave clock, syncable clock*
media component	The basic building block for all Time Media frameworks. Media components model real-world objects, such as speakers, mixers, and filters, but are usually implemented entirely in software. A media component has one or more input ports and/or one or more output ports through which it can be connected to other media components. Media data flows from the output ports of one component to the input ports of the next component or components.
media network	A series of connected media components. SEE ALSO *media component*
media player	In the Time Media frameworks, a media component that is capable of presenting media data or recording it in a media sequence. Media players can set the starting point, control the rate of playback, and synchronize media sequences. They are usually implemented entirely in software. SEE ALSO *media component, media sequence*
media port	In the Time Media frameworks, an input or output port that can accept or send media data across a connection between two media components.

media port surrogate

In the Time Media frameworks, media input port surrogates and media output port surrogates are used in place of actual input and output ports to prevent clients and media components from attempting to write data to a port simultaneously. The actual input and output ports are used to transfer media data across a connection between two media components.

media presenter

In the Time Media User Interface framework, an object that provides a bridge between the Time Media frameworks and the Document framework. It can be used to play or record a media sequence from within an embeddable component or from within a simple lightweight view that doesn't inherit all the characteristics of embeddable components.

SEE ALSO   *embeddable component, media sequence*

media sequence

In the Time Media frameworks, a stream of media data, such as a clip of audio, video, or MIDI data. A media sequence is characterized by a duration and a list of data types. Media sequences are played by media players.

SEE ALSO   *media player*

member

In C++, a data member or a member function of a particular class.

SEE ALSO   *class, data member, member function*

member function

In C++, a function defined by a particular class.

SEE ALSO   *data member*

memory segment

A contiguous and usually rather large block of raw or unmanaged memory. Memory segments never overlap. A given address can be contained in, at most, one heap, and a memory segment cannot be owned by more than one heap.

SEE ALSO   *address space, heap*

metadata

In Object Runtime Services, a means of representing the types of instances based on the ANSI C++ extensions for checked casts, casting from virtual bases, and RTTI.

SEE ALSO   *Run-Time Type Identification (RTTI)*

microkernel

An operating system kernel designed to be as small as possible by including only essential services such as processor and memory allocation but not services such as networking, the file system, or (usually) device drivers.

minimizer	An icon in the title bar of a window that lets the user reduce the window to its title tab and enlarge it again to full size.
mixin class	A class used via multiple inheritance to enhance the characteristics of a derived class, complementing those that the derived class inherits from its primary base class. By design, a mixin class should not be used as a sole base class. By convention, mixin classes in the CommonPoint system begin with an "M," for example, MGraphic. SEE ALSO *base class, class, class hierarchy, derived class, inheritance*
model	In the Compound Document framework, the fundamental abstraction for a data object. A model encapsulates its data and provides the rest of the system with the means for accessing the data. SEE ALSO *command, presentation, selection*
monomorphic streaming	A form of streaming that involves calling an object's streaming operators directly and requires previous knowledge of the object's type. SEE ALSO *polymorphic streaming, streaming*
multiple inheritance	A mechanism for structuring inheritance relationships among classes that allows a class to have more than one base class. The Taligent programming model supports multiple inheritance by means of mixin classes. SEE ALSO *base class, class, class hierarchy, inheritance, mixin class*

N

network	In networking and communications, a group of computers and peripheral devices that are connected by communications facilities. A network can be a local area network (LAN) or a wide area network (WAN).
network service	In the Service Access framework, a service that a client, either on the same host or across the network, can access by providing a network name. SEE ALSO *client*
notification	An object that conveys news of an event to a receiver. When a sender receives an event for which it has defined an interest, it uses the appropriate interest, and possibly additional notification-specific data, to create a notification. The sender then sends the notification to the receivers that want it. SEE ALSO *interest, notifier, receiver, sender*

notifier	An object used by several different senders to provide notification of a particular event. SEE ALSO *receiver, sender*
NURBS	Nonuniform rational B-spline curve. *Nonuniform* means that the parameterization of the curve or surface can be changed to allow kinks, gaps, and smooth joins. *Rational* means that rational polynomials are used to allow exact representations of circles, ellipses, and other conic sections. *B-spline* stands for basis spline, a spline curve similar to the Bézier curve except that it facilitates better curve fitting and modeling.

O

object	In OOP, a software entity made of data (nouns) and definitions of actions that can be performed on the data (verbs). An object can represent a programming entity such as a pushdown stack or a window, or it can represent an abstraction of a real-world entity such as a chess piece or a invoice. An object is an instance of a class, and the class serves as a template for creating objects. In C++, objects can be created either at compile time or at runtime. SEE *class, instance*
orthogonal color space	In color display technology, an uncalibrated color space in which the components that make up the color space are at right angles to each other (for example, the RGB color space and the CMY color space). SEE ALSO *color space*
override	Replace the definition of a member function provided by a class higher in the class hierarchy with a new definition. COMPARE *class hierarchy, member function, polymorphism, subclassing*

P

page	In the Basic Printing framework, one side of a leaf in a book or printed manuscript or its digital representation before printing. SEE ALSO *folio, page description*
page description	In the Basic Printing framework, an object that describes the media and page metrics for every page in a folio, including page bounds, duplex capability, mismatch options, page orientation, and media sources on the target printer. SEE ALSO *folio, page*

page iterator

In the Basic Printing framework, an object that can iterate through the pages in a folio and establish page order.

SEE ALSO   *folio, page*

paginated page folio

In the Basic Printing framework, a folio that represents a large canvas area partitioned into pages. It contains page-sized tiles arranged in a two-dimensional array with optional borders and gaps. It can be used as a pagination aid when pagination is required in a model presentation.

SEE ALSO   *folio, page*

palette

A special window that floats above the layer of document windows. A palette typically contains a cluster of cursor tools, colors, or other related items.

SEE ALSO   *cursor tool*

part

In OpenDoc, a representation of data that can be embedded in a compound document.

SEE ALSO   *part handler*

part handler

In OpenDoc, code written by a developer that allows users to view and edit data presented in parts.

SEE ALSO   *part*

parts palette

A *cp*Constructor window that displays ready-made user interface elements, such as windows, controls, buttons, icons, and colors, that a programmer can drag into other *cp*Constructor windows to create or modify the user interface for a specific application.

SEE ALSO   *archive viewer, editor, gallery viewer, inspector*

People

People elements provide a consistent representation of people throughout the Taligent human interface. A person's attributes, such as name, telephone number, address, and email address, are collected in elements such as Business Card objects. Collections of People elements can be organized into phone books, group icons, mailing lists, departments, organization charts, and so on.

SEE ALSO   *Places, Task-Centered Computing, Things*

People, Places, and Things	The unifying metaphor that implements Taligent's vision of Task-Centered Computing for organizations. Based on the traditional schoolbook definition of a noun, this metaphor represents objects and relationships in ways the correspond to real objects and relationships. Instead of learning elaborate rules for making the computer do things, users interact with a diverse range of familiar objects using a consistent language of gestures and representations. SEE ALSO *People, Places, Task-Centered Computing, Things*
Places	Place representations are collaborative environments, usually based on real-world models such as meeting rooms, stores, and offices, that allow users to organize shared information and tasks in meaningful contexts. A Place representation is distinguished by the presence of users and a unique organization of the interface objects that appear within it. Users can create a Place environment and modify the behavior of its interface objects to reflect the requirements of a particular task or set of tasks. SEE ALSO *People, Task-Centered Computing, Things*
player	SEE *media player*
polymorphic streaming	A form of streaming that involves calling the FlattenPointer and Resurrect functions, which use RTTI to look up the object's shared library and type. SEE ALSO *monomorphic streaming, Run-Time Type Identification (RTTI), streaming*
polymorphism	The ability to hide different implementations behind the same name. Polymorphism allows a programmer to use the same name with many different kinds of objects to trigger the same effect without having to deal with the underlying mechanisms, which may be quite different. SEE ALSO *class, class hierarchy, override, subclassing*
preemptive	A scheduler characteristic: any thread can be made to yield control of the CPU at any time. The Taligent scheduler is preemptive. SEE ALSO *thread*
presentation	The manifestation of data to the user. Most presentations are visual displays, but other formats are possible, such as sounds or mechanical controls. The Presentation framework provides generic elements of a typical presentation, such as a main content view, menus, dialog boxes, and palettes. SEE ALSO *command, selection, view*

previewer	A *cp*Constructor window that allows a designer to display a user interface object as it will appear in the application and perform preliminary testing. SEE ALSO *action monitor*
printable rectangle	In the Basic Printing framework, the portion of the physical page on which a particular printer can print.
printer handler	An object that prepares spooled print jobs for a particular printer, usually represented on screen by a printer appliance icon. A printer handler maintains a connection to its printer over the network or via one of the computer's ports and provides printer objects when needed for print job descriptions. To print a spooled print job file, a printer handler resurrects the streamed data and uses the Graphics system to send it to its printer via a drawing port and graphics device driver. SEE ALSO *printer object, print job description*
printer object	An object that is supplied by a printer handler and represents a real printer. SEE ALSO *device job description, printer handler, resurrecting*
print job description	An object that encapsulates a client job description, which contains information from the document being printed, and a device job description, which contains information from the printer object about the actual printer. SEE ALSO *client job description, device job description, printer object*
priority queue	A collection ordered partly by an internal (automatic) sorting mechanism, and partly by external manipulation (that is, according to the order in which an element is added.) COMPARE *dictionary, sequence, set*
privileged cocoon	In the OODDM, an interface that executes in privileged mode and is used by interrupt handlers. COMPARE *user cocoon* SEE ALSO *device ensemble, interrupt handler*
property	An identifier used to keep track of small collections of heterogenous instances when type safety is important or for handling general-purpose objects that may originate on a different machine COMPARE *attribute*

	proxy	A reference to a document. A document window's title bar includes a proxy icon that a user can drag and drop just as if it were the document's icon on the desktop.
		SEE ALSO *alias*
	pure virtual function	A virtual function that must be overridden because it doesn't provide its own default implementation.
		COMPARE *override, virtual function*
Q	**queue**	A data structure for storing entities, typically in first-in, first-out (FIFO) order. Data Structures and Collections implement queues via deques.
		COMPARE *deque, sequence, stack*
R	**receiver**	An instance that registers an interest in and responds to notifications from a sender. Receivers get notifications through a connection. Each receiver generally owns a connection instance.
		SEE ALSO *connection, interest, notification, sender*
	record source	A read-only sequence of records with the same type structure. Record sources are used to transfer records from arbitrary sources (such as the Data Access framework, spreadsheets, or databases) to arbitrary destinations.
	reference link	A link between two anchors that allows a user to navigate between them by clicking a button or performing some other action.
		COMPARE *anchor, data link, link*
	remote object call	In ROC Services, a member function call that spans tasks (address spaces). The tasks may be on the same machine or on separate machines on a network. Remote object calls are transparent; they appear as local calls even though they access remote functions. Also known as a remote procedure call.
		SEE ALSO *address space, member function, task*
	request	In the View framework, an object that encapsulates a function call (including parameters) and a target object on which to invoke the function.
		SEE ALSO *event, request queue, view*

request handler	In the View framework, an object that serially removes requests from a request queue and dispatches them to their targets. SEE ALSO *event, request, request queue*
request queue	In the View framework, a first-in, first-out (FIFO) queue of requests. SEE ALSO *event, request, view*
request-reply interface	In Message Streams, an implementation of a communications model that involves an alternating exchange of messages between a source and a receiver. The source makes a request; the receiver handles the request and returns a reply. COMPARE *datastreams interface*
resurrecting	The reverse of flattening. Resurrecting a flattened object involves using the Resurrect member function defined in TStream to restore the object to a state in memory that is equal to its state at the time it was flattened. SEE ALSO *flattening, polymorphic streaming, streaming*
Run-Time Type Identification (RTTI)	An ANSI C++ extension that allows enquiries about or comparisons of the types of most objects. SEE ALSO *metadata*

S

script	A writing system, such as Cyrillic or Arabic. SEE ALSO *Unicode*
selection	(1) In the Basic Document framework, a specification of a set of data elements in a model that can be acted on by a command. (2) In a user interface, the data that the next command will apply to, often indicated by highlighting. SEE ALSO *command, model*
sender	Instances that use the Notification framework to notify other instances of changes to themselves; exactly which changes are up to the sender. The sender defines an interest that's specific to the notification for a particular kind of change. Senders can perform the notification themselves, or they can share a notifier with other senders. SEE ALSO *connection, interest, notification, receiver*

sequence	An ordered collection. The Collections classes include three kinds of sequences: sorted sequences, arrays, and deques. SEE ALSO *array, deque, sorted sequence*
service	In Communications, any remote functions available to a client. COMPARE *client*
service adapter	An extension to the Service Access framework that encapsulates information about non-Taligent services for use by the framework.
service definition	In the Service Access framework, an object created by a service to register itself as available to clients.
service reference	In the Service Access framework, an object created by a client to access a service through a service definition.
set	An unordered collection that contains no duplicate members. Adding a duplicate member to a set simply replaces the original member. SEE ALSO *collection, dictionary, sequence*
shared heap	A heap that is shared among tasks, across address spaces. One task creates the shared heap and passes knowledge of it to the other tasks by using standard streaming operators. SEE ALSO *address space, heap, task*
shared library	A class library used by multiple programs. A shared library is typically a software file, but it can also be implemented on a bus card, in ROM, or in a disk partition. A shared library is usually loaded at runtime, including programmatically.
shrink-wrapped software vendor	SEE *commercial developer*
slave clock	In Time Services, a clock that is synchronized to another clock. SEE ALSO *master clock*
sorted sequence	A sequence ordered automatically according to lexical or numeric rules of comparison such as alphabetical order. SEE ALSO *collection, sequence*

stack	(1) A data structure for storing elements in last-in, first-out (LIFO) order. In the Collections classes, stacks are implemented via deques. (2) A portion of memory used for temporary storage within a procedure and for implementing calls and returns between procedures. Data on the stack is added (pushed) and removed (pulled or popped) in LIFO order. COMPARE (1) *deque, queue.* (2) *heap*
stationery pad	A template that is represented by a characteristic icon and used to create new documents and containers. An object created from a stationery pad has the same properties as the original: layout, fonts, and the like. Any document or container can be turned into stationery, and a user can "tear off" any number of sheets from a stationery pad to create new objects. SEE ALSO *container, document, embeddable component*
streaming	The process of flattening objects into a byte-encoded stream or restoring them in the opposite direction. The CommonPoint system's streaming mechanism underlies all forms of object persistence, including sending objects to other objects, writing them to disk, or sending them across a network to another machine. SEE ALSO *context, filing, monomorphic streaming, polymorphic streaming*
style	(1) In typesetting, a stylistic modification of a basic typeface such as bold, italic, or underline. (2) In the Text system, an object derived from TStyle that defines a single style element associated with either text characters or a paragraph. Each style object is described by a name and a value: for example, the name "text color" and the value "red," or the name "justification" and the value "flush left."
subagent	A client of the Management Agent framework that is independent of particular management protocols. A subagent can be used with all underlying master agents and implements the management interfaces of a particular application or service. COMPARE *management agent, master agent*
subclassing	Deriving a new class from an existing class by adding to or overriding the members of the original class. SEE ALSO *class hierarchy, override, polymorphism*
subclassing API	A framework API that programmers use by subclassing new classes and overriding member functions. *calling API, client API, customization API*

syncable clock

In Time Services, a clock that can be synchronized with another time source. A syncable clock can be a master clock or a slave clock.

SEE ALSO   *master clock, slave clock*

syncable clock surrogate

In Time Services, a syncable clock surrogate is used to synchronize one syncable clock to another.

T

target class

In the Test framework, the class being tested.

SEE ALSO   *decision function*

task

In Microkernel Services, a collection of one or more threads that share a single address space and, usually, a single purpose. A task provides a particular application or service (like a server). Multiple tasks can exist simultaneously.

COMPARE   *address space, thread*

Task-Centered Computing

The paradigm that underlies Taligent's People, Places, and Things metaphor and related human interface policies. Task-centered computing uses the completion of human tasks as its basic organizing principle, as opposed to dividing tasks into applications and their documents. Instead of learning to manipulate applications, users can bring their knowledge of the real world to their computing environment and can rely to some extent on the same rules and expectations they take for granted in their everyday lives.

COMPARE   *human interface policies, People, Places, Things*

telephone call

In the Telephony framework, the representation of a telephone call. It provides a low-level interface to the functions associated with telephone calls, such as creating, placing, and answering.

telephone handset

In the Telephony framework, the representation of the physical telephone terminal equipment (such as the dialer, cradle, and receiver). It provides a low-level interface to functions associated with such equipment.

telephone line

In the Telephony framework, the representation of the physical telephone line. It provides a low-level interface to simple functions associated with telephone lines, such as initiating telephone call connections, determining the hook status of the line, and accessing telephone line features.

telephone line feature	In the Telephony framework, the representation of telephone line features such as call holding, conference calls, and call forwarding.
text formatter	An object that fits lines of text displayed by the Line Layout framework into text panels on the basis of line-breaking algorithms and high-level paragraph and page styles. The Text Editing framework includes a standard text formatter.
text modifier	An object such as a transliterator or lexical tool that modifies text. SEE ALSO *lexical tool, transliterator*
Things	User interface objects such as documents folders, stationery pads, components, appliances, and cursor tools, including business objects such as forms, reports, and invoices. SEE ALSO *People, Places, Task-Centered Computing*
thread	An individual unit of execution—that is, a single series of instructions that execute in a logical sequence. COMPARE *task*
time	In Time Services, a quantity of picoseconds. SEE ALSO *clock*
time media	Forms of data that change meaningfully with respect to time. Audio and video are common examples of Time Media. Also called time-based media or multimedia. SEE ALSO *media player*
token	An object that encapsulates unstyled Unicode character arrays for internal manipulation of text strings that do not need to be displayed.
transaction	A sequence of operations, managed by the Concurrency Control and Recovery classes, whose execution is atomic, consistent, isolated, and durable. Transactions allow applications to work with shared recoverable data.
transcoding	Converting character codes from one standard character set to another; for example, from ASCII to Unicode.
transformation matrix	In graphics processing, a matrix for applying custom algebraic operations to the set of coordinates that define a 2-D or 3-D graphic object.

transliteration	The process of substituting a character or character sequence for another character or character sequence within the same encoding system.
transliterator	An object that transliterates text input based on a specific algorithm or set of rules; for example, converting the keystrokes "a" and "`" into the character "à". Transliterators differ from transcoders in that they convert Unicode characters into other Unicode characters, not to an external character set. In addition to accent composition, transliterators can be used to change the case of certain letters, enable "smart quotes," or transcribe phonetically between scripts, for example from a Roman "a" to a Greek "α".
	SEE ALSO *lexical tool, text modifier, transcoding*
type negotiation	A mechanism for determining which of several possible data formats should be used for a particular operation. For example, commands and selections use a default type negotiation that attempts to find a type the destination selection understands so that inserted data is absorbed as native data.
	SEE ALSO *absorption, command, embedding, model, selection*
typing configuration	An object that encapsulates language-specific information about keyboard layout, text modifiers, and (optionally) input methods for entering ideographic text from nonideographic keyboards.
	SEE ALSO *input method, lexical tool, text modifier, transliterator, virtual keyboard*
typing interactor	An interactor that converts keystrokes into character data on the basis of information supplied by a typing configuration.
	SEE ALSO *interactor, typing configuration*

U

Unicode	A fixed-width 16-bit character-encoding system that provides a code for every character in every major writing system, along with an extensive set of symbols, punctuation, and control characters. Unicode is part of the internationally recognized standard ISO 10646.
	SEE ALSO *script*
user cocoon	In the OODDM, an interface that executes in user mode and is used by device access managers.
	COMPARE *privileged cocoon*
	SEE ALSO *device ensemble, device access manager*

user interface	The buttons, windows, dialog boxes, and other elements (including nonvisual elements such as sounds or tactile controls) by means of which a user can communicate with and control a computer. SEE ALSO *human interface policies*	

V

video
In the Video framework, any graphical information that can be sequenced with respect to time.

view
An object that can draw itself on a display device such as a computer monitor or a printer. It defines a portion of a virtual drawing surface in which a program can draw. A view doesn't necessarily have to appear on the screen.

SEE ALSO *event, interactor, presentation, request*

viewer
In the *cp*Professional development environment, a specialized view that can be arranged with other viewers within a browser to display specific program elements or their properties.

SEE ALSO *browser*

view hierarchy
An arrangement of views in parent-child relationships that correspond to the way the views are related to each other (nested or side-by-side) when displayed.

SEE ALSO *view*

virtual function
A function that can be overridden but also provides its own default implementation.

COMPARE *pure virtual function*

virtual keyboard
An object that maintains a set of mapping rules between a virtual key code, or a combination of modifier keys and a virtual key code, and either a single Unicode character or multiple Unicode characters. These mappings are independent of the layout of the physical keyboard. Each virtual keyboard can also have localizable names for use with the locale mechanism.

SEE ALSO *input method, locale, typing configuration, Unicode, virtual key code*

virtual key code
A code that represents a specific physical key on a keyboard device. Virtual key codes are mapped to Unicode characters to allow text input by keyboard typing.

SEE ALSO *virtual keyboard*

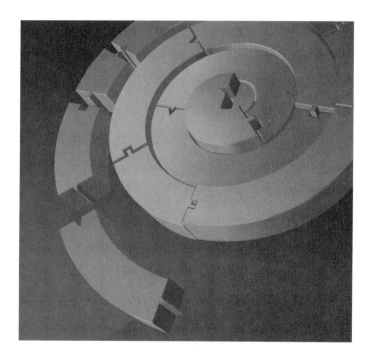

BIBLIOGRAPHY

This bibliography lists some of the sources that Taligent recommends for learning about object-oriented technology.

For more information, see Taligent's home page on the World Wide Web (`http://www.taligent.com`). The document *Object Technology Resources,* which is available via the home page or directly from Taligent, provides a complete listing of recommended resources.

BOOKS AND ARTICLES

The books and articles listed here provide a starting point for learning about object-oriented technology and related topics. Many of them are recommended reading for Taligent's own software engineers.

Object-oriented technology

Booch, Grady. *Object Oriented Design with Applications.* 2d ed. Redwood City, CA: Benjamin/Cummings, 1994. One of the best books available on object-oriented design. Highly recommended for Taligent engineers.

Budd, Timothy. *Introduction to Object-Oriented Programming.* Reading, MA: Addison-Wesley, 1991. A Smalltalk-oriented approach to OOP.

Goldstein, Neil, and Jeff Alger. *Developing Object-Oriented Software for the Macintosh.* Reading, MA: Addison-Wesley, 1992. Another excellent book on object-oriented design. It explodes some common myths. Despite the title, it can also be useful for non-Macintosh programmers. Recommended for Taligent engineers.

Meyer, Bertrand. *Object-Oriented Software Construction.* Englewood Cliffs, NJ: Prentice Hall, 1988. The first part of the book is a guide for object-oriented designers. Recommended for Taligent engineers.

Taylor, David A. *Object-Oriented Information Systems: Planning and Implementation.* Reading, MA: Addison-Wesley, 1992.

———. *Object-Oriented Technology: A Manager's Guide.* Reading, MA: Addison-Wesley, 1990. An introduction to object technology for business and technical managers. Highly recommended as a primer for anyone new to the area.

Wirfs-Brock, Rebecca, et al. *Designing Object-Oriented Software.* Englewood Cliffs, NJ: Prentice Hall, 1990. A guide for object-oriented designers. Recommended for Taligent engineers.

Programming with C++

Taligent's Guide to Designing Programs: Well-Mannered Object-Oriented Design in C++. Reading, MA: Addison-Wesley, 1994. This book reflects years of experience building large, object-oriented C++ systems. It is based on an internal programming style guide used by Taligent engineers, by early Taligent application developers, and in Taligent training courses. It helps programmers understand the philosophy behind Taligent's system designs and suggests ways of using object-oriented design and C++. Highly recommended for Taligent engineers.

Cargill, Tom. *C++ Programming Style.* Reading, MA: Addison-Wesley, 1992. This book contains that rare and useful information—examples of bad code with analyses. Like the original *Elements of Programming Style,* this book is quite helpful because it shows what not to do. It provides detailed guidance on issues such as abstraction, consistency, inheritance, virtual functions, operator overloading, wrappers, and efficiency. Highly recommended for Taligent engineers.

Ellis, Margaret, and Bjarne Stroustrup. *The Annotated C++ Reference Manual.* Reading, MA: Addison-Wesley, 1990. This book (known as "the ARM") has been supplanted by the current working papers for the draft ANSI C++ standard. The ARM reflects the state of the language at the start of the standardization process a few years ago. Neither this book nor the working papers are light reading. However, it's essential to have one of them close at hand to make optimum use of C++. If you can get a copy of the working paper, that is preferable to using the ARM.

Meyers, Scott. *Effective C++.* Reading, MA: Addison-Wesley, 1992. Presents 50 good rules for designing and writing with C++. Highly recommended for Taligent engineers.

Prata, Stephen, *C++ Primer Plus: Teach Yourself Object-Oriented Programming.* Corte Madera, CA: Waite Group Press, 1991. A well-organized introduction to OOP for beginners. This book is more approachable than Stroustrup's and assumes that you don't know C.

Stroustrup, Bjarne. *The C++ Programming Language.* 2d ed. Reading, MA: Addison-Wesley, 1991. In addition to being the best introduction and reference to the language (except for the ANSI draft specification), this book includes excellent chapters on object-oriented design and management of object-oriented projects. These chapters are full of experience from the man who invented C++ and has worked on more C++ projects than anyone else. Highly recommended for Taligent engineers.

Frameworks and related topics

The Power of Frameworks. Reading, MA: Addison-Wesley, 1995. Describes how to use a simple framework, provided on the accompanying CD-ROM, that runs on Windows software. Written by Taligent engineers, this book introduces basic programming concepts that are used throughout the CommonPoint application system.

Alexander, Christopher. *Notes on the Synthesis of Form.* Cambridge, Mass.: Harvard University Press, 1964.

Alexander, Christopher, et al. *A Pattern Language.* London: Oxford University Press, 1977.

————. *The Timeless Way of Building.* London: Oxford University Press, 1979.

————. *A New Theory of Urban Design.* London: Oxford University Press, 1987.

Coleman, Derek, et al. *Object-Oriented Development: The Fusion Method.* Prentice Hall, 1994.

Gabriel, Richard. "The quality without a name." *Object Magazine,* September 1993.

————. "Pattern languages." *Object Magazine,* January 1994.

————. "The failure of pattern languages." *Object Magazine,* February 1994.

Gamma, Erich, Richard Helm, Ralph Johnson, and John Vlissides. *Design Patterns: Elements of Object-Oriented Software Architecture.* Reading, MA: Addison-Wesley, 1994.

Johnson, Ralph E. "Documenting frameworks using patterns." Notes from OOPSLA, 1992, pp. 63–76. Discusses the application of Christopher Alexander's work to framework design and documentation.

————. "How to design frameworks." Notes from OOPSLA, 1993.

Johnson, Ralph E., and Vincent Russo. "Reusing Object-Oriented Designs." University of Illinois tech report UIUCDCS 91-1696, 1991.

Love, Tom. "Timeless design of information systems." *Object Magazine,* November/December 1991.

Lynch, Kevin. *The Image of the City.* Cambridge, MA: MIT Press, 1960. A classic contribution to large-scale design theory that is also short and readable.

Opdyke, William F., and Ralph Johnson. "Refactoring: An aid in designing application frameworks and evolving object-oriented systems." Proceedings of Symposium on Object-Oriented Programming Emphasizing Practical Applications (SOOPPA), September 1990.

Potel, Mike, and Jack Grimes. "The architecture of the Taligent system." *Dr. Dobb's Special Report,* Winter 1994/95.

Text and graphics

Beatty, John C., Brian A. Barsky, and Richard H. Bartels. *An Introduction to Splines for Use in Computer Graphics and Geometric Modeling.* Los Altos, CA: Morgan Kaufmann, 1986.

Farin, Gerald. *Curves and Surfaces for Computer Aided Geometric Design: A Practical Guide.* 3d ed. Boston: Academic Press, 1993.

Foley, J. D., et al. *Introduction to Computer Graphics.* Reading, MA: Addison-Wesley, 1994. A new introductory text on computer graphics adapted from the longer and more comprehensive *Computer Graphics: Principles and Practice* (2d ed.).

The Unicode Standard, Version 1.0. Reading, MA: Addison-Wesley, 1991.

Unicode Technical Report #4. Unicode Inc., 1993.

Computer industry

Gibbs, W. Wayt. "Software's Chronic Crisis." *Scientific American,* September 1994.

Early Adopters of Object Technology. Cupertino, CA: Taligent, 1992. A Taligent white paper that summarizes the lessons learned by a group of companies engaged in significant object-based application development.

O'Connor, Rory J. "Windows delayed again: operating system may not be released until next August." *San Jose Mercury News,* December 21, 1994, Morning Final, Business Section, 1F.

PERIODICALS AND NEWSLETTERS

The following magazines and newsletters contain articles, announcements of conferences and classes, and other information about OOP:

C++ Report
    SIGS Publications, Inc.
    588 Broadway, Suite 604
    New York, NY 10012
    212 274-0640 (voice)
    212 274-0646 (fax)

First Class
    Object Management Group
    Framingham Corporate Center
    492 Old Connecticut Path
    Framingham, MA 01710
    508 820-4300

Journal of Object-Oriented Programming
    SIGS Publications, Inc. (for address see *C++ Report*)

Object Magazine
    SIGS Publications, Inc. (for address see *C++ Report*)

OO Strategies
    Cutter Information Corp.
    37 Broadway
    Arlington, MA 02174-5539
    617 648-8702 (voice)
    617 648-1950 (fax)

ASSOCIATIONS AND CONFERENCES

C++ World
SIGS Publications, Inc.
588 Broadway, Suite 604
New York, NY 10012
212 274-0640 (voice)
212 274-0646 (fax)

European Conference on Object-Oriented Programming (ECOOP)
Kaiserlauten, Germany
DFKI in cooperation with ACM
Contact the Association for Computing Machinery (ACM)
1515 Broadway
New York, NY 10036
212 869-7440 (voice)
212 869-0481 (fax)

Object Expo
Contact SIGS Publications, Inc. (address under *C++ Report*) for information.

Object World
IDG World Expo
111 Speen Street
P.O. Box 9107
Framingham, MA 01701
800 225-4681 (voice)
508 972-8237 (fax)

Object-Oriented Programming Systems, Languages and Applications (OOPSLA)
Contact ACM for information.

Patricia Seybold's Object Technology Conference
Patricia Seybold Group
148 State Strteet, Seventh Floor
Boston, MA 02109
617 742-5200

USENIX
USENIX Association
2560 Ninth Street, Suite 215
Berkeley, CA 94710

INDEX

C

C++
  ANSI extensions, 406
  *cp*Professional support for, 133
  exceptions, 404
  guidelines for using, 168
  and heaps, 400, 401
  and object-oriented technology, 151
  optimizing compiler and linker, 138
  Safe Pointers, 358
C, *cp*Professional support for, 133
calibrated colors, 245, 246
calling API, vs. subclassing API, 60–61
Caucus framework, 105, 380
CIE. *See* Commission Internationale de l'Eclairage
class diagram conventions, 169–171
classes, 44–45
class hierarchies, 50–51
class libraries
  benefits of, 51
  frameworks vs., 62–63
  limitations of, 52
class name conventions, 169
  for Graphics classes, 236
client API, vs. customization API, 63–64
client-server support, 112–116, 307–325, 376–388
clocks, 395–398
  rate, 396
  representing timing dependencies, 398
  syncable, 396–398
  times, 397
collaboration, 71, 84, 105–106, 112–114, 188
collation, 304
collections, 347–351
  arrays, 349
  class hierarchy, 348
  deques, 350
  dictionaries, 350
  priority queues, 350
  queues, 350
  sequences, 349–350
  sets, 351
  stacks, 350
  types of, 347–351
Color frameworks, 245–247

colorimetric color matching, 247
coloring a graphic, 249
Color Matcher framework, 245, 247
Color Model framework, 245
color profiles, 245
commands, 184–190
  incremental, 190
  streaming, 188
commercial CommonPoint software, 121–124
commercial developers, 9–12, 126–127, 132–135
Commission Internationale de l'Eclairage (CIE), 246
CommonPoint application system
  Application frameworks, 161–163, 173–305
  Application Services, 162–163, 226–305
  architecture, 157–420
  benefits of developing for, 125–129
  commercial software for, 121–124
  cross-platform development for, 133
  deployment of, 117–120
    on Windows NT and Windows 95, 120
  Desktop frameworks, 68, 173–211
  development leverage, 33–35
  documentation, 154
  Embeddable Data Types, 161, 213–224
  Enterprise Services, 164, 307–325
  Foundation Services, 165, 327–373
  host operating systems, 22, 167
  integration with host user environments, 107–109
  interoperability with host applications, 23, 107–109, 284–287
  introduced, 22–26
  name, 114
  OS Services, 166, 375–420
  overview of, 159–167
  portability of, 24
  and Taligent product suite, 23–24
  target industries, 114–115
  technical support, 154
  tools for working with, 132–150
  training, 154
  use of frameworks in, 66–72

D

O